Theodoret of Cyrus
Commentary on the Letters of St. Paul

Theodoret of Cyrus

Commentary on the Letters of St. Paul

Volume One

Translated with
an Introduction
by
Robert Charles Hill

HOLY CROSS ORTHODOX PRESS
Brookline, Massachusetts

© Copyright 2001 Holy Cross Orthodox Press
Published by Holy Cross Orthodox Press
50 Goddard Avenue
Brookline, Massachusetts 02445

Library of Congress Cataloging–in–Publication Data
Theodoret, Bishop of Cyrrhus.
Commentary on the letters of St. Paul/Theodoret of Cyrus ; translated with an introduction by Robert Charles Hill.
p. cm.
Includes bibliographical references.
ISBN 1-885652-52-6 (v. 1 : pbk. : ailk. paper) — ISBN 1-885652-53-4 (v. 2 : pbk. :alk. paper)
1. Bible. N.T. Epistles of Paul—Commentaries. I. Hill, Robert C. (Robert Charles), 1931-II. Titles

BS2650.3 .T48 2001
227'.077—dc21
                                        2001039569

To William J. Dalton
of the Society of Jesus,
distinguished Pauline commentator and teacher,
in friendship and esteem

Rejoice insofar as you are sharing Christ's sufferings,
so that you may also be glad and shout for joy
when his glory is revealed.
1 Peter 4.13

Contents

Abbreviations

ABR	*Australian Biblical Review*
AJP	*American Journal of Philology*
Bib	*Biblica*
CCG	*Corpus Christianorum Graecorum*
ClR	*The Clergy Review*
DB Supp.	*Dictionnaire de la Bible, Supplément*
EstBib	*Estudios Bíblicos*
ETL	*Ephemerides Theologicae Lovanienses*
FOTC	Fathers of the Church series
HeyJ	*The Heythrop Journal*
ITQ	*Irish Theological Quarterly*
JECS	*Journal of Early Christian Studies*
LXX	Septuagint (Greek Old Testament)
NJBC	*New Jerome Biblical Commentary*
OCA	Orientalia Christiana Analecta
PG	*Patrologia Graeca*
PL	*Patrologia Latina*
SC	*Sources Chrétiennes*
StudP	*Studia Patristica*
SVTQ	*Saint Vladimir Theological Quarterly*
TGL	*Theologie und Glaube*
TRE	*Theologische Realenzyklopädie*
TS	*Theological Studies*
VC	*Vigiliae Christianae*
VTS	*Vetus Testamentum*, Supplement

Introduction

1
PLACE OF THE COMMENTARY AMONG THEODORET'S WORKS; HISTORICAL CONTEXT

I t is a remarkable feature of the life of Theodoret, bishop of Cyrus from 423 for over thirty-five years, that despite the ecclesiastical and theological turmoil of the period, in which he was closely involved, he could claim authorship of as many literary works.[1] "Little backwater"[2] though Cyrus may have been, the diocese still had responsibility for over 800 parishes, and Bishop Theodoret was credited with many social and civic improvements as well. Born in Antioch a dozen years after the second ecumenical council held at Constantinople in 381 (whose creed leaves its imprint on his writings), the bishop was caught up in the currents swirling about the sessions of the third council at Ephesus in 431, and was briefly deposed by the Robber Synod there in 449, returning from deposition to take the lead in having the fourth council convoked at Chalcedon in 451 against the monophysites.

While these currents and movements can be detected in his works, what is particularly admirable is the volume of his literary output in this turbulent period. Of especial interest here are his numerous exegetical works. Though he intended to begin his work on "the divine Scriptures," in traditional fashion, with a commentary on the Psalms, as he tells us in its preface,[3] he was first obliged to respond to requests for commentary on the Song of Songs, Daniel, Ezekiel and the Twelve (minor) Prophets. There followed commentaries on Isaiah and Jeremiah. Strangely, Theodoret did not turn his hand to a commentary on any of the Gospels;[4] but before completing his literary output with a series of *Quaestiones* on the Octateuch, probably after Chalcedon in his declining years, he composed some few years before that council a Commentary on the Fourteen Letters of St Paul, in this following the example of his great predecessors in the School of Antioch, Theodore of Mopsuestia and John Chrysostom (their mentor, Diodore of Tarsus, also having commented on some Pauline letters). His indebtedness to their work, if not specifically acknowledged, is discernible in his Commentary.

Theodoret's correspondence furnishes statements that enable us to date the Pauline Commentary to the mid-440s,[5] though some scholars still contest the date.[6] Internal evidence is less cogent: in the process of commentary Theodoret is reticent about current events. In commentary on 1 Cor 7.32-34, where Paul is speaking of virginity, Theodoret remarks that he has treated of the topic at greater length in his *logoi* on the subject; but we do not know when such a work was composed. More conclusive is his response to the quotation at 2 Cor 4.13 of Ps 116.10, which the Septuagint (Paul's text) numbers 115.1; in commenting on this occurrence Theodoret quotes also Ps 116.8-9 (LXX 114.8-9). But at those places in his Commentary on the Psalms (which can be dated between 441 and 448, and which makes no mention of a work on Paul when listing previous exegetical works)[7] he did not refer to Paul's citation, frequent though scriptural documentation is in that latter work – a fact which would be unusual if he had already done a commentary on Paul's text, and which perhaps confirms the generally held view of the posteriority of the Pauline Commentary. Another possible indicator of the lateness of this Commentary comes from his treatment of the Christological hymn at Phil 2.6-11, which Theodoret turns into an arsenal against all possible trinitarian and Christological heresies; he admits he has treated of these matters in other works: could he be including the *Eranistes*, dated at 447?

Even if the commentator at his desk has blinkers on, however, we can glean certain information as to his times and his church. He emerges as a shrewd observer of contemporary (sexual) mores: in commenting on the Pastorals' insistence on monogamous clergy, he cites the limited efficacy of imperial decrees on monogamy; and when Paul in 1 Cor 7.3-4 proposes an equality of esteem between husbands and wives, the bishop observes,

Human laws, you know, tell women to be continent, and punish those breaking the law, whereas of husbands they do not require the same continence: men, being makers of the law, were not concerned for equality, instead granting themselves license.[8]

He has no problem with the institution of slavery in his society. He paraphrases Paul's comment on it at 1 Cor 7.21 this way: "So do not shun slavery as unworthy of the faith; rather, even if it is possible for you to attain your freedom, remain in service, and look for reward." Even though he sees some element of "exaggeration" in Paul's sentiment, we feel he has no difficulty with the principle; he can even be patronizing to mere servants who prove an ornament to their Christianity (on Titus 2.10), and he is really staggered by Paul's writing on behalf of a slave in Phlm, the letter closing in a way that suggests the apostle's thinking is too advanced for him. Significantly, in quoting Col 3.11, "Where there is no longer Jew or Greek, circumcision or uncircumcision," he conveniently omits the further phrase "slave or free."[9] He remarks on the continuing tendency to angelolatry, a phenomenon (prompting the concern also of Severian before him) he sees Col 2.18; 3.17 referring to, and documents it from the prevalence of chapels to St Michael in Phrygia.

He grew up in the church of the years following the council of Constantinople; he seems to cite its credal terminology in commentary on 2 Cor 4.4, for example. Predictably as a bishop, he likes to think his church is structured and "orderly," a feature he sees Paul wanting to find in Corinth.[10] The frequent emphasis he lays on the abuse of the gift of tongues at Corinth suggests he feels the orderliness of his own church at risk from the same problem. Yet in comment on Rom 14.5 to do with the proper use of freedom of conscience he admits legitimate diversity in ascetical practices in the churches of his own day. As elsewhere in his work, Bishop Theodoret abjures any notion of clerical monopoly of spiritual things. He acknowledges the practice of consecrated life, which he had experienced in his youth at nearby Apamea, where he would return during his brief period of deposition in 449. Beyond these incidental references, we learn nothing from the Commentary of his life and times other than theological currents and controversies.

2

THEODORET'S TEXT OF PAUL; THE TEXT OF THE COMMENTARY

Theodoret, like Chrysostom before him, seems generally (if not consistently),[11] to be using a text of Paul's letters we know as the Koine text, resulting from a major revision of Greek manuscripts at the end of the third century and the beginning of the fourth that produced also a "Western" text in North Africa-Egypt. On the testimony of Jerome, this Koine (or Byzantine) text, which spread widely with the spread of bishops from Antioch, was attributed to the scholar of Antioch, Lucian.[12] Such attribution has come under recent scrutiny, Jerome's testimony being now thought suspect.[13] But it is owing to the preservation of its readings in the works of Chrysostom and Theodoret that scholars are now appreciating the antiquity of the Koine text.[14]

These distinctive readings of the Koine text are represented in Theodoret's Commentary on Paul's letters. A modern commentator on Paul like Joseph Fitzmyer will dismiss some as an "inferior reading,"[15] a "weakly attested reading,"[16] an "anachronistic interpretation;"[17] but Theodoret has no difficulty assimilating them to his argument. A different reading can affect his interpretation: when his text of 1 Cor 11.11 reads, "Yet neither is man independent of woman nor woman of man *in the world* (not, in the Lord)," his comment is, "Through intercourse and sharing the race is propagated." He can make a case for the Koine *gennômenon*, "born" (of a woman), in preference to *genomenon* in Gal 4.4 for Christological purposes, and yet employ the latter in quoting the verse in comment on Rom 5.8 and Heb 3.1 (he cites Col 4.8 in two forms). Some Koine readings represent a longer form [18] or contain an extra phrase.[19] At times one gets the impression he is aware his text is atypical, and tries to get around it.[20] More significantly, the doxology that occurs in modern texts as Rom 16.25-27 is placed in Theodoret's text at the end of chapter 14, not at the letter's end or (as in some other traditions) in both places.

Of the text of Theodoret's Commentary on these letters we have no modern critical edition. To hand is the nineteenth century reprint found in J. P. Migne's *Patrologia Graeca* 82 of the eighteenth century edition by J. L. Schulze, based on the first edition of all Theodoret's works by Jacob Sirmond in the early seventeenth century, Schulze having access also to two sixteenth century codices, Augustan and Bavarian.[21] Schulze reports no major discrepancies in this fortunately direct transmission of Theodoret's Commentary, unlike the widely-varying forms (shorter and longer) of his Psalms Commentary. Perhaps the matter of greatest textual moment is the occurrence of brief codicils to individual letters dealing with place of composition and dispatch, whose authenticity Schulze doubts, generally on the grounds of contradiction of factual detail.[22] In short, we have a generally reliable text from the commentator's hand to enable us to estimate the character and success of his work, of which Schulze observes, "quo nil melius tota antiquitas habet post Chrysostomum."[23] High praise, and therefore high time for its first appearance in English.

3

THE NATURE AND STYLE OF THE COMMENTARY

a) purpose and readership

There is no dispute about this work's being a commentary, *hermeneia*, by a pastor and desk theologian on a great Christian classic, the fourteen letters of Paul (Hebrews also included, occurring in his text before the Pastorals, and providing much grist to his theological mill). Theodoret is scrupulous about the limits to the desk commentator's role; even more than is true of his work on the Psalms, any direct address to the readers is rare, apart from the conventional doxologies that serve to conclude each of the *tomoi* that evidently contain a sufficiently sizable amount of commentary. Nor are there any signs of orality, such as rhetorical patterns that leave the reader of Chrysostom's Commentary on the Psalms wondering whether the text is a similar desk work or represents homilies actually delivered.[24] No, the bishop is clearly and professedly concerned with a cognitive exercise – "to demonstrate the profundity of the apostle's wisdom and strip away the veils from the writing so as to offer those willing to partake of it the due benefit," as he admits at the opening of the preface, aware doubtless of the caution about the letters' lack of transparency sounded from as early as 2 Peter 3.15-16. Finding Paul's meaning less than transparent in Rom 7.17, for example, he observes: "This is short on clarity, requiring greater explanation," which he proceeds to supply. How well he succeeds we must examine in detail.

Though Theodoret in his time thus shares something of the purpose of today's commentators on Paul like C. K. Barrett, Matthew Black, F. F. Bruce, Rudolf Bultmann, Joseph A. Fitzmyer, Jerome Murphy-O'Connor and John A. T. Robinson, we note also some differences, not to mention the various skills patristic and modern commentators bring to the task – not always to the relative credit of the latter.[25] At the opening of commentary on Romans, he shows none of our contemporary interest in sociological matters like the composition of the Roman church. It is rare for him to relate our knowledge of Paul's background to the material in the letters; in comment on 2 Cor 2.6-7 referring to the community's punishing the wrongdoer in response to his directive, Theodoret remarks, "Tentmaker though the writer was, he was capable of such an effect owing to the power within him." He leaves till 2 Thess the similarities in letter writing between Paul's time and his own. His accent falls on doctrinal matters, moral directives and parenesis being of less moment: when on Romans he reaches chapter 12, he steps up the pace of commentary on this basis, "The knowledge of the divine nature as well as both faith and a proper disposition to it are the summit and the true foundation of good things," mere exhortation not calling for much comment. As was true also of his work on the Psalms by comparison with preacher Chrysostom's,[26] moralizing is quite absent, aware as he is of the desk theologian's different role; even a sobering account of human sinfulness like Rom 1 does not tempt him to desert the desk for the pulpit.[27] At this desk he keeps his wits about him and is conscious of the need of his readers for guidance in the movement of Paul's thought; as notes to this translation highlight, he frequently enough provides helpful overviews of a letter's development for the reader's assistance, as in chs 4,5,7,9 of Romans, at 9.19 and the opening of ch 15 of 1 Cor, at 2 Cor 2.12, at the opening of Col, 1 Thess, 2 Thess, Heb, 1 Tim, 2 Tim, Titus.

Just who are these readers? They are not his peers; the opening to the preface, which is not explicit about readership, implies a principle of his that clerics have no monopoly on spiritual things, and he goes on to account for his brevity of treatment on the grounds that it "encourages even those prone to easy ways to do some reading." He is evidently writing for lay people in the world (the adequacy of his spiritual guidance of them something we shall have to examine later) and possibly also for religious like the community at Apamea.[28] Does he envisage women reading his Commentary? Certainly he takes Genesis 3 in a much less anti-feminist way than does Chrysostom in his homilies on that book,[29] man and woman shown by Theodoret sharing the guilt.[30] But he is no more sensitive than Paul in 1 Cor 11.7-9 on the creation story of Gen 1, apostle and bishop both taking *anthropos* to refer solely to the male to bring out superiority.[31] Certainly he does, as we have seen, chide his own society for its sexual inequality. He takes an interest in the Phoebe of Rom 16, not so much for her ministerial status as for the degree of attention she receives, which he finds disproportionate. He goes out of his way to explain the mention of Prisca ahead of husband Aquila in 2 Tim 4.19 as due to her greater zeal for good causes. The odd passage would suggest he does not contemplate women having access to his material: when Paul rehearses the decalogue at Rom 13.9, Theodoret paraphrases him exclusively thus,

> The man (*aner*) who is well disposed to someone does not do away with the man he is fond of, does not commit adultery with his wife, does not filch anything of his friend's possessions, does nothing that may cause him harm.[32]

And when Paul in Gal 4.2 speaks of children inheriting at maturity, he speaks of that time only as "manhood" (though the term may reflect an inability by women in that society to inherit).

b) influences on the commentator

Theodoret is well aware that he is not the first to turn his hand to a work of commentary on Paul. He was familiar with the commentaries of fellow Antiochenes Theodore of Mopsuestia and John Chrysostom,[33] and through them to earlier works by commentators of the same school like Severian of Gabbala. He faced the same initial discouragement in commencing the work as Augustine faced from Jerome in contemplating work on the Psalms: if your predecessors did well, your work will be superfluous; if badly, it will be presumptuous.[34] In his preface he confronts his likely critics from the outset:

> I am aware that in turning my hand to a commentary on the teaching of the divine Paul I shall not escape the criticism of fault-finders. They will represent me as guilty of presumption and over-confidence for having the effrontery to undertake commentary on the apostle in the wake of this person or that, the world's luminaries.

But he claims to have something to contribute,[35] citing biblical examples of people passed over but proving their credentials, like Eldad and Medad in the book of Numbers and the young Samuel. So he is content to follow in the wake of his great predecessors "like some kind of mosquito, buzzing about the apostolic meadows along with those famous bees" (we shall have cause to note his gifts of imagination).

The honey from those bees he samples at regular intervals, not acknowledging them by name but citing their opinions anonymously and evaluating them, not hesitating to differ from them.[36] Jean-Noël Guinot in his authoritative work on Theodoret has traced forty-six such references to his Antiochene predecessors in this Commentary,[37] as he is indebted in his other exegetical works; unlike a work such as his Commentary on the Psalms, where he could access Alexandrian exegesis through Eusebius of Caesarea, on Paul he did not go beyond Antioch. The works of his illustrious predecessors he regarded, *pace* Jerome, not as grounds for disqualification but as a resource on which to call in his own efforts. We have to admire him for this, as also for his balance in assessing these alternative views.

c) attitude to the text

It is perhaps proverbial to apply the term "uncritical" to the great majority of the Fathers in their approach to the biblical text, especially of the Old Testament. This is probably also the moment to make the point that "exegesis" is a term less applicable to their work than "commentary," though in dealing with a Greek text from the New Testament the Fathers (at least those in the East) suffer from fewer exegetical handicaps, obviously. Theodoret's lack of Hebrew does not often prove a limitation: he fails to appreciate Paul's play upon the similarity in form of the Hebrew words for "Jew" and the verb "praise" in Rom 2.28-29;[38] with Paul he cannot match the quibble raised by modern commentators as to the true significance of the name Abraham in the citation of Gen 17.5 at Rom 4.17 or the identity of the nations mentioned there – though with Syriac as his native tongue[39] he is in a position to comment fully on *Abba* at Rom 8.15 and *Maran atha* at 1 Cor 16.22, where he disabuses Chrysostom of the idea that the word is Hebrew, not Aramaic.

Theodoret differs from modern commentators such as those cited above in his unquestioning acceptance of details now impugned. "Blessed Paul wrote fourteen letters," he tells us in the preface, accepting the Pauline authorship of Hebrews that had become traditional at least since Cyril of Jerusalem a century before, despite Origen's abandonment of the idea. He entertains no suggestion of a distinction between proto-Pauline and deutero-Pauline letters;[40] even the identical closure to Ephesians and Colossians raises no critical quibble. He does not enter into a discussion of the various forms of authorship when there is mention of a scribe at the end of Romans or his autograph at the end of 2 Thess.[41] The Corinthian correspondence gives rise to no consideration of the number of letters or the possibility of lost letters, though he notes oddities in details of the text.[42] He has no qualms about the degree of correspondence between the evidence of Acts and of the letters (in Gal 2, for example). He is independent enough to observe in the preface that despite Paul's authorship of all fourteen letters, "I believe the order in which they occur in the Bible is not of his doing," using the compilation of the Psalter (the preface to that Commentary revealing a like flexibility) as a parallel; and he proceeds to deal with the obvious question of the order of the letters. On this and the question of place of composition, with which most of the preface is occupied, he can utilize internal evidence and statements in the Acts; the inclusion of Hebrews precludes the possibility of his thinking in terms of an order based on relative length, nor does he allow for letters to churches being placed before those to individuals. Today's commentators would address also other introductory questions – Paul's life, conversion and commissioning, the purpose of the letters in general, their authenticity, their use in the churches of his day – but Theodoret treats of these, if at all, only incidentally.

d) appreciation of Paul

On the other hand, at times one feels modern commentators could do with reading Fathers closer to Paul's time, like Theodoret, to acquire a better grasp of the letters and an empathy with their composer.[43] The bishop shows not only a close understanding but also a warm admiration of his subject,[44] whom he rarely refers to as Paul, generally "the divine apostle;" like all the biblical authors he is acknowledged as being divinely inspired, *thespesios*. He is therefore proof against personal criticism: where a modern commentator would draw to our attention an imprecise quotation by the composer (as at 1 Cor 2.9; 10.8), Theodoret is silent (though his silence could in cases be due to inadvertence, we shall see). When Paul admits to poor penmanship at the end of Galatians, Theodoret has to check with his predecessors how to interpret the admission. He clearly relishes the task of commenting on his *beau ideal*, being much more expansive and confident than, say, on the less congenial material in the Psalter.

We admire his sureness of touch in commenting on Paul's thought. He reveals a fine understanding of the relationship developed in Romans (and Galatians) between the Law, grace and faith, eschewing from the outset any interest in a narrow "pangs of conscience" interpretation and instead setting the composer's thinking in the wider context of the Incarnation. When he comes to chapters 9 to 11 of that letter, he realizes (in a way Reformation theologians did not) that he had reached "the heart of Romans," and with one of his sweeping summaries of the material that are of great help to a reader, he unerringly situates the chapters in the letter's developing theology:

> The divine apostle explicitly demonstrated that the Incarnation of our God and Savior was necessary and was a source of ineffable goods to the believers. In fact, he proved Jews to be liable to heavier accusation because of the giving of the Law, and all the others to be transgressors of the law of nature. Exposing the threat of punishment, he explained the gifts of the evangelical grace, and gave a glimpse of the salvation coming from faith. Lest the Jews complain, supposing the Law to be under attack, and lest heretics hostile to the Old Testament take occasion from making of the comparison for calumny against the Law, he was obliged to bring out the usefulness of the Law and commend it with great eulogy. Since, however, the Jews in turn put forward the patriarch Abraham and the

promises made him by God, and attempted to show the apostles' preaching to be at variance with these, he was obliged to give attention to these arguments; with great wisdom he demolished them, employing opportunely both scriptural testimonies and ancient examples, and clearly showing the real meaning of the divine promises.

Unlike some modern versions, he is in touch with the full sense of Paul's use of *mysterion* at its occurrence in Romans and 1 Corinthians – no mere "secret" but the whole divine plan revealed to us[45] – and of other key Pauline terms like *oikonomia*. With typical Eastern optimism he understands Paul's true accent on healing in the movement from Fall to restoration in Rom 5.12-14: "Just as that first human being by sinning fell under the norm of death, and the whole race followed the first parent, so Christ the Lord by fulfilling the utmost righteousness destroyed the power of death, and being the first to rise from the dead he led the whole human race back to life." His vision of *anakephalaiosis* of all things in Christ in Eph 1.10 is magnificent, and is one we associate rather with Irenaeus (in its Latin version *recapitulatio*) and Maximus Confessor. In company with all the Greek Fathers before John Damascene he rightly takes ἐφ' ᾧ in Rom 5.12 not with Adam as antecedent but in the sense "because," commenting, "In other words, it is not because of the sin of the first parent but because of their own that each person is liable to the norm of death."[46] He refuses to accept a notion of predestination that would later be based on Rom 8.30. He will conscientiously wrestle with items in a *crux interpretum* like Rom 1.3 or the phrase "from faith to faith" (Rom 1.17), where he acknowledges the traditional but inadequate interpretation before offering an improvement. He appreciates the irony in texts like 1 Cor 4.8, and is concerned readers of Galatians are sensitive to Paul's unusually irate tone there.

His commentary, so much in sympathy with the composer's thought, only suffers when Theodoret allows his ever present theological concerns to obtrude into his work, prompted by some remark of Paul's in another direction and leading to a distracting digression. We shall note them below in studying his theology; they betray the theological climate in which the Commentary was composed, in which older errors such as Arian and Pneumatomachian positions were still to be countered and newer, monophysite doctrines were yet to be dealt with in a Chalcedonian council still a few years away.[47] A more serious defect on this Antiochene commentator's part is his resistance to Paul's own thought when it threatens to undermine positions held at Antioch, such as the question of the gratuity of God's grace; as the insistence on a balance, somewhat weighted one way, between this gift and human effort in the process of salvation characterized also Theodoret's work on the Psalms (and Chrysostom's before him),[48] so again and again – particularly in the heart of Romans where the mystery of divine election is being canvassed – the commentator perversely resists the writer's acceptance of gift ahead of personal zeal, *prothumia*. In another area the commentator refuses to accept at face value the recurring phrase "God and Father of the Lord Jesus," insisting we make a break and apply the former term only to ourselves lest some element of subordinationism enter our thinking. In these instances we truly observe a commentator who, in the words of John A. T. Robinson, is wrestling with Romans (and with places in other letters).

e) scriptural familiarity; hermeneutics

Scriptural documentation is not a feature of this Commentary to the extent that it characterizes Theodoret's work on a more challenging Old Testament text like the Psalter; meaning emerges more immediately from the text, not requiring to anything like the same extent elucidation from other scriptural statement. Nor does this indicate any disparagement of Old Testament authors; all are inspired, like Paul himself, and all of them, as distinct from New Testament composers, are styled *prophetai* in that sense of inspired OT composer (not simply the "prophets" in the sense used in our Christian Bible, but psalmists as well). Theodoret can speak of the Old Testament as "holy Scriptures," and insist against Marcion, Valentinus and the Manichees that "the old Scripture is divine,... inspired by God." Both the Old and the New are spiritual realities of the kind mentioned in 1 Cor 2.13.

Interpretation of these Old Testament texts cited by Paul or himself is in the manner of his school, where in fidelity to Diodore's principles the literal sense was preferred to the allegorical,[49] and where typology was acceptable only with the encouragement of Scripture itself. He feels he has to explain to his readers what Paul means by an allegorical sense to the Hagar and Sarah story at Gal 4.22-26; interestingly, he does not – *pace* Albert Vaccari[50] – see the allegorical sense cancelling the historical. When Paul speaks of Christ as the true mercy seat,[51] Theodoret beautifully develops this typological picture of Christ in its Old Testament setting in a way that delivers a resounding negative to Matthew Black's tentative question as to whether "expiation" is an adequate notion for *hilasterion* in Paul's thinking at this point – a further example of the rich resource that patristic commentary is for modern scholars prepared to read it. He further relishes Paul's encouragement at 1 Cor 10.1-4 to take in typological fashion (and even sacramental, as is his wont) the narratives from Exodus of Moses feeding the people in the wilderness and giving them to drink; and he frequently acknowledges the use of typology by the author of Hebrews.

As emerges also in his other works, Theodoret's sureness of touch deserts him when he moves from understanding of Paul's text to citation of other biblical loci. Though sitting at his desk with Bible at hand, he can err in his recall of details: the seventy who pass Eldad and Medad over in the Numbers text he cites in the preface are in fact not judges but elders, nor does the text of 1 Sam support Samuel's being accorded a vision as claimed there; the Joseph story as recounted in Rom 2 is faulty in some details; it is Paul's skin, not his garments, that is the healing agent in the incident cited (twice) from Acts 19.12; and so on. He is also less than textually precise when quoting verses from Old and New Testaments.[52]

f) characteristics of the commentator

In the preface, Theodoret makes it a rule of thumb for his task of commentary, "My particular concern is for conciseness: I am aware that brevity encourages even those prone to easy ways to do some reading;" perhaps the prolixity of a preacher like Chrysostom, open before him, prompts this aspiration. And, as elsewhere in his commentaries on the Bible, he adheres to that norm, only departing from it (as we noted) when a Christological or trinitarian issue leads him to digress.[53] Within the variation we noted of ebb and flow that marks the attention to the letters' moral and dogmatic sections, respectively, he produces a work of commentary that has to be rated as measured and balanced.[54]

As with his Antiochene fellows, his attention to the text is marked by the virtue of *akribeia*, precision both in the biblical author and in the commentator. When Paul claims in Rom 1.9 he is serving God "through the Gospel of his Son," Theodoret insists it is "not idly or to no purpose" that both Father and Son receive mention, and he goes off on another brief trinitarian clarification. The phrase occurs very frequently, as it occurs likewise in Chrysostom,[55] and the attitude pays off: while a modern like Barrett claims Paul is using only elegant variation in speaking diversely of "gifts," "ministries" and "activities" at 1 Cor 12.4-6, Theodoret proves him wrong by establishing in Antiochene fashion the individual sense of each word. Good theology depends on linguistic precision, he says in picking his way through Hebrews: "It is therefore necessary for us to realize that some names are appropriate to the divinity, some to the Incarnation." He can build an argument, convincingly or not, on morphological details: when Paul says at 2 Cor 5.2, "We groan, longing to be clothed with our habitation from heaven," Theodoret notes that a further prefix gives *ependusasthai* precedence over *endusasthai*, claiming, "He did not say 'put on' but 'be clothed,' since instead of putting on another body, this corruptible body is clothed with incorruptibility." When Paul at 1 Thess 3.11 prays to "our God and Father and our Lord Jesus Christ," Theodoret sees him stressing the equality of persons: "He used not the preposition *through* but the conjunction *and*." The term "of himself" in the Koine reading of Heb 1.3 he reminds the reader must be read with an aspirate, and finds in the reflexive pronoun considerable Christological significance. Trifling and exaggerated though this adherence to details of the text may seem, it is not difficult to trace its adoption by the Antiochenes to their thoroughly incarnational soteriology, Christology and spirituality.

As befits one who situates himself in the line of his predecessors like "some kind of mosquito buzzing about the apostolic meadows along with those famous bees," Theodoret does not allow Paul's figurative expressions to go without notice or appreciation (as he had responded well to the psalmists' imagery in his earlier work). When Paul says in 1 Cor 9.26, "I am not like a boxer beating the air," he first develops the figure and reminds the readers whence Paul derives it:

I see good things as an object of hope, my crown is not obscure nor am I shadow-boxing to no effect; instead, I land a blow on the invisible adversaries. He employed this expression by way of a metaphor from the pugilists: in training they flay the air with their hands.[56]

He frequently calls on his own imagination to bring home Paul's point. When in Rom 1.16 the Gospel is spoken of as God's power for every believer, Theodoret brings out its hidden efficacy by examples from nature: "For example, pepper has the appearance of being cool, and to the unwary it betrays no sense of being hot; but whoever crushes it with their teeth gets a taste of fiery heat."[57]

g) attitude to Jews

As is true also of commentary on the Psalms, Theodoret is not so expansive or so mordent as Chrysostom in polemic against the Jews of his day. Admittedly, he does bring out in both his works the evidently conventional attribution of current Jewish misfortunes to the crucifixion, finding encouragement for this in statements of Paul like 1 Cor 2.8: he agrees the awful offense was pardonable, but the Jews did not repent, even when confronted with the apostolic miracles; "they persisted in their infidelity and so he consigned them to the siege." On the other hand, he does not wax eloquent on Paul's devastating disparagement of the Old Covenant in 2 Cor 3-4 or Gal 3, nor elaborate on Paul's diatribe in 1 Thess 2.15-16; he seems somewhat embarrassed by the insistence in Titus 1 that Jewish converts are the principal nuisance, remarking, "We have taken on the task of commentary, not of criticizing Jews." Judaism in the past is commendable, he seems to be saying, and the Jews' practice of its rituals and institutions admirable – in the past, not in the present; of contemporary Judaism (a term he does not employ, even when Paul uses it in Galatians) he betrays little knowledge.[58] Circumcision was commendable, he maintains in comment on 1 Cor 7.19, not as a fact but as observance of a divine commandment. The Law was an advantage the Jews (of old) enjoyed, and he upholds its dignity against Marcion; "the Old Scripture is divine," inspired like the New. In commentary on Colossians, which he sees directed against Judaizers, again and again he denies the Law is in Paul's sights – just obsolete adoption of it.[59] Interestingly, he seems to see Jewish Christians bringing a rich background to the faith: when Paul speaks of the churches of Macedonia and Achaia contributing to the welfare of the church in Jerusalem, Theodoret glowingly sketches that background, from the patriarchs to Jesus to the apostles, before saying it is only right that the Gentile churches, who were given a share in that rich background, "should give a share in the less."[60]

4

CHRISTOLOGICAL AND TRINITARIAN CONCERNS

Whereas Theodoret is scrupulous about maintaining his role as desk commentator and keeping his distance from the reader, not straying into the preserve of the parenetic homilist, he is not so successful in explicating Paul's thought completely within the circumstances and theological currents of the mid-first century. Understandably, and in the manner of many another commentator, even within the Bible, he allows contemporary movements and currents to break through the surface and, as we have seen, affect the progress of commentary. One even gets the impression occasionally that Theodoret feels Paul is directly addressing later ecclesiastical and theological developments. Romans is written thus, he says at its opening.

> (Paul) was aware that Jews were excessively attached to the Law, while those infected with the teachings of Marcion and Valentinus, and of course Manichees, criticized it severely. So just as some excellent general, surrounded on all sides by enemies, repels one lot after another and sets up the trophy, so the divine apostle demolished both the column of the heretics and the force of the Jews through divine grace.[61]

By contrast, he will rewrite Paul if he feels the apostle's phrasing unhelpful, as he does the term "the Son of his love" in Col 1.13.

It is not the relative status of the Law, however, that recurs as a continuing concern throughout the Commentary. The person of Christ, the *homoousion* of the Spirit, and the Trinity are more generally in focus. In fact, Theodoret finds it hard to move them out of focus, even when his text is moving in another direction. When Paul is treating of the false worship of impious pagans in developing his important diptych in the opening chapter of Romans, Theodoret cannot resist what he considers a more urgent issue closer to home: "Whereas they ought to have worshipped the true God, they offered reverence due to God to a creature. They also are liable to these accusations who call the only-begotten Son of God a creature while adoring him as God...," and off he goes on this tangent.[62] The subordinationism of "those who hold the position of Arius and Eunomius" is a constant worry to him, the phrase popping up a score of times, relevant to Paul's theme or not.[63] Concomitantly, he is worried about Paul's phrase "God and Father of the Lord Jesus," and insists with his readers that a break is to be made between the two terms; he will even presume to rewrite the phrase, as at Rom 15.6, "He called God our God, and Father of the Lord Jesus: the God of us all is his Father."[64] All major trinitarian and Christological heresies of the previous two or three centuries come in for mention and rejection in comment on the hymn at Phil 2.6-11, which he finds an apologetic compendium. He also uses the hymn at Col 1.15-20 against Arian subordinationism.

There are signs the Commentary was composed during the years of the monophysite controversy preceding the council of Chalcedon,[65] Theodoret being keen to labor the distinction of natures in Jesus (as he is in the Commentary on the Psalms in the same decade). Paul gains his commendation for doing likewise at the beginning of Romans with the phrase in 1.3, "of David's line according to the flesh;" Theodoret comments, "in mentioning David's line the divine apostle of necessity added 'according to the flesh' to teach us clearly how on the one hand he is God's Son and on the other he is styled David's."[66] Insistence on the distinction has earned him suspicion of underplaying the hypostatic union (no phrase of his, of course).[67] Certainly there are passages in the Commentary where he shows reluctance to concede the *communicatio idiomatum*:[68] on 1 Cor. 2.8, "If they had realized it, they would not have crucified the Lord of glory," Theodoret comments, "Now, he called the crucified one 'Lord of glory,' not to associate the passion with the divinity, but to show the degree of lawlessness of the sinners." When Rom 5.10 reads, "We were reconciled to God through the death of his Son," Theodoret has to head off an unacceptable interpretation by commenting, "Once more, of course, he gives the name 'Son' to Christ the Lord, who is both God and man; and it is clear, in my view, even to heresiarchs, which nature was involved in the passion."[69] His theological justi-fication of his Koine reading of Gal 4.4 as "born of a woman" (*gennômenon*) is that it avoids any idea of sending of the divinity. His reading of Heb 2.10 leads him to say, "The nature assumed is source of our salvation: rising from the dead, it procured resurrec-tion for us all."

To a greater degree than the Paul of the letters, Theodoret is concerned to stress with his readers the equality of status of the persons of the Trinity (and by the time of this Commentary, at any rate, there is nothing Nestorian in his use of *prosopa*, as emerges from his comments on the trinitarian blessing that closes 2 Cor). Without encouragement from the text, he maintains that when Paul at the opening of the letters claims to have been "set apart for God's Gospel," it was "Father, Son and Holy Spirit who set him apart," finding scriptural support elsewhere for each so as to bring out the necessary equality. Ephesians closes with a blessing from Father and Christ, but Theodoret insists it is also from the Spirit (cf. 2 Thess 3.5). The community's gifts, ministries and activities may be diverse, he concedes at 1 Cor 12.4-6, and may be said by Paul to be imparted by the Spirit, but "they are supplied by the all-holy Spirit, by the Lord, and by the God and Father... He did not claim, as some of the foolish heretics supposed, that some are activated by the Spirit, others by the God of all." It is a question in particular of defending the *homoousion* of the Spirit ("the Spirit that proceeds from the Father,"[70] of course – not also from the Son); and with Athanasius and the Cappadocians he comes out in several places against the subordinationism of Origen, Eusebius of Caesarea, the later Arians and the Pneumatomachians (without citing them).[71]

5

OTHER THEOLOGICAL ACCENTS; THE SPIRITUALITY OF THE COMMENTARY

Those are the principal theological concerns emerging in the Commentary, generated less by Paul's text than by the climate of the time. What the nature of the textual material does account for is (by comparison with the figurative expression of the Psalms) relative lack of warning to the reader not to infringe divine tran-scendence by misinterpreting anthropomorphisms, which of course occur less frequently in the letters. It is rare for Theodoret to give the reminder arising from Rom 1.18, "By 'God's wrath' he refers to retribution, not because God punishes in a passion, but to instil fear into the opponents by mention of his name." (Chrysostom would have gone on to speak of the divine *synkatabasis* of such anthropomorphic expressions; but it is not a term found in Theodoret's vocabulary here.)

It is predictable that the bishop would respond to the sacramental, and particularly baptismal, dimension to Paul's thinking, especially on the process of justification. In fact, he will find this dimension even where the composer did not intend it, occasionally even projecting on to Paul an understanding of the immersion ritual of baptism that was probably not liturgical practice in the first century; for instance, he embroiders Paul's reference to the sacrament in Rom 6.4 thus:

> The sacrament of baptism itself taught you to shun sin. Baptism, in fact, represents a type of the Lord's death, and in it you have had a share with Christ in both the death and the resurrection.[72]

That difficult phrase "from faith to faith" in Rom 1.17, on which Theodoret cites first the traditional but "certainly inadequate" interpretation (in Fitzmyer's view also), is then taken sacramentally, belief in Christ leading through baptism to belief in further verities such as resurrection of the dead. Many a time the process of justification is seen by the commentator to involve participation in the sacraments.[73]

The Commentary thus provides useful data for historians of sacramental practice and theology. In Theodoret's church, initiation into the community was a single rite, performed at the moment of baptism (of adults, presumably): on 1 Cor 12.13 he comments, "We were all renewed by one Spirit, we all enjoyed the same gift in baptism, we all alike received forgiveness of sins, we all participated similarly in the eucharist."[74] The context here is the treatment of the charismata; on v. 7 of that chapter, "To each is given the manifestation of the Spirit," his comment reveals a theology and practice different from the western thinking on a sacrament of confirmation: "He said, not 'the gift,' but 'the manifestation:' the grace even today is given to those thought worthy of all-holy baptism, but not in obvious fashion" (unlike the working of the charismata in the Corinthian community). As there is no separate moment of confirmation in his church,[75] nor it seems is there a separate rite of reconciliation: forgiveness comes with baptism, and he warns his readers of its unicity: "Do not, therefore, look forward to any other forgiveness through baptism."[76] Yet he can condemn Novatian rigorism in denying the possibility of pardon of sin after baptism, as he does at the close of comment on 2 Cor 12, on Gal 4.19, Heb 6.4-6; 10.26-27; 12.17 (Novatian already having come in for censure for ruling out second marriages).[77] Treating of the eucharist in 1 Cor 11, he presents the sacrament in a paschal theology, and reminds his readers that their term for it is not quite Paul's: "By 'the Lord's Supper' (*kyriakon deipnon*) he refers to 'the Lord's sacrament' (*despotikon mysterion*)" – *mysteria* being his term for sacraments generally.

In this context, too, with the prominence given to baptism, it is interesting to see the bishop maintaining his principle that clerics have no monopoly on spiritual goods. When, in taking issue with the parties in Corinth that traced their origin back to the minister of baptism, Paul claims he was sent by Christ to preach and not baptize, this desk commentator modestly concedes the priority of the former role:

> Preaching is more important than baptizing: baptizing is easy for those thought worthy of priesthood, whereas preaching is proper to a few, who have received this gift from a divine source.[78]

We have noted Theodoret's sound grasp and endorsement of Paul's thought on the relationship of Law, grace and faith. When Paul comes to treat of faith in Rom 3.28, "We therefore hold that a person is justified by faith apart from the works of the Law," with the aid of Antiochene precision he avoids the later error of Hilary, Ambrosiaster and then Luther in inserting "only" after faith, and seconds the warning of James not to exclude all works from the process of justification, commenting, "The law he is referring to is the Mosaic Law; yet he said not, We hold a Jew is justified by faith, but 'a person,' a name referring generally to human nature."[79] He is likewise clear on Paul's distinguishing the Law from the natural law; in v. 20 of that chapter he helpfully distinguishes the natural law, its expression in the Decalogue, and temporary prescriptions for the Jews by way of cultic practices.[80] He joins the ranks of commentators ancient and modern in wrestling with that puzzling phrase in Rom 12.3, "Each according to the measure of the faith God has assigned," and gives a plausible interpretation.

Though he expresses a preference for the dogmatic sections of the letters and tends to be even more concise in commenting on the moral sections, he cannot avoid taking moral positions. We have noted that moralizing he regards as beyond his purpose; he does not fulminate against sin in the manner of a preacher, and just as he avoided going into details when commenting on David's sin in Psalm 51, so he does not expatiate on sexual excesses when Paul touches on the subject in Rom 1.26-27. We saw that when he came to that key text in Rom 5.12 on the Fall and the consequence of death for all, he was anxious to insist that it is individual sin that brings us under the norm of death. He would give no encouragement to pelagians with his acceptance of the Fall, and yet with typical eastern accent on healing rather than wound he can present it almost as a *felix culpa*:

> From the beginning the creator arranged our condition this way, and foreseeing Adam's transgression he prepared in advance a remedy suited to the wound.[81]

In pointing up Theodoret's deficiencies as a spiritual director, then, Gustave Bardy is probably wide of the mark in tracing his ambivalent position on grace and free will to a problem with original sin (though, predictably, the term does not occur in his text).[82] We saw him, rather, wrestling with Paul's insistence on the gratuity of divine grace because, on the basis of Antioch's incarnational theology generally, it seemed to impugn the role of free will and human effort in the process of salvation – as it would thus undercut that school's Christology, soteriology and approach to (the literal sense of) Scripture. It is quite logical for him, therefore, to resist a notion of predestination limiting free will that developed in later interpretation of Rom 8.30, "Those whom he predestined he also called;" capitalizing on his imaginative gifts, he warms to Paul's theme as he sees it:

> It was not the foreknowledge that made them like that – rather, God from afar foresaw the future as God. In other words, if I were to see a bucking horse champing at the bit and in no way tolerating the rider, and say he was riding for a fall, and then things turned out according to my word, it would not be I who brought the horse

down; rather, I put into words what was bound to happen, relying on the horse's lack of control as a sign. The God of all from a distance knew everything as God; he did not apply pressure to such-and-such a one to practice virtue, nor to another to commit evil. After all, had he forced them in each case, it would not be right for him to celebrate and award the former and sentence the other to punishment.

We bear a considerable degree of responsibility for our own salvation, he is saying; in the divine economy human effort counts for much: "faith is not sufficient for salvation," as he says by way of paraphrase of 2 Cor 5.9 – our response to our divine benefactor is also required.[83] It was by not responding that the Jews lost God's favor through their own free will (*gnome, proairesis*): such is his diagnosis of biblical history in chs 9-11, "the heart of Romans." Not that there is no role for divine grace: the Commentary repeatedly insists on it; but in his desire to maintain that "symmetrical" balance the commentator can come out with statements that seem at least ambivalent and would give heart to the pelagians – for example, "Grace comes to the assistance of those who contribute the proper enthusiasm (*prothumia*)."[84] At other times the balance, though still unhappily expressed, is more deliberate, as in commentary on Rom 12.11-12:

> The Spirit is quenched in the case of those unworthy of grace: they do not keep the eye of the mind clear, and so do not receive that ray... The one who is fervent in spirit serves the Lord with enthusiasm, looks forward to the enjoyment of the good things hoped for and proves superior to the onset of trials, pitting endurance against their assaults and calling unceasingly on divine grace for assistance.

Our effort and enthusiasm make us "worthy of grace," and yet we depend on and pray for "divine grace for assistance" – a balance, if teetering somewhat. He is more secure in comment on Phil 1.29: "Free will (*gnômê*) of itself, devoid of grace, can achieve no good work: there is need of both, our enthusiasm and divine assistance. In other words, the grace of the Spirit is not sufficient for those lacking enthusiasm, nor in turn is enthusiasm which is devoid of it capable of amassing the riches of virtue."[85]

Predictably, in Theodoret we find no suggestion of impairment of human nature;[86] he retains his eastern optimism on its goodness, and would not want his readers to think Paul is of a different mind in passages like Rom 6.13: "He presented the body not as evil but as a creation of a good God: it is capable, when guided by the soul in a fit and proper manner, of worshipping God." He would have no truck with modern commentators like Bultmann who constantly find in the text a gnostic background to Paul's thinking. He takes issue with heretics who want to see a dualistic antithesis of body and spirit in the letters, especially in passages contrasting two principles of action, like Rom 8.13:

> Here, of course, the divine apostle saw the blasphemy of Marcion, Valentinus and Mani, and proposed the teaching with great precision, saying not, You put to death the body, but 'the actions of the body,' that is, the mindset of the flesh, the impulses of the passions; after all, you have the Spirit's cooperating grace.

He insists in comment on Gal 5 that Paul's antithesis of flesh and spirit is to do with attitude, *phronêma, gnômê*, no criticism of the body being involved. He tells his readers (probably lay people in the world, we concluded) that there is no need to cut themselves off from the world; he paraphrases 1 Cor 5.10 to mean, "I impose no difficult requirement on you; I am not bidding you be completely cut off from those not of the faith, this being tantamount to dispatching you to some other world."[87] He is concerned lest the dictum (if not of Paul, of the Corinthians themselves) in 2 Cor 5.6 be taken amiss, "While at home in the body, we are away from the Lord," and he insists, "He does not say, We are at a distance from the Lord in still being joined to the mortal body; rather, We do not see him here and now with the eyes of the body, whereas we shall see and be in his company." Bodily existence is no obstacle to union with the Lord. He rejects as "obvious servitude and abolition of the dignity given to us" the rigorous asceticism of deviants in the Colossian church.

It is sound, balanced, practical advice to his readers for living their spiritual life, even if he does not go into further detail than Paul himself; this he would see more appropriate to a preacher. Theodoret would probably have been content with Louis Bouyer's summary – an "asceticism without mysticism"[88] – of Antioch's reaction against impractical Alexandrian mysticism. As is true also of the Commentary on the Psalms, in this work Theodoret does not aspire to the role of spiritual director, or (as we have noted) engage the reader in a discourse of spiritual direction; when Paul at 1 Thess 5.17 urges his listeners to "pray without ceasing," he passes on with a mere one-liner. He realizes his readers, who as lay people are not in the habit of reading much and are "prone to easy ways" in that regard, are not bent on ascending Mount Carmel. Generally, they are married people; he is aware Paul had contemporary misunderstandings about marriage to confront, and he himself wants to uphold the institution against later heretics assailing it. The occasion comes, of course, with the reply to queries on the subject of virginity and marriage from Corinth at 7.32-37 of the first letter. Taking a lead from Paul, Theodoret first concedes the double function of virginity, pragmatic and eschatological: "The person practicing virginity has a soul free of idle and pointless concerns, and reproduces the future life as far as possible;" he adds the fact that his work on this topic (not known to us) goes into greater depth. He then relates the two ways of life without detriment to marriage: "He brought out the good in one case and the better in the other, and stopped the mouths of the heretics who malign marriage," citing as well Novatian's condemnation of second marriages (an issue also in the Pastorals). In the light of his general defense of life in the world and the compatibility of body and spirit in the Christian life, this brief endorsement would have encouraged his readers, as it did Paul's community.

6

THEODORET'S ACHIEVEMENT

Theodoret tells us at the outset that he was aware that "in turning my hand to a commentary on the teaching of the divine Paul I shall not escape the criticism of fault-finders," especially on the score of the task having been completed by illustrious predecessors. Augustine, we noted, faced the same rejoinder in contemplating a work on the Psalms in the wake of dozens of others before him; but we likewise do not now regret that he was unswayed by Jerome's discouragement. Seeing the work of Chrysostom and Theodore rather as resource than as obstacle, Theodoret was content, "like some kind of mosquito, to buzz about the apostolic meadows along with those famous bees." He thus evinced a virtue of modesty with which, significantly, he frequently credits Paul, just as in his Commentary on the Psalms it was gentleness that he found most appealing in David. His achievement, in fact, is considerable, whether viewed as "exegetical" (in a loose sense of the word), theological or spiritual. He demonstrates a fine grasp of Pauline thinking, brings Antiochene precision to the text, even if like his contemporaries eschewing historical, sociological and other critical issues examined by modern commentators – who, however, we agreed, could benefit from reading his comments on many a passage. The litmus test must be whether Paul comes through to us more clearly from his Commentary, and the verdict is indisputably affirmative.

Where his objectivity as exegete/commentator falters is when his ever-present theological concerns not only obtrude into the text but bring him to see his positions, which are those of his school, as irreconcilable with those apparently espoused by "the divine apostle," with implications for theology and spirituality. This is true particularly of his reluctance to accept Paul's views on divine election and the gratuity of grace; free will and human effort must be upheld if Antioch is to maintain a necessary "balance." So, like a celebrated modern commentator, Theodoret can be seen wrestling with Romans (in particular – though these convictions permeate most letters). We can learn from his Commentary much of the Christological and trinitarian currents of the time (the decade before Chalcedon, it would seem), and also of contemporary eastern sacramental discipline. Within his self-imposed limits as a desk commentator as distinct from a preacher, the spiritual guidance he offers is also characterized by the balance of his textual commentary. He can reasonably claim to have succeeded in his modest aim of "demonstrating the profundity of the apostle's wisdom and stripping away the veils from the writing," and the work ("quo nil melius tota antiquitas habet post Chrysostomum," its editor assures us) deserves to be more widely known by now appearing in English.

Bibliography

Aland, K., Aland, B., *The Text of the New Testament*, 2nd ed., Eng.trans., Grand Rapids, 1989

Ashby, G. W., *Theodoret of Cyrrhus as Exegete of the Old Testament*, Grahamstown, 1972

Azéma, Y., *Théodoret de Cyr. Correspondance* II,III, Sources Chrétiennes 98,111, Paris, 1964,1965

Bardy, G., "Théodoret," *DTC* 15, Paris, 1946

_____ , "Interprétation chez les pères," *DBSupp* IV, Paris, 1949

Barrett, C. K., *The First Epistle to the Corinthians*, New York, 1968

Black, M., *Romans*, New Century Bible Commentary, 2nd ed., Grand Rapids, 1989

Bouyer, L., *The Spirituality of the New Testament and the Fathers*, Eng.trans., London, 1963

Bruce, F. F., *1&2 Thessalonians*, Word Biblical Commentary 45, Waco TX, 1982

Bultmann, R., *The Second Letter to the Corinthians*, Eng.trans., Minneapolis, 1985

Byrne, B., "The Letter to the Philippians," *NJBC* 791-97

Canivet, P., *Histoire d'une entreprise apologétique au Ve siècle*, Paris, 1957

Dalton, W., *Galatians Without Tears*, Sydney, 1992

Fitzmyer, J., "The Letter to the Romans," *NJBC*, 830-68

Guinot, J.-N., *L' Exégèse de Théodoret de Cyr*, Théologie historique 100, Paris, 1995

Hay, C., "Antiochene exegesis and Christology," *ABR* 12 (1964) 10-23

Hill, R. C., "*Akribeia*: a principle of Chrysostom's exegesis," *Colloquium* 14 (Oct. 1981) 32-36

_____ , "The mystery of Christ: clue to Paul's thinking on wisdom," *HeyJ* 25 (1984) 475-83

_____ , "Psalm 45: a *locus classicus* for patristic thinking on biblical inspiration," *StudP* 25 (1991) 95-100

_____ , "The Fathers on the biblical Word," *Pacifica* 7 (1994) 255-72

_____ , "A pelagian commentator on the Psalms?" *ITQ* 65 (1998) 263-71

_____ , *Theodoret of Cyrus. Commentary on the Psalms*, FOTC 101, 102, Washington DC, 2000, 2001

_____ , "Theodoret, Commentator on the Psalms," *ETL* 76 (2000) 88-104

Houlden, J. L., *Paul's Letters from Prison*, SCM Pelican Commentaries, London, 1977

Kelly, J. N. D., *Early Christian Doctrines*, 5th ed., New York, 1978

_____ , *Golden Mouth. The Story of John Chrysostom, Ascetic, Preacher, Bishop*, Ithaca NY, 1995

MacNamara, K., "Theodoret of Cyrus and the unity of the person in Christ," *ITQ* 22 (1955) 313-28

Mandac, M., "L'union Christologique dans les oeuvres de Théodoret antérieures au Concile d'Ephèse," *ETL* 47 (1971) 64-96

Murphy-O'Connor, J., "The First Letter to the Corinthians," *NJBC* 798-815

Parvis, P., *Theodoret's Commentary on the Epistles of St Paul*, Oxford, 1975

Schäublin, C., "Diodor von Tarsus," *TRE* 8, 763-67

_____ , *Untersuchungen zu Methode und Herkunft der Antiochenischen Exegese*, Köln-Bonn, 1974

Smalley, B., *The Study of the Bible in the Middle Ages*, 3rd ed., Oxford, 1983

Vaccari, A., "La θεωρία nella scuola esegetica di Antiochia," *Bib* 1 (1920) 3-36

Viciano, A., "Theodoret von Kyros als Interpret des Apostels Paulus," *TGl* 80 (1990) 279-315

Weaver, D., "The exegesis of Romans 5:12 among the Greek Fathers and its implications for the doctrine of original sin: the 5th-12th centuries," *SVTQ* 29 (1985) 132-59

Young, F., *From Nicaea to Chalcedon*, Philadelphia, 1983

_____ , *Biblical Exegesis and the Formation of Christian Culture*, Cambridge 1997

NOTES

[1] As he does in a letter to the monks of Constantinople in 451 (*Théodoret de Cyr. Correspondance* III, ed. Y. Azéma, Sources Chrétiennes 111, 176).

[2] A term from Frances Young, *From Nicaea to Chalcedon*, 267. Cyrus lay about 100 km NE of Antioch.

[3] Cf. my translation, *Theodoret of Cyrus. Commentary on the Psalms.*

[4] "Strangely," except perhaps for the fact of the classic commentaries by his Antiochene predecessor John Chrysostom on the Gospels of Matthew and John (the former being so celebrated in later times that Thomas Aquinas said of it that he would give the whole town of Paris to have composed it) that might have discouraged his admirer from rivaling them.

[5] A letter to an unknown recipient, dated by editor Azéma a little before 448 (*Correspondance* II, Source Chrétiennes 98, 20), says, "I gave your holiness, as a judge both wise and dependable, my book written on the divine apostle;" a letter to Eusebius of Ancyra, dated December 448 (II, 202), gives Theodoret's claim to have commented on "all the prophets, the psalter, and the apostle;" a letter to Pope Leo, dated in 449 (III, SC 111, 64), reads, "Thanks to divine grace, commentaries by me have been composed on both the apostolic (or New Testament) and the prophetic (or Old Testament) oracles."

[6] Including Paul Parvis and Alberto Viciano, who would place the work a decade earlier.

[7] For evidence of dating, see the Introduction to my translation of that Commentary in the Fathers of the Church series.

[8] Today's social workers and criminologists would agree with the bishop's analysis of the effects of indolence and unemployment in commentary on Eph 4.28, "Let thieves be thieves no more," where he sees theft as a symptom of idleness.

[9] In commentary on 1 Cor 15 (see note 25 there). His position is similar in commentary on the Household Code at Eph 6; cf. comment on 1 Tim 5.21; 6.1.

[10] Cf. comment on 1 Cor 14.31.

[11] He can cite the Koine text of a letter, and then comment not on it but on the alternative reading, e.g., Col 4.7-9 (cf. Phlm 14); Heb 10.34; cf. 2 Tim 2.25; 4.14. It would thus seem he has – at least at times – two texts open before him.

[12] So K. Aland, B. Aland, *The Text of the New Testament*, 51-71. Lucian had been given credit also for the form of the Septuagint found in Antioch and represented in the Old Testament commentaries of Chrysostom and Theodoret (also on the word of Jerome, likewise under review).

[13] Cf. B. Aland, K. Wachtel, "The Greek miniscule manuscripts of the New Testament," in B. D. Ehrman, M. W. Holmes (edd.), *The Text of the New Testament in Contemporary Research*, Grand Rapids, 1995, 45: "We can no longer maintain without reservation the view that was still held by the present author (B. Aland) in *The Text of the New Testament*, 64-66, that the Koine text is to be attributed to a recension produced by Lucian... One simply cannot determine if and to what extent Lucian was involved in producing a recension of the New Testament."

[14] A change in attitude from that expressed earlier in the century by paleographers like E. Mangenot, "Texte du Nouveau Testament," *DB* V, 2122: "C'est un mauvais texte." Of course, there are times when the text in our

edition is not proof against human error on the part of copyists; see, e.g., note on Phil 4.7.

[15] Cf. Rom 3.22, "God's righteousness through faith of Jesus Christ for all *and upon all*" (Theodoret's distinctive element in emphasis).

[16] Cf. Rom 4.1: "So what shall we say our father Abraham found *according to the flesh*?" Cf. Heb 2.9, which Theodoret turns to his advantage; also 11.8.

[17] Cf. Gal 4.4.

[18] Cf. Rom 11.6.

[19] Cf. Rom 8.1; Eph 4.6; Phil 3.16; Col 2.7; Heb 1.3; 11.37; 1 Tim 2.7; 4.12; 6.5.

[20] Cf. 1 Cor 10.28; 2 Cor 12.1; Eph 4.6. On the "Sleeper, awake" hymn at Eph 5.14 Theodoret cites and follows a reading from "some of the manuscripts" – though Guinot reminds us he is only doing what Theodore and Chrysostom had done before him.

[21] Cf. also G. Bardy, "Théodoret," *DTC* 15, 325.

[22] There is also the matter of the lacuna, apparently inexplicable, of eight and a half verses, Gal 2.6b-14.

[23] PG 82.1. Page numbers of PG 82 are given in the text of the translation below.

[24] Theodoret's awareness of the distinction in roles emerges in commentary on the picture of the ideal pastor in Titus 1.9, where he notes that preference goes not to eloquence but to "helpful instruction." For a discussion of orality in patristic works, and of the means available to the Fathers for recording their oratorical works, see my "Chrysostom's Commentary on the Psalms: homilies or tracts?" in P. Allen et al (edd.), *Prayer and Spirituality in the Early Church* I, Brisbane, 1998, 301-18.

[25] Occasionally, too, we regret that those responsible for modern versions have not consulted the Fathers. On the requirement in 1 Tim 3.2, for instance, that an overseer should be a husband of one wife, Theodoret with the encouragement of Theodore and Chrysostom allows the possibility of a second marriage for these clergy after the death of their first wife (against Novatian rigorists) – which the NRSV's "married only once" does not canvass.

[26] See my translation and Introduction to it, *St John Chrysostom. Commentary on the Psalms*, 2 vols, Brookline MA, 1998.

[27] A solitary exception would be his comment on the litany of sins of the last days given in 2 Tim 3.1-5, which he regrets (if briefly) refer to his own society.

[28] He can leave to them decision on moot points, like the debated question of whether Paul had been to Colossae before writing to the community (where he differs from Theodore and Chrysostom).

[29] See my translation and Introduction to *St John Chrysostom. Homilies on Genesis* 1-17 (Father of the Church 74), Washington DC, 1986.

[30] Cf. commentary on Rom 1.17; 7.10. He does not respond to the misogynist cue in 2 Tim 3.6-7 to expatiate on *gynaikaria*, whereas he makes a gratuitously grudging remark about the Apphia in Phlm 2 he thinks is

Philemon's wife.

[31] One could get the impression from Theodoret's opening to his Commentary on the Psalms that he is sexually egalitarian. He takes issue with Ps 1.1, "Blessed is the man," which in both his LXX text and the original refers to the male, commenting, "Now, no one seeing only a man declared blessed here should think that womankind are excluded from this beatitude. I mean, Christ the Lord in delivering the Beatitudes with men in mind did not exclude women from possessing virtue: his words include men and women." This impression, however, is undermined both by the backhanded way he upholds women's place and by his reverting in his own usage to exclusive language.

[32] Cf. Phil 4.15-16; Heb 9.10; 11.31; 1 Tim 2.9.

[33] It is unlikely he was closely acquainted with either one of "the world's luminaries." Both exercised their episcopal ministry beyond Antioch, Chrysostom moving to Constantinople in 397 to die in exile a decade later, Theodore to Mopsuestia in Cilicia in 392 until his death in 428.

[34] Ep 112.20, written about the end of 404 (PL 22.928). Neither monitum proved efficacious.

[35] As he likewise did in working on the Psalms, claiming that, in addition to what he gained from his predecessors, "what we learnt from the Holy Spirit we were anxious to offer to posterity" (the brief conclusion to the Psalms Commentary, PG 80.1997). One has therefore to doubt the close acquaintance with the text of either Commentary on the part of those who deny originality to Theodoret, like Gustave Bardy, "Interprétation chez les pères," DBS IV, 582: "Il n'a aucune prétention à l'originalité;" Alberto Viciano, "Theodoret von Kyros als Interpret des Apostels Paulus," 279: "Es ist keine originelle Arbeit, sondern ein Werk das die Kontinuität der kirchlichen Überlieferung wahrt."

[36] The unusual length he goes to in disallowing their opinions on composition of Ephesians seems to suggest he feels uncomfortable in taking a stand against Severian, Theodore and Chrysostom together. Cf. Col 2.1.

[37] L'Exégèse de Théodoret de Cyr, 644-66, to which one could add a forty seventh reference, on Col 2.16.

[38] On "the Isaac of God" in Gal 6.16 he confuses the etymology of Jacob's cognomen with that of Peniel in the same incident in Gen 32.28-30; he thinks he sees Adam ('adam) in the red ('ademah) heifer of Num 19.2 referred to in Heb 13.11.

[39] So P. Canivet, Histoire d'une entreprise apologétique au Ve siècle, 26-27, a view confirmed by his access to the Peshitta Bible in commenting on the Psalms.

[40] He notes the author's quotation from Luke in 1 Tim 5.17 (fifth in order of composition, he decided in the preface), but does not advert to any issue this raises about respective dates of composition if Paul (whose death by beheading under Nero he accepts in commentary on Phil 1.25-26) is to be upheld as the author.

[41] Cf. the end of Col. At the end of Gal he takes Paul to mean he wrote the

whole letter personally. Cf. comments on Phlm 19.

[42] E.g., at 1 Cor 5.9; 2 Cor 1.15-16; 2.12-13; 7.8; 10.

[43] For example, when Paul says in 1 Cor 4.13, "We have become the world's garbage, " Barrett comes up with the unlikely notion of "scapegoats," leading one to wish he could have read Theodoret's comment on the verse: "We are no different, he is saying, from what is thrown out in households as superfluous – vegetables, scraps and other things like that; in similar fashion we are reputed by most people to be worthless." Bruce, by contrast, frequently checks with the Fathers' views (though not Theodoret's).

[44] Keeping to his self-imposed limits as a desk theologian, Theodoret generally does not give vent to this admiration, unlike a preacher such as Chrysostom; but the pathos of the relationships Paul skillfully exploits in making his appeal to Philemon gets the better of him.

[45] Cf. my "The mystery of Christ: clue to Paul's thinking on wisdom."

[46] David Weaver ("The exegesis of Romans 5:12," 152-53), with the support of John Meyendorff, thinks that, despite the clarity of this statement, a meaning "on account of which" is preferable to "because" for Theodoret's interpretation of Paul here.

[47] Unlike modern commentators such as Rudolf Bultmann, who find gnostic ideas ever in Paul's sights, Theodoret is drawn to comment formally on the gnostics only when the text obliges him to do so, at 1 Tim 6.20 (though Valentinus is more than once included in a group censured for its dualistic approach to the Incarnation).

[48] See my "A pelagian commentator on the Psalms?"

[49] Cf. C. Schäublin, "Diodor von Tarsus," 8.756. Derek Krueger cannot have read Theodoret's exegetical works to claim typology as a "standard method" of Antiochenes in his article, "Typological figuration in Theodoret of Cyrrhus's *Religious History* and the art of postbiblical narrative," *JECS* 5 (1997) 407.

[50] "La θεωρία nella scuola esegetica di Antiochia," 12: "La essenziale differenza fra teoria e allegoria consiste in ciò, che l'allegoria esclude di sua natura il senso letterale." The term *theoria* occurs in Theodoret's text in connection with discernment of sacramental realities (on Heb 8.4-5).

[51] Rom 3.25.

[52] Details occur in the appropriate places in the text below.

[53] An exception would be the length he goes to in disallowing views of several Antiochene predecessors about the composition of Ephesians.

[54] Bardy rightly classes Theodoret's exegetical work as "modéré," justifying its esteem by later ages as "le noyau ou le terme de comparaison indispensable" ("Interprétation chez les pères," 582). Ashby concurs, seeing him "representing a later and more balanced stage of Antiochene exegesis" than Theodore and Chrysostom.

[55] See my "*Akribeia*: a principle of Chrysostom's exegesis."

[56] Cf. Phil 3.8,13-15; Col 2.17,18; 1 Thess 2.7-8,11; 5.2-3; Heb 5.13-14; 1 Tim 4.2; 2 Tim 1.6,13.

[57] Cf. Rom 2.25; 6.13; 7.12; Gal 5.6; Eph 4.25; Phil 3.7; 1 Thess 4.17; 2 Thess

2.9-10; Heb 10.24; 11.6; 1 Tim 1.16; 6.5; 2 Tim 2.15.

[58] He does not know extrabiblical Jewish literature, like *Jubilees*, that would have helped commentary on Col. He is unaware of errors about Jewish ritual by the author of Heb. He knows the Mishnah – or at least the meaning of the word (*deuterôsis*) – but disallows its value (1 Tim 1.4; cf. 4.7; Titus 1.13-15). The mention of parchments in 2 Tim 4.13 elicits a reference to Sefer Torah scrolls kept by the Jews.

[59] Cf. Heb 7.18-20; 9.9-10; 10.3; 1 Tim 1.8; 4.7; Titus 1.16.

[60] Rom 15.26-27. He even speaks, on Eph 5.27, of the Church existing before Christ's coming, though in "her former servile condition," which is now stripped away by Christ's death. Cf. comment on Timothy's Jewish Christian mother Eunice, 2 Tim 1.5.

[61] Cf. Heb 1.1-3.

[62] Rom 1.25; cf. 11.36; 1 Cor 11.3; 2 Cor 4.6; 13.4; Gal 1.1,15-16; Phil 4.7; 2 Thess 1.1-2.

[63] Rom 11.36; 1 Cor 1.24; 3.9; 3.23; 8.6; 15.25,27-28; 2 Cor 3.17; Phil 2.6; 1 Thess 4.2; 2 Thess 2.16; 1 Tim 2.5; 6.13. He is aware of texts called into service by the Arians, such as John 17.3 (in comment on 1 Thess 1.9).

[64] Cf. 2 Cor 1.3; 11.31; Eph 1.3; Heb 2.11. Docetism is also a concern for a commentator who always has in mind the oikonomia of the Incarnation as the backdrop to textual statement on Jesus. At 1 Thess 4.14 he sees Paul speaking in consoling fashion of "those who have fallen asleep" but insisting bluntly that "Jesus died." Cf. Heb 5.7-10; 1 Tim 4.1; 2 Tim 2.8.

[65] The terminology of the Chalcedonian formula occurs at times, e.g., on Eph 5.32; 1 Tim 6.15. It is odd that an article by Camillus Hay entitled "Antiochene exegesis and Christology," *ABR* 12 (1964) 10-23, could make no mention of Theodoret, confining itself to the commentaries on John's Gospel of Theodore and Chrysostom.

[66] Cf. Eph 1.19-22; Heb 1. Such efforts at achieving a balance have helped earn his thinking the term "symmetrical" from K. McNamara, "Theodoret of Cyrus and the unity of person in Christ," 326, McNamara attributing the term to Alois Grillmeier. If meant pejoratively by McNamara, "symmetrical" can also be taken as a fair statement of Theodoret's balanced and disciplined approach.

[67] Cf. M. Mandac, "L'union Christologique dans les oeuvres de Théodoret antérieures au Concile d'Ephèse," 96: "Il est vrai qu'il ne sut pas exprimer avec toute la clarté désirable ce qu'on appelle aujourd'hui l'union hypostatique et ses conséquences, mais qui connaît la longue histoire de ce dogme ne lui en fera pas grief." J. N. D. Kelly, *Early Christian Doctrines*, 325, is prepared to concede he does not sacrifice one dogma for the other: "His guiding principles, we should note, were the completeness and distinction of the natures (cf ἡ λαβοῦσα and ἡ ληφθεῖσα φύσις), and their union in one person." The latter principle can succumb to accent on the former, resulting in statements that sound Nestorian: in comment on Heb 5.7-10 Theodoret observes, "The divinity allowed the humanity to experience (the passion)."

[68] Cf Viciano, "Theodoret von Kyros als Interpret des Apostels Paulus," 288: "Er hebt die *unio hypostatica* nicht genügend hervor. Das gilt auch für die *communicatio idiomatum.*"

[69] Cf Gal 1.1; Heb 1.12; 7.25-26; 1 Tim 3.16. 1 Thess 1.10 prompts him to comment, "It is as a human being that he suffered, and as a human being that he rose."

[70] His comment on Rom 8.11; 1 Cor 2.12; Heb 9.8,14; 1 Tim 4.1.

[71] Cf Rom 8.11; 1 Cor 3.17; 2 Cor 3.17; 1 Tim 6.13. On the classic text on divine inspiration of the Scriptures, 2 Tim 3.16, his comment is simply that as the Spirit is involved, the Spirit must be God.

[72] In commentary on Col 3.9-14, the ritual of baptism, in which neophytes don the baptismal robe, is much on the bishop's mind. Cf 2 Tim 2.11.

[73] Cf Rom 4.25; 5.1-2; 8.30; 11.26-27; 13.14; 2 Cor 3.9; 5.17; Gal 2.19; Heb 3.14.

[74] Cf Gal 6.15. He also speaks of catechising as a preparatory stage to initiation (Eph).

[75] Mention of sealing with the Holy Spirit in Eph 4.30 evokes no comment on a sacrament of confirmation, as it might in the West.

[76] Rom 6.9-10; cf 4.25; Col 1.14.

[77] At the close of comment on 1 Cor 7; cf 1 Tim 3.2; 5.9,14.

[78] 1 Cor 1.17; cf 1 Tim 5.17.

[79] One must "confirm faith with deeds," he says more than once in comment on 1 Tim.

[80] Cf Gal 2.16; 3.21; Eph 2.15; 6.3; Heb 7.18-20; 9.9-10; 1 Tim 1.11.

[81] 2 Cor 5.5.

[82] "On voit sans peine les insuffisances et les lacunes de cette doctrine (of original sin). Lorsqu'il s'agit de la grâce et de sa nécessité, Théodoret n'est pas moins incomplet" ("Théodoret," 323).

[83] His comment on Titus 3.8 is, "For those devoid of good works faith is not sufficient for salvation." When Eph 2.8 says unambiguously, "By grace you are saved through faith..., not from works," Theodoret concurs, but sees faith as our response to the gift, and after baptism the practice of virtue, thus maintaining the balance; and on 4.8 he remarks that it is our faith that elicits divine grace. Cf Heb 4.2; 1 Tim 1.14; Titus 1.1.

[84] 1 Cor 7.7; 1 Tim 4.13. As with Chrysostom, *prothumia/rhathumia* are binomials (to adopt the terminology of F. Asensio) basic to the spiritual life in Theodoret's thinking. See my "A pelagian commentator on the Psalms?"

[85] But in the next chapter, 2.13, he rephrases Paul, finding him too even-handed. Cf 2 Thess 3.5: "We need both, good intention and cooperation from on high;" also 2 Tim 1.9. Kelly defends both Theodore and Theodoret against charges of pelagian theology, admitting only "an intensified emphasis on individualism" (*Early Christian Doctrines*, 373).

[86] Cf Weaver, "The exegesis of Romans 5:12," 136: "It will be seen that such concepts as 'sin of nature,' inherited sin, or inherited guilt are virtually impossible for Greek theologians, not only the orthodox, but also for those entertaining heterodox opinions in other matters."

[87] But that other-worldly dictum in Heb 13.14 leads him (as it has led many another preacher) to an unhelpful comment for lay people, "Let us despise things of this life."

[88] *The Spirituality of the New Testament and the Fathers*, 444.

The Blessed Theodoret
Bishop of Cyrus

Commentary on the Fourteen Epistles of the Holy Apostle Paul

Preface

I am aware that in turning my hand to a commentary on the teaching of the divine Paul I shall not escape the criticism of fault-finders. They will represent me as guilty of presumption and over-confidence for having the effrontery to undertake the commentary on the apostle in the wake of this person and that, the world's luminaries. [1] Nevertheless, I shall endeavor – not by relying on myself but by imploring divine grace – to demonstrate the profundity of the apostle's wisdom and strip away the veils from the writing so as to offer those willing to partake of it the due benefit. [2]

Now, I beseech those who cannot forbear criticizing others' efforts to study the divine Scripture carefully: they will find many similar examples. Eldad and Medad, remember, did not get the popular vote, nor were they numbered among the seventy judges; [3] instead, even the mighty Moses left them in the company of the crowd. But they were accorded divine grace, and enjoyed a gift of prophecy. The prophet Samuel when still a youngster was not permitted by the priests to take part in even the least important act of worship, his immaturity being an impediment to worship; yet he was granted a divine appearance, enjoyed a vision of God and received the sound of the Lord God in his ears despite not yet knowing anything of God. [4] Elijah, of course, believed he was the only prophet left alive (37); but he was told there were seven thousand free of error regarding the idols and offering due honor to God. [5] And you could find innumerable such accounts in the divine Scripture.

So it is not out of place for us, too, like some kind of mosquito, to buzz about the apostolic meadows along with those famous bees. The Lord, after all, makes poor and makes rich, he humbles and he exalts, he lifts up the needy from the earth and raises the poor from the dungheap to seat them in the company of the mighty ones of the people and on a throne of glory. The Lord gives knowledge to the blind, turns the clever back on their tracks and renders their plans futile. [6] This is the very reason why, by begging to attain the ray of light for the mind, I shall be so bold as to attempt the commentary and assemble resources from the blessed Fathers. [7] Now, my particular concern is for conciseness: I am aware that brevity encourages even those prone to easy ways to do some reading. [8]

Firstly, however, I shall endeavor to make clear the chronological sequence of the apostle's letters. While blessed Paul wrote fourteen letters, [9] I believe the order in which they occur in the Bible is not of his doing. Instead, just as the divine David composed the sacred Psalms when in receipt of the action of the all-holy Spirit, whereas some other people compiled the collection as they pleased at a later stage, and though emitting the spiritual fragrance they do not retain the original sequence, so it is possible to see this happening likewise with the apostle's letters. [10] The one written by the most divine Paul to the Romans, for example, was assigned first place, whereas it was written last of all of those dispatched from Asia, Macedonia and Achaia. In fact, I believe the first to be written was First Thessalonians: the divine Paul sent it from Athens, as he made clear in writing to them, speaking this way in the middle of the letter, "Hence, being unable to bear it, we decided to be left alone in Athens, and sent our brother Timothy, God's faithful minister and our fellow worker in the Gospel of Christ, to strengthen and encourage you for the sake of your faith." [11] And after a short passage of time he sent the second one to the same people.

We learn from the story of the Acts that on leaving Athens the divinely-inspired Paul reached Corinth and spent a great deal of time there. I believe the first letter to the Corinthians was written after those ones; at all events, he sent it while living at that time in Ephesus. This he himself made clear: towards the end of the letter he says, "But I shall stay in Ephesus until Pentecost; a wide door for effective work has opened up for me, and the adversaries are numerous."[12] Now, he arrived at Ephesus (40) after preaching to Macedonians, Athenians and Corinthians, as the story of the Acts makes clear. I believe the second letter to the Corinthians was written after this one: reaching them in keeping with his promises and spending a short time in Macedonia, he sent it from there, and in turn indicated this in the letter itself. After describing the tribulations in Asia and in Troas, remember, he went on to say this in the middle, "Even when we came to Macedonia, in fact, our bodies had no rest; instead, we were afflicted in every way – contests on the outside and fears within. But the one who consoles the lowly consoled us with the coming of Titus, and not only with his coming but also with the consolation with which he was consoled about you;" and again, "Now, we make you aware, brethren, of the grace of God given to the churches of Macedonia;" and further, "Should Macedonians come with me."[13]

The fifth letter I believe to be the first one sent to Timothy: after the introduction he speaks this way, "As I urged you to wait in Ephesus when I was on my way to Macedonia."[14] Now, the story of the Acts also teaches us that when he arrived for the first time in Macedonia, he had not yet been to Ephesus: "They had in fact been forbidden by the Spirit to speak the word in Asia," it says. Timothy at any rate accompanied him; the story of the Acts also teaches this clearly: when the Jews from Thessalonica arrived in Beroea and incited the multitude to revolt, the divine apostle set sail for Athens, "whereas both Silas and Timothy remained there," it says. And again, when the composer described what happened in Corinth and taught how the divine apostle spoke in the synagogue on the Sabbath and the fact that he convinced both Jews and Greeks, he added, "When both Silas and Timothy arrived from Macedonia, Paul was occupied with preaching, testifying to the Jews that Jesus was the Christ."[15] It is therefore clear that when for the second time blessed Paul arrived in Macedonia from Ephesus, he then left the excellent Timothy there to care for those who had accepted the saving message. I suspect that after that letter the one to Titus was written: while still living in those parts he urged him to join him, as he says in these words, "When I send Artemas to you, or Tychicus, lose no time in coming to me in Nicopolis, as I have decided to spend the winter there." [16] Now, they say Nicopolis was a Thracian city but close to Macedonia.

The seventh letter he sent to the Romans: he himself makes clear that he wrote it after all those others, speaking this way, "At present, however, I am on my way to Jerusalem to minister to the saints; Macedonia and Achaia have agreed to do some sharing of goods (41) with the poor among the saints at Jerusalem." [17] Now, of these goods he speaks in the first letter to the Corinthians: "So that collections be not taken up at the time when I come; instead, when I get there, I shall send those whom you approve of by letter to bring your gift to Jerusalem. But if it seems appropriate for me also to travel, they will travel with me." [18] On sailing with this money to Jerusalem, he said to the elders from Ephesus in Miletus, "None of you, among whom I have gone about proclaiming the kingdom of God, will see my face anymore." [19] In fact, he was denounced as a criminal in Jerusalem and ran the risk of the supreme penalty, but was set free by the tribune from the Jews' clutches; lodging an appeal, under Festus he made his way to Rome. [20] Now, the fact that he wrote the letter to the Romans from Corinth its own conclusion clearly teaches us: he first commends Phoebe, saying she is a deacon of the church in Cenchreae, Cenchreae being a Corinthian town. Then he goes on to say this: "Gaius, host to me and the whole church, greets you," [21] giving the name "host" to someone who entertains guests. Now, the fact that Gaius was a Corinthian can easily be discovered from First Corinthians; he writes to them this way, "I thank God that I baptized none of you except Crispus and Gaius." [22]

Consequently, the letter to the Romans was the last one written from Asia, Macedonia and Achaia, and is seventh in order, as we have shown from the apostle's writings. The others, in fact, he sent from Rome. I believe the one to the Galatians was written first: before his departure for Macedonia he traveled through Phrygia and the region of Galatia preaching the Gospel. Then, after spending some time in Macedonia, Achaia and of course Asia, he left for Judea. From there he arrived at Rome after Ephesus; and learning that some people were confusing the religious teachings, he provided them with a remedy from his writings. From Rome he wrote to the Philippians after them, and the letter's conclusion suggests it: "Those of the emperor's household greet you,"[23] he says, remember. At the same time, however, he wrote also to the Ephesians and the Colossians, employing the one messenger for both letters: at the end of each he says, "For you also to know how I am and what I am doing, Tychicus will inform you of everything; he is my beloved brother and faithful minister in the Lord, whom I sent to you for that very purpose, for you to be aware of our circumstances, and to comfort your hearts."[24]

At least in the letter to the Colossians he also makes mention of Onesimus: "Along with Onesimus," he says, remember, "my faithful and beloved brother, (44) who is one of you. They will inform you of everything here."[25] So the letter to Philemon is located before those two: in it he urges that Onesimus be welcomed as a recipient of the spiritual birthpangs in prison,[26] whereas in the Colossians he ranks him with the ministers. After them he wrote to the Hebrews, at least to those from Rome, as the conclusion indicates: "Those from Italy greet you,"[27] he says, remember. Last of all he wrote the second letter to Timothy; it is likewise easy to discover this from his own writings: "As for me," he says, remember, " I am being poured out like a libation, and the time of my departure is at hand." From this it is possible to learn that he sent both the letter to the Ephesians and the letter to the Colossians from Rome: "I sent Tychicus to Ephesus,"[28] he says, note.

While this is the chronological order of the letters, people have given pride of place to the one to the Romans on the grounds of its containing instruction of all kinds and to the greatest extent offering precision in the doctrines. Some, on the other hand, claim that it is out of respect for the city that presides over the world and holds the scepter of kingship that they placed at the beginning the letter written to them. In my view the former seems the truer reason.[29] Nevertheless, if God sees fit, we shall write on the themes of the other letters at the proper time, and put each one's forward. For the time being at least, however, we shall speak on the purpose of the letter to the Romans at the beginning.[30]

NOTES

[1] Theodoret feels the need to account for his attempting a work already undertaken by others, such as famous predecessors of his in Antioch (like Diodore, Severian, Theodore and Chrysostom), not to mention Origen. He offered the same apologia in beginning commentary on the Psalms, where he also – as here – still claimed to have something peculiar to contribute.

[2] Even from the time of 2 Peter (cf. 3.15-16) it was admitted that Paul's letters offered the student difficult challenges.

[3] Cf. Num 11.24-29, where in fact the chosen seventy are elders.

[4] Cf. 1 Sam 3.1-14, where the text does not specify a vision of God. Bishop Theodoret is not above abjuring any monopoly by clerics on dealings with the divine.

[5] Cf. 1 Kgs 19.14-18.

[6] Cf. 1 Sam 2.7-8; Ps 113.7-8. At unusual length Theodoret is laboring his relative incompetence for the task.

[7] The works of previous commentators Theodoret regards not as grounds for disqualification but as a resource on which to call in his own work (as was true of his earlier work on the Psalms, an example he proceeds to cite).

[8] Conciseness, if not the chief virtue of a commentator, is the one Theodoret prizes, as he admitted also in the preface to his Commentary on the Psalms. He seems to be presuming that his readers include those not disposed to read a lengthy commentary.

[9] Though it is two centuries since Origen had abandoned the Pauline authorship of Hebrews, Theodoret prefers to follow the attribution of this letter (or, more precisely in the case of Heb, epistle – to follow G. Deissmann's distinction) to Paul along with those bearing his name, a tradition stemming from Cyril of Jerusalem a century before Theodoret.

[10] As a biblical critic Theodoret, despite some exegetical shortcomings (more significant in dealing with the Hebrew Scriptures), shows commendable flexibility, being prepared here to challenge the traditional order of the letters (as he did some matters affecting the Psalms). His independent examination of internal evidence of chronology does not allow for the possibility of letters to churches being placed before those to individuals, nor for the fact of decreasing length within those two groups; inclusion of Hebrews prevents his considering such principles of the ordering of letters.

[11] 1 Thess 3.1-2.

[12] 1 Cor 16.8-9.

[13] 2 Cor 7.5-7; 8.1; 9.4.

[14] 1 Tim 1.3.

[15] Acts 16.6; 17.14; 18.5.

[16] Titus 3.12. Modern cartographers would rather place Nicopolis as a western coastal city of Macedonia.

[17] Rom 15.26.

[18] 1 Cor 16.2-4.

[19] Acts 20.25.

[20] Acts 21;25.

[21] Cf. Rom 16.1,23.

[22] 1 Cor 1.14. Theodoret impresses us with his careful crosschecking as he goes about his seemingly independent ordering of the letters.

[23] Phil 4.22.

[24] Eph 6.21-22; Col 4.7-8. Occurrence of the identical closure in both letters prompts no critical comment in Theodoret, distinction between proto- and deuteropauline letters being a consideration beyond his critical horizons.

[25] Col 7.9.

[26] Cf. Phlm 10.

[27] Heb 13.24.

[28] 2 Tim 4.6,12.

[29] Since the placement of Hebrews distracts Theodoret from finding in mere length a principle of the ordering of the letters, he considers two other factors frequently offered as reasons for the series beginning with Romans, rightly disallowing the latter, as it would not account for the relative placement of some other letters, such as Galatians and Ephesians.

[30] In his preface Theodoret has thus addressed the question of the order of the letters, but said nothing on introductory questions such as Paul's life (he deals with its close in commenting on Phil 1.25), conversion and commissioning, the purpose of the letters, their authenticity, their use in the churches of his day – questions which often interest commentators, and which he addressed in connection with the Psalms in the preface introducing them.

The Letter to the Romans

THEME

On the one hand, the divine apostle offers in these writings a teaching that is manifold and varied. On the other, this aim of the letter is universal.[1] While the mystery of the divine Incarnation is something awesome and worthy of the deepest adoration by those who sincerely believe,[2] manifestly instructing us as it does in God's (45) lovingkindness, those who are beset by the gloom of unbelief and are yet to receive the illumination of light for the mind ridicule that which even the throngs of the angels fail to praise worthily in song. The divinely-inspired apostle brought this out clearly in writing to the Corinthians: "Whereas the message about the cross is folly to those who are perishing, to those who are being saved it is God's power."[3] Accordingly, in writing to the Romans he shows the saving proclamation is necessary, and for all people, both Jews and Greeks,[4] it is useful and advantageous. This is surely the reason why he convicts Greeks ahead of the rest of brazenly corrupting the distinction of good and its opposite and of transgressing the laws of nature, and of course Jews, who despite being recipients of written instruction in divine laws declined to take benefit from it and instead proved liable to greater retribution. After this he refers to the appearance of our God and savior, which occurred not for judgment and retribution for the transgressors but to grant forgiveness of sins, promise the end of death and proclaim eternal life.

He was aware, however, that Jews were excessively attached to the Law, while those infected with the teachings of Marcion and Valentinus, and of course Manichees, criticized it severely.[5] So just as some excellent general, surrounded on all sides by enemies, repels one lot after another and sets up the trophy, so the divine apostle demolished both the column of the heretics and the force of the Jews through divine grace. What in fact does he do? He neither extols the Law unduly, owing to Jews' impudence, nor does he provide the impious heretics with an occasion for criticism. Instead, he shows it giving the necessary instruction and proposing the teaching of righteousness, though unable to achieve this on account of the weakness of those on whom the law was imposed. Then he teaches that faith put into effect the aim of the Law: what the latter was willing but unable to achieve faith brought to completion through the grace of the all-holy Spirit. [6]

Now, in all this we learn that the God who created us and who always exercises providence towards human beings achieved his goal. That is to say, he first placed in nature the distinction between good and its opposite. Then through creation he guided the well-intentioned towards piety: even if not all wanted to see the truth, yet those desiring it attained what they desired. In addition to this, however, he leaves us also with this lesson, that it was by no change of heart that the God of all arrived at this method of salvation; rather, from the outset he foretold it through the divine prophets. He also brings out the reason for the rejection of the Jews, and (48) exhorts the believers from the Gentiles not to exult over them, urging them to outstrip the others in accepting the message. [7] With words of instruction he mingled also counsels of practical virtue, at one and the same time giving lessons in the truth and guiding behavior.

This, then, is the letter's theme; commentary on individual verses instructs us more precisely in it all.

CHAPTER ONE

Paul, a servant of Jesus Christ, called to be an apostle (v.1). Viceroys and generals place at the head of their writings their honorific titles, putting on airs and cultivating an exalted sense of their importance. The divine apostle, by contrast, calls himself one born out of due time, styles himself first of sinners, and claims to be unworthy of apostleship. [8] Nevertheless, in writing he prefaces the letters with the titles imposed by grace for the benefit of the recipients: on learning of the importance surrounding the writer, they accepted them with greater zeal and enthusiasm. The first name he gives himself is *Paul*, not getting this name originally from his parents but being given it after his calling, as Simon was given Peter, the sons of Zebedee sons of Thunder, Jacob Israel, and Abram Abraham. Next, *servant of Jesus Christ*, whom all the unbelievers called a corpse, crucified, son of the craftsman, whereas he embraced his service in preference to any kingship. Then he gives himself the name *called* in a reference to the calling from on high. And he adds the name *apostle* to bring out that this was also granted him: since it was the Lord who gave this title to the Twelve, the divine apostle claims it as well, not taking it by force but receiving it from the Lord himself; "Go," he said to him, remember, "because I shall send you far away to Gentiles." [9]

Set apart for God's Gospel. I am not self-appointed, he is saying; rather, I received the ministry of preaching from God himself. The Father, the Son and the Holy Spirit set him apart. The fact that the Father set him apart he personally teaches in the letter to the Galatians: "But when God, who from my mother's womb had set me apart and called me through his grace, was pleased to reveal his Son to me so that I might bring the good news of him to the Gentiles." [10] The fact that the only-begotten Son also did the very same the apostle likewise says in the Acts, that the Lord appeared to him in the Temple and bade him hurry up and leave, Jews not accepting his preaching, and added, "Go, because I shall send you far away to Gentiles." He said the very same thing also to Ananias, who was showing reluctance: "Go, because he is an instrument whom I have chosen to bring my name before Gentiles and kings and sons of Israel." Blessed Luke for his part teaches us that when the prophets in Antioch (49) were worshipping the Lord and fasting, the Holy Spirit said, "Set apart for me Barnabas and Saul for the work to which I have called them." [11] From this, then, the equality of the Trinity is also clear.

At this point he also called the Gospel God's, whereas a little later he says it is the Son's, speaking in these terms, *God, whom I serve with my spirit through the Gospel of his Son, is my witness* (v.9). It was not idly or to no purpose that he made this observation, [12] but to show that the teachers of truth refer the same things indiscriminately to the Father at one time and the Son at another. Now, he called the preaching *Gospel* for being a promised source of many good things: it brings good news of God's reconciliation, overthrow of the devil, forgiveness of sins, the end of death, the resurrection of the dead, eternal life, the kingdom of heaven.

After saying that he had been set apart for God's Gospel, the divine apostle at once shows its antiquity ahead of all things in case some foolish person should reject it in the belief that it was recent; he says, *Which he promised beforehand through his inspired authors in holy Scriptures* (v.2): the Old Testament is full of the prophecies about the Lord. Now, it was not idly that he employed the term *holy*; rather, it was firstly to bring out that he was aware that the Old Scripture is divine, then to distinguish it from all foreign composition: only Scripture inspired by God has contents that are beneficial. [13]

He also mentions the nature of the promise: *about his Son, who was of David's line according to the flesh* (v.3). Through all the inspired authors, he is saying, he made prophecies about the Son, who was begotten of him by nature before the ages, and styled son of David for assuming human nature of David's line. Of course, in mentioning David it was quite necessary for him to add the phrase *according to the flesh* lest he be considered David's son by nature and God's by grace: the addition of *according to the flesh* implies that he is truly son of God and Father according to divinity. After all, you do not find the phrase *according to the flesh* occurring in reference to those who are only what they seem. The evangelist Matthew is witness to this: after saying, "Abraham begot Isaac, Isaac begot Jacob, Jacob begot Judah," [14] and going through the whole of the rest of the genealogy, at no point did he add the phrase "according to the flesh:" such qualification did not apply to them, human beings that they were. In this case, on the contrary, since he is not only a human being but also eternal God, God the Word incarnate, in mentioning David's line the divine apostle of necessity added *according to the flesh*, teaching us clearly how on the one hand he is God's Son and on the other he is styled David's. (51)

Appointed Son of God through power, according to a Spirit of holiness, from resurrection of the dead, Jesus Christ our Lord (v.4). Before the cross and passion Christ the Lord did not seem to be God, not only to the other Jews but even to the apostles themselves: they were misled by human appearances, seeing him eating and drinking, sleeping and growing weary, and not even the miracles brought them round to this impression. So as soon as they beheld the miracle on the sea, they said, "What sort of person is this, that even the sea and the winds obey him?" [15] This is surely the reason the Lord also said to them, "I have many things to say to you, but you cannot bear them now. When that person comes, the Spirit of truth, he will guide you to the whole truth;" [16] and again, "Stay here in this city until you are clothed with power from on high when the Holy Spirit comes upon you." [17] Before the passion, then, they had such impressions of him, whereas after the resurrection and ascension into heaven, coming of the all-holy Spirit and the various wonders they worked by calling on his holy name all the believers came to know that he is God and God's only-begotten Son. Accordingly, here too the divine apostle taught that, while styled David's son according to the flesh, he was appointed and assigned Son of God through the power exercised by the all-holy Spirit after the resurrection from the dead of our Lord Jesus Christ himself. [18]

Through whom we have received grace and apostleship with a view to obedience of faith among all the gentiles for the sake of his name (v.5): it was he who proposed us as preachers, entrusting to us the salvation of all the Gentiles, and regaling us with grace suited to preaching so that they might heed us and believe the word, now that we have received the message. *Among whom you also are numbered, called to belong to Jesus Christ* (v.6): you too are from these Gentiles, with whose tending I have been entrusted. Do not think I am usurping what belongs to another and seizing pastures allotted to others: the Lord appointed me preacher to all the Gentiles.

To all God's beloved who are in Rome, called to be saints (v.7). He both honored them with the divine titles and repressed their arrogance. Firstly, note, he did not distinguish them from the other Gentiles on the score of being rulers of the world; rather, he combined them with the others. Then he addresses all together, combining servants, beggars, manual laborers, those abounding in wealth, those invested with influence. The fact that there were believers also from the latter groups, remember, he brings out in the letter to the Philippians: "Those from the emperor's household greet you." [19] (53) He made clear, of course, that he is writing not to unbelievers but to those who have already come to faith;

hence he calls them *called* and *saints*, commending them with spiritual encomiums and enkindling a desire for the benefactor. *Grace to you and peace from God our Father and the Lord Jesus Christ.*

Thus he completed the letter's opening formula: *Paul, a servant of Jesus Christ, to all God's beloved who are in Rome, called to be saints, grace to you and peace from God our Father and the Lord Jesus Christ.* He inserted other things in between, bringing out whose preacher he was appointed, what he was bidden to preach, and to whom he was assigned to propose these things. For them he prays firstly for God's grace: through that all the believers enjoyed salvation; then for peace, by which he is referring to the practice of virtue – peace with God, after all, being the lot of the one who embraces the evangelical way of life, who is zealous in serving him in everything. And he shows the provider of these gifts to be not only the Father but also the Son: *from God our Father and the Lord Jesus Christ*; through this he clearly taught us the equality of Father and Son. [20]

Firstly, I thank my God through Jesus Christ for you all for the fact that your faith is proclaimed in the whole world (v.8). The apostle put this in, not to flatter them but to admit the truth: what happened in Rome could not escape the notice of those living throughout the world. The Roman emperors had their palaces there, after all, and from there were dispatched both the rulers of the nations and those exacting tribute from the cities; and, of course, to that city all who sought royal favors directed their steps. By means of all these people it was bruited abroad that even the city of Rome had accepted the teaching about Christ. This was a source of great benefit to the listeners; hence the divine apostle praised the Lord for these developments.

Since, however, he claimed to have been appointed teacher of all the Gentiles, and a considerable time had elapsed without his going to them or through his writings guiding them to the truth, of necessity he both offers an apology and calls the Lord God to witness his kindly feelings for them. *God in fact, whom I serve with my spirit through the Gospel of his Son, is my witness that I make constant mention of you. I always in my prayers beg that there might sometime be a way to succeed in coming to you by God's will* (vv.9-10). There are many forms of worship: the one who prays worships God, as does the one who fasts, the one who heeds the divine sayings, and of course also the one who cares for strangers. (56) For his part the divine apostle claims to worship God by proposing the Gospel of his Son to the Gentiles, and to worship *with the spirit*, that is, with the gift given; this is the way he knows the honor of the Only-begotten to be pleasing to God. Employing a precise expression, however, he did not simply say he had begged to make the journey to them, but *by God's will* – if this is pleasing to the governor of all things, he says. But if where the salvation of such vast numbers was concerned the divine apostle asked nothing indiscriminately and instead associated the divine will with his request, what excuse would we deserve if we talk and pray about material things and do not depend on the divine will in our concerns? [21]

I am, in fact, longing to see you so as to share with you some spiritual gift (v.11). His words are redolent of a humble attitude: he did not say "to give" but *to share*: I give some of what I received. And since the mighty Peter was the first to offer them the evangelical teaching, of necessity he added, *for confirming you*: I wish to offer you no other teaching, but rather endorse that already offered and offer irrigation to the plants already planted. Then in turn he fills his words with great moderation: *This is for our mutual encouragement through our faith in one another* (v.12): I wish not only to give but also to receive from you. The zeal of the disciples also encourages the teacher.

I do not wish you to be ignorant, brethren, that I often longed to come to you and so far have been prevented (v.13). He both revealed the intention and indicated the divine plan: [22] divine grace governs me as it wishes, he is saying. After inserting the phrase *so far I have been prevented*, he brings out more clearly the reason he wanted to come to them: *so as to have some fruit among you also as among the other Gentiles as well. I owe a debt both to Greeks and to barbarians, to wise and to simple – hence eagerness on my part to preach the good news also to you in Rome* (vv.13-15): I was appointed teacher of all the Gentiles; this is the reason I owe a debt of teaching to all, not only to Greeks but also to barbarians. On this account, to be sure, the grace of the Spirit gave me also different tongues, and the debt ought to be discharged both to those puffed up with learning and those innocent of knowledge (calling *wise* those bragging about a gift of the gab, and *simple* those so-called by the so-called wise for their lack of learning). [23] And since not everyone accepted the preaching of the Gospel, he was right to add *eagerness on my part*: it is for me to preach, but for the listeners to believe.

And since he often called the preaching (57) Good News, whereas it contained reference to passion and cross and death, and these things seemed to be suggestive of dishonor to those who had not yet come to faith, it was appropriate for him to add, *I am not ashamed of the Gospel of Christ, in fact: it is God's power for salvation for every believer, for Jew first and also for Greek* (v.16). I am not focusing on the apparent dishonor, he says, but on the beneficence that springs from it: the believers reap salvation from it. In like manner many material things also contain their own hidden operation. For example, pepper has the appearance of being cool, and to the unwary it betrays no sense of being hot; but whoever crushes it with their teeth gets a taste of fiery heat. This is the reason, to be sure, that medical practitioners prescribe it for its potency for heat, on the grounds that, while not seeming to be like that, it is capable of proving to be such. In like manner grain has the capacity to be root and stalk and ear, but does not appear to be like that before being sown in the furrows of the soil. [24] Hence it was right also for the divine apostle to call the saving preaching *God's power* as being a power revealed to the believers only and regaling them with salvation. Now, he said that this is available to all, both Jews and Greeks; but he gave the Jews precedence to the Greeks since Christ the Lord also sent the sacred apostles as preachers first to them. This is what God also said through the prophet, "I appointed you as a covenant of a race, as a light to nations," [25] calling the Jews "race" since it was from them he came according to the flesh.

God's righteousness, you see, is revealed in it from faith to faith (v.17): it is not revealed to everyone, but to those who have the eyes of faith. Now, the divine apostle teaches us that God from the beginning managed things this way in our regard, he forecast these events through the inspired authors, and before the inspired authors he kept hidden within him this purpose concerning them; he says so elsewhere as well, "The mystery hidden in God, the creator of all things," [26] and again, "We speak a wisdom hidden in mystery, which God determined before the ages for our glory." [27] So at this place he did not say righteousness is "given" but is *re-*

vealed: formerly hidden, it is made clear to the believers. He says *from faith to faith*: it is necessary to place credit in the inspired authors of the Old Testament, and through them to be guided to the faith of the Gospel. [28] But it also has another meaning: the one who believes in Christ the Lord and is the recipient of the grace of all-holy baptism and receives the gift of sonship is guided through these to believing in the future goods – (60) I mean resurrection from the dead, eternal life, the kingdom of heaven. He means God's righteousness is revealed through the Gospel, not only the righteousness provided to us but also that shown openly in the very mystery of the divine plan. That is to say, it was not in power that he arranged our salvation, nor did he overthrow death's sway by command and direction; rather, he tempered justice with mercy. The only-begotten Word of God in person put on the nature of Adam, preserved it innocent of any sin and offered it for our sake, and by paying the debt of nature he canceled the indebtedness common to all human beings.

The divine apostle, however, teaches us this more clearly in what follows. Let us nonetheless continue to comment on details. Having said, then, that salvation accrues to both Jews and Greeks who wish it, he confirms his statement with scriptural testimony, saying, *As it is written, Now, the righteous one will live from faith.* [29] He put this in for the sake of Jews, to teach them not to cling to the way of life of the Law but to follow their own inspired authors, these having from the beginning preached salvation in advance through faith.

From this point, then, he desists from his initial accusation of the Jews, and accuses all the other people of fearlessly breaking the law placed in nature by the creator. In any case, by accusing them he provides a defense of the Maker: in creating them he did not allow them to live like brute beasts, but dignified them with the gift of reason, gave them a sense of right and wrong, and implanted in them a recognition of good and its opposite. [30] Those living before the Mosaic Law who were distinguished for piety and virtue testify to this gift of reason, as do those who took the opposite path: on breaking the commandment and tasting the fruit forbidden him, Adam at once endeavored to hide, his conscience reproaching him; then, when called to judgment he neither denied the crime nor offered ignorance as a defense, and instead shifted the responsibility for the accusation to his wife. [31] This fact he teaches clearly, that nature had the power to judge between actions. Cain likewise slew his brother in secret, and when asked, "Where is your brother Abel?" [32] he denied it and sought to hide the crime, but convicted he admitted the punishment to be fair, concurred with the judge, and said he had sinned beyond the limits of pardon. And you could find countless such examples in the divine Scripture.

For this reason the divine apostle said, *God's wrath in fact is revealed from heaven against all impiety and iniquity of people who suppress the truth by iniquity* (v.18): nature taught them both things, that God is creator of everything, and how to shun iniquity and embrace righteousness. But they did not make use of the teachers given them as they should; hence he threatened them also with the punishment to come. Now, he was right to use *revealed* here, too, for the reason that those who have not experienced what is threatened will in any case see the truth of the (61) words. By *God's wrath* he refers to retribution, not because God punishes in a passion, [33] but to instil fear into the opponents by mention of his name. And he said *it is revealed from heaven* because it is from there that our God and Savior will appear: the Lord himself said so, "Then you will see the Son of Man coming on the clouds of heaven with power and great glory." [34]

Because what is to be known of God is clear to them (v.19). Who is the giver of this knowledge to them? *God in fact made it plain to them.* How and in what fashion? *That is, the things that are invisible about him have from the creation of the world been understood through his creatures and perceived, both his eternal power and divinity* (v.20). Creation, he is saying, and what is made in creation, changes in seasons and alteration in times, succession of night and day, opening of clouds, gusts of wind, fruitfulness of plants and seeds, and all the other similar things clearly teach us both that God is maker of everything and that he wisely holds the tiller of creation. After all, having made everything through lovingkindness alone, he would never leave untended what he had made. This is the reason, to be sure, that the divine apostle said not "the thing that is invisible" but *the things that are invisible,* namely, his creation, his providence, his just verdict on everyone, and his various arrangements. This is the real reason why those who enjoyed such teachers were undeserving of pardon, for taking no benefit from such extraordinary lessons; he added, in fact, *with the result that they have no excuse*: the facts themselves well-nigh bellow out that they have no grounds for liberation from the evils threatened.

Hence despite knowing God they did not honor him as God or give thanks (v.21): they themselves testify to knowing he is God; they bandy about this venerable name, but are not prepared to entertain beliefs about him. *Instead, they were futile in their ideas, and their senseless heart was plunged into darkness*: they followed their mindless thoughts, and willingly adopted the gloom of unbelief. *Claiming to be wise they became fools* (v.22). He augmented their guilt with the name: though giving themselves a name for being wise, they revealed themselves in fact to be mindless. *They exchanged the glory of the incorruptible God for a likeness of an image of a corruptible human being* (v.23): refusing to realize that the creator of everything is proof against corruption and superior to visible things, they gave the name of gods to the images of their own bodies. (64) Carvers, sculptors and painters, in fact, make images not of invisible souls but of corruptible bodies. They were not satisfied with impiety of this kind, however: they worshipped the representations of birds, four-legged beasts and reptiles. But they should have realized that some of these things they eat as being edible, while others they abominate as being unclean, and others they avoid as being treacherous. Yet out of folly and utter stupor they deified images of what they ate, what they abominated and what they slaughtered.

Hence God also gave them over in the lusts of their hearts to impurity so that they failed in respect for their bodies among themselves (v.24). He used *gave over* for "permitted." Now, he means that on observing them wanting neither to be guided through creation to the creator nor through judgment in their thinking to choose the better things to be done and avoid the worse, he deprived them of providence and let them be tossed about like a vessel adrift, refraining from giving direction to those falling foul of extreme impiety, which gave rise also to a lawless life. *They exchanged the truth about God for a lie, and reverenced and worshipped the creature in place of the creator, who is blessed for ages. Amen* (v.25). Impiety, he is saying, is the foundation of lawlessness; on both accounts they were deprived of divine grace. Now, by *the truth about God* he refers to the name "God," and by *a lie* the idol made by human hands: whereas they ought to have worshipped the true God, they offered reverence due to God to the creature. They also are liable to these accusations who call the only-begotten Son of God a creature while adoring him as God: they ought either, if they confess him to be God, associate him not with a creature but with God who begot him, or, if they call him a creature, not offer reverence to him as divine. [35]

Let us, however, proceed with the rest of the commentary. *For this reason God gave them over to ignominious passions: their women exchanged natural intercourse for unnatural; likewise the males, too, forsook natural intercourse with women, and were consumed with passion for one another, males involved in shameless behavior with males* (vv.26-27). Lawlessness is related to impiety: just as they exchanged God's truth for a lie, so they turned the lawful enjoyment of desire to unlawful. [36] *Receiving in their own persons the due penalty for their error.* Ignominy is the ultimate penalty for this passion: what no enemy ever attempted to commit against them (64) they embraced with complete enthusiasm; and the penalty no judge ever awarded against them they inflicted on themselves.

And what was the cause of the evils? *And as they did not see fit to keep God in mind, God handed them over to unseemly thoughts of doing what is improper* (v.28): had they really been prepared to acknowledge him, they would have followed the divine laws; but since they denied the creator, they were completely deprived of his providence. For this very reason they brazenly reach to every form of wickedness: *They were filled with every kind of iniquity* (v.29). By *iniquity* he refers to what is diametrically opposed to righteousness: from it springs practically every kind of thing that is reprehensible, *immorality, wickedness, avarice and evil; they were full of envy, murder, strife, deceit and malice; slanderers, detractors, God-haters, insolent, haughty, arrogant, inventors of evil, rebellious towards parents, short on sense and short on faith, heartless, ruthless, merciless* (vv.29-31). By *immorality* he refers to intercourse engaged in outside of marriage, [37] by *wickedness* the savage mentality, by *avarice* the longing for more and taking what is not due, by *evil* the inclination of the soul to inferior things and the thought directed to harming the neighbor, by *full of envy* the feeling of severity, reluctant to put up with the neighbor's success; this gave rise also to *murder* and conceived *deceit*: Cain was smitten with envy, employed deceit as his assistant, took his brother out into the open country and committed murder. [38] By *malice* he refers to those putting their minds to scheming and plotting the neighbor's harm; by *slanderers* those assailing the ear and speaking badly of those present, by *detractors* those brazenly applying calumnies against the absent, by *God-haters* those hostile to God, by *insolent* those inclined to violence, by *haughty* those carried away with a great sense of their own superiority, by *arrogant* those who despite lacking any basis for a sense of importance are puffed up to no purpose, by *inventors of evil* those who not only practice an evil lifestyle but also set their minds on other crimes, by *rebellious against parents* the most inappropriate vice of all, with nature as its accuser, by *short on sense* those driven headlong to the lawless life and forfeiting their status as rational beings, by *short on faith* those embracing an unsociable and evil life, by *heartless* those unwilling to learn the norms of friendship, by *ruthless* those heedlessly breaking their commitments, by *merciless* those reproducing the savagery of wild beasts. (68)

They know God's ordinance, that those who practice such things deserve to die, yet they not only do them but even congratulate those who do them (v.32). We have shown how nature teaches both the choice of good and avoidance of its opposite; yet (he is saying) there are those who do not find it sufficient to do these things but even come up with commendation for those who perform the like. Now, this is the final extremity of lawlessness; after all, one should not only hate others' lawlessness but also abhor one's own. [39]

CHAPTER TWO

Then in a different fashion he once more shows us in possession of the judgment between good and its opposite. *Hence you are without excuse, mortal that you are, everyone who judges: by the judgment you pass on the other you condemn yourself, doing as judge the very same things* (v.1): but even in this situation, if you were to receive the right of judging from someone, you would punish the lawbreakers as guilty; you possess the judgment between good and its opposite. [1] It should be realized, however, that on the same basis as you judge others to be deficient you subject yourself to the identical verdict, committing the same lawlessness. *But we know that God's judgment on those who commit such things is in keeping with truth* (v.2): it is clear to those of good sense that according to the divine verdict those guilty of lawlessness are punished.

Do you believe, mortal being that you are, judging those committing such things and doing the same yourself, that you escape the judgment of God? Or do you despise the riches of his goodness, forbearance and longsuffering? (vv.3-4). While we know that the righteous judge will at the right moment inflict the punishment on each transgressor, you on the contrary (he is saying), who punish others but refuse to see your own transgression, suppose that you will escape the divine tribunal. But it is not like that: he is showing forbearance and longsuffering in expectation of your repentance. In fact, he added, *ignoring the fact that God's goodness leads you to repentance.*

But in your hard and impenitent heart you are heaping up for yourself wrath on the day of wrath and revelation and God's righteous judgment, when he will repay everyone according to their works (vv.5-6): since you have a stubborn attitude and persist in your wickedness, you will pass a penal sentence on yourself, which for the time being God in his mercy will postpone, but will reveal on the day of reckoning, and will provide repayment corresponding to deeds. Now, the phrase *you are heaping up for yourself* was well put, showing that none of our words or deeds will be consigned to oblivion; instead, the lovers of virtue will store up for themselves good things, and the evildoers will do the same. *To those who by persistence in good work seek glory and honor and incorruption, eternal life* (v.7). He brought out the labors virtue involves, and gave a glimpse of the crown, (69) the phrase *by persistence in good work* indicating the labors. It is necessary, in fact, to persist and practice virtue, and thus await its crown. While the labor is passing, however, the profit is eternal – yet *eternal* is true not only of the *life* but also of *glory and honor and incorruption.*; he wanted to show the reward of good in further ways.

But for those motivated by selfseeking, and who are responsive not to the truth but to iniquity, there will be anger and rage, tribulation and distress for every human being practicing evil, Jew first and Greek (vv.8-9). As in the other section he did not simply promise good things to anyone at all nor to those practicing virtue carelessly, but to those not loath to withstand its hardships, so also in the case of vice he leveled harsh threats not at those who stumble into it through circumstances, but to those who practice it with great relish; this emerges from the phrases *motivated by selfseeking, responsive not to the truth* and *practicing evil.* In similar fashion, he is saying, both Jews and Greeks he will punish if they transgress, and reward with a crown if they attend to piety and righteousness. Now, by *Greeks* at this point he refers not to those who have made their approach to the divine preaching, but to those living before the divine Incarnation. He did not actually promise eternal life to those adoring idols, but to those living their life beyond the Mosaic Law, yet embracing godliness and devoting themselves to righteousness.[2] *But glory, honor and peace to everyone doing good, Jew first and also Greek* (v.10). It was not without purpose that he included this; rather, it was to connect the theme with what follows: he intends now to introduce the accusation against Jews.

With God, you see, there is no partiality: all who sinned apart from the Law will also perish apart from the Law; and all who sinned under the Law will be judged by the Law (vv.11-12). God the creator of all, he is saying, will in fact likewise be judge of all, and will require an account of the Jews on the basis of the Mosaic Law, while those not accepting it (he speaks of them as being *apart from the Law*, note) and then sinning he will justly punish on the basis of the knowledge implanted by nature. *It is not the hearers of the Law, after all, who are righteous before God; rather, it is the doers of the Law who will be justified* (v.13): law was surely not given to us for this reason, to be pleasing to our ears, but to lead us to the performance of good. *In fact, when Gentiles not having the Law perform the works of the Law by nature, despite not having the Law they are a law unto themselves* (v.14): because the divine Law involves action, those before the time of the Mosaic Law give witness by their use of pious thoughts and (72) by embellishing their life with good actions, and thus becoming lawgivers for themselves.

They show the performance of the Law to be written on their hearts; their conscience bears witness to it, and their thoughts will respectively accuse or defend them on the day when God will judge people's secrets, according to my Gospel, through Jesus Christ (vv.15-16). He indicated the law of nature to be written on their hearts, and the accusation and defense of conscience to be adorned with truth. Now, for my part I think it worthwhile to clarify the point with an example. When the remarkable Joseph devised the scheme involving Benjamin, and he took steps to take him as a slave on the grounds of his stealing a cup so as to test the brothers' intentions by fire, the force of the witness of conscience was openly displayed: at that time, of course, at that time they were scarcely minded to pay attention to this tragedy, whereas they recalled the crime committed twenty two years before. While some said, "He will require our younger brother's blood at our hands," Reuben reminded them of the recommendations he had made to them. [3] In keeping with this comparison let us describe the tribunal to come and the conscience of those living outside the law, at one time offering an excuse and feigning ignorance, at another accepting the accusation and proclaiming the justice of the verdict imposed. Thus Abimelech also, with the witness of conscience, said to God, "Lord, will you slay an ignorant and righteous people? Did he not tell me himself, She is my sister, and she herself say, He is my brother? I did this thing with a pure heart." [4]

After teaching these things in this fashion, the divine apostle transfers his attention to the Jew in the words, *Lo, you call yourself a Jew* (v.17). This name is common, in fact, and once was honorable; hence he did not say, You name, but *You call yourself. And you take your stand on the Law*: you have no problem, like someone living beyond the Law, looking for what has to be done; instead, you have the Law teaching you everything clearly. *And your boast is in God* as giving you preference to all the nations throughout the world, as according you great care, giving you the Law and guiding you through the inspired authors. *You know his will* (v.18) – that is, God's – *and determine differences* – that is to say, opposites: righteousness and iniquity, temperance and licentiousness, piety and impiety. *By holding to the Law*: it has proved your teacher in these matters. [5] *You believe you are a guide* (73) *to the blind, a light to those in darkness, instructor of simpletons, teacher of infants* (vv.19-20). Here he brought out their sense of importance, and laid bare the superior attitude they adopted to the proselytes. *Having in the Law the embodiment of knowledge and truth*: the divine Law provided you with the imprint of all these things.

So do you who teach the other not teach yourself? do you who preach against stealing steal? do you who say not to commit adultery do so yourself? do you who deplore idols commit sacrilege? do you who boast in the Law dishonor God by breaking the Law? (vv.21-23) He showed that the Jew gained no benefit from the giving of the Law, and instead found in the text alone grounds for conceit; while presuming to teach others, he flouted the prescriptions in practice, and to no purpose boasted in the Law. He also adduces testimony to confirm the accusation: *In fact, God's name is blasphemed among the nations because of you,* [6] *as Scripture says* (v.24): you not only proved responsible for praise of God, but also moved many tongues to blasphemy; seeing your lawless way of life, they openly blasphemed God for choosing you.

After showing in this way that they gained no advantage from the Mosaic legislation, he shifts the focus to circumcision, and shows the lack of advantage in it as well when it is not associated with other works. *Circumcision is of benefit, in fact, if you carry out the Law; but if you break the Law, your circumcision has become uncircumcision* (v.25). The divine apostle followed the inspired words: the God of all says through the prophet Jeremiah, "All the nations are uncircumcised in their flesh, whereas the house of Israel is uncircumcised in their hearts," and again, "Circumcise yourselves to God;" and to show what kind of circumcision he means is pleasing to God, he added, "And remove the hardened foreskin of your hearts." [7] Warming to this theme, the divine apostle showed circumcision to be of no value if not circumcision in terms of the soul; that is the purpose for which it was given. After all, if that is not forthcoming, no benefit stems from it: it fills only the function of a badge. When we have gold or silver or precious stones or rich garments, we normally apply seals; but when nothing of the sort is contained within, placing of seals is pointless. [8]

If, then, the uncircumcised keep the ordinances of the Law, will not their uncircumcision be taken for circumcision? (v.26). The Law requires performance, he is saying; so if you who are circumcised do not have it whereas the uncircumcised person does, is it not right for you (76) to be called lawless whereas that person takes your honorable name, and is no longer called uncircumcised in your abusive manner but rather called circumcised for circumcising the soul's wickedness? *The uncircumcised by nature who keep the Law will judge you who break the Law in writing and circumcision* (v.27). The extraordinary degree of the apostle's wisdom is worthy of admiration: he did not oppose the natural law to the written one, but the shameful name to the august one, uncircumcision to circumcision. The former is free of accusation, he is saying: no one is born like this of free will, but the creator it is who forms nature in this way. Hence no harm comes from it for the lovers of virtue. You, on the other hand, accepted the sign of circumcision from your parents, and you have the Law to let you see what has to be done, but by your actions you frustrate the purpose of the Law.

After thus showing circumcision to be given as a sign and later proving pointless, he then shows even the name of the Jew to have no advantage. *In fact, a Jew is not the one who is so in appearance, nor is circumcision that which is in appearance in the flesh. Rather, a Jew is the one who is so inwardly, and circumcision that which is of the heart in spirit, not in writing; praise of it comes not from human beings but from God* (vv.28-29). Here he wisely takes refuge in the testimonies of the inspired authors, which we cited above: "Remove the hardened foreskin of your hearts."[9]

CHAPTER THREE

After putting paid in this way to the Jews' boastfulness and showing them to have no grounds for taking pride in circumcision, in the Law and the name of Jew, he adds, in case anyone should think him to be doing this out of hostility or malevolence, *So what is extraordinary about the Jew? what is the good in circumcision?* (v.1) If some of the foreign nations who are adorned with godliness and virtue enjoy the divine commendation, he is saying, why on earth did God mark out Israel from the nations, and give them circumcision (the phrase *what is extraordinary about the Jew* meaning preference to the nations)? Then he adds, *Much, in every way* (v.2): he chose their forebears, freed them from the clutches of the Egyptians, made them celebrated through various marvels, gave them the Law for their assistance, appointed prophets – this the meaning of *Much, in every way*.

Being reticent about all these, however, he cites only the giving of the Law: *First, remember, their being entrusted with God's sayings*: this is the greatest honor, that while the other nations had only the (77) discernment that comes from nature, they received also the giving of the Law.[1] *What, in fact, if some did not believe? Will their lack of faith nullify the faithfulness of God? Far be it* (vv.3-4). God knew from the beginning, he is saying, both those who would keep the Law and those who would break it; consequently, the unbelievers did not in any way undermine the divine favors. After all, even if all human beings proved ungrateful to him, their ingratitude would not lessen God's glory; he made this clear, in fact, in what follows.

Let God be proved true, although every human being is a liar (v.4). Let us in fact concede, he is saying, that no human being offers him a due song of praise, and instead all are smitten with ingratitude (this being the meaning of *although every human being is a liar*): what loss does God's glory suffer from that? Blessed Paul referred to it elsewhere as well: "If we are faithless, he remains faithful, unable as he is to deny himself."[2] At this point he also invokes a scriptural testimony: *As it is written, So that you may be justified in your words, and prevail in your judging.*[3] Now, *so that* here does not supply a reason so much as declare an outcome: we do not sin for the purpose of revealing God's lovingkindness; rather, it is he who provides a flood of beneficence in bringing about the salvation of everyone. Human beings, on the other hand, endowed with free will as they are, give pride of place to worship of God in some cases, and in others take the opposite path, and find a fitting end to that path. God, however, showing kindness even to them, has a reason to judge them in his manifold attention to them. Thus he also said to Israel, "My people, what have I done to you? or what grief have I caused you? Answer me;"[4] then he reminds them in detail of his kindnesses. Thus also he cries aloud through Jeremiah, "What fault did your fathers find in me that led them to move far from me, go after worthless things and become worthless?"[5] And again he introduces the list of kindnesses.

The divine apostle conducts an argument from the viewpoint of the adversaries: *But if our iniquity confirms God's righteousness, what shall we say? Surely in inflicting wrath God is not unjust? I speak in human terms: perish the thought* (vv.5-6). Of necessity he adduced the contrary position proposed by the other side, and demonstrated its inappropriateness by refutation. It is not I who am saying this, he says: I marshaled the thoughts of the others (the meaning of *in human terms*). *For how does God judge the world? I mean, if through my falsehood God's truth abounded to his glory, why am I still* (80) *judged as a sinner?* (vv.6-7). To say this is quite absurd, he is saying: God's verdict is fair, and my recklessness does not procure for God glory from his lovingkindness. After all, it would be injustice at its worst if those who procured his glory paid the penalty at his hands and suffered eternal punishment: not even the worst of the worst would do this, let alone the one from whom spring the fonts of righteousness.

And not as we are misrepresented, and as some people claim we say, Let us do evil so that good may come; their condemnation is just (v.8). We say nothing of the kind, he is saying, but are wrongly presented by others as saying it; they will pay for their calumny. It should be acknowledged, however, as the sacred apostles say, "Where sin increased, grace did more abound;" [6] some devotees of piety employ falsehood against them, claiming they hold, *Let us do evil so that good may come*. But this was not the thrust of the apostolic teaching: they prescribed exactly the opposite, for everyone to desist from any kind of lawlessness. On the other hand, they bade all those acceding to the all-holy message to be of good cheer on the grounds of the forgiveness of their former sins granted by God.

Now, at this point we suspend the commentary to give our mind a rest, sing the praises of him who gave some people speech and made some deaf and dumb, and beg to understand the thinking behind the apostolic teaching; our request will be fully granted by him who says, "Ask and it will be given to you, seek and you will find, knock and it will be opened to you." [7] To him is glory due and magnificence, together with the Father along with the all-holy Spirit, now and forever, for ages of ages. Amen.

We have already remarked that the divine apostle wishes to show that the Incarnation of our God and Savior Jesus Christ happened of necessity. It was for this reason, after all, that he directed his attention to those outside the Law and of course those living under it as well, and refuted both those who break the natural law and those who break the Mosaic Law, who deserve the extreme punishment. He imitated an excellent physician, who first conveys to the patients the severity of the complaint, and thus offers next the help of the remedies that ward off disease. This is also the way, in fact, that after refuting the lawlessness of the one group and the other, and showing them liable also to punishment, he next offers the remedy of faith and brings out the lovingkindness of the divine plan in the words, *So what advantage do we have? We have already alleged, after all, that both Jews and Greeks are all under sin, as it is written, There is no one who is righteous, not even one; there is no one who has understanding, there is no one who seeks God. All turned aside, together they became worthless; there is no one who works for good, there is not even one. Their throat an opened grave* (81), *they used their tongues to deceive. Venom of asps is on their lips, their mouth is full of cursing and bitterness. Their feet are swift to shed blood; ruin and misery in their paths, they have no knowledge of the path of peace. There is no fear of God before their eyes* [8] (vv.9-18). In what was said before, he first compared the situations of the circumcised and the uncircumcised, and added, *So what is the advantage of the Jew?* (v.1) And at this point he wanted to show the extraordinary degree of the evangelical grace and said, *So what advantage do we have?* In other words, We showed that both those beyond the Law and those living under the Law have sinned. He brought to bear also the Davidic testimony for its great relevance to the present argument; he does it with a particular eye to brevity: he could have summoned all the inspired authors to accusation of the Jews, having as they do similar things to say about them and even less relevant things than these.

Hence he added, *We know that whatever the Law says, it speaks to those under the Law* (v.19). He expressed this, too, with great precision, saying not "about those under the Law" but *to those under the Law*: it says much also about Babylonians, Persians, Medes and Egyptians, and very many other nations, yet it offered to Jews also the prophecies about them. *So that every mouth may be stopped and the whole world become accountable to God.* He employed *so that* in a particular sense: it is not that the God of all gives laws and offers human beings exhortations for the purpose of rendering them liable to punishment; rather, he does it in his care for their salvation, whereas they take the opposite path and bring punishment on themselves.

Then, intending to show the gifts of faith, he first shows all who need it, and in advance of the others those in particular who pride themselves on the Law. *Because no human being will be justified in his sight* [9] *by works of the Law* (v.20). Some parts of the Mosaic Law correspond with natural knowledge, like "You shall not commit adultery, you shall not murder, you shall not steal, you shall not give false witness against your neighbor, honor your father and your mother," [10] and the like: even those who are not in receipt of the Law knew that each of these involves not only accusation but actual punishment as well. But other parts the lawgiver imposed on Jews for that particular time, like circumcision, sabbath, sacrifices, washings, prescriptions about leprosy and menstruation, and things like that; they are symbols of other things, but their performance does not suffice to make the performer righteous. This was also the reason the divine apostle said, *Because no human being will be justified in his sight by works of the Law* (84). And in case anyone should think he was criticizing the Law, he added, *It is through the Law, after all, that knowledge of sin comes.* The Law, he is saying, imparted to human beings a more precise knowledge of sin, it made the charge against it more severe; but human beings are not sufficient of themselves for the practice of virtue.

Having thus shown the Law to be only a teacher of good things, he gives a glimpse of the power of grace: *Now, however, apart from the Law the righteousness of God has been revealed, attested by the Law and the inspired authors* (v.21). Who could show sufficient admiration for the force of the apostolic wisdom? At one and the same time, note, he showed the Law both coming to an end and also supporting grace. It was also appropriate for him to use the phrase *has been revealed*: it made clear to everyone the hidden mystery of the divine plan. [11] In relating grace and Law he showed the excellence of the victory, casting the Law itself and the inspired authors in the role of witnesses to grace. *God's righteousness through faith of Jesus Christ for all and upon all who believe* (v.22). In other words, since he said, *The righteousness of God has been revealed*, and then inserted something, he had to repeat the phrase and show that they enjoy this through faith in Christ the Lord, [12] whether they be Jews or Greeks who long to attain it.

He then continues to make the point more clearly: *There is in fact no distinction: all have sinned, and fall short of the grace of God* (vv.22-

23). He briefly showed all to be guilty and in need of grace. *Justified gratuitously by his grace through the redemption that is in Christ Jesus* (v.24): bringing faith alone, we received the forgiveness of sins, since Christ the Lord offered his own body as a kind of ransom for us. *Whom God put forward as a mercy seat by his blood effective through faith* (v.25). The mercy seat was of gold leaf, situated on the ark; on either side it had the carvings of the cherubim. From there God's benevolence was revealed to the high priest as he ministered. The divine apostle, then, teaches that Christ the Lord is the true mercy seat: the old one had the function of a type of the latter. [13] Now, the title belongs to him as man, not as God: as God he gave a response through the mercy seat, while as man he receives this name as he does others, like sheep, lamb, sin, curse and suchlike. Whereas the old mercy seat was without blood, insofar as it was lifeless, and drops of the blood of the victims fell on it, Christ the Lord is God and (85) mercy seat, high priest and lamb, and with his own blood worked our salvation, requiring from us only faith.

As a demonstration of his righteousness, with a view to the tolerance of the sins previously committed, in God's forbearance for a demonstration of his righteousness in the present time (vv.25-26). God showed his characteristic goodness, exercising longsuffering to the greatest extent towards the people who transgressed, [14] and he made his righteousness clear to everyone. Now, to prove that it was not without purpose that he put up with the people who transgressed but to prepare ahead of time this remedy of salvation for them, he says, *that he himself is righteous and makes righteous the one who has faith in Christ Jesus.* In other words, both truths should be acknowledged, that the God of all manages things in our regard justly and lovingly, and that everyone believing in Christ the Lord reaps the benefit of righteousness from faith.

Having thus shown briefly the gifts of grace, he reverts in turn to his treatment of the Law, and shows it yielding to grace. *So what place is there for boasting?* (v.27) Then the reply: *It is shut out.* He said, not "shut in," but *shut out* – that is, it has no place. [15] Now, by *boasting* he refers to the Jews' superior attitude: they gave themselves airs as alone enjoying divine providence; but once divine grace came on the scene and was poured on all the nations, the Jews' cause for boasting came to an end, God having given faith as a short cut to salvation for human beings. This, in fact, is what Paul taught in what follows: *By what kind of law – a law of works? No; rather, by a law of faith.* It was not without purpose that he called faith *a law*; instead, it was to recall the prophecy of Jeremiah, "In those days and at that time I shall make a new covenant with the house of Israel and the house of Judah, not according to the covenant I made with their forefathers." [16] Now, if the Mosaic Law is called a covenant and in turn the New is likewise called a covenant, the latter prescribing belief in Christ, the divine apostle in inspired fashion connected the title of law with faith.

Then he developed his treatment of faith. *We therefore hold that a person is justified by faith apart from the works of the Law* (v.28). The law he is referring to is the Mosaic Law; [17] yet he said not, We hold a Jew is justified by faith, but *a person*, a name referring generally to human nature. Hence he added in argumentative fashion, *Is God the God of Jews only? And not of the nations as well? Yes, of the nations as well* (v.29). Then he makes it proof against contradiction. *Since God is one, and he will justify the circumcised from faith and the uncircumcised through faith* (v.30). The God of all is one, he is saying, (88) the creator of all is one; and it is not possible that he would take care of some and leave others go neglected. Consequently, he offers salvation to all who believe. Now, by *the circumcision* he refers to Jews, and by *the uncircumcised* the nations. He also solves the objection, *But do we abolish the Law by faith? Perish the thought: rather, we uphold the Law* (v.31): from the beginning the Law and the prophets made pronouncements on faith; so by receiving faith we endorse the Law. He then offers examples of these.

CHAPTER FOUR

Though being in a position to provide numerous testimonies from the inspired authors, he goes to the very root of Judaism, and shows the patriarch Abraham acquiring righteousness through faith, and says, *So what shall we say our father Abraham found according to the flesh?* (v.1). What sort of righteousness of his did we hear happening through works before Abraham believed in God? *According to the flesh* in fact means the kind achieved through works, since it is through the body we perform the works. [1] *After all, if Abraham was justified through works, he has something to boast about –*

but not before God (v.2). The doing of good works crowns the doers themselves, but does not demonstrate God's lovingkindness. Faith, on the other hand, makes both clear, the attitude of the believer towards God and the love of God, because the receipt of faith allows a person to celebrate the one who is responsible for it.

He confirms this with scriptural testimony. *What in fact does Scripture say? Abraham believed God, and it was reckoned to him as righteousness*[2] (v.3): blessed Abraham did not attain divine testimony by living according to the Law;[3] rather, by believing in the one who called him he reaped the riches of righteousness. *To the worker, on the other hand, wages are not reckoned as a gift but as his due* (v.4): the doer of righteousness looks for wages, whereas the righteousness from faith is a gift of the God of all. He says as much also in what follows.

But to the person without works who believes in the one who justifies the ungodly their faith is reckoned as righteousness (v.5). Having thus shown through the patriarch Abraham that faith is more ancient than the Law, he invokes the inspired author and king David as still another trustworthy witness to this. To him the God of all renewed the promises made to Abraham: as he promised the patriarch Abraham that he would bless all the nations in his offspring, likewise he said to the most divine David as well, "Once I have sworn by my holiness, I shall not be false to David: his offspring will abide forever, and his throne like the sun before me, and like (89) the moon it will be made perfect forever, and be a faithful witness in the heavens;" and again, "I shall set his hand on the sea, and his right hand on rivers;" and further, "All the kings of the earth will bow down before him, all the nations will serve him,"[4] and other things like those. As he showed blessed Abraham attaining righteousness through faith, and Abraham lived before the giving of the Law, he had to show David, who lived under the Law, witnessing to grace; he says, *As David also declares blessed the person to whom God reckons righteousness apart from works, Blessed are those whose iniquities are forgiven, and whose sins are covered over; blessed the man to whom the Lord does not impute sin*[5] (vv.6-8). The Law, he is saying, inflicted punishment on sinners, whereas the inspired author declares blessed those receiving forgiveness of sins. It is therefore clear that he declares blessed our situation and foretells the gifts of grace.

He shows it available to everyone, saying so in the form of a question: *Is this blessing, then, for the circumcised, or also for the uncircumcised?* (v.9) Then he further supports the foregoing from the patriarch Abraham. *We say that faith was reckoned to Abraham as righteousness. So how was it reckoned: in his being circumcised or in being uncircumcised?* (vv.9-10). He showed that faith was more ancient, not only than the Law but also than circumcision itself, and that before circumcision the patriarch received the testimony of righteousness according to faith. How, then, did he need circumcision, having won righteousness from faith? He brings this out clearly: *He received a sign of circumcision as a seal of the righteousness of the faith that he had while being uncircumcised* (v.11). Circumcision, he is saying, is not righteousness but a testimony and seal of righteousness, a sign of the faith of which he gave evidence before circumcision.

So that he might be father of all who believe despite not being circumcised in order that righteousness be reckoned also to them, and father of the circumcised (vv.11-12). Here there is need of distinction: he shows the patriarch as father first of those who believed while uncircumcised, since he himself while still uncircumcised offered God the gift of faith, then of course also of Jews on the grounds of their sharing circumcision with him. He brings out this same truth more clearly in what follows: *who are not only circumcised but also follow the traces of the faith that our father Abraham had while uncircumcised*: if anyone who sprang from the Gentiles and is not in receipt of circumcision follows that faith of the patriarch that he demonstrated before circumcision, they will not fall short of that kinship. (92) I mean, the God of all, foreknowing as God both that he would gather together one people from Gentiles and Jews and through faith would provide them with salvation, foreshadowed both in the patriarch Abraham; after showing him in possession of righteousness through faith before circumcision, and after circumcision not living according to the Mosaic Law but abiding by the guidance of faith, he gave him the name father of the nations so that both Jews and Greeks should fix their eyes on him, not the former on his circumcision and the latter on his uncircumcision, but both imitating his faith. The divine Scripture, after all, gave the name *justification* not to circumcision nor to uncircumcision but to faith.

Having thus shown faith to be more ancient and more venerable than the Law, he shows in turn the Law to be more recent than the promise made to Abraham, revealing grace to be antecedent to the Law: it was about it that the promises were made to Abraham. He promised to bless all the nations in his offspring, [6] and the promise had its fulfillment in Christ the Lord. *It was not through the Law, in fact, that the promise was made to Abraham or his offspring that he would be heir to the world, but through the righteousness of faith* (v.13): by believing in God, and not by living according to the Mosaic Law, he received the promise of the blessing of the nations. *After all, if from the Law they are heirs, faith is made void and the promise abolished* (v.14): if by living according to the Law they attain the promised goods, it was in vain that Abraham had faith in God, and the promises made to him by God proved false and untrue. *The Law, you see, produces wrath* (v.15): the Law's way is to punish the transgressors, *wrath* being the name he gave to punishment. *But where there is no law, neither are there transgressors*: the Law punishes transgressors, law being associated with observance and transgression; whereas some through attention to virtue choose to observe it, others through sloth have no hesitation at all in transgressing it.

This is the reason, to be sure, that it is from faith, so that according to grace the promise may be confirmed for all the offspring, not only those from the Law but also those from the faith of Abraham, who is father of us all (v.16). He suppressed the Jews' pride, by *Abraham's offspring* referring to those imitating Abraham's faith, even if by race they are foreigners. Now, if the Law punishes transgressors, while grace accords the gift of forgiveness of sins, the latter confirms God's promise by according the nations the blessing. Since, however, he called Abraham father of both the Gentiles and the Jews, he confirms his remarks with the testimony of Scripture: (93) *As it is written, I have made you father of many nations* [7] (v.17). Then he endorses the testimony with an example: *Before God in whom he believed, who gives life to the dead and calls into existence what does not exist.* As God is maker of everything, he is saying, and both God and carer of all, so too he appointed Abraham father of all, not Jews only but all the believers.

He brings out also the extraordinary degree of Abraham's faith:

Hoping against hope, he believed that he would become father of many nations, according to the saying, This is how your offspring will be;[8] *he was not weakened in faith when he considered his own body was already dead (being about a hundred) and the barrenness of Sarah's womb* (vv.18-19): though he saw his partner sterile and the weakness of old age affecting them both, and in human terms the hope of children being slim, without any previous example to encourage him, he faithfully accepted the divine promise. *Against hope* refers, note, to the human possibilities, while *hoping* to God's promise. *He was not led by unbelief to have doubts about God's promise; instead, he grew strong in faith, giving glory to God, fully convinced he was capable also of doing what he promised* (vv. 20-21): far from having regard to the weakness of nature, he trusted unhesitatingly in its maker.

Therefore it was reckoned to him as righteousness (v. 22) – faith, that is. Having in this way shown faith to be flourishing both among those under the Law and among those before the Law, he transfers his attention to the foregoing theme. *Now, it was not for him alone that it was written, Faith was reckoned to him as righteousness, but for us, too, to whom it will be reckoned as believers in the one who raised our Lord Jesus from the dead* (vv. 23-24). The patriarch, though seeing his partner's womb barren, believed that it was easy for God to fulfill his promise; and we, when hearing Jews speaking of our Lord as dead, believe that he is risen. Let us also, therefore, gather the fruit of faith, and reap the righteousness that springs from it; it was not without purpose that record was kept of what the Lord God did in Abraham' case, but that on seeing it we might give evidence of a like faith. The phrase, *the one who raised our Lord Jesus*, of course, he spoke in reference to the humanity: in what he suffered, in this he also was raised; the suffering was of the flesh, not of the divinity, which is immune from suffering. [9]

Who was handed over for our trespasses and raised for our justification (v.25): he endured the suffering for the sake of our sins, to pay our debt, and so that his resurrection might effect the resurrection shared by everyone; through it we also gain the basis of justification, and when buried together in baptism we receive the forgiveness of sins. [10]

CHAPTER FIVE

Having thus shown (96) the power of faith, and laid bare the gifts of grace, he shifts the focus to exhortation, urging them to give a thought also to the practice of virtue. Since, you see, he had said that with the appearance of faith the Law is idle, and showed that the patriarch attained the righteousness that comes from faith, it was necessary, if those addicted to sloth were not to find grounds for neglecting the practice of virtue on the plea that faith suffices for being made righteous, [1] for him to include moral advice as well. So he says, *Justified by faith, then, we have peace with God through our Lord Jesus Christ, through whom we now have obtained access by faith to this grace in which we stand, and we boast in the hope of the glory of God* (vv.1-2). While faith bestowed upon us forgiveness of sins, and rendered us stainless and righteous through the regeneration of the washing, [2] it behoves us to preserve the peace made with God. The Only-begotten by becoming man reconciled us to him when were at odds, after all, but sin produced that enmity. Righteousness, then, will preserve the peace that is made. We ought spare no pains in going in search of it, considering the hope given to us and the glory which has been promised would be given us by God; he called the reward of our labors not payment, note, but *glory*, to show the extraordinary extent of the response.

Since, however, they sustained many troubles at that time, plagued, harassed, subjected to countless forms of death, it was right for him to offer consolation about them as well. *Not only that, however: we even boast in our tribulations* (v.3). He gave clear evidence of his own unsurpassed magnanimity: he said, not We sustain the tribulations, but *We even boast in the tribulations*. We take pride, he is saying, and congratulate ourselves on being sharers in the Lord's sufferings. He did not say as much directly: to think this way is a mark of those perfect like him; instead, he consoles the others with the prospect of the future.

Knowing that tribulation produces endurance, endurance character, character hope, and hope does not disappoint (vv.3-5). When troubles beset someone, provided they bear it nobly, they are shown to have character and are buoyed up by the hope of future things. It is reliable and truthful; he said so, in fact: *it does not disappoint*, whereas it is those who hope and fail who are ashamed and embarrassed.

Because the love of God love has been poured out in our hearts through the Holy Spirit who has been given to us: the grace of the all-holy Spirit, which we received in baptism, enkindled in us the desire for God. [3]

While we were still helpless, you see, (97) *at the right time Christ died for the ungodly. After all, rarely will anyone die for a righteous person; perhaps for a good person someone might possibly be ready to die* (vv.6-7): we believe that while we were still transgressors and suffering from the ailment of impiety, Christ the Lord accepted death for our sake; and from this we learn the depths of the lovingkindness. After all, perhaps someone would accept death for a righteous person; but in his case it was in the excess of love that he underwent death for sinners. In fact, he added, *But God proves his love for us in that while we were still sinners Christ died for us* (v.8): God, on the contrary, shows the extraordinary degree of his love for us in that the death of Christ happened not for righteous people but for sinners; now we have been justified through faith in him, but when he accepted death for us, we were still caught up in sins of all kinds. Now, *at the right time* means in time, at the appropriate time; he says as much in the letter to the Galatians, "But when the fullness of time had come, God sent his Son, born of a woman, born under the Law, so as to buy back those under the Law so that might enjoy adoption." [4] *Much more surely, then, now that we have been justified in his blood, shall we be saved through him from the wrath* (v.9): it is perfectly clear that, having accepted that accursed death for impious and lawless people, he will also free those who have come to faith in him from the punishment to come (by *wrath* referring to the punishment to come).

After all, if while enemies we were reconciled to God through the death of his Son, much more now that we are reconciled shall we be saved by his life (v.10): if while adversaries and enemies we were granted such care that he gave over to death the Son for us, how could it be that with reconciliation made we do not have a share in eternal life? Once more, of course, he gives the name *Son* to Christ the Lord, who is both God and man; and it is clear, in my view, even to heresiarchs, which nature was involved in the passion. [5] *Not only that, however: we even boast in God through our Lord Jesus Christ, through whom we have now received reconciliation* (v.11): not only do we await eternal life; rather, even in the present life we take pride in being God's familiars, considering what happened to Christ our Lord, who by becoming our go-between brought about peace.

From this point on he reveals the mystery of the Incarnation, and brings out the reason for becoming man. *⁶ Hence, just as through one human being sin* (100) *entered the world, and through sin death, and thus death spread to all human beings for the reason that all sinned* (v.12). On creating Adam and dignifying him with the gift of reason, the Lord God gave the single commandment of exercising his reason; it was impossible that, sharing in reason and enjoying the discernment of good and its opposite, he should live his life apart from any law. He was deceived and broke the law; and from the beginning the lawgiver linked the threat of punishment to the commandment. Becoming subject to the rule of death, then, Adam begot Cain, Seth and the others. All of them, therefore, on the grounds of their lineage from this man, had a nature subject to death; such a nature is in need of many things – food and drink, clothing and habitation, and diverse skills. Use of these things, however, often stimulates the passions to intemperance, and intemperance generates sin. Consequently, the divine apostle means that, since Adam had sinned and death had occurred through sin, both spread to the race: *death spread to all human beings for the reason that all sinned*. In other words, it is not because of the sin of the first parent but because of their own that each person is liable to the norm of death. ⁷

Up to the Law, you see, sin was in the world, but with no Law it is not imputed (v.13). He accuses, not those before the Law, as some supposed, but all together: *up to the Law* means not as far as the beginning of the Law but as far as the end of the Law ⁸ – in other words, As long as the Law was in force, sin had force; with no law it is impossible for transgression to occur. *But death reigned from Adam to Moses, even over those who did not sin in a manner similar to the transgression of Adam, who is a type of the one to come* (v.14). By *Moses* he refers to the Law; we find this also in the Gospels, "They have Moses and the prophets," ⁹ and the divine apostle speaks likewise in the second letter to the Corinthians, "But to this day, whenever Moses is read, a veil lies over their heart" ¹⁰ – that is, the Law. So death reigned, he is saying, from Adam until the coming of the Savior: then the Law reached its end. "The Law and the prophets prophesied up to John," Scripture says, remember; "but from the days of John the kingdom of heaven has suffered violence, and violent people take it by force." [11] *Death reigned, however, even over those who did not sin in a manner similar to the transgression of Adam.* After all, even if they did not break the commandment, they still committed other lawlessness. Now, he referred to Adam as a type of Christ, whom he calls *the one to come* on this reasoning, that just as (101) that first human being by sinning fell under the norm of death, and the whole race followed the firstparent, so Christ the Lord by fulfilling the utmost righteousness destroyed the power of death, and being the first to rise from the dead he led the whole human race back to life. [12]

Since he called Adam a type of Christ, he shows the preeminence involved. *But the gift is not like the fall* (v.15). How is it, rather? *If the many died through the fall of the one, much more did the grace of God and the gift abound for the many, thanks to the one person Jesus Christ.* In imposing punishment, he is saying, the Lord God preserved the norm of righteousness, and the whole race followed Adam's sin and consignment to death. It was unquestionably more proper for justice to be preserved through God's lovingkindness and for all human beings to share in the resurrection of Christ the Lord. Now, here he called Christ the Lord a *person* so as to bring out precisely the type of Adam, because just as in that case death came through one human being, so in this case the overthrow of death came though one human being.

The gift was not like what happened with one sin: the judgment from one involved condemnation, whereas the grace from many falls involved justification (v.16). The liberality of the grace, he is saying, surpasses the norm of justice: in the former case the whole race experienced the punishment for one sin, whereas in this case, though all people were godless and sinful, he did not inflict punishment, but accorded life. *If, after all, by one person's fall death reigned through the one, much more will those who receive the abundance of grace, gift and righteousness reign in life through the one Jesus Christ* (v.17): if one person's transgression strengthened the power of death, it is clear that those in receipt of the bounteous gifts of God will prevail over death and share with Christ in the indestructible kingdom and eternal life.

Therefore, just as the effect of one fall was condemnation for all people, so too the effect of one righteous act is justification of life for all people (v.18). Have no doubt, he is saying, of what is said by me when you have regard to Adam: if this is true, as in fact it is, and if with his transgression the whole race fell under the norm of death, it is patent that the righteousness of the Savior achieves life for all people. He says the same thing again, varying the expression and constantly turning it in different directions, so as to teach us more clearly the mystery of the Incarnation. *In other words, just as through the one person's disobedience the many were made sinners, so too through the obedience of the one the many will be made righteous* (v.19). Here he was precise (104) in using the word *many* in respect both of Adam and of grace: among those in the past we find some who were proof against the worse sins, like Abel, Enoch, Noah, Melchizedek, the patriarchs, and of course those who were outstanding in the time of the Law; and after grace there were many who adopted the lawless life.

Having thus shown us from Adam's story the causes of the divine Incarnation, [13] he counters the objection and supplies the solution. Now, the objection concerns the Law, which was given between Adam and the coming of the Savior; hence the divine apostle said, *But the Law made its appearance with the result that the fall was multiplied* (v.20). Now, he employed the phrase *with the result that*, not to touch on causes, but in a peculiar sense. His meaning is that God did not leave human beings neglected even in the former time; rather, he gave Jews the Law, while by means of their diligence he also gave the other nations a glimpse of the light of godliness. Now, it was appropriate for him to employ the term *made its appearance* since Christ was the fulfillment of the promise given to the patriarch, "All the nations of the earth will be blessed in your offspring." [14] Between Abraham and Christ, however, the Law *made its appearance*; it taught more precisely that sin is an evil, but was powerless to stop it, and instead greatly augmented it: the more commandments that were given, the greater the transgressions occurring. The divine apostle, on the contrary, in a few words supplied the answer: *But where sin was multiplied, grace abounded all the more*. It did not undermine God's generosity, he is saying; instead, it revealed the extraordinary degree of his goodness.

So that as sin reigned through death, so too grace reigned through righteousness, unto eternal life through Jesus Christ our Lord (v.21). With this he completed the chapter. He teaches that, just as sin in giving birth to death reigned in mortal bodies, prompting the passions to intemperance, so grace in according the believers the righteousness that comes through faith has a kingdom that is not of equal duration with sin but eternal and unending. After all, whereas the former has power over bodies, it ceased its reign with their death: "The one who has died is acquitted of sin," [15] according to the divine apostle. After the resurrection, on the other hand, when our bodies have become imperishable and immortal, grace will reign in them, sin then having no place; when the passions come to an end, you see, sin will have no place.

CHAPTER SIX

He next cites once again a further objection that emerges, and easily dispatches it. *What, then, shall we say? Shall we persist in sin so that grace may abound? Far be it* (vv.1-2). He showed the absurdity by the negative, which he employed because of what had already been said, *Where sin was multiplied, grace abounded all the more.* He was not content, however, (105) with a simple negative; instead, he conducts the argument in other ways as well. *How will we, having died to sin as we have, still live in it?* And how did we die? *Are you unaware, brethren, that all who were baptized into Christ Jesus were baptized into his death?* (v.3). You denied sin, he is saying, became dead to it and were buried with Christ; so how is it possible for you to take sin on?

We were therefore buried with him through baptism into death, so that just as Christ rose from the dead by the glory of the Father, so we too might walk in newness of life (v.4). The sacrament of baptism itself taught you to shun sin. Baptism, in fact, represents a type of the Lord's death, and in it you have had a share with Christ in both the death and the resurrection. [1] Now, by *glory of the Father* he refers to the divinity of Christ; in another letter he says, remember, "that the God of our Lord Jesus Christ, the Father of glory," [2] and the Lord in the Gospels, "Destroy this temple, and in three days I shall raise it up." [3] If the heretics were not to accept this interpretation, however, they would not in this way detract from the glory of the Only-begotten: even if it was the Father who raised him, it was as man that he raised him, as it was as man also that he experienced the passion.

I mean, if we have grown together with him in the likeness of his death, we shall certainly also be in the likeness of his resurrection (v.5). Since he referred to saving baptism as a type of his death, he clearly touched on resurrection by the change of name: what is properly planted grows. *Knowing that our old self was crucified with him so that the body of sin might be destroyed with a view to our no longer being in thrall to sin* (v.6). It was not nature that he referred to as the *old self*, but the wicked attitude; he said this was put to death by baptism so that the body might become unresponsive to sin, using the words, *so that the body of sin might be destroyed with a view to its being nevermore in thrall to sin*. Then he shows this more clearly from another image as well. *The one who dies, after all, is acquitted of sin* (v.7): who ever saw a corpse that was violating another's marriage, or bloodying its hands with murder, or committing anything else improper?

But if we died with Christ, we believe we shall also live with him (v.8). It therefore behoves us, too, buried with Christ as we are, to be dead to sin on the one hand, and on the other to look forward to the resurrection. Then he cites the model once again: *Knowing that Christ, being raised from the dead, will never die again; death no longer has dominion over him. After all, the death he died he died to sin, whereas the life he lives he lives to God* (vv.9-10). His teaching was clear enough in these words in his wish to keep the believers apart from sin. Christ died once, he is saying, and it is impossible for him to die twice: he now has an immortal body. This is surely the reason we also enjoy one baptism; do not, therefore, look forward to any other forgiveness through baptism.[4] It was also well said that he was *dead to sin*: not that he was subject to death, having committed no sin, but he accepted death on account of our sin.

Likewise in your case, too, consider yourselves to be dead to sin and alive to God in Christ Jesus (v.11): in your case, too, accordingly, show your limbs to be dead to the action of sin, and embrace the vitality of Christ, through which you will attain immortal life. We ought all heed this teaching, shun the wiles of sin and summon to our assistance Christ who has saved us: on being called he will appear and offer us his grace. To him glory belongs and majesty, with the Father and the all-holy Spirit, now and forever, for ages of ages. Amen. [5]

Let sin, therefore, not reign in your mortal body to the point of obeying it in its desires (v.12). The rule of a tyrant differs from this in that, whereas the tyrant exists against the will of his subjects, its rule is over those willing to be ruled. So he urges them never to submit to the influence of sin: by becoming man the Lord destroyed its rule, and in legislating for them in their state of still being mortal and having a body subject to passions he gives laws accommodated to their limitations. He says, not Let it not dominate, but *Let it not reign*: the former is characteristic of sin, the latter of our free will – that is to say, the movement and disquiet of the passions are naturally innate within us, whereas the performance of forbidden things depends on free will. He also brought out the temporary nature of the conflict by calling the body *mortal*: as it is subject to the norm of death, the onset of the passions also comes to an end. He therefore bids us, not to bring the tyranny of sin to an end, but to give no obedience to its intemperate inflaming of the body's yearnings. [6]

Nor make your limbs available to sin as weapons of iniquity (v.13). After mentioning kingship, he necessarily showed also its armory, and instructed us in the way to conquer: sin employs our limbs as weapons against us. (109) *Instead, make yourselves available to God like people brought back from the dead.* He had already said as much, *Likewise in your case, too, consider yourselves to be dead to sin and alive to God in Christ Jesus*, that is, You were buried with Christ and rose with him, so you are dead to sin and seek a different life. *And your limbs to God as weapons of righteousness.* He presented the body not as evil but as a creation of a good God: it is capable, when guided by the soul in a fit and proper manner, of worshipping God. [7] The tendency of the will to the worse offers the limbs to sin like weapons of some kind, and conversely the disposition of free will in regard to the good fits the limbs for serving the divine laws. The tongue, for instance, when the artist is of sober mind, offers the God of all fitting hymnody, whereas when the musician is drunk and disorderly, it insanely utters the discordant sound of blasphemy. [8] In a similar fashion it also gains adornment from true speech and defilement from false. Likewise, too, an eye gazes upon both the sober and the seamy, the cruel and the kind; likewise, too, a hand delivers both death and deliverance, and, in a nutshell, all parts of the body prove weapons of righteousness when the mind is so disposed, and conversely weapons of sin when it embraces the power of sin.

The divine apostle shows the ease of victory from other points of view as well. *Sin, after all, will no longer have dominion over you* (v.14), he says: instead of nature any longer conducting the struggle on its own, it has the grace of the Spirit working with it. He added, in fact, *I mean, you are not under the Law but under grace.* He teaches that before grace the Law taught only what had to be done, but offered no assistance to those under obligation, whereas grace before imposing obligation provides reinforcement as well. This is the reason, to be sure, why the obligation of grace is more to the point than that of the Law, since the assistance overcomes the difficulty.

Then in turn he deals with the objection. *What, then? Shall we sin because we are not under the Law but under grace?* (v.15) He posed the challenge on account of those keen to find fault. He first of all denied it, showing its absurdity in the words, *Far from it.* Then he brings out the opposite at length. *Are you not aware that if you make yourselves available as slaves to anyone to the point of obedience, you are slaves of the one you obey, either of sin to the point of death or of obedience to the point of righteousness?* (v.16) Whomever you choose to serve you must obey when they give orders: it is impossible to serve two masters at the same time. Now, righteousness and sin are diametrically opposed; the Lord also said in the sacred Gospels, "No one can serve two masters."[9]

Thanks to God, however, you were once slaves to sin but you obeyed from the heart a form of teaching to which you were entrusted (v.17). He brought out their transformation (112), and revealed his satisfaction with it by offering praise to God. You were slaves to sin, he is saying, but by free will you rejected its lordship and embraced the spiritual teaching. *Freed from sin, you became slaves to righteousness* (v.18): you shook off the slavery of sin, and submitted to the yoke of righteousness; so it is impossible for you, bearing the latter, to yield to the commands of the former.

I am speaking in human terms because of the limitations of your flesh (v.19): I accommodate exhortation to nature, knowing that the passions are moved by the mortal body. *You see, just as you made your limbs available in the service of impurity and lawlessness with a view to lawlessness, so now make your limbs available in the service of righteousness with a view to sanctification.* He brought out in this as well that it is not the body that deserves accusation but the free will giving it evil guidance. Now, he is asking nothing beyond our powers; rather, what we put at the disposal of sin is all he asks us to offer to righteousness. And indeed whereas we obeyed the unlawful directions of the former, the latter will procure our sanctification if we obey it.

In fact, when you were slaves to sin, you were at liberty in regard to righteousness (v.20): you carried out the orders of the former alone, but did not accept the laws of righteousness. Then he brings out the difference from another viewpoint as well. *So what benefit did you gain then?* (v.21) You cited the advantages of sin; instead, it is pointless to inquire what they are: without saying a word you admit the harm, enveloped in shame as you are. He added this, in fact: *from what you are now ashamed of.* That is, even if someone is completely brazen, after the end of the enjoyment they feel shame. In addition to this, however, he brings out the worse and harsher effect of sin: *The end of those things is in fact death.* By death he means not this passing one but the eternal one.

Now, on the contrary, you have been made free from sin but enslaved to God, and so you enjoy the fruit of it for sanctification and its end eternal life (v.22). In this he made God the opposite of sin, sanctification of shame, and eternal life of eternal death. *The wages of sin, after all, is death* (v.23). Since it once ruled and now has become a tyrant, and he called the limbs that are badly guided *weapons*, it was right for him also to give the reward the name *death*. This is the term he likes to use, in fact, for the military allowance: in the letter to the Corinthians he says, "Who ever pays his own wages for serving as a soldier?" [10] *God's gift, on the other hand, is eternal life in Christ Jesus* (113) *our Lord*. Here he used not *wages* but *gift*, eternal life being God's gift: even if one practiced the highest degree of righteousness, the everlasting goods would not be commensurate with the temporary hardship.

CHAPTER SEVEN

After speaking of the sins that should not be committed by those living a life in keeping with grace, he shifts his attention in turn to a comparison of the Law and grace, showing the force of the one and the weakness of the other, and teaches that with the coming of grace the Law came to an end. He begins this way: *Are you not aware, brethren (I am speaking to those who are familiar with the Law), that the Law dictates to a person for as long as they live?* (v.1) You have a clear knowledge, he is saying, especially you who were raised in the Law, that the Law is in force while life lasts. He also introduces an example bearing on the subject in hand, saying, *The married woman, remember, is by the Law bound to her husband while he is alive, but if the husband dies she is released from the law about the husband* (v.2). Then he gives clearer teaching about it: *While the husband is alive, then, she is styled an adulteress if she lives with another man, whereas if the husband dies, she is free from the Law so that she is not an adulteress if living with another man* (v.3). The Law calls unfaithful, he is saying, not the woman who has relations with another after the death of her spouse, but the one who has intercourse with another while her partner is still around, ordering this one to be punished for violating the law of marriage. It is obvious, therefore, that when the husband reaches the end of his life, the widow marries another lawfully, not unlawfully. The divine apostle was aware, of course, that the Law also granted the living the dispensation to dissolve the marriage when it was not agreeable. But he heeded the Lord's teaching, which said Moses granted this in view of the Jews' hardness of heart, whereas the law of nature did not provide for it;[1] God created them one husband and one wife, he said, imposing the law of marriage in their very formation.

This is surely the reason that on leaving that point he moved on to the law about the dead, adding, *And so, my brethren, you too died to the Law through the body of Christ so as to belong to another, the one who has been raised from the dead* (v.4). In fact, in keeping with the example it was appropriate to say, the Law died, that is, ceased to have effect. In his concern for the Jews' weakness, however (they held the Law in great respect, remember), and not wishing to give an occasion for criticism to heretics in their opposition to the Old Testament, he did not say the Law had ceased to have effect; instead, he said that we are dead to the Law through saving baptism, [2] and then having risen in turn (115) we are joined to another, to the one who has been raised from the dead, that is, Christ the Lord. And since he called faith in the Lord relationship and marriage, it was right for him to show also the fruit of the marriage, saying, *in order that we might bear fruit for God*. What is the fruitfulness? Our members becoming instruments of righteousness. Now, he very wisely let it be seen that the Law itself urges our being related to Christ; it was not opposed to the wife being married to another husband, he is saying, after the death of the former one.

Then in turn he brings out the difference. *When we were living in the flesh, you see* – that is, in the way of life according to the Law, calling *flesh* the regulations given to the flesh, about food, drink, leprosy and matters similar to them – *the sinful passions that are due to the Law were at work in our members* (v.5). He did not say "by the Law" but *due to the Law*: it is not the Law itself that brings about sin; rather, it levels the accusation of sin. Sin made wrongful use of good. Neither did our members bring about sin; rather, the inclination of our spirit in the wrong direction achieves its effect through our members. Now, what is the result of this? *For bearing fruit for death*. In this he teaches us that before grace, while were living under the Law, we suffered worse impulses of sin, the Law letting us see what had to be done but lacking the power to provide assistance.

But now we are quit of the Law (v.6). He persisted in his caution; he did not say, The Law is abolished, but *we are quit of the Law* – that is, for us the Law is otiose, we no longer live by it. And how are we quit? *dead to the grasp it held*: subject to the Law, we approached baptism, and dying with Christ and rising with him we were related to the lawgiver, and have no further need of the way of life of the Law, having received the very grace of the Spirit. What follows, in fact, indicates this: *so that we serve in newness of spirit, and not in ancient ways of the letter*. He opposed the spirit to the letter, the new to the old, to refer to the Law by *the letter* and its cessation by *the ancient ways*; God says through Jeremiah, remember, "I shall make a new covenant with the house of Israel and with the house of Judah, not like the covenant I made with their fathers in the day when I took them by the hand and led them out of Egypt." [3] And so the difference is brought out through the prophet, and with the coming of the New Covenant the Old must yield.

Having said as much, and by reason of his being accorded spiritual grace foreseeing that some heretics (117) would take this as criticism of the Old and consider the Old Law to be from some other god, of necessity he also raises objections and provides solutions. [4] *What then should we say – that the Law is sin?* (v.7) He had cited many things in what was previously said that would have provided those wishing to speak irreverently of the Law with grounds for criticizing the Law had he not adduced the solution addressing the questions: *The Law made its appearance with the result that the fall was multiplied*, and *The Law produces wrath*, and *No human being will be justified in his sight by works of the Law*,[5] and statements similar to these. Hence for a solution of these very points he raised the objection. Firstly he proved the question to be blasphemous, using a word of denial, *Far from it*. Then he brings out the utility of the Law: *Yet I would not have known sin except through the Law*. Not only, he is saying, is the Law not a teacher of sin – far from it – but on the contrary it is even an accuser of sin: I would not have known what evil is if it had not taught me. *In fact, I would not have been aware of covetousness if the Law had not said, You shall not covet*. The phrases *I would not have been aware* and *I would not have known* are not completely indicative of ignorance here; rather, they mean, Through the Law I got a more precise grasp of differences arising from nature.

Sin, however, taking occasion from the commandment, gave rise to all kinds of covetousness in me (v.8). He uses every means to show the Law to be free from blame: after saying sins abounded with the imposition of the Law, he is obliged lest anyone suspect the Law to be guilty to give an idea of sin's way of proceeding – namely, sin seized upon the giving of the Law as an occasion for a struggle so as to fight against reason in its greater weakness. *Apart from the Law sin was dead*: with no law to show what had to be done and to forbid what was not to be done, there was no room for sin. He then makes this clear from an example. *I lived at one time apart from the Law* (v.9): before the Fall Adam had no fear of death.[6] *But once the commandment came, sin came to life again, whereas I died* (vv.9-10). As soon as God gave the commandment about the trees, the devil made his approach to the woman in a serpent and employed those deceitful words. She fell for it, noticed the beauty of the fruit and was captivated by the pleasure while at the same time breaking the commandment; immediately she together with Adam became subject to the norm of death, he having been a sharer in the eating. *The commandment that was meant for life proved to be death.* In every way he defends the Law and the commandment, while (120) establishing the evil of sin: the commandment was a source of life (he says), whereas the movement to its opposite produced death. It was appropriate for him to employ the word *proved* so as to bring out that while the Law's purpose is one thing, owing to sin its outcome is another.

Sin, in fact, took occasion from the commandment to deceive me, and through it killed me (v.11). He said the same thing in a different fashion. *And so the Law is holy and the commandment is holy, righteous and good* (v.12). By *Law* he refers to the Mosaic Law, and by *commandment* to that given to Adam. He extolled it with many commendations for the reason that it was the object of much criticism on the part of many: those addicted to sloth and not embracing the hardships of virtue criticize the Lord God for imposing the commandment. If he was unaware of what would happen, they claim, how is he God in not foreseeing the future? Yet if he imposed the commandment while foreseeing the Fall, he himself is responsible for the Fall. They should have realized, however, that the discernment of good and its opposite is proper to those endowed with reason. The wolf is rapacious, for example, the lion carnivorous, and bears and leopards are similar, having no sense of sin or a conscience pricked by their actions. Human beings, on the contrary, even if no one is present during their actions, blush at and feel guilt for their crimes, conscience manufacturing the accusation. [7] How, then, could those in possession of such a nature live a life apart from law? This is surely the reason God gave the commandment, so that they might acknowledge their own nature and fear the lawgiver.

Now, it is possible to recognize also the lawgiver's lovingkindness: the law he imposed was not difficult to practice but actually very easy to observe. He permitted the enjoyment of all the plants, forbidding a share of one only, not out of envy of

them in this case (how could he, after all, after giving them authority over everything?) but to instruct them in the limits of service,
to teach them to be well-disposed to the Creator, and to provide
the rational being with an occasion for exercising that faculty. If,
on the contrary, they did not observe the commandment and thus
fell under the norm of death, the blame was due not to the one
who imposed it but to the one who transgressed it. A physician,
after all, in bidding the patient abstain from cold drinks, does so
not out of illwill but from concern for health; but if the patient
does not keep the command and takes some water, he is the one to
suffer harm, whereas the physician is innocent of blame. The Lord
God, of course, regaled Adam in person and all his race with care
of all kinds. And – to pass over other details and get to the heart of
the matter – for the sake of him and his race the Only-begotten
Word became man and put an end to the reign of death which had
begun with him; he gave a promise of resurrection (121) and made
ready the kingdom of heaven, and so he both knew his Fall and
prepared in advance the remedy to come. This is surely the reason
the divine apostle called the commandment *holy, righteous and good*
– *holy* as teaching what is proper, *righteous* as lawfully delivering
the sentence on the transgressors, and *good* as making life available to those who keep it. [8]

He next raises the question in turn, *Did the good prove to be death
for me?* (v.13), and in turn denies it in his customary way, *Not at all.*
He demonstrates the cause of problem: *Rather, it was sin causing
death in me by means of the good so that sin might be shown up.* It is
lacking in clarity on account of the conciseness; what he means is
this, that by means of the good – namely, through the Law and
through the commandment – sin is shown to me, that is, evil and
wickedness. How is it shown? By causing death: from the fruit I
know the tree, and with death before my eyes I hate its mother.
Now, the Law is my instructor in this; accordingly, by teaching me
this the Law is not evil – sin is, the source of death. Our will's
inclination towards worse things brings about sin. *In order that
through the commandment sin might prove to be sinful beyond measure*:
even if nature lets us see it, nevertheless the Law taught us more
clearly the excess of its wickedness. Now, the phrase *might prove* is
incomplete: *obviously* is understood, as we said also in what pre-

ceded, *Rather, it was sin causing death in me so that sin might be shown up in order that through the commandment sin might prove to be sinful beyond measure* – in other words, in order that through the commandment it might be obvious that sin is sinful (that is, wicked) beyond measure.

Then, like an excellent painter, he depicts the struggle between our nature and sin. [9] *We know that the Law is spiritual* (v.14). Again he extols the Law with commendation; what is more honorable than this title? It was written by the divine Spirit, he is saying; by sharing in this grace blessed Moses composed the Law. [10] *But I am of the flesh, sold into the slavery of sin.* He introduces the human being before grace, beset by passions, using the term *of the flesh* for not yet attaining spiritual assistance. Now, let us take the phrase *sold into the slavery of sin* in the usage of the prophet, "Lo, because of your sins you were sold into slavery." [11] This is his meaning here, too: I threw in my lot with sin, and sold my self into its service.

I mean, what I do I do not understand (v.15). Overcome by pleasure and carried away also by the passion of anger, he has no clear knowledge (124) of sin, whereas at least after the cessation of the passion he has a sense of the evil. *That is to say, what I want I do not do; rather, I do what I detest.* This is the effect of the Law, teaching what is evil and instilling hatred of it in the soul. Of course, the phrases *what I do not want* and *what I detest* imply not compulsion but weakness: we fail, not under the impulse of any compulsion or force; rather, under the spell of pleasure we do what we loath as unlawful. *Now, if I do what I do not want, I concede that the Law is good* (v.16): the very hatred I have for sin I have on receipt from the Law. Consequently I defend the Law, and admit its proper function.

As it is, however, it is no longer I that do it but sin dwelling within me (v.17). This is short on clarity, requiring greater explanation. [12] The body, mortal as it became after the transgression of the commandment, felt the effect of the passions; the course of the present life depends on them. For example, it requires desire, not only for nourishment but also for procreation, agriculture and for the sake of the other trades; where it is lacking, none of them functions. It is also responsible for our practice of virtue: the person with no longing for it shies away from the hardships it involves. It also produces in us the longing for God. So, on the one hand, moderation in desire is an aid to the good, and on the other its excess is productive of intemperance: it causes interference in the marriages of others, hankering after what is improper, brigandage, grave robbing, homicide and other such crimes. This is surely the reason why the God of all linked anger with it, to repress its lack of restraint. Yet this passion also is in need of what restrains its insatiability. Just as, then, we apply heat to what is very cold, and conversely with what is very cold we temper the heat, so in creating us God instilled these two passions, diametrically opposed to one another, and taught us to temper the one with the other. [13] He put the mind in charge of them, you see, like a charioteer with ponies, and imposed the harness of service on them, obliging them to bear it equally. But if at some time it happened that desire slipped out of control, he gave directions for anger to be spurred so that once aroused it might bring the harness level again, whereas if anger experienced the passion of excess, he urges desire in turn to be stimulated, and check anger's excess. The mind, then, when sober and discrete, preserves this style; but should it become negligent and drop the reins, it causes the ponies to bolt, it loses its footing, and with them tumbles into holes and crevices. The divine apostle said as much here, *As it is, however, it is no longer I* (125) *that do it but sin dwelling in me*, referring by *sin* to the servitude of the mind and the dominance of the passions. He himself does not do it, since he hates what is done; the dominance of the passions has this effect.

I know, in fact, that good does not dwell within me, that is, in my flesh (v.18). He means the control of the passions, which the body turned mortal has brought to the fore and the mind's negligence has augmented. *Willing what is right is within my possibilities, but performing it I cannot reach on*: the zeal for what is right I gained from the Law's teaching, yet I lack strength for its performance, not having any further assistance. *In other words, the good I intend I do not do; instead, the evil I hate is what I perform. Now, if I do what I do not intend, it is no longer I that do it but sin dwelling in me* (vv.19-20). He said the same thing more clearly.

So I find the Law is that when I intend to do what is right (v.21). Here a distinction is required: *evil is close beside me*. Again, owing to the conciseness he put it obscurely; he means, And the Law seems right to me. In other words, I extol what is stated by it as right, and likewise I love what is right and hate what is opposed to it. [14] Yet *evil is close beside me* – that is, sin – through having a body that is subject to death and suffering, and through the soul's indifference and weakness. Then he shows more clearly the struggle between the mind and the passions: *I mean, I delight in God's Law in my inner self* (v.22). By *my inner self* he means the mind. *But I see another law in my members making war against the law of my mind, and holding me a prisoner of the law of sin which is in my members* (v.23). He gives sin the name *law of sin*. Now, it is in force when the body's passions are activated, on the one hand, and on the other when the soul is incapable of checking them owing to the indifference occurring from the outset, and instead forfeits its own freedom and agrees to be enslaved to them. Yet, though enslaved, it hates its slavery, and praises the accuser of the slavery.

The apostle treated of all this so as to show what we were like before grace, and what we became after grace; and as though taking on the viewpoint of those who before grace were beset by sin, as it were finding himself in the midst of the enemy, taken captive (128) and obliged to serve, with no assistance in sight from another quarter, he groans deeply and laments, and shows the Law incapable of helping, saying, *Wretch that I am, who will rescue me from the body of this death? I thank my God through Jesus Christ our Lord* (vv.24-25). Now, he speaks of a *body of death*, as though made subject to death – that is, mortal, the soul being immortal. Our Lord Jesus Christ alone, he is saying, freed us from that harsh domination, undoing death and promising us immortality, an existence free from hardship and grief, and a life without hostility and sin. Of course, we shall receive the enjoyment of these things in the future life, whereas in the present, enjoying the grace of the all-holy Spirit, we are not alone in being drawn up in battle array against the passions, and instead with that to help us we are able to prevail over them.

Then he offers a solution to all that has been said: *In my mind, then, I am a slave of God's law, but in the body a slave of the law of sin.*

CHAPTER EIGHT

Now, therefore, there is no condemnation for those who are in Christ Jesus, who walk not according to the flesh but according to the Spirit [1] (v.1): the passions now do not prevail over us who resist, since we have received the grace of God's Spirit. *The law of the Spirit of life in Christ Jesus, after all, freed me from the law of sin and death* (v.2). As he used the term *law of sin* of sin, so he called the lifegiving Spirit *law of the Spirit of life.* Its grace, he is saying, has through faith in Christ bestowed on you two freedoms: it not only destroyed sin's domination, but also brought to an end death's tyranny.

He also gives a glimpse of the manner of the destruction. *That is, what was impossible for the Law, because it was weakened by the flesh.* The Law, then, was not evil; yet, though good, it was impotent, proposing obligations to those invested with a mortal nature: in the present life it is through all-holy baptism that we receive a pledge of immortality.[2] *God sent his own Son in the likeness of sinful flesh, and as far as sin is concerned he condemned sin in the flesh* (v.3). He did not say, In the likeness of flesh, but *in the likeness of sinful flesh*: while he took human nature, he did not take human sin – hence he called what was taken not likeness of flesh but *likeness of sinful flesh*: though having the same nature as we have, he did not have the same mindset as ours. Now, he means that, with the Law being incapable of fulfilling its own purpose on account of the weakness of those under its obligation (129), their nature being weak and mortal, the only-begotten Word of God became man and in human flesh destroyed sin,[3] fulfilling all righteousness while incurring no blame from sin, and as though a sinner he endured the death of sinners and brought a charge of sin's injustice in handing over to death a body not subject to death. Yet it was this very act, you see, that destroyed both sin and death: as one not subject to death (he had not committed sin, after all) and still accepting it through sin's unjust verdict, he became a ransom for those justly held in death's grip, while himself free among the dead.

In fact, he taught as much in what follows. *So that the ordinance of the Law might be fulfilled in us, who walk not according to the flesh but according to the Spirit* (v.4). He paid our debt, he is saying, and discharged the Law's purpose. Now, what was that? Making righteous those accepting the Law. If, then, the divine plan involving Christ the Lord put into effect the Law's purpose, the Law deserves not accusation but commendation. After commencing the treatment of righteousness, however, he introduces exhortation: having said, *who walk not according to the flesh but according to the Spirit*, he added, *Those who live according to the flesh, you see, think in terms of the flesh, whereas those who live according to the Spirit think in terms of the Spirit* (v.5). Likewise, too, in another place, "So if we live by the Spirit, let us also be guided by the Spirit."[4] Now, by *Spirit* here he means the grace of the Spirit, and he teaches that the person following it both thinks and does what is pleasing to it, whereas the person in thrall to the flesh – that is, the body's passions – has been deprived of freedom.

The mindset of the flesh, after all, is death (v.6). He did not say The flesh, but *the mindset of the flesh*, that is, the impulses of the passions; death in fact is the penalty for those who have sinned. *Whereas the mindset of the Spirit is life and peace*: the person who lives in spiritual fashion shares in peace with God. *Hence the mindset of the flesh is hostility towards God* (v.7). Once more he criticized the mindset of the flesh – that is, the influence of the passions – and said it was at war with God. *It does not subject itself to God's Law, you see, being unable to do so.* How could it, after all, falling under the influence of the passions as it does, embrace the service of God, since it still chooses to be enslaved to sin? *Those living by the flesh cannot please God* (v.8). He does not bid us live outside our bodies, but to be rid of the mindset of the flesh, teaching us this also in what follows.

You, on the contrary, do not live by the flesh but by (132) *the Spirit if the Spirit of God really dwells in you* (v.9). It is clear that those accepting this teaching were not bodiless; rather, he said they were proof against the bodily passions, and had the grace of the all-holy Spirit dwelling within. Likewise the Lord also said the apostles were not of the world,[5] not because they came from somewhere else, but because they were dead to the world. *Anyone who does not have the Spirit of Christ, by contrast, does not belong to him.* Since he said *anyone*, and this is indefinite, he was right to add that the person not sharing in this grace has no communion with Christ. And since this was sufficient to disturb those listening to it, he offers the remedy in what follows: *But if Christ is in you, the body is dead because of sin whereas the spirit is life because of righteousness* (v.10). He made clear what was indefinite, and showed that he accuses not the flesh but sin: he ordered the body to be dead to sin, that is, not to be involved in sin. Now, here he called the soul *spirit* for being already made spiritual. He bids it go in quest of righteousness, whose desirable fruit is life.

Now, if the Spirit of him who raised Jesus from the dead dwells in you, he who raised Christ from the dead will give life also to your mortal bodies on account of his Spirit dwelling in you (v.11). He provided consolation with the hope of future realities, and gave zeal sufficient for the present struggles. Before long, he is saying, your bodies will be immortal, and will prove superior to the passions now causing disturbance. It is the God of all himself who will do this, who now generously provides you with the pledge of the Spirit. Now, he taught us also in this the one nature of the divinity: he spoke of the all-holy Spirit belonging to God and to Christ, not because, in the view of the execrable heretics, he has been created from the Father through the Son, but because he is of the same substance as Father and Son, and proceeds from Father in keeping with Gospel statement, while his grace is supplied to those worthy through Christk. [6]

Now, he goes on to teach how we must overcome the passions of the flesh. *So then we are debtors not to the flesh, to live according to the flesh* (v.12): having attained salvation from Christ the Lord and received the grace of the Spirit, we owe the debt of servitude to him. *After all, if you live according to the flesh, you are destined to die* (v.13). *According to the flesh*, that is, following the passions of the flesh (133); he means the death that is eternal. *But if by the Spirit you put to death the actions of the body, you will live.* Grace brings this advantage over and above the Law, that while the latter taught obligation, the former brings also the Spirit's cooperating grace. Here, of course, the divine apostle saw the blasphemy of Marcion, Valentinus and Mani, and proposed the teaching with great precision, saying not, You put to death the body, but *the actions of the body*, that is, the mindset of the flesh, the impulses of the passions; after all, you have the Spirit's cooperating grace, life being the fruit of victory. [7] *In fact, whoever are led by God's Spirit are God's sons* (v.14): those living a spiritual life share the dignity of sonship. Here he also goads the Jews, teaching them not to be self-important, since others were also called sons; they were actually deprived of the dignity that comes from the all-holy Spirit, having no share in grace.

After all, you did not receive a spirit of slavery to fall back into fear;

rather, you received a spirit of sonship (v.15). Once more he compares grace with the Law, and calls the way of life under the latter *slavery*. Yet he teaches that the grace of the Spirit wrote that as well. So by *a spirit of slavery* he refers not to the all-holy Spirit but to the imposition of the Law and its occurring through the divine Spirit. [8] Now, if he refers to the all-holy Spirit as *a spirit of slavery*, it is clear the *spirit of sonship* is something else. They are quite different: the all-holy Spirit is one, but his gifts are many and varied. "To one is given through the Spirit the utterance of wisdom," remember, "to another the utterance of knowledge according to the same Spirit, to yet another faith in the same Spirit," [9] and so on. Showing that we have truly attained the dignity of sonship, he added, *in whom we cry, Abba, Father*: when offering the mystical prayer to the Lord, we are bidden to call him Father, and say, "Our Father, who art in heaven." [10] Now, he inserted *Abba* to bring out the confidence of those who call: children, of course, addressing their parents with greater confidence (not having complete discernment, you see), frequently employ this word. We too likewise call the maker of all *Father*, as we are bidden, on account of his ineffable lovingkindness and immeasurable goodness; but we are ignorant of the degree of difference between him and us, (136) neither understanding ourselves perfectly nor recognizing his nature completely. *The Spirit himself, you see, confirms the witness of our spirit that we are children of God* (v.16). He refers to the nature of the Spirit as *Spirit*, and the grace given us as *our spirit*: the terms are used interchangeably. He means that we offer the prayer in obedience to the spiritual teaching; we are not criticized for doing so because we are carrying out a divine law.

But if we are children, we are heirs as well (v.17): freedom from slavery was not sufficient for us, nor was the grace of freedom – instead, we were also adorned with the dignity of sonship; and we were given the name not only of sons but also of God's heirs and Christ's fellow-heirs. He added as much, in fact, *heirs of God and fellow-heirs with Christ*. Since not every son is an heir of the begetter, it was right for the divine apostle to combine inheriting with sonship. And since in many cases a servant receives some inheritance from the master without being left on equal terms with the son, he necessarily added *fellow-heirs with Christ* so as to make utterly clear the lovingkindness that beggars description. *Provided we suffer with him in order to be glorified with him as well*: not all those granted saving baptism enjoy these goods – only those who in addition accept fellowship in the Lord's sufferings. Now, it was not without purpose that he added this: it was for the consolation of those receiving the letter; after all, they had undergone all kinds of onset of trials, were plagued, racked, imprisoned and subjected to countless forms of death. For that reason he composes words of comfort, consoling them with future prospects, and urging them to bear the present situation nobly.

I consider, in fact, that the sufferings of the present time are not comparable with the glory due to be revealed for us (v.18): the crown surpasses the contests, the rewards are out of keeping with the hardships; insignificant the hardship, great the benefit hoped for. This is surely the reason he called the expectation *glory*, not reward. *I mean, the anticipation of creation is for the revelation of the sons of God* (v.19). Do you not see, he is saying, heaven, earth, sea, sky, sun, moon, all visible creation, and invisible beings in addition to these – angels, archangels, powers, authorities, dominations? All these look forward to your perfection. *You see, the creation was subjected to futility, not of its own will but on account of the one subjecting it in hope* (v.20). He calls decay *futility*. Shortly afterwards he teaches that *creation itself will be freed from the bondage to decay*. He teaches that all visible creation shared a mortal nature, especially since the maker of all foresaw the Fall of Adam (137) and the sentence of death imposed on him; it was not right or just, after all, that the things made on his account should share incorruption while he, for whose benefit they were made, should be subject to death and suffering. But with his eventual receipt of immortality through the resurrection, they too in similar fashion share incorruption. Accordingly, he says that visible creation awaits the transformation of things, having become subject to change through no fault of its own but in response to the decree of the creator. But perceiving the care of us, it holds hope of transformation, that creation itself will be freed from the bondage to decay. Now, the divine David also witnesses to creation's being subject to change: after mentioning heaven and earth, he added, "They will perish, but you will abide." [11]

Because creation itself will also be freed from its bondage to decay with a view to the freedom of the glory of God's children (v.21): when the latter are revealed to be what their name suggests, and emerge as sons of God in immortality, the former also will undergo complete freedom from decay. Now, he said this, not to imply that visible creation has the use of reason, but by employing personification; this is typical of the inspired authors, one saying that the pine trees cry aloud, another that the trees rejoice, the mountains skip, and the rivers applaud. [12] *We know, in fact, that the whole of creation has been groaning and giving birth until now* (v.22). Here, too, he includes the invisible creation, saying *the whole of creation.* For a more precise grasp of the text, I shall recall the evangelical saying: the Lord said, Even the angels in heaven rejoice over one sinner who repents. [13] Now, if they rejoice at sinners repenting, they are obviously distressed to see our transgressions.

Not they alone, however, but we ourselves also, who have the firstfruits of the Spirit; we ourselves groan within us (v.23). What surprise is there if creation has this experience on our account? After all, we ourselves, who have received many pledges of future realities as well as the grace of the Spirit before the others, groan as we long for freedom; he indicates this in what follows, *awaiting adoption, the redemption of our body.* He actually stated that we received a spirit of adoption; yet he teaches more clearly that while in this life we received the name, we shall then share the reality when our bodies are freed from decay and put on immortality. He used *firstfruits* to imply that in the present life (140) we shall receive the manifold grace of the Spirit; if what is given now is *firstfruit* and pledge, it is clear that the future gift will be more abundant than it.

I mean, by hope we were saved (v.24): we have not yet attained resurrection, but by receiving the promise we are comforted with hopes. *Now, hope that is seen is not hope: what is left to hope for in the case of someone who sees? But if we hope for what we do not see, we await with patience* (vv.24-25). Do not take it hard, he is saying, to see problems: we did not make false promises to you. That is, we told you to await the enjoyment of the good things, but the good things expected are not visible to the body's eyes: if they were seen, they would no longer be expected, whereas if they are expected, we must wait for them and not cast away the anchor of hope.

In addition to this he shows also further assistance given. *Likewise, the Spirit also offers support in our weaknesses* (v.26): we have adequate succor, the grace of the Spirit. *I mean, we do not know how to pray as we ought; but the Spirit himself intercedes for us in unspeakable groaning.* Do not ask for relief from distress, he is saying: unlike the God who guides us, you do not know what is for the good. Surrender yourselves to the one who holds the tiller of the universe: even if you ask for nothing and only groan under the impulse of the indwelling grace, he will wisely govern your circumstances and provide what will be for your good. He added as much, in fact: *The one who searches the hearts knows what is the mind of the Spirit, because in God's plan he intercedes for holy ones* (v.27). *Spirit* here means not the promise of the Spirit but the grace given to the believers: stimulated by it we feel compunction, inflamed by it we pray more fervently, and *with unspeakable groanings* we entreat God the Savior. The divine apostle wrote this even on the basis of what he had suffered; he had asked in his own case as well for relief from trials, not once or twice but even thrice, and was unsuccessful in his petition. He was told, in fact, "My grace is sufficient for you: my power is made effective in infirmity." On learning this he embraced what he had prayed to be rid of, saying, "So I shall boast all the more gladly of my infirmities so that the power of Christ may dwell in me." [14]

Now, we know that for those who love God all things work together for the good, for those who are called according to purpose (v.28). They *work together*, not for everyone, but for *those who love*; and not simply work together, but *work together for the good*: if you were to ask for what is not beneficial, (141) you would be disappointed in your request since it is not beneficial to attain it. Now, it was with great precision that he linked *purpose* to *calling*: he does not call indiscriminately, but those with purpose. Hence in Corinth he said to the apostle, "Speak and do not be silent: there are many in this city who are my people." He forbade the preaching of the word in Mysia; in Asia, on the contrary, he first constrained them, but later bade them do so. For this reason also in Jerusalem he said to him, "Hurry, leave here quickly: they will not accept your testimony." [15] Hence here too he said *for those who are called according to purpose*; what follows is also consistent with this.

Because those whom he foreknew he also predestined to be conformed to the image of his Son so that he should be firstborn among many brethren (v.29). Saying everything with precision,[16] he did not say *conformed to his Son* but *conformed to the image of his Son*. He put it more clearly in the letter to the Philippians: after saying, "But our citizenship is in heaven, and from there we are also expecting a savior, the Lord Jesus Christ," he added, "who will transform the body of our lowliness, so that it becomes conformed to the body of his glory."[17] Likewise here, too, he spoke of those thought worthy of the call as *conformed to the image of the Son*, that is, the Son's body: since the divine nature is invisible but the body visible, he is adored through the body. *So that he should be firstborn among many brethren.* The truth of the teaching gives testimony to this: he is called *firstborn* as man, while being Only-begotten as God; as God he has no brethren, but as man he calls the believers *brethren*. He is *firstborn* among them, though he is not a different person from the Only-begotten; rather, in himself he is both Only-begotten and firstborn.[18]

Those whom he predestined he also called, those whom he called he also justified, and those whom he justified he also glorified (v.30). He glorified from the beginning those whose purpose he foreknew; having predestined he also called them; then having called he justified them through baptism;[19] and having justified he glorified them, calling them sons and granting them a gift of the Holy Spirit. Let no one say, however, the foreknowledge is responsible for them:[20] it was not the foreknowledge that made them like that – rather, God from afar foresaw the future as God. In other words, if I were to see a bucking horse champing at the bit and in no way tolerating the rider, and say he was riding for a fall, and then things turned out according to my word, it would not be I who brought the horse down; rather, I put into words what was bound to happen, relying on the horse's lack of control as a sign. The God of all from a distance knew everything as God; he did not apply pressure to such-and-such a one to practice virtue, nor to another to commit evil. After all, had he forced them in each case, it would not be right for him to celebrate and award the former and sentence the other to punishment. But if God is righteous, as he certainly is, he gives encouragement to goodness and forbids the opposite, and he commends those who do good and punishes those who willingly embrace evil.

So what shall be our response to this? If God is for us, who is against us? (v.31) With God as ally, are we afraid of people? Everything is included in that *who?* – kings, generals, mobs, mob leaders, the whole world together. Then he brings the supreme example to the fore: *How will he who did not even spare his own Son but gave him up for us all not also grant us everything along with him?* (v.32) He gave us the greater gift, and will he not add to it the lesser gift? He granted the Son, and will he hold back material things? We should acknowledge, of course, that the person of the Son is one, whereas human nature has been given for us by the divinity. "The bread that I shall give," he says, remember, "is my flesh, which I shall give for the life of the world;" and "I have authority to lay down my life, and I have authority to take it up again." [21]

Who will bring a charge against God's chosen? It is God who justifies. Who is to condemn? (vv.33-34). After saying, With God to help us, who will harm us? he added, With God making us righteous, who will succeed in condemning us? *Christ it is who died and was even raised, who is at God's right hand – he it is who also intercedes for us* (v.34). What will you look for in excess of this? Christ the Lord died for you, rose, and is seated with the Father, and has not stopped his care for you in this way; instead, revealing the firstfruits he assumed from us and giving evidence to the Father of their blamelessness, through them he begs salvation for us. He expressed it this way, of course, in reference to the humanity: as God he does not beg but provides. If, however, (145) the heretics were to claim that the Son does so in his divinity as well, they would not thus reveal his glory to be any the less. [22] Let us take the example of two kings of equal standing: a lieutenant or general offends them both, and one of them, who is the first to receive the appeal of the offender, petitions his associate in kingship for reconciliation with the offender – does this diminish the petitioner's standing? By no means. Nor can you say so in this case: what is decided by the Son is decided jointly by the Father, and one decision comes from both. So the expression is devised by the apostle in his wish to bring out the extraordinary degree of care.

Who will separate us from the love of Christ? Will tribulation, oppression, persecution, hunger, nakedness, danger, the sword? As it is written, [23]

On your account we are dying all day long, we were thought of as sheep for slaughter (vv.35-36). The citation is relevant to the theme: it is spoken on the part of men with the identical purpose, the all-holy Spirit having written a psalm about the remarkable Maccabees through the divinely-inspired David. *But in all this we are more than conquerors through him who loved us* (v.37): setting the love for us by the God of all over against all these things, we prove superior to the troubles. We consider it the height of absurdity, in fact, that while Christ the Lord accepted death on behalf of sinners, we do not undergo execution for him with great willingness.

I am in fact convinced that neither death nor life, neither angels nor principalities nor powers, neither present nor future, neither height nor depth nor any other creature will be able to separate us from the love of God that is in Christ Jesus our Lord (vv.38-39). He balances all creation as one against love for God, and associates spiritual things – angels, principalities and powers – with visible things, hoped for goods (and actually even the threat of punishment, *depth* being in my view his name for hell, *height* for the kingdom) [24] with present ones, and in addition to these eternal life and eternal death; and perceiving even this part to be incomplete, he seeks to add something else, and not finding it he weaves the rest of creation of this kind in great variety into his theme without seeing all this matching love for God. In other words, it is not necessary, he is saying, to love him for the promises of good things, but to desire them for his sake; the one who is well disposed to some rich person does not love him for his affluence but for his reciprocal attitude, and (148) is fond of the possessions belonging to him. That is what the divine apostle is saying, too. I would prefer, he says, not to have the kingdom of heaven, things visible and spiritual, and twice or thrice as many other such things without love for God. If, on the other hand, someone proposed to me troubles both present and future, death in this life and for eternity, and lengthy punishment in hell, I would gladly and eagerly opt for them along with love for him in preference to those other attractive things wonderful and beyond words while deprived of love.

Let us also, then, pray and be zealous for it so that by following in the apostle's footsteps we may be found worthy of the apostolic dwellings, thanks to the grace and lovingkindness of our Lord Jesus

Christ, to whom with the Father and the all-holy Spirit belong glory and majesty, now and forever, for ages of ages. Amen.

Chapter Nine

The divine apostle explicitly demonstrated that the Incarnation of our God and Savior was necessary and was a source of ineffable goods to the believers. In fact, he proved Jews to be liable to heavier accusation because of the giving of the Law, and all the others to be transgressors of the law of nature. Exposing the threat of punishment, he explained the gifts of the evangelical grace, and gave a glimpse of the salvation coming from faith. Lest the Jews complain, supposing the Law to be under attack, and lest heretics hostile to the Old Testament take occasion from making of the comparison for calumny against the Law, he was obliged to bring out the usefulness of the Law and commend it with great eulogy. Since, however, the Jews in turn put forward the patriarch Abraham and the promises made him by God, and attempted to show the apostles' preaching to be at variance with these, he was also obliged to give attention to these arguments; with great wisdom he demolished them, employing opportunely both scriptural testimonies and ancient examples, and clearly showing the real meaning of the divine promises. [1]

With the intention of criticizing the Jews' unbelief, he first reveals the affection he has for them, saying, *I am speaking the truth in Christ, I am not lying, my conscience confirming it by the Holy Spirit* (v.1). He showed that what he would say was free from falsehood and bore the mark of truth, calling to witness the grace of the divine Spirit along with conscience so as to persuade them by all this not to lose faith in his words. *The fact that I have deep distress, and the pain in my heart is unremitting* (v.2). The composition of the sentence is incomplete: he ought to have added, On account of the Jews' rejection or unbelief the distress is unremitting. But by recourse to understatement, instead of using those words he conveys their folly through what follows.

He speaks this way: *In fact, I personally prayed to be cut off from Christ for the sake of my brethren, my kindred in the flesh* (v.3). *Cut off* has two senses: what has been dedicated to God is called *cut off*, and what is foreign to him has the same name. The second meaning the divine apostle brought out in the letter to the Corinthians, "Let anyone who does not love the Lord be cut off."[2] Common usage also brings out the former (our calling the offerings to God *cut off*), the God of all himself bidding the city of Jericho to be *cut off*.[3] Here, of course, the blessed Paul used the second sense to bring out the affection he had for his kith and kin. He did not say, I *wanted*, but *I prayed* to be alienated from Christ so that my kindred in the flesh might be related to him and reap the fruit of salvation. Now, it was very appropriate for him to insert the extra word *I personally*, reminding them of what had already been said about the love for Christ, and saying, as it were, I, *whom neither life nor death, neither the present nor the future, nor any other creature will be able to separate from the love of God in Christ Jesus*, would gladly be separated from him for the sake of the salvation of Jews. It is clear, however, that he said this, not by way of esteeming them ahead of the savior, but indicating both his love and longing for them, longing to see them all making their submission and willingly accepting the saving message.[4]

Now, to render his statement believable, he supplies evidence both of their former nobility and of the wealth of the gifts divinely bestowed, saying, *They are Israelites* (v.4). This name was celebrated, remember, imposed on the ancestor by God, like someone bequeathing it as an inheritance on his progeny. *Theirs the sonship*: they shared this name; "Israel is my firstborn son,"[5] Scripture says, remember. *And the glory*: they became famous for the marvels. *And the covenants*: he promised to give them not only the Old but also the New, "I shall make with the house of Israel a new covenant, not according to the covenant I made with their ancestors, which they refused to accept."[5] *And the giving of the Law*: he gave them the Mosaic Law. *And the worship*: esteeming them above the other nations, (152) he taught them a liturgy in keeping with the Law. *And the promises*: equally those made by God to the ancestors and those proposed through the inspired authors.

Theirs the fathers (v.5): they were both famous and celebrated, whose god was styled God. Then he cited the summit of good things: *And theirs the Christ according to the flesh, who is God over all, blessed forever. Amen.* The addition of *according to the flesh* was sufficient to indicate the divinity of Christ the Lord; but as at the beginning he said, *who was of David's line according to the flesh*, and added, *appointed Son of God through power*, likewise here after saying *according to the flesh*, he added the clause, *who is God over all, blessed forever. Amen*, to show the distinction of natures and to bring out the justification for the lament, that though the God over all came from them according to the flesh, they forfeited their nobility and proved foreign to their kindred. He resembled the wives of men departed and lamented who include in their laments loss of charm of body, height of powers, fame of offspring, affluence and power.

Having thus betrayed his affection for Jews, he then sets about the theme proposed. *Now, it cannot be that the word of God has failed* (v.6). I not only wanted, he is saying, but also prayed to be alienated from Christ if only through my alienation Jews could attain the good things promised. Nevertheless, despite their opposition and refusal to reap the harvest of salvation, the promises to the fathers remain valid. How so? *Not all the descendants of Israel, you see, are Israel*: God's interest is in kinship not of nature but of virtue. Then he brings this out more clearly: *Nor are the offspring of Abraham all his children* (v.7), that is, of God; he promptly brings this out: *Instead, Through Isaac descendants shall be named for you.*[6] After citing God's promise, he explains it, with the explanation making the argument clear: *In other words, the children of the flesh are not God's children but it is the children of promise who are regarded as descendants* (v.8). Now, he calls *children of the flesh* those born according to the line of nature, and *of promise* those given according to grace.

This, in fact, was the text of the promise, At this time I shall come, and Sarah will have (153) *a son*[7] (v.9): nature being deficient, he became a father by divine generosity. This is what he means, that Ishmael was Abraham's son, and his firstborn son. Why, then, O Jew, do you have an exalted sense of your own importance as though you alone bore the name of offspring of Abraham? If, on the contrary, you considered that that son was rejected from kinship on account of being half a slave, you would consider wrongly: the divine Scripture customarily traces descent from fathers, not from mothers. Paul could also have adduced the example of the sons of Keturah and shown that though born of a free woman they were not called

Abraham's offspring. [8] It would have been simple for him also to cite the twelve sons of Jacob from different mothers, four of them half slaves, [9] all styled Israel, not at all rejected for their mothers' condition as slave. Making sparing use of proofs, however, he passed up this opportunity and prevailed with the remainder: after quoting what was said by God to Abraham, *Through Isaac descendants will be named for you*, he shows that not even all his line shared this blessing: while one received the blessing, the other missed out on it.

In fact, he added as much: *Not only that: Rebecca conceived children by one husband, our ancestor Isaac; before they had been born, and had done anything good or bad (so that God's purpose regarding election might continue, not by works but by his call), it was said to her, The elder will serve the younger* [10] (vv.10-12). If you think, he is saying, that it was on Sarah's account that Isaac was given precedence over Ishmael and the sons born of Keturah to Abraham, what would he say about Rebecca? In this case there was one mother, one father and one conception, the sons being twins; this was what he meant, in fact, *she conceived children of one husband*, that is, she conceived both at the same time. Yet one was dear to God, the other unworthy of the divine care. God did not await the outcome of events, but instead foretold the difference between them while they were still in the womb. Now, he foretold it from knowing in advance their purpose; election, far from being unjust, is in keeping with people's purpose. [11] Then Paul proposes as well the inspired testimony, *As it is written, I loved Jacob but hated Esau.* [12] So, instead of attending to nature, he looks for virtue alone; this he confirms from further examples.

So what shall we say? Surely not injustice on God's part? Perish the thought (v.14). The divine verdict contains no injustice, he is saying; instead, it bears all the marks of justice. He was able to prove this and bring out clearly that God's way is not to attend to nature, but that he looks for an excellent mindset, and to remind them that they were frequently handed over to numerous enemies, enjoying no mercy on their forebears' account because (156) they did not imitate their virtue, and that whereas they were all handed over to the Babylonians, Abimelech, though a slave and an Ethiopian, attained salvation through godliness. [13] While his intention in doing this was not to terrify them, he shows the divine arrangements surpassing human reason, and that whereas many people commit crimes, not all pay the penalty. In the wilderness, for example, most people adored the image of a calf like a god, not all paid the penalty; instead, some were punished and others came to their senses through the others' punishment. Likewise, by punishing Pharaoh, he thus benefited many.

These cases the divine apostle cited, putting it this way: *He says to Moses, remember, I shall have mercy on whomever I have mercy, and shall pity whomever I pity* [14] (v.15). The Lord said this at the time of making of the calf. Now, he had to mention Moses as well so as to bring out the trustworthiness of the words through the one who spoke and the one who listened. *So it depends not on the one willing or the one making the effort but on God, who has mercy* (v.16). Instead of giving the solution, he expands the question by the addition of examples. *Scripture says to Pharaoh, remember, I raised you up for the very purpose of demonstrating my power through you so that my name might be proclaimed in all the earth* [15] (v.17). Then he proceeds in turn by way of argument: *So he has mercy on whom he chooses, and hardens the heart of whom he chooses* (v.18). These texts are clear, he is saying; I assemble and offer them from no other source: you heard God himself saying, *I shall have mercy on whomever I have mercy, and shall pity whomever I pity.* The words spoken in turn to Pharaoh are from the same person; he it was who passed over Ishmael and the sons of Keturah and chose Isaac; he it was also who gave precedence to Jacob ahead of Esau, despite their being formed at the same time in the one womb. So why are you surprised if he has done this very thing now as well, and has accepted the believers from your midst and rejected those not accepting this ray of light?

Instead of saying as much for the time being, however, he increases the difficulty of the questions, saying, *You will say to me, then, Why does he still find fault? I mean, who opposed his will?* (v.19) In other words, if *he has mercy on whom he chooses, and hardens the hearts of whom he chooses*, people's mindset depends on his will. But if this is so, it would not be just for him to inflict punishment on the sinners: his decisions could not be resisted. Having thus increased the difficulty with the number of the questions and raised all the objections, he added, *Nay rather, mortal that you are, who are you to argue with God?* (v.20) Since you said, he means, (157) *Who opposed his will?* tell me, who are you? are you not mortal? how, then, do you argue and pry into the divine arrangements? I mean, if you were not independent and had no free will to choose what has to be done, instead being subject to the necessity of the divine will, you would keep silent in the fashion of lifeless things, content with the arrangements. But being endowed with reason, you say and do what you please and also have no liking for what happens, looking instead for the reasons for the divine arrangements. *Surely the artifact will not say to the artificer, Why did you make me like this? Has the potter no authority over the clay to make out of the same lump one vessel for special use, another for ordinary use?* (vv.20-21). Consider the potter's clay, which has no share in reasoned discernment and so offers no objection to the maker: even if it is assigned to the work of an ordinary vessel, it accepts in silence what happens. You, on the contrary, resist and object. You, then, are not constrained by natural necessities nor transgress in defiance of free will; instead, you embrace evil willingly, and accept the hardship of virtue of set purpose. The sentence of the God of all is therefore right and just: he justly punishes the sinners for presuming to do this with free will. [16] And there is justice in the presence of lovingkindness as well: it takes occasion from us to extend mercy. Some claim, however, that the verse, *Nay rather, mortal that you are, who are you to argue with God?* is said by way of reproof; first reproving those who pry into divine things, he is saying, and showing their vileness, he arrived at the solution in that way.

Now, the solution is as follows: *But if* (v.22). Here there is need of a further distinction: he means, If you desire to learn why it is that, though most people sin, he punishes some but is kind to others by means of them, and though many practice virtue, he renders some illustrious while through them giving others a glimpse of the future, listen to what follows. *Desiring to give evidence of his wrath and make known his power, God bore with great longsuffering vessels of wrath prepared for destruction, and in order to make known the riches of his glory for vessels of mercy, which he prepared in advance for glory, including us, whom he called not only from Jews but also from Gentiles?* (vv.22-24). God was not the author of Pharaoh's wickedness, he is saying; instead, he exercised longsuffering in customary fashion. But Pharaoh took his longsuffering for weakness, and counting on it he augmented his own disobedience. The wise governor of all things, however, inflicted punishment on him justly, and also from his wickedness he prepared a remedy for the others to ward off evil. Just as surgeons do not themselves make vipers (160), but with them prepare a remedy useful for people, so God did not intend Pharaoh to taste punishment; yet since he was hell-bent on ferocity, he inflicted manifold punishments on him and demonstrated to all people his characteristic power. Hence he said, *I raised you up for the very purpose of demonstrating my power through you so that my name might be proclaimed in all the earth*. Now, the phrase *I raised you up* means, I allowed you to attain kingship, and though in a position to check you I did not check you, foreseeing the benefit that would come from it for the others. By *vessels of wrath prepared for destruction* he refers to those who turned out that way through their own free will; he wrote the same message also to Timothy, "In a large house there are vessels not only of gold and silver, but also of wood and clay, some for special use, some for ordinary." And to bring out that a person willingly becomes one or other, he added, "So if you cleanse yourself of such things, you will be a vessel consecrated to special use and useful to the Master, prepared for every good work." [17] And he writes to the Corinthians thus, "Now, if anyone builds on this foundation with gold, silver, precious stones, wood, hay, straw," [18] openly stressing people's faculty of independence. In the same way he called those deserving of divine lovingkindness *vessels of mercy*, whereas by the phrase *which he prepared in advance for glory* he indicates divine foreknowledge, something he had said previously, *those whom he foreknew he also predestined to be conformed to the image of his Son*. In other words, for the apostle the purpose is to show that only the God of all, and not a single human being, knew those deserving of salvation.

Now, having said that *he called us not only from the Jews but also from the Gentiles*, he confirms his words with scriptural testimony in the words, *As he says also in Hosea, I will call the one not my people My people, and her who was not beloved Beloved. In the place where it was said to them, You are not my people, there they will be called Sons of the living God* [19] (vv.25-26). Now, God said this not about the nations but about the Jews themselves: bidding Hosea take an unfaithful wife, and in fact an adulteress, he bade the children that were born to be given the names in one case Not my people and in the other Not beloved, forecasting the fate of Jews. Yet he promised them prosperity in turn, *the one not my people will be called My people, and she who was not beloved Beloved.* So consider, he is saying, that even you did not always enjoy the same condition; rather, at one time you were a people, at another not a people, and in turn you came to be styled a people; at one time you were beloved, then not beloved, and in turn you were beloved. So nothing novel is happening at the present time: it was habitual for you to be rejected, but if in turn you wish it, [20] you will be called people and beloved; the nations, who were not my people, are now styled my people.

He added a further testimony to his argument. (161) *And Isaiah cries out for Israel, If the number of the sons of Israel were like the sand of the sea, the remnant will be saved: the Lord will make his word take effect promptly on the earth* [21] (vv.27-28). It was very apposite for him to cite this testimony, bringing out that the God of all had prior knowledge from the beginning both of those who came forward in faith and those who were afflicted with unbelief. Since the Jews said, you see, that few of them had accepted the message whereas all the others had shunned it as an imposture, he showed this had been foretold from the beginning, and that even if they surpassed that number in size and resembled the sand of the sea, it would not be all of them who would attain salvation, but those adorned with faith. He referred to faith, note, by *a word taking effect promptly*: what the Law taught in many commandments without being able to provide salvation in its completeness the confession of Christ achieved, procuring faith; it is concise, in need of no lengthy discourse, making its judgments by the soul's disposition and preaching through the tongue. *And as Isaiah prophesied, If the Lord of hosts had not left us offspring, we would have become like Sodom and been made like Gomorrah* [22] (v.29). Those whom he called *a remnant* above he named *offspring*, and on account of them the prophet said Jews would not suffer the fate of Sodom and Gomorrah, which underwent complete ruin.

Having thus brought out that the God of all has no regard for kinship according to nature but looks for the fellowship of faith, he brings out more clearly why Jews forfeited their ancestral nobility while the nations gained a share in salvation, saying, *What then shall we say?* (v.30). It must be read as a question by those making a distinction; then the following by way of reply: *That Gentiles, who did not pursue righteousness, achieved righteousness, but the righteousness of faith, whereas Israel, who pursued the Law for righteousness, fell short of the Law of righteousness* (vv.30-31). Be aware, he is saying, that faith is responsible for the good things enjoyed by the nations: it made worthy of the righteousness that comes by grace those who were once in error and who neither enjoyed righteousness nor wished to look for it, whereas Israel, though having possession of the Law and pursuing the righteousness that comes from the Law, failed in their quest and did not attain righteousness.

Then he goes on with another question: *Why so?* (v.32) Do you want to learn the reason for this? he asks. *Because they acted not from faith but as though from works of the Law.* They thought the way of life according to the Law would suffice for them to gain righteousness, and they scorned faith. For this very reason they neither shared in the gifts of faith nor possessed righteousness on the basis of that way of life. He then brings out the reason why they did not enjoy the good things of faith. (164) *In fact, they stumbled over the stumbling stone, as it is written, I am laying in Sion a stumbling stone, and the one believing in it will not be ashamed.*[23] People usually stumble if their minds are distracted and they are not prepared to keep their eye on the path. This happened to Jews: taken up with the vacuities of the Law, they were not prepared to recognize the stone foretold by the prophets, even though they clearly prophesied that the one believing in him would attain the greatest goods – *would not be ashamed*, in his words, because those who hope but are disappointed in their hope are *ashamed*.

CHAPTER TEN

Having thus mildly chided them, he once more shows the affection he has for them lest the rebuke give an impression of hostility; the heavier charges he kept, in fact, till last. *Brethren, my heartfelt wishes and prayer to God for Israel are for their salvation* (v.1). By *heartfelt wishes* here he referred to desire; in my desire, he is saying, I also pray that they attain salvation. *In fact, I testify of them that they have zeal for God, but not an enlightened zeal* (v.2). He combined censure with commendation, as though concealing a hook under bait of some kind so that the benefit of his message might prove acceptable to them. [1]

That is to say, ignorant of God's righteousness and seeking to set up their own righteousness, they did not submit to the righteousness of God (v.3). He called the untimely observance of the Law *their own righteousness*: they are anxious to observe it though it has ceased to have effect; on the other hand, he gave the name *God's righteousness* to that which happens according to grace through faith. He added as much, note: *Christ in fact is the end of the Law, bringing righteousness for everyone who believes* (v.4): faith in Christ is not opposed to the Law – rather, it is very much in harmony with it. It was the Law, after all, that guided us to Christ; so the one who believes in Christ the Lord fulfills the purpose of the Law. Now, it was good for him say once again *for everyone who believes,* thus including all human nature: if they believe, be they Greek or barbarian, they have a share in salvation.

Then he brings out once again the difference between the Law and grace, and introduces the lawgiver Moses as teacher of both, saying, *Moses, remember, writes about the righteousness that comes from the Law, The person who does these things will live by them* [2] (v.5): the one who has fulfilled all the prescriptions of the Law enjoys life as the fruit of observance, while any chance transgression involves punishment. (165) *But the righteousness from faith speaks this way* (v.6), that is, It is not Moses who says this regarding the righteousness from faith, but the God of all through Moses. *Do not say in your heart, Who will ascend into heaven (that is, to bring Christ down)? or who will descend into the abyss (that is, to bring Christ up from the dead)? What instead does Scripture say? The word is near you, in your mouth and in your heart* [3] (vv.6-8). The God of all said this about the Law to teach Jews that they accepted without hardship the instruction about obligations, and were not committed either to ascent into heaven nor descent into Hades. *The word is near you:* knowledge of the requirements is given you. The divine apostle, however, took up these words for a treatment on faith, teaching that there should be no prying into the Lord's plan, or doubting that the Only-begotten Son of God became man and by accepting the passion achieved resurrection; rather, we should reap salvation as fruit of faith. *The word is near you, in your mouth and in your heart.* Then he adds, *That is, the word of faith, that we proclaim*: what Moses said about the commandments of the Law we say about faith.

Because if you confess with your mouth Jesus is Lord, and believe in your heart that God raised him from the dead, you will be saved: belief is from the heart unto righteousness, and confession by the mouth unto salvation (vv.9-10): there is need of both, of faith true and firm, and of confession made with confidence, so that the heart may be adorned with the certitude of faith, and the tongue made resplendent by fearless proclamation of the truth.[4] Then once more he calls to mind the testimony of Scripture: *Scripture says, in fact, No one believing in him will be put to shame*[5] He also comments on *No one. There is no distinction between Jew and Greek, the same Lord being Lord of all, generous to everyone and to all who call upon him; after all, everyone who calls upon the name of the Lord will be saved*[6] (vv.12-13). Then he teaches that Jews willingly were deprived of salvation, refusing to accept the message offered. Instead of proposing this argument openly, however, he develops the point in a different fashion. (168)

How, then, will they call upon one in whom they have not believed? And how will they believe in one of whom they have not heard? And how will they hear without a preacher? And how will they preach unless they are sent? (vv.14-15). It is necessary, he is saying, first to believe, then to call. But it is impossible to believe if one does not have the benefit of the teaching, and this could not happen with no preachers, and deputation in turn is responsible for them. After citing these points in this manner by way of Jews' defense, he uses them to add to the accusation against them; the last one, that relating to the sending of the preachers, he put first to show that it was forecast from the beginning. It was, in fact, logical to give it pride of place ahead of the others: the first need is for the preachers to be deputed, then the preaching, then the listening to the preachers, and at that point the coming to faith. Accordingly, he adduces the prophecy of Isaiah in the words, *How charming the feet of those who bring news of peace, of those who bring good news;*[7] the Lord, remember, bade the apostles say on entering a house, "Peace be to this house:"[8]

they indicated divine reconciliation, and brought the good news of the enjoyment of good things. He calls their feet *charming* for running the good race, for being washed by the Lord's hands.

Having thus adduced the testimony to the preachers, he says in question form, *But have they not all obeyed the Gospel?* (v.16) Then, by way of response, *Isaiah says, Lord, who has believed our report?* [9] Not even the divine Scripture kept silent about it; instead, God actually foretold it from the beginning through Isaiah. Then, by way of logical argument, *So faith comes from hearing, and hearing through the word of God* (v.17): the one who does not believe, therefore, shows utter distrust for the divine sayings, and the one who believes and accepts divine words offers the fruit of hearing, faith.

But I ask, Have they not heard? (v.18) This, too, must be read as a question. Then, by way of response, *On the contrary: Their sound has gone out to all the earth, and their words to the world's limits* [10] (v.18): how could Jews not have heard when the nations throughout the world did hear? The preachers offered the message of truth to them first, the Lord himself said to them , "Go by preference to the lost sheep of the house of Israel;" [11] and in the Acts of the Apostles, "It was necessary that the word of God be spoken first to you." [12] The (169) divine apostle persisted in this style, making his argument clearer by question and answer; again it should be read as a question: *But I ask, Was Israel in ignorance?* What follows is by way of response: *First Moses says, I shall make you jealous of what is not a nation, with a heedless nation I make you angry* [13] (v.19): he called us *heedless* to give evidence of our lack of comprehension prior to faith. The divine apostle also said as much, remember, "We ourselves, you know, were also heedless of a time, disobedient, errant, in thrall to lusts and manifold pleasures, living in vice and envy, despicable, hating one another." [14] With this in particular God tormented Jews: not slavery, dispersion or loss of the Temple so distresses them as the godliness of the nations and also their fame.

Isaiah also made so bold as to say, I was found by those who did not seek me, I made myself visible to those who did not ask for me [15] (v.20). He showed at the one time the prediction of the nations coming to know God and the Jews' bloodguiltiness, the phrase *he made so bold* indicating it. He was not put off, the meaning is, by Jews thirsting for blood and falling into frenzy; instead, he forecast with great confidence the salvation of the nations. He also prophesied the Jews' unbelief; what follows makes it clear: *But to Israel he says, All day long I held out my hands to a people unbelieving and contrary* [16] (v.21). The phrase *all day long* implies persistence; Symmachus and Aquila, in fact, rendered it *the whole day*.

CHAPTER ELEVEN

Having thus shown the remarkable prophets both accusing Jews and heralding the nations' faith, he gives the impression through what follows of offering them comfort, but augments the accusation of the unbelieving. *I ask, then, surely God has not rejected his people? Far from it* (v.1). Then, though in a position to provide the proof of this from many other instances, such as parading the three thousand who came to faith in Jerusalem, [1] the countless numbers of whom the mighty James spoke [2] and those throughout the world from amongst Jews who accepted the message, he puts forward himself in evidence in preference to all these, saying, *I am an Israelite, after all, from the line of Abraham, of the tribe of Benjamin. God has not rejected his people, whom he foreknew* (v.1-2): if he had rejected them, I too would be one of those under accusation; after all, I sprang from that stock, and boast of Abraham as forebear and Benjamin as chief of my tribe, and I glory in the name of Israel.

Do you not know what Scripture says in Elijah, that he intercedes with God against Israel? Lord, they killed your prophets and overthrew your altars; I am left solitary, and they are after my life. But what divine response does he give him? I reserved seven thousand men for myself who did not bend the knee to Baal [3] (vv.3-4). At that time, he is saying, there were countless numbers of Israelites, and all were called Israelites; but the God of all named himself the God of the seven thousand, disqualifying all the others: *I reserved seven thousand men for myself*, he said, *who did not bend the knee to Baal*. The prophet, of course, did not know even this much, believing the remnants of godliness that were saved were confined to him. It is, therefore, not novel or surprising if you likewise are ignorant of those who have come to faith in the Savior from your number, whom the God of all calls his people. Now, it was timely for Paul to parade the mighty Elijah, who had written the text against them for not only slaying the prophets but also rooting up the altars. I mean, let us concede that they were hostile to the prophets for predicting harsh outcomes – but what did they have against the divine altars? Rather, through the abuses they committed they made clear that they hated their God.

The divine apostle moves from the scriptural testimony to his own argument in the words, *Likewise, then, in the present time, too, a remnant has appeared by the election of grace. But if it is by grace, it is not from works, since grace would no longer be grace. But if it is from works, it is no longer grace, since the work would no longer be work* (vv.5-6). [4] As in the past, he is saying, (173) only seven thousand free from impiety were reserved out of countless thousands, so in these times, too, non-believers were more numerous and believers enjoying the divine grace fewer. I mean, the way of life according to the Law did not justify them (what he means by *from works*); rather, God's grace saved them – hence salvation is also called *grace* since it happens by divine liberality. He says this also in what referred to the patriarch Abraham: *To the worker, on the other hand, wages are not reckoned as a gift but as his due.* [5]

What, then? (v.7) At this point a further distinction is to be made, occurring as a question, with the meaning, So what can we say? The rest follows as a reply: *What Israel is seeking it did not attain; the elect attained it, but the rest were hardened.* He calls *elect* those of their number who were believers. Now, he means this: In adhering to the Law Israel failed in its aim; it now keeps the Law unlawfully, and reaps no fruit of righteousness. Those of their number who were believers, on the other hand, attained it, *but the rest were hardened*, that is, unbelief caused their heart to be hardened. He shows this was also prophesied from olden times. *As it is written, God gave them a spirit of stupor, eyes not for seeing and ears not for hearing, to this very day* [6] (v.8). The word *gave*, like *gave over*, means allowed: God did not cause them to be unbelieving – how could even he instil unbelief in them, and himself penalize them for it? The prophet also brought this out more clearly, "The heart of this people has been dulled, they listened stolidly with their ears and shut their eyes." [7] So it was no one else who blinded them: they shut their own eyes and refused to see the light. He used the term *a spirit of stupor* of their mindset resistant to change: as the person enjoying a commendable slumber is not liable to a turn for the worse, so those surrendering themselves completely to wickedness do not make a choice of a change for the better. *And David says, Let their table become a snare, a trap, a stumbling block in their way and retribution for them. Let their eyes be darkened so that they do not see, and bend their backs forever* [8] (vv.9-10). He called luxury *table*, and predicted it would be changed into the opposite.

So I ask, have they stumbled so as to fall? Not at all. But through their stumbling salvation has come to the nations so as to make them jealous (v.11): those of their number who believed offered to them first (176) the saving message; but when they opposed it and did not accept the teaching, they offered the divine Gospel to the nations, who by contrast believed and enjoyed salvation. Now, this is sufficient to provoke the Jews in their opposition, rouse them to jealousy and procure for them a share in salvation; they see the last have become first. *Now, if their stumbling means riches for the world, and their defeat means riches for Gentiles, how much more their full membership?* (v.12): if, while most did not believe, those of their number who did believe offered the riches of the knowledge of God to the nations, it is obvious that, if all believed, they would be responsible for greater goods to all people. After all, it would be easier for all to believe if the others did not offer opposition and instead preached the truth along with them.

At this point he offers encouragement to those coming to faith from Gentiles, advising them to exercise a moderate attitude, and achieving two ends at once, namely, repressing their arrogance and prompting them to fear; he also turns Jews back to a share in their ancestral inheritance. He begins this way, *I am in fact speaking to you Gentiles: inasmuch as I am an apostle of Gentiles, I glorify my ministry so as to make my kin jealous and save some of them* (vv.13-14): since God designated me preacher of the Gentiles, I necessarily concern myself with the salvation of the Gentiles, direct my words on their behalf and show the divine prophets foretelling it from of old so as by this means at any rate to prompt Jews to jealousy and cause some of them to share in salvation. In fact, he calls the Jews his *kin* as sharing only kinship with him, while being at odds in attitude.

You see, if their rejection means the reconciliation of the world, what will their admission mean if not life from the dead? (v.15). If with their refusal to believe, he is saying, the Gentiles were admitted and freed from their previous ignorance, it is clear that if they all were prepared to believe, there would be nothing else left remaining but resurrection of the dead. The Lord himself also said as much, "This Good News of the kingdom will be preached to all the nations as a witness to them, and then will come the end."[9] It must be acknowledged, however, that the divine apostle said this, measuring his words deliberately so as to instruct those who had come to faith from Gentiles to keep their head, and also to extend a hand to the unbelievers amongst the Jews and give them a glimpse of salvation through repentance. What follows brings this out more clearly.

If the first batch is holy, the whole lump is, too; (177) and if the root is holy, so too are the branches. But if some of the branches were broken off and you, a wild olive, were grafted on them and succeeded to a share in the root and the richness of the olive tree, do not boast over the branches (vv.16-18). He calls Christ the Lord in his human nature *first batch,* the patriarch Abraham *root,*[10] the people of the Jews *branches of the olive tree* for springing from him, and the instruction in piety *richness of the olive tree.* So he urges the believers from Gentiles not to lord it over the unbelieving Jews, which he calls *branches cut away;* keep in mind, he is saying, that you came from different stock and were grafted on to it, and you were recipients of the richness of the pious root. *But if you do boast, it is not you that supports the root, but the root you:* consider this as well, that the root carries you, not you the root; you need it, not it you.

So you will say, The branches were broken off so that I might be grafted on. True: *they were broken off through unbelief, whereas you hold firm through faith. Do not get carried way; be afraid, rather* (vv.19-20): unbelief put even them at odds with the root, and faith attached you to the root and caused you to share in its richness; so instead of becoming self-important, you should fear and tremble. Why? *After all, if God did not spare the natural branches, perhaps he will not spare you, either* (v.21): if natural affinity was of no help to them since they did not exercise the same option,[11] much more likely is it that if you do not preserve grace, you will be at odds with the root. *Behold, then, God's goodness and severity: severity towards the fallen, but goodness towards you provided you abide in the goodness – other-*

wise you will be cut off (v.22): see now how in the one case God lopped them off for not imitating their forebears' faith, whereas he accorded you lovingkindness and made you share in a foreign root with which you would be completely at odds if you did not preserve the gift that has been given.

Even those others, however, provided they do not persist in their unbelief, will be grafted on (v.23): it is in accord with God's righteousness, though you have been thought worthy of that root of theirs in defiance of expectation and in turn have not preserved the grace given, to separate you once more from the root, and also to attach again to it those who have been rid of their unbelief. It was good for him also in addition to that to employ the term *they will be grafted on* for the reason that though unbelief cut them off completely, faith attaches them to the root in a manner like the Gentiles. *After all, God is able to graft them on again.* He gave evidence of the ease of the process for God's power, (180) and cites an example that is neither foreign nor out of date but relevant and novel, calling them in witness to it in the words, *I mean, if you have been cut from what is naturally a wild olive and, contrary to nature, grafted on to a cultivated olive, how much more easily will these natural branches be grafted on to their own olive* (v.24): if you, though a wild olive (in other words, you had not the Law to raise you, nor the inspired authors to irrigate and prune you and give you due attention), were separated from godless parents and kindred, made sharers in the faith of Abraham, and gloried in him as root and father and forebear, not by dint of nature but as a result of divine generosity, much more in accordance with both reason and nature, of course, will they be attached to their own root when they come to believe.

Now, he says this, as I mentioned, both to teach those from Gentiles who believe to keep a grip on themselves and to propel to salvation those of the Jews who did not believe. And what follows is in harmony with this. *You see, I want you, brethren, not to be unaware of this mystery, lest you be wise in your own way of thinking* (v.25). A mystery is what is intelligible not to everyone but only to those who have trust. [12] So he means, I want you to learn a mystery that we know about the question in hand lest you consider yourselves very smart and thence gain an impression of self-importance. Now, what is the mystery? *A hardening has come upon part of Israel until the full number of the Gentiles has come in, and thus all of Israel will be saved* (vv.25-26). He said *part* to teach that not all failed to believe: many even of them did believe. But his advice is not to despair of the salvation of the others: after the Gentiles' acceptance of the message, even they will come to faith with the mighty Elijah's coming and offering them the teaching of the faith; the Lord also said as much in the sacred Gospels, "Elijah is coming, and will restore all things." [13]

He also adduced the testimony of the inspired author: *As it is written, Out of Sion will come the deliverer, and he will banish impiety from Jacob. This is the covenant between them and me, when I remove their sins* [14] (vv.26-27). If the way of life according to the Law grants forgiveness of sins, the inspired word would have prophesied it. But if the Law punishes transgressors, while the charge of lawlessness was constantly leveled at Jews, it is clear that the text indicates forgiveness provided through baptism. [15] Now, he speaks of all Israel as believers, whether they be from Jews as having a natural kinship with Israel or from Gentiles as attached to it from the kinship of faith. (181) *In respect of the Gospel, they are hostile on your account, whereas in respect of election they are beloved on account of the ancestors* (v.28): when I focus on you, with whose instruction I was entrusted, I form the impression of them as hostile and ill-disposed, taking every step for your harm. But when I have regard for the forebears, and consider that God chose them out of the whole world, I am fond of them as well on your account.

God's gifts and calling, after all, are not subject to review (v.29). He says all this by way of exhortation of the Jews: to the fact that the goods God gives he takes back when he sees the recipients suffering from ingratitude Saul is witness, having enjoyed spiritual grace and then being deprived of it later. [16] Solomon likewise enjoyed peace through divine generosity and was bereft of the gift after his fall. The Jews themselves, too, constantly enjoyed attention from Old Testament inspired authors, but at the present time are deprived of this care. He delivered this threat also to those from Gentiles who recently came to faith: provided, that is, you abide in goodness, he is saying – otherwise you too will be cut off. [17] *I mean, just as you also were once disobedient but now have enjoyed mercy through their disobedience, so too they have now been disobedient through the mercy shown to you so that they also may have mercy shown to them* (vv.30-31): remember that all were guilty of impiety for a long time, and the loving Lord had no regard to that protracted and severe impiety; instead, to those willing he granted ineffable lovingkindness, and when they proved unbelieving he called you in their place. It is therefore not unlikely that those who at present voice their opposition have also been accepted by God if willing to believe, and attain the same lovingkindness. Now, he once more employed *so that* in his own peculiar usage: it was not that they were disobedient for the purpose of having mercy shown them; rather, they were disobedient on account of obstinacy of mind, but had mercy shown them by recourse to repentance. [18]

God, in fact, has imprisoned all in disobedience so as to show mercy to all (v.32), using *imprisoned* for censured. He censured the Gentiles for having natural discernment and enjoying creation as a teacher of knowledge of God and yet failing to gain any benefit from the one or the other. He censured the Jews for being in receipt of more abundant teaching, receiving in addition to nature and creation the Law and the inspired authors instructing them on obligations and yet proving liable to heavier penalty. Nevertheless, to both the former and the latter, though deserving of utter destruction, he granted salvation, provided they were ready to believe. [19]

After recounting all this and perceiving the depths of the divine lovingkindness and the incomprehensibility of his wisdom, he cried aloud, *O the depths of the riches and wisdom and knowledge* (184) *of God!* (v.33): from the very beginning he foreknew this, in his foreknowledge he wisely made his plans, and in his planning he gave a glimpse of the riches of his lovingkindness. *How unsearchable his judgments and how inscrutable his paths!* The pattern of the divine plans surpasses human understanding, and the providence of the God of all escapes the unseen powers. *Who has known the mind of the Lord,* remember, *or who has been his counselor? Who has given him a loan for him to be in debt?* [20] (vv.34-35). He cited these three verses to match the three attributes wealth, wisdom and knowledge: *Who has known the mind of the Lord?* matching knowledge, *Who has been his counselor* wisdom, and *Who has given him a loan for him to be in debt?* wealth – in other words, the wealth of his goodness is immeasurable because he gave existence to those who did not have it and grants to those alive a good existence; he repays no one, only gives good things. Being loving he calls giving repayment.

Because from him and through him and to him are all things. To him be glory forever. Amen (v.36): he made everything personally, as controller he personally brings to completion all things that have been made. It behooves everyone to look to him, giving thanks for what they have, and asking for providence in the future. They ought also offer him due praise. Through these expressions the divine apostle showed that he did not acknowledge a difference in purpose between *from whom* and *through whom,* the former (as though indicating something greater) belonging to the Father, and the latter (as conveying something less) referring to the Son: he applied both to each person. Whether those holding the position of Arius and Eunomius were to claim it belongs to the Father, they would find *through whom* linked to *from whom;* or whether they referred it the Son, they would see *from whom* linked to *through whom.* If, on the other hand, *from whom* signifies something greater and *through whom* something less, and both apply to each person, it would be logical to think the same person is greater than himself owing to *from whom* and less owing to *through whom.* [21] Let us instead leave this aside and glorify both our creator and our savior, to whom belongs the glory for ages of ages. Amen.

CHAPTER TWELVE

The knowledge of the divine nature as well as both faith and a proper disposition to it are the summit and the true foundation of good things: what the eye is to the body faith and knowledge of divine things are to the soul. They still require, nonetheless, the practice of virtue, as the eye does hands, feet and the other parts of the body. Now, for this reason the divine apostle added moral teaching as well to the doctrinal instruction (185) so as to develop complete virtue in us, through the Romans offering the benefit to all people.

He begins this way: *So I urge you, brethren, through the mercy of God* (v.1). He lays down laws, keeps authority under cover, proposes teaching along with entreaty, and calls to mind the divine lovingkindness on which he had spoken at length in the preceding section. Now, to what does he urge them? *To present your bodies as a living sacrifice, holy, pleasing to God, the worship of your reason.* He had already recommended them to turn their limbs into instruments of righteousness and to present themselves like those raised from the dead. [1] But here he urges the bodies to become also a sacrifice, and calls it the *living sacrifice*: he does not bid the bodies to be slaughtered, but to be dead to sin and not to accept any of its operation. He named this sacrifice *holy, reasonable, pleasing*, comparing it to the immolation of brute beasts and showing the Lord God pleased with it. In all the inspired authors, so to say, God finds fault with the sacrifices of brute beasts, remember, and lays down this single requirement, "Sacrifice to God the sacrifice of praise," and "A sacrifice of praise will glorify me." [2] And you can find countless such statements in the divine Scripture.

Far from being configured to this age (v.2). By the figures of the present age he is referring to things like wealth and influence and other pomp and circumstance, implying future things are stable and lasting. Likewise elsewhere, too, "The figure of this world is passing away, after all." [3] Many people, in fact, have undergone a change in state from the height of affluence to extreme penury, while others growing up in poverty have been entrusted with the highest offices; still others, on the other hand, puffed up and filled with a sense of their own importance, and believing themselves superior to everyone else, have suddenly lost their footing and been turned into stinking dung. The divine apostle, accordingly, wants us not to long for such things nor fall in love with the figure of this life, but rather go after those things that bring life everlasting. *Be reformed by the renewing of your mind so as to discern what is the will of God, good, pleasing and perfect.* Here he is also urging those taking a turn for the worse to make a change for the better, suggesting this by *Be reformed*. He also brought out the extent of the difference between present realities and virtue, calling the former *figure* and virtue *form*. Form betrays things in reality, whereas figure is something easily lost. [4] He brought out also the soul's independence, bidding it renew its judgment and distinguish better from (188) worse; he said this is service of God. He also teaches what this is, disallowing conceit before everything else and requiring humility.

I tell you, in fact, by the grace given me, to everyone among you not to

form a higher impression of yourself than you ought, but to form an im-
pression leading to sober judgment (v.3). He has this to say by way of
giving directions not of himself but the grace of the Spirit speaking through him; I am its instrument, he is saying. Now, he called
a healthy mind *sober judgment* here to bring out that haughtiness is
a disease of the mind. He imitated his own Master, of course: the
Lord also declared blessed in the first place those exercising humility, "Blessed are the poor in spirit because theirs is the kingdom
of heaven." [5] Paul makes this requirement of everyone, poor and
rich, slaves and masters, men and women: *everyone among you* suggests as much. He also gives the measure of self esteem: *Each*
according to the measure of faith God has assigned, [6] here calling grace
faith: the giving of grace is made through faith, and the gifts of
grace are supplied according to the measure of faith. He bids them
measure out the soul's self-esteem to match the grace given.

As we have in one body many members, you see, and not all the mem-
bers have the same function, likewise though many we are one body in
Christ, and individually we are members one of another (vv.4-5). The
resemblance to the teaching on love is fitting: [7] each of the parts of
the body is useful not for itself alone; rather, it brings benefit to the
body as a whole. Accordingly, it likewise behooves people receiving some grace from on high to acknowledge clearly that they
received this gift for the common good; the believers form one body,
while each of us discharges the function of a limb.

We have gifts that differ according to the grace given to us (v.6). It is
to be understood this way: We are members of one another, *having*
gifts that differ according to the grace given to us; even if they differ,
they are supplied by divine grace for the common good. *Inspired*
utterance in keeping with the faith, ministry in ministering, the teacher
in teaching, the exhorter in exhorting (vv.7-8). The supplier of good
things measures out the grace to match each one's faith. Now, he
calls *inspired utterance* not only the knowledge of the future but
also the knowledge of what is hidden, *ministry* the service of preaching, *teaching* instruction in the divine truths, *exhorting* (189) urging
to virtue. *The sharer in simplicity,* not hankering after the good opinion of others but meeting the needs of the needy, not falling into a
quandary as to whether one has sufficient for oneself or not but
trusting in God and making generous provision.

The leader in zeal, the merciful in cheerfulness. Let love be without simulation (vv.8-9). He makes all these requirements with intensity, and bids their care be zealous lest the name go unmatched by the deed. He associates joy with beneficence, giving a glimpse of the gain of sharing: those who gain are normally happy. He said so also in writing to the Corinthians, "Not gloomily or under obligation: God loves a cheerful giver." [8] And he urges that their love be sincere and they dismiss a facade of simulation. *Abhorring what is evil, holding fast to what is good.* Again he did not simply say, Shun, pursue; instead, on the one hand he urged them hate evil vehemently, and on the other he bade them cling closely to the doing of good, exercising affection like a kind of glue. *Loving one another with mutual affection, outdoing one another in showing esteem* (v.10): have an ardent affection for one another as becomes brethren; let each relinquish pride of place to the neighbor, this being a sign of true love.

Not backward in zeal (v.11): showing unalloyed enthusiasm for the good, and completely rejecting sloth. *Fervent in spirit*, calling grace *spirit*; he bade enthusiasm give substance to it, like wood on fire. He says the same thing elsewhere, too, "Do not quench the Spirit." [9] Now, the Spirit is quenched in the case of those unworthy of grace: they do not keep the eye of the mind clear, and so do not receive that ray. [10] Likewise for those who blind their body even the light is darkness, and in the middle of the day they are in thrall to gloom. Hence he bids us *be fervent in spirit*, and have a warm desire for the divine, adding as much, *Serving the Lord, rejoicing in hope, being patient in tribulation, persevering in prayer* (vv.11-12): the one who is fervent in spirit serves the Lord with enthusiasm, looks forward to the enjoyment of the good things hoped for and proves superior to the onset of trials, pitting endurance against their assaults and calling unceasingly on divine grace for assistance. [11] He said this, after all, *persevering in prayer*, that is, doing it unceasingly.

Sharing necessities with the saints (v.13). With the mention of *sharing* he urges them to generosity: who does not choose to contribute resources and (192) become a sharer of virtuous deeds? He said as much also in writing to the Corinthians, remember, "Your abundance for their need so that likewise their abundance may be for your need." [12] *Extending hospitality to strangers.* He calls *strangers* not only the saints but also those arriving from any quarter what-soever in need of attention, for whom he bids them take care. *Bless those who persecute you, bless and do not curse* (v.14). This is the Lord's law: the Lord proposed it to the divine apostles. [13] *Rejoice with those who rejoice, weep with those who weep, being of one mind with one another* (vv.15-16): share with one another, both in grief and in its opposite, one being a mark of sympathy, the other of friendship that is free of the blame of envy. *Instead of being standoffish, associate with the lowly.* Again he eliminates the hauteur of arrogance, and requires they mix with those of humble appearance. *Do not puffed up with your own importance*, that is, do not be content with your own ideas, but take advice from others.

Do not repay anyone evil for evil (v.17). This is a mark of the most mature virtue and close to the achievement of freedom from passion. *Planning for what is noble in the sight of all.* Likewise elsewhere as well, "Give no offense to Jews or Greeks or the Church of God." [14] *If possible and within your capacity, be at peace with everyone* (v.18). The addition of *If possible* and *within your capacity* is done with precision. Do not be responsible for any trouble, he is saying; instead, apply every means in the cause of peace. It is also in keeping with the preceding: the one who blesses the persecutor and takes no vengeance on the wrongdoer – what hostility does he indulge in? *Do not avenge yourselves, dearly beloved; but leave room for wrath. It is written, remember, Vengeance is mine, I shall repay, says the Lord.* [15] *So if your enemies are hungry, feed them, if thirsty, give them to drink; by doing this, you see, you will heap coals of fire on their heads* [16] (vv.19-20). By giving a glimpse of the judge and laying bare his righteous judgment (the sense of *Vengeance is mine, I shall repay, says the Lord*), he bids them nobly bear the injustices inflicted, reward the wrongdoers with the opposite and supply the needs of their opponents. This is the stuff of the crowns of those with true values, after all, while augmenting the retribution of the wrongdoers. You must understand, of course, that it is not appropriate to encourage our adversaries to the point where they become liable to even heavier penalties; the divine apostle added this in his wish to quench the anger of the wronged, (193) not in any attempt to heighten evil with good. [17] What follows also brings out the fact that he bids them have true values. *Do not be overcome by evil; rather, overcome evil by good* (v.21): whereas taking vengeance betrays defeat, repaying evil with good is victory beyond dispute.

Chapter Thirteen

Having thus given them a lesson in morality, he urges them accord also those in power due respect; being in receipt of the grace of the all-holy Spirit in rich measure, he foresaw that some, exercising conceit rather than zeal, would despise the earthly rulers, regarding themselves as of greater importance on account of their knowledge. He did this for the particular purpose of cutting their self-esteem down to size; they had formed the false impression that they should overturn the laws obliging all in common. Some said, "The people who have been turning the world upside down have come here also," [1] while others, They introduce different morals. [2] Accordingly, he thought it useful to legislate also on this.

Let every person be subject to higher authorities (v.1): be they priest or archpriest or someone professing the solitary life, let them yield to those entrusted with office. Obviously on condition it is in keeping with godliness: breach of God's commandments may not be allowed the rulers. *There is, in fact, no authority except from God, and the authorities in force are ordained by God.* These depend on God's providence: he it is who in his care for the general order has arranged for some to rule and be ruled, bringing upon wrongdoers fear of the rulers like a kind of bridle. It should be realized, of course, that the divine apostle made ruling and being ruled dependent on the providence of God, not the appointment of this one or that: the authority of unjust people is not by God's mandate – only the provision for government. Being kindly, of course, he gives rulers who have a respect for justice; "I shall give them shepherds after my own heart," he says, remember, "who will shepherd them as shepherds with understanding;" [3] and again, "I shall give you judges as before and counselors as at the beginning," and in his wish to correct the fallen he even allows them to be ruled by wicked rulers, "I shall appoint youngsters as their rulers, and deceivers will rule them." [4]

It is time, however, to return to commentary on what follows. *And so the one resisting authority resists God's ordinance* (v.2). He said enough to scare them. *And those who resist will bring judgment on themselves,* that is, they will become liable to retribution. Then he brings out also the usefulness of government. (196) *The rulers, after all, are a terror not to good works but to bad* (v.3): they punish those living an evil life. *Do you wish to have no fear of authority? Do good, and you will earn commendation from it; it is, in fact, God's servant for you for your own good* (vv.3-4). He made it appear deserving of respect, calling it *God's servant.* He also urged them to the practice of good works, saying the rulers commended good works. *But if you do evil, be afraid: it does not bear the sword in vain; it is God's servant, after all, executing wrath on the wrongdoer:* if you love the good, respect authority as the one legislating for it; but if you are involved in the opposite, fear its verdict, for it is divinely commissioned to punish the wicked.

Hence it is necessary to be subject, not only because of wrath but also because of conscience (v.5). He calls retribution *wrath.* He bids them be subject on two scores, both for fear of retribution and for discharging one's dues, referring to this as *conscience. For this reason, in fact, you also pay taxes; they are actually God's ministers in performing this very role* (v.6): while you sleep, he is engaged in the concerns of all; you sit at home while he is embroiled in war for the sake of peace. *So render to everyone their due: tribute to the one due tribute, revenue to the one due revenue, fear to the one due fear, respect to the one due respect* (v.7). He calls *tribute* what is the contribution for the land, *revenue* what is expended for commerce, *dues* not only these but also *fear* and *respect,* these being due the rulers from the ruled.

Owe no one anything except to love one another (v.8), not to avoid discharging the debt of love – we ought, in fact, discharge it before everything else – but to increase it by discharging it: repayment multiplies the debt, rendering love more ardent. *The one who loves the other, remember, has fulfilled the Law.* How and in what fashion? *The commandments, You shall not commit adultery, You shall not murder, You shall not steal, You shall not covet,* [5] *and any other commandment are summed up in this word, You shall love your neighbor as yourself* [6] (v.9): the man who is well disposed to someone does not do away with the man he is fond of, does not commit adultery with his wife, does not filch anything of his friend's possessions, does nothing that may cause him harm. [7] He went on to say as much, in fact, *Love does no wrong to the neighbor* (v.10); then as a logical conclusion, *love, therefore, is the fulfillment of the Law*. Likewise the Lord also, when asked what is the first commandment, both stated the first and added the second, "You shall love the Lord your God with all your heart, and with all your soul, and with all your strength, and with all your mind, and (197) your neighbor as yourself." [8] He shows the speculative virtue being achieved in the first, and the practical in the second. Likewise the divine apostle, *love is the fulfillment of the Law*.

Then he adds, *As well, you know the moment, that it is time for us to rise from sleep* (v.11), in other words, The truth is that it is time not for sleeping but for getting up. *I mean, salvation is nearer to us now than when we came to faith*: each day we are closer to the Lord's coming. *The night is far spent, and the day is at hand* (v.12). He calls *night* the time of ignorance, and *day* the time after the coming of the Lord: the Sun of Justice has arisen and illuminated the world with the rays of the knowledge of God. *So let us put aside the works of darkness, and put on the armor of light*. He calls *darkness* the time of ignorance, and *the works of darkness* the lawless actions; knowledge he terms *light*, and the performance of good *armor of light*. *Let us walk becomingly as in the day* (v.13). He brings out spiritual things from bodily: those adopting the life of lawlessness commit the latter by night, but in daytime they wrap themselves in the appearance of seemliness. He wishes them to be rid of evil, then, as night passes and ignorance comes to an end.

He teaches something else as well: *Not in reveling and drunkenness, not in debauchery and intemperance, not in quarreling and jealousy*. Some people are accustomed to revel at banquets, and pollute their tongue with vile songs; drunkenness is the cause of it, and of course is also the mother of intemperance and the teacher of quarreling and strife. *Let us instead put on the Lord Jesus Christ* (v.14), not for them to receive baptism again but for them to see the garment in which they are clad. [9] *And have no concern for the desires of the flesh*. Here he also stops the mouths of the heretics accusing the flesh: he did not forbid care of the body; rather, he outlawed luxury and intemperance. He did not say, note, Have no concern for the flesh, but Have no concern for its desires, that is, Do not cause it to get out of hand through luxury. [10]

Chapter Fourteen

After discoursing on this once more with regard to the practice of virtue, he returns again to doctrinal matters. Now, it is necessary first of all to state the purpose of the apostolic teaching so that the commentary on the text may be more easily grasped. The believers from Gentiles embraced the evangelical way of life. Many of those, on the other hand, who had come to the evangelical teaching from Jews, were bound to the provisions of the Law, adopting the observance of days and partaking of a diet which the Law prescribed. From this (200) there developed disagreement, and in fact conflict: the latter condemned those from Gentiles for partaking of foods indiscriminately, while the former scorned the others for scrupulous and superfluous observance of the Law. To heal this trouble, then, the divine apostle offers exhortation befitting each party. Firstly he urges those from Gentiles to mutual regard.

Welcome the person weak in faith, but not for the purpose of a difference in opinion (v.1). He calls *weak* the person who is in thrall to the observances of the Law. *One person believes in eating anything* (v.2) – namely, the believer from Gentiles – *whereas the weak eats vegetables*. Some say that those from Jews were ashamed of those from Gentiles and abstained not only from pork but also from other meat on the pretext of self-denial and temperance. [1] For this reason the divine apostle said, *whereas the weak eats vegetables*: not having a mature faith, they were under the impression they would be defiled by this food.

Let the one who eats not despise the one who does not eat (v.3). You see, those from Gentiles loathed those from Jews for not having sincere faith and for this reason refusing to share the same food. *Let the one who does not eat not judge the one who eats*. Those from Jews, of course, condemned those from Gentiles, thinking the indiscriminate enjoyment of food lawlessness. *God, in fact, welcomed that person*, namely, the Gentile. He goes on developing the address to the Jew: *Who are you to judge someone else's servant? It is before their own Lord they stand or fall* (v.4). It is true of all servants that, by living they are valuable to their own master, and by dying they in turn incur loss for him. This servant, then, the Lord of all acquired, giving his own blood as payment. And since he had said, *It is before their own Lord they stand or fall*, he had to continue, *And they will stand.* He confirms his statement from the power of God: *The Lord is able to make them stand, after all.*

After saying this about foodstuffs, he shifts the focus to days. *Some people judge one day different from another, others judge all alike* (v.5): some continually abstained from foods forbidden by the Law, others on individual days. *Let everyone be content with their own decision.* He did not lay this down as a general principle: in regard to the divine teachings he does not recommend this attitude; in fact, he condemns those presuming to teach the opposite to the truth, "If anyone proclaims to you a gospel contrary to what you received, let them be accursed." [2] So it is only in connection with foodstuffs that he allowed scope for individual decision. (201) In fact, this custom has continued in the churches, to be sure, even up to the present day, one person adopting abstinence, another having no qualms about partaking of foods, the latter not judging the former nor the former censuring the latter, but both distinguished by the harmony of the law.

The one who observes the day observes it for the Lord, and the one who does not observe the day does not observe it for the Lord; the one who eats, eats for the Lord, giving thanks to God, and the one who does not eat does not eat for the Lord, and gives thanks to God (v.6). He says this out of considerateness, being concerned to bring harmony to the Church. The God of all knows, he is saying, the intention of those who eat and that of those who do not eat; he not only attends to the deed, but also weighs up the purpose of the action.

None of us, you see, lives for ourselves, and none of us dies for ourselves: if we live, we live for the Lord, and if we die, we die for the Lord. So whether we live or die, we are the Lord's (vv.7-8): we are not our own, we are bought at a price. So in living we are the Lord's, and in dying we are the Lord's. In other words, you are not his master, nor he yours: we all have one master, the Lord. *It was also for this that Christ died, rose and came to life again, to be Lord of both dead and living* (v.9): he is the Lord of all, giving himself to death for us, destroying the power of death, and promising resurrection to us all. We are subject to him, therefore, as recipients of life from him.

You, on the contrary, why do you judge your brother? [3] (v.10). He says this to the Jew. *After all, we shall all stand before the judgment seat of Christ.* Then he confirms his statement with a scriptural testimony: *It is written, remember, As I live, says the Lord, every knee shall bow to me, and every tongue confess to God* [4] (v.11): he is our judge, he is our arbiter, we must appear before that dread tribunal. The inspired testimony, of course, refers to the eminence of the divinity of the Only-begotten: after saying through the prophet, "I am God eternal, I am God first, I am God later, and into the future I am God," and "Before me there was no other God, nor will be after me, and apart from me there is none," and "Besides me there is no one righteous and saving," he then added, "By myself I have sworn, says the Lord, To me every knee shall bow, and every tongue confess to God." [5]

Let us, however, go on to the rest of the commentary. *So each of us will give an account of themselves to God* (v.12). Since he had given a glimpse of the Lord's tribunal, (204) he had to urge them not to judge one another but to await that verdict. In fact, he went on to say as much: *Let us therefore no longer judge one another, but resolve rather not to put a stumbling block or hindrance in the way of the brother* (v.13). Here he develops his remarks towards those from Gentiles who did not show considerateness for the weakness of the believers from Jews, and instead formed the impression that indiscriminate consumption of foodstuffs was the height of virtue and ardent zeal. First he teaches that none of them is accursed and unclean, putting it this way: *I know and am convinced in the Lord Jesus that nothing is unclean thanks to him* (v.14). He had to add the phrase *in the Lord Jesus* on account of the weakness of the Jews: lest they say, Who are you to oppose Moses? he focused on Moses' Lord to bring out that it was he who brought the observances of the Law to an end and permitted them to regard no food as unclean – *thanks to him,* that is, as a result of his provision in the Gospels. He it was, remember, who said also to blessed Peter, "Do not declare unclean what God has made clean." [6] If, however, someone thinks this food is unclean and eats it, it is unclean, not by nature but by the judgment of the eater.

Having thus made these distinctions, he goes on to reprove those from Gentiles for not putting up with Jews' weakness. *But if your brother is upset about food, you are no longer walking in love* (v.15). He highlighted the obligation of love in revealing the one engaged in this practice. Then he further shows the absurdity of what happens: *Do not let food be the cause of the downfall of the one for whom Christ died*: Christ underwent death for that person's sake, whereas you are not prepared to be the cause of their life by abstention from the food, instead devising their death by eating. *So do not let what is good for you be misrepresented* (v.16). Again the obligation along with commendation, referring to faith as *good*. I commend you for your faith, he is saying, but I do not want it to become a cause of harm and misrepresentation.

The kingdom of heaven, after all, is not eating and drinking, but righteousness, peace and joy in the Holy Spirit (v.17): do not think this is the greatest achievement, procuring for you the kingdom of heaven; it is procured by true righteousness, and by the harmony and zeal in peace and love, from which springs the happiness from God. (205) *The one who serves Christ in these things, you see, is pleasing to God and meets with people's approval* (v.18): the God of all requires this of us; as well, it brings benefit to human beings. Of course, it should be remarked that he said that serving Christ is pleasing to God; but if serving Christ is pleasing to God, surely honoring Christ is pleasing to God. Consequently, blaspheming Christ and endeavoring to diminish his honor is displeasing to the God of all.[7]

Let us, then, pursue what makes for peace and for mutual edification (v.19): we ought therefore esteem beneficial harmony ahead of everything else, and do everything for the sake of the benefit of one another. *Do not for the sake of food destroy the work of God* (v.20). The Lord said the *work of God* is believing in him, "This is the work of God, believing in the one he has sent."[8] So since it was likely that some of the Jews, impatient of the reproaches of the believers from Gentiles, desisted from believing, it was right for him to say, *Do not for the sake of food destroy the work of God.* Lest in turn those of Jews take occasion from this to confirm the observance of the Law, he makes provision for it in the words, *Everything is clean.* None of these foods, he is saying, is unclean. *But it is wrong for any person whose eating is a cause of stumbling*: eating brings harm to you since you are unconcerned about the neighbor's welfare, and despite your insight you scorn the one who is harmed. *It is good not to eat meat or drink wine or do anything to make your brother stumble or be hindered or weakened* (v.21): I urge you not in any way to partake not only of meats but also of wine if this causes any harm to the neighbor.

Do you have faith? Have it on your own before God (v.22): by exercising faith you keep the law; it is a great possession, it is a virtue worthy of praise – but let it not harm the neighbor. *Blessed are those who do not bring judgment on themselves through what they approve.* The verse suggests that the believers from Gentiles even forced the Jews to eat what they did not want to. So he teaches that while one believer receives no harm from eating, another eats with some uncertainty and consumes the food as though unclean. Hence he declares blessed those not bringing judgment on themselves, that is, having no uncertainty. He went on to make this interpretation: *The one who is uncertain and eats is condemned* (v.23). He brings out the reason: *Because it is not from faith.* (208) *Everything which is not from faith is sin*: the one who believes eats to no harm, whereas the one who eats with some uncertainty passes sentence on himself.

To emphasize that he prescribes what is pleasing to God, he offers an earnest prayer for them. *Now, to him who is able to confirm you.* [9] And what is the manner of the strengthening? *According to my Gospel.* What Gospel does he bring? *And the message of Jesus Christ.* And to highlight the antiquity of the message, he adds, *According to revelation of mystery*: it did not happen now, but it is now that the mystery kept secret has been revealed; he says as much in what follows, *kept secret from eternity.* Then he adds as well the witnesses: *But now disclosed through the inspired writings by direction of the eternal God*: what he foretold through the inspired authors in obscure fashion the creator of the ages now disclosed. What is the fruit of the message? *For obedience of faith*: all who hear what is said ought believe. And who are they? *Made known to all the Gentiles.* It is to be understood this way: According to my Gospel and the message of Jesus Christ made known to all the Gentiles. *To the only wise God through Jesus Christ, to whom be the glory for ages. Amen.* After showing the mystery of the divine plan, arranged from the beginning, then foretold by the inspired authors, and later made manifest in reality, he marveled at God's wisdom and uttered the due hymn of praise. [10] Now, if the heretics were to say that only God is given the name wise, let them learn that Christ the Lord is not only wise but is also called wisdom. But if they have the habit of depriving the Son of this name wise, let them not call him immortal, either: the apostle himself says of God, "Who alone has immortality." [11]

Let us, however, leave them to their foolish talk, and take up the sequel: after uttering these prayers for them, the divine apostle offers exhortation, composing words of praise for those from Gentiles and naming them *strong* on account of their faith.

CHAPTER FIFTEEN

We who are strong, on the other hand, ought bear with the weaknesses of the infirm, and not please ourselves. Let each of us please the neighbor for the good purpose of edification (vv.1-2): I know you have strength, and faith has rendered you strong. I urge you, however, to extend a hand to the weak, and not look to your situation only but make provision for the benefit of the neighbor as well. He did not simply say *please the neighbor* but *for the good purpose of edification* also: it is possible to please the neighbor to their detriment as well. Then the example: *Christ did not please himself, remember; instead, as it is written, The reproaches of those who reproach you* (209) *have fallen on me* [1] (v.3): the Lord himself did not look to his own good, but gave himself over to death for our salvation; close to the passion, remember, we hear him praying in the words, "Father, if it is possible, let this cup pass from me; yet not as I wish but as you wish." [2] He also accepted the Jews' blasphemies, and what those living in lawless fashion offered of old to his Father they also employed against him. That is the reason Paul supplied also the testimony of the Old Testament author. *Whatever was written of old, you see, was written for our instruction so that by endurance and the encouragement of the Scriptures we might have hope* (v.4): mindful of our welfare, God both offered us written instruction and also preserved the stories of the saints in writing. [3]

Now, may the God of endurance and consolation allow you to be of one mind with one another in accordance with Christ Jesus (v.5). Once more by the addition of *according to Christ Jesus* he brings out that it is not indiscriminately that he prays for them to enjoy harmony; rather, he asks for pious accord. By mention of *endurance and consolation* he brings the treatment around to love so that they may be adorned by it and bear the neighbor's defects, and that through counsel and consolation they might show the way to perfection. *So that with one accord and with one voice you may glorify the God and Father of our Lord Jesus Christ* (v.6). He called God *our God* and *Fa-*

ther of the Lord Jesus: the God of us all is his Father. [4]

Hence, welcome one another just as Christ also welcomed us, to God's glory (v.7): Christ the Lord loved us, not that we were righteous; rather, he took us as sinners and made us righteous. We too, therefore, ought also bear with the weakness of the brethren and take every step for the sake of their salvation. Since, however, those who came faith from Judaism made an issue also of the Lord's circumcision, claiming that even he adopted the way of life in keeping with the Law, the divine apostle thought it worthwhile to write what was needful about this matter, too, saying, *I tell you that Christ Jesus became a minister of the circumcision for the sake of God's truth so as to confirm the promises of the fathers, and so that the Gentiles might glorify God for the sake of his mercy* (vv.8-9) The God of all promised to Abraham that in his offspring he would bless the nations, and the patriarch in his own person accepted the sign of circumcision along with all his tribe. It was therefore necessary also for the one named his offspring according to the flesh and communicating the blessing to the nations to have the sign of kinship so that the realization of the divine promise might be clearly revealed, and the nations on receipt of the grace might sing the praises of the source of the lovingkindness.

Then he adduces scriptural (212) testimonies to bring out that the salvation of the Gentiles was foretold from of old. *As it is written, Hence I shall confess to you among nations, and sing praise to your name.* [5] *And again it says, Rejoice, nations, along with his people.* [6] *And again, Praise the Lord, all the nations, and magnify him, all the peoples.* [7] *And again Isaiah says, There will be the root of Jesse, the one rising to rule nations; in him nations will hope* [8] (vv.9-12). He quoted all these scriptural testimonies, of course, to teach believers from Jews not to be upset by the salvation of the nations but believe the inspired writings about them. Once more he prays for them, showing his fatherly compassion: *May the God of hope fill you with joy and peace in believing so that you may abound in hope by the power of the Holy Spirit* (v.13). He said also in what was commented on above that hope which is within our vision is not hope;[9] hence he also calls God *God of hope* for giving the nations the hope of blessing from old and confirming the promise in deeds. Now, this is a pledge of the good things hoped for: the one who made those promises and then fulfilled them will fulfill completely also what he promised us in our time. He bids us, however, not only hope but also *abound in hope*, that is, hope sincerely and believe we see the good things hoped for. This, he says, the grace of the Spirit supplies.

After this exhortation and prayer he offers praise, by this means urging them to better things. *I too am personally persuaded about you, brethren, that you also are filled with goodness, replete with all knowledge, capable also of admonishing others* (v.14). I am aware, he is saying, that you do not need instruction: you have sufficient knowledge, and you are full of all kinds of good things so as to offer also to others appropriate exhortation. *To some extent, however, I have written to you rather boldly as if giving you a reminder as a result of the grace given me by God* (v.15). He revealed the moderation of his thinking, admitting he showed boldness in teaching; and he indicated the grace given, stressing that he wrote what was appropriate to it. Now, what was the grace given to you? *To be a minister of Jesus Christ to the Gentiles in the priestly service of the Gospel of God* (v.16): I am commissioned as teacher of the Gentiles, and perform this service to Christ the Lord. What benefit stems from it? *So that the offering of the Gentiles may be acceptable, sanctified by the Holy Spirit*: I zealously bear every hardship so that the nations may be confirmed in the faith and attain the grace of the Spirit. He called preaching (213) *priestly service*, and sincere faith *acceptable offering*: [10] so nothing I did was ineffectual (he is saying), even if *I have written rather boldly* and taken issue with sinners.

I have reason to boast in Christ Jesus, then, of what pertains to God (v.17). Then he brings out the form of boasting: *I shall not presume to mention anything other than what Christ has accomplished through me for the Gentiles' response, in word and deed, by the force of signs and wonders, by the power of the Spirit of God* (vv.18-19): I pride myself not on my labors but on the gift of Christ the Lord; he gave me the grace of the all-holy Spirit for the working of signs and wonders so that the Gentiles might be taken captive through them and receive the illumination of the knowledge of God. He also brings out the great number of nations he preached to: *so that from Jerusalem right round to Illyricum I gave full service to the Gospel of Christ*: I cultivated not only the nations situated on the direct route but also took a wide arc around the eastern and Pontic regions, and in addition to these I discharged my role of teaching to those in Asia and Thrace (*right around* suggesting this).

And thus I take every effort to preach the good news, not where the name of Christ has been sounded, so that I do not build on someone else's foundation, but as it is written, Those who have not been told of him shall see, and those who have not heard shall understand [11] (vv.20-21). This indicates the zeal displayed in the tireless activity: he took on neglected fields for his work, sowed the seed, had waving crops to show for it, and matches the outcome to the prophecy. *This was also the reason I was for so long prevented from coming to you* (v.22): my involvement with the others prevented my being with you. *Now, however, having no place any longer in these regions, and with my desire for many years to come to you, I shall make my way to you when I travel to Spain. I hope to see you on my journey and to be sent on by you after first enjoying your company for a time* (vv.23-24). He cited two reason for going to them, the fact that the others had accepted the message and no nation was left without hearing the evangelical instruction, and his longing for them. The former obstacles having ceased to apply, you see, longing prompted him to make the journey. He says the longing was of much longer standing than his coming: I longed to see you *for many years,* he says. Now, he predicts that he will not only see them, but will even reach Spain. And in case they might think his coming to them was a secondary purpose of the journey, he added, *And* (216) *I may be sent on by you after first enjoying your company for a time*: I desire to see you first, and after you the others.

Now, however, I make for Jerusalem to minister to the saints (v.25). He calls the distribution of the money *ministry.* He mentions also the donors: *Macedonia and Achaia were gracious enough, you see, to share their resources with the poor among the saints in Jerusalem* (v.26). The divinely-inspired Barnabas and Paul had come to this agreement with the blessed apostles – namely, Peter, James and John – and after taking on the instruction of the Gentiles they promised to urge the believers from the Gentiles to meet the needs of the faithful in Judea. He brings this out clearly in the letter to the Galatians: "Peter, James and John, considered pillars of the community, extended the hand of fellowship to me, agreeing that while they went to the circumcised, we should go to the Gentiles. One thing was that we were to keep in mind the poor, which was the very thing I was anxious to do." [12] He says this here, too, marveling at the willingness of Macedonia and Achaia.

He also calls this beneficence an obligation: *They were in fact pleased to do so, and they are indebted to them* (v.27). Whence came this obligation? *I mean, if the Gentiles had come to share in their spiritual goods, they also ought minister to them in the things of the flesh.* The patriarchs were their fathers, he is saying, the promises were made to them, their prophets foretold the goods enjoyed in common, from them came Christ the Lord in his human nature, from them the apostles, preachers to the world, through them were distributed the gifts of the Spirit. [13] So it was fair that those who received a share in the greater things should give a share in the less. This is the reason he called the donation of the money *sharing* above and *ministry* further on, to suggest repayment by *sharing* and discharging a debt by *ministry*.

So when I have performed this task and have put my seal on this fruit for them, I shall set out by way of you for Spain (v.28). By the expression *having put my seal on this fruit for them* he refers to the Macedonians and Achaians: by the hands of the saints I put the offerings in God's right hand; he will keep them safe and sound. [14] *I know that in coming to you I shall come in the fullness of blessing of the Gospel of Christ* (v.29). By *the fullness of blessing of the Gospel* he referred to the perils he had endured in Jerusalem, as emerges from what follows.

I therefore urge you, brethren, through our Lord Jesus Christ and through the (217) *love of the Spirit, to second my efforts in prayer for me to God so that I may be rescued from the unbelievers in Judea, and my ministry to Jerusalem may prove acceptable to the saints* (vv.30-31). What encomium would suffice to crown this blessed – in fact, thrice blessed – head? I mean, firstly, he knew what would happen and foretold it: in Miletus he said to the elders from Ephesus, "The Spirit testifies to me in city after city that bonds and tribulations await me;" and when Agabus forecast the same things, and everybody lamented and tried to detain him, the divine man said, "Why do you weep and pull at my heart strings? I am ready not only to be bound but also to die for the name of our Lord Jesus Christ." [15] Here too he prophesied that he would see Rome and Spain. Now, he added that he would also *come in the fullness of blessing of the Gospel of Christ*. Then, as though enjoying a precise vision of the Jews' frenzy, he required also their prayers, on account not only of the unbelievers but also of the believers: they were not well disposed to him, regarding him as a transgressor of the Law. This was the reason that he added, *and that my ministry to Jerusalem may prove acceptable to the saints*. He made the collection with countless hardships, proposing exhortation of all kinds to the disciples, and he brought pressure to bear on the recipients not to let hatred overcome need.

So that I may come to you in joy, God willing, and have a rest in your company (v.32). Not even upright things is he prepared to do independently of the divine will. *The God of peace be with you all. Amen* (v.33). It was not without purpose that he called God here *God of peace*: it was as though in need of it himself, on account both of those openly hostile and those laboring under suspicion of him. He also prayed for it for them in view of the arguments they were having with one another over the observances of the Law. [16]

Chapter Sixteen

Now, I commend to you our sister Phoebe, a deacon of the church in Cenchreae, so that you may welcome her in a manner befitting the saints, and assist her in whatever she may require of you, patron as she herself has been to many including myself. Greet Priscilla and Aquila, my fellow workers in Christ Jesus (vv.1-3). Cenchreae is the largest town in Corinth, so the impact of the preaching calls for admiration: in a short time it filled with piety not only the cities but also the towns. And so large was the congregation of the church of Cenchreae that it even had a woman deacon, [1] one both famous and celebrated: she had so great a wealth of virtuous actions as to earn such encomiums from the apostolic tongue – *patron as she herself has been to many including myself*, he says, note. Now, by *patronage* I am inclined to think he refers to her hospitality and care, and he rewards her with multiple compliments. I mean, it is likely she received him into one house for a short time – namely, the period he spent in Corinth – whereas he introduced her to the world, and on all land and sea she became famous: not only the Romans and Greeks knew of her but also all the barbarians.

The woman mentioned after her, however, surpassed even her: Priscilla, or Prisca (you can find both forms in the books), and Aquila he calls *fellow workers* and adds the phrase *in Christ Jesus* in case anyone should get the idea of a professional association, they being tent makers like him. [2] He mentions also a further trial: *Who risked their necks for me* (v.4). He links the common with the private: *To whom not only I myself give thanks but also all the churches of the Gentiles.* He mentions also another praiseworthy virtue, greeting *also the church in their house* (v.5); the text indicates the extraordinary degree of piety: it is likely they taught all the servants the highest virtue, and earnestly performed in the home the divine services. The divine Luke also mentions them, and brings out how they led Apollo to the truth. [3]

Greet my beloved Epainetus, who is the firstfruits of Achaia for Christ. It is likely he was the first of all the nation to come to faith; hence he received the title *firstfruits. Greet Mary, who has worked hard for you* (v.6) – still another woman crowned by her own labors. *Greet Andronicus and Junias, my kinsmen and fellow captives, notable among the apostles, who also were in Christ before me* (v.7). [4] Many compliments at the one time, firstly for being sharers in the divine Paul's perils; [5] he called them *fellow captives* for sharing his sufferings. Then he says they were not among the disciples but among the teachers – not any sort of teachers but the apostles. He commends them also for their time in the faith, saying, *they were in Christ before me,* meaning, I was called after them. Everywhere I admire the modesty of this divinely-inspired person. (221)

Greet Ampliatus, my beloved in the Lord (v.8). This, too, is no slight compliment, naming him *beloved in the Lord,* indicative of virtuous behavior. *Greet Urbanus, our fellow worker in Christ, and my beloved Stachys* (v.9). He bedecked Urbanus with greater commendation, calling him fellow worker in the preaching of Christ and the contests. *Greet Apelles, who has not been found wanting in Christ* (v.10). Testimony to the highest virtue: to have no base element is the summit of good things. *Greet those of the household of Aristobulus, my kinsman Herodion, and those of the household of Narcissus* (v.11). Obviously the households had found the faith; of that of Narcissus, at any rate, he says *those in the Lord,* since there were presumably others as well who to that point were not so.

Greet Tryphaena and Tryphosa, laborers in the Lord (v.12). Again the crown in return for labors; the term suggests labor, or hospitality, or fasting, or some other virtue. *Greet the beloved Persis, who labored much in the Lord.* The commendation is greater than the previous one, her industry being greater. *Greet Rufus, chosen in the Lord, and his mother and mine* (v.13). This again is a desirable compliment: "Many are called," remember, "but few are chosen." [6] And his mother he celebrates for many virtuous deeds; on no other grounds, after all, would she have deserved to be called Paul's mother: nature made her Rufus's mother, respect for virtue the divine Paul's.

Greet Asyncritus, Phlegon, Hermas, Patrobas, Hermes and the brethren who are with them (v.14). This is another household of believers, deserving Paul's greeting. *Greet Philologus, Julia, Nereus and his sister, Olympas and all the saints who are with them* (v.15). These in turn were living together, and gained the apostolic salutation on account of the virtue they had. Having thus saluted them by name, he then urges them all to greet one another: *Greet one another with a holy kiss* (v.16). In other words, since in his absence he could not embrace them personally, he does so through them, urging them to greet one another, and convey their greeting *with a holy kiss*, respectful, chaste, honest, sincere and free of all deceit. *All the churches of Christ greet you.* He gave greetings from the whole world, so to say, to the city presiding over the world. (224)

Now, I urge you, brethren, to have an eye to those responsible for quarrels and obstacles in defiance of the teaching you learnt, and keep your distance from them (v.17). In this he refers to the evil advocates of the Law, whose teaching he bids them avoid, praising the preaching of the head of the apostles: the expression *acting in defiance of the teaching you learnt* comes from one full of admiration for the teaching they acquired. *Such people, after all, serve not Christ our Lord but their own belly* (v.18). It is clear from this that he says these things about Jews: he is ever accusing them of gluttony, saying elsewhere, "Whose god is their belly." [7] *And by smooth talking and flattery they deceive the hearts of the innocent.* He called praise *flattery*, suggesting also some were taken in by them: *they deceive the hearts of the innocent*, he says. Of course, it was the malice, not the simplicity, that he blamed.

Then he lifts their spirits with further praise. *Your obedience, you see, has reached everyone* (v.19), the fact that you eagerly accepted the apostolic teaching. *So I rejoice in you.* Yet even while commending them he continues teaching them: *But I want you to be wise where good is concerned, but guileless where evil is concerned.* The Lord also proposed this law to the apostles, saying, "Be prudent like serpents and guileless like doves." [8] The dominical saying also implies rejecting the schemes proposed by our adversaries but not taking vengeance on the wrongdoers. *The God of peace will promptly crush Satan under your feet* (v.20). Since he urged them to be on their guard against the adversaries, it was timely for him to beseech God to crush the teacher of the schemes and put him under the feet of those who believe. *The grace of our Lord Jesus Christ be with you.* After revealing the enemy, he let them see the ally: those enjoying divine grace are invincible.

My fellow worker Timothy, Lucius, Jason and Sosipater, my kinsmen, greet you (v.21). One enjoys the distinction of fellowship in work, the others kinship; the fellow worker, however, is far more estimable than the kinsman. Now, Timothy is the one whom he circumcised in Lystra [9] and to whom he wrote two letters; Jason is mentioned in the story of the Acts. [10] *I Tertius, the writer of the letter, greet you in the Lord* (v.22). He, too, was one of those who was accorded the apostolic teaching, thanks to which he benefited from the birth pangs of the holy soul by word of mouth, and was bidden to commit them to writing. [11] (225)

Gaius, host to me and the whole church, greets you (v.23). This is also a very great testimony and commendation, his throwing open his house to the nurslings of the faith, and along with everyone else tending to the needs of the teacher of the world himself; he calls the one who receives strangers *host.* He was a Corinthian, and the divine apostle gave us this information in the letter to the Corinthians, "I thank my God that I baptized none of you except Crispus and Gaius." [12] *Erastus, the city treasurer, greets you, and brother Quartus.* He calls him *treasurer* not of the church but of the city for being entrusted with a certain responsibility for everything; he mentions him also in the letter to Timothy, speaking this way, "Erastus stayed in Corinth; Trophimus I left ill in Miletus." [13]

The grace of our Lord Jesus Christ be with you all. Amen (v.24). Once more he imparts to them the spiritual blessing, and invests them with the grace of the Lord as with a kind of wall of steel. He did this as an opening to the letter and likewise used it as a conclusion. Let us also share in it so as to prove superior to the wiles, so that illuminated by it we may travel the straight and narrow without being led astray, and by following in the apostolic footsteps we may be allowed to see the teacher and through his intercession enjoy the Lord's favor. May we thus attain the promised goods, thanks to the grace and lovingkindness of our Lord Jesus Christ, to whom with the Father together with the all-holy Spirit belong glory and magnificence, now and forever, for ages of ages. Amen.

It should be understood that the letter to the Romans was written from Corinth. [14]

Notes to the *Letter to the Romans*

CHAPTER ONE

[1] Theodoret thus avoids that "pangs of conscience" approach to Romans we associate with Reformation hermeneutics that concentrated on personal human predicament without acknowledging the wider context of the whole mystery of salvation, and particularly the place in it of both Jew and Gentile – a most sensitive issue for Paul the Jew.

[2] For Theodoret as for Paul, of course, *mysterion* is no "puzzle" but a great sacred reality, God's design for the world, or an aspect of the plan, such as the Incarnation.

[3] 1 Cor 1.18. As in the preface Theodoret conceded David's gift of the Spirit in composing the Psalms, so he sees Paul also enjoying the influence of divine inspiration in composing the letters.

[4] Theodoret does not open his commentary, as do modern commentators, by identifying the composition of the Roman church. But he is aware that Paul speaks early of Jews and Gentiles, and that of the latter he distinguishes Greek speakers and non-Greek speakers, *barbaroi*. It is not clear of which group Theodoret uses the term "Greeks."

[5] To take Theodoret at face value, he is implying Paul in writing has in mind these heretical groups of the second and third centuries – all distinguished by a distortion of biblical creation stories and, particularly in Marcion's case, scorn for Old Testament revelation as a whole. It is interesting to see him faulting them for this disparagement of the Hebrew Scriptures, while faulting the Jews for "excessive attachment" to them.

[6] Theodoret shows a fine understanding and succinct expression of Paul's basic theme of the role of faith and grace in achieving the end of the Law.

[7] Theodoret returns to the basic dynamic of the letter, the tension between the respective places of Jews and Gentiles in the plan of salvation – not the later polemic about respective roles of faith and works, or the means of justification. His focus here is on the heart of Romans, chs 9-11. He proceeds to observe that this (and other Pauline letters) has both a dogmatic and moral character.

[8] Cf. 1 Cor 15.8-9.

[9] Acts 22.21.

[10] Gal 1.15. Theodoret, whose thinking elsewhere also is strongly trinitarian, is anxious (without explicit support from the text at this point) to see the Father, Son and Spirit involved in Paul's commissioning. He is also at pains to stress the equality of persons in the Trinity.

[11] Acts 22.21; 9.15; 13.2.

[12] The Antiochene character of Theodoret's commentary emerges from this phrase we see occurring frequently in commentators of that school, nothing in the text being thought to occur "idly." As precision, *akribeia*, marks the text, so should it characterize also the commentator.

[13] As elsewhere, Theodoret asserts his conviction of the divine influence or inspiration affecting Old Testament composers, or *prophetai* (a term that includes all, not simply those listed as "prophets" in the Christian Bible) – a term he will not apply to NT authors. Again, as before against Marcion and others, he upholds the value of these Jewish Scriptures; they are *theopneustai*.

[14] Matt 1.2. Theodoret, of course, had grown up with the creed of Constantinople of 381, and evidence suggests the Commentary on Paul comes from the decade prior to Chalcedon's dealing with the monophysite controversy in 451. He is therefore very careful to draw distinctions between divine and human natures in Jesus.

[15] Matt 8.27.

[16] John 16.12.

[17] Cf. Luke 24.49, where in fact the text does not mention the coming of the Spirit; *akribeia* has its limits.

[18] This verse, of course, constitutes a notorious *crux interpretum*, offering a particular affront to readers with its suggestion that Jesus was not God before the resurrection. Theodoret deals with every difficult phrase, especially that faulty suggestion, speaking of Jesus being "appointed" (not "predestined" like Augustine and Pelagius) and "assigned" (a sense given to *apodeiknumi* by Herodotus in place of "manifested"), and taking the power to be that of the Spirit in the wake of (his interpretation of *ex*) the resurrection. He acknowledges no assistance from previous commentators in this exercise; likewise, not all modern commentators would concur totally with his interpretation.

[19] Phil 4.22.

[20] It has been helpful to his readers for Theodoret to present a brief synopsis of this most elaborate of Paul's opening formulas, separating the traditional structure from the dogmatic elaborations contained within it. He also highlights the equally traditional greeting, grace and peace, without mentioning the Old Testament background (cf. 2 Macc 1.1) particularly of the latter term; and he takes the occasion to bring out again the trinitarian dimension.

[21] Bishop Theodoret as a desk theologian does not often engage his readers in pastoral interchange, choosing to confine himself to comment on the text and not proceeding to apply it to his readers' lives; so this challenge is rare.

[22] Again Theodoret highlights the backdrop to Paul's thinking on his mission and this letter, the divine plan, *oikonomia*, as he did in stating the letter's theme (see note 2 above). Modern commentators speak of the "theological passive" here, God intervening to stay his journey.

[23] Modern commentators, more interested than Theodoret in sociological issues, would like to find in v.14 an index of the composition of the Roman church. Theodoret is less concerned to elaborate on the distinction between Greek and non-Greek speaking Gentiles than on the attitudes of some.

[24] Just as Theodoret shows appreciation of the figurative language of the Psalms, so he has the ability to use telling examples from nature to bring out the hidden power of the Gospel.

[25] The significance of the temporal adverb does not escape Theodoret, nor is he inclined to diminish the sense of the Jews' priority denoted by it.

[26] Eph 3.9.

[27] 1 Cor 2.7 (see note 2 above).

[28] This interpretation of the puzzling phrase, which goes back to Origen, a modern commentator like Joseph Fitzmyer calls "certainly inadequate." Theodoret seems to agree, offering an additional understanding of it, without reneging on his further endorsement of the Old Testament (*prophetai* here again having that sense) as distinct from the New (the Gospel). The additional sense has a sacramental dimension, not uncommon with the bishop, and develops into a beautiful statement of the mystery of salvation – vindicating Theodoret's claim for his commentary of respecting the old and improving on it.

[29] Hab 2.4; cf. Gal 3.11; Heb 10.38. Modern commentators – though not Theodoret – are quick to point out that Paul has somewhat misquoted Habakkuk for his purposes, though not (as is clear from Theodoret's comment) to the effect of reinforcing the Reformers' reading, "justification by faith alone" (by Matthew Black, e.g.).

[30] Theodoret is clearly aware of Paul's distinction between the Mosaic Law and natural law.

[31] Theodoret, who in his commentaries can – inconsistently – uphold the status of women as characters in and readers of the Bible, is perhaps aware that he is running counter to a commentator like Chrysostom on Genesis 3, who is prepared to see Adam as the unwitting victim of a guilty wife.

[32] Gen 4.9.

[33] Antiochene as he is, Theodoret cannot pass over anthropomorphisms in the text without warning the reader against a literalist misinterpretation that might infringe divine transcendence.

[34] Mark 13.26 loosely recalled – a habit of Theodoret's, less pardonable in a desk theologian.

[35] Theodoret feels the general theme of impious pagans could give way to an example closer to home, if less in line with Paul's thought – namely, Arian theology, which denied the generation of the Son; hence here insistence on begetting and only-begotten.

[36] Bishop Theodoret does not expatiate on these moral excesses, viz, female and male homosexuality. As in his Commentary on the Psalms he declined to go into details of David's sin, despite mention of it occurring frequently enough in that context, so he delicately prefers reticence here. For similar reticence in a modern commentator, see Black.

[37] Unlike modern commentators, who at this point simply observe that Paul is rehearsing a familiar list of sins that is Hellenistic or Jewish-Hellenistic (Black) or "an echo of the early Church's *didache*" (Fitzmyer), Theodoret helpfully – for us and for his readers – unpicks each member of the catalogue as understood in his time.

[38] Cf. Gen 4.5-8.

[39] Bishop Theodoret is not one for moralizing; this he leaves to the preachers, despite the moral content of these verses, which he sees it his role simply to clarify.

CHAPTER TWO

[1] Whom does Theodoret take Paul as referring to as the person sitting in judgment? Though Fitzmyer claims it is to "the secular judge or Roman authority" that he and Chrysostom are referring at this place, his commentary seems rather to speak of the normal human being enjoying the faculty of moral judgment but likely to be easier on himself or herself than on others. Some moderns suggest Paul has a Jew specifically in mind (on the basis of v.17); not so Theodoret.

[2] This clarification, if tardy, is helpful; see note 4 on ch 1.

[3] Theodoret chooses an appropriate example in the Joseph story, but has the details somewhat garbled: the figure of twenty two years (the biblical sum is no more than sixteen) he may arrive at by thinking of two periods of ten years, not seven, for plenty and famine respectively, while the words about the younger brother (Gen 42.22) are also Reuben's.

[4] Gen 20.4-5.

[5] Though Theodoret in places can exemplify the contemporary polemic against Jews on the grounds of the crucifixion in particular, he generally concedes the advantages those in the Old Testament enjoyed; and here he gilds the apostle's lily on the subject.

[6] Cf. Isa 52.5; Ezek 36.20.

[7] Jer 9.26; 4.4.

[8] Again Theodoret, without recourse to polemics, helpfully develops Paul's point on the vacuity of physical circumcision with an apposite comparison. We continue to receive the impression of someone who appreciates thoroughly the apostle's line of thought.

[9] Sympathetic as Theodoret is with Paul's thinking, his lack of Hebrew (not such a liability here as in his Old Testament commentaries) precludes his detecting Paul's play upon the similar words in Hebrew for "Jew" and (the hiphil form of) the verb "praise" in v.29 noted by modern commentators.

CHAPTER THREE

[1] The phrase "God's sayings," which at face value would seem to refer to the sacred writings generally, the normal sense also in the Septuagint, Theodoret takes more narrowly to refer to the Law.

[2] 2 Tim 2.13.

[3] Ps 51.4.

[4] Mic 6.3.

[5] Jer 2.5.

[6] Rom 5.20.

[7] Matt 7.7. The bishop at his desk calls a halt like a preacher with his congregation, concluding with a doxology (commentary on the longer letters required several *tomoi*). In resuming he reverts for a moment to the big picture, as he did at the opening of the first chapter, stepping back from the details of the argument – a perspective Paul would have commended.

[8] Cf. Pss 14.1-3; 53.1-4; 5.10; 140.4; 10.7; 36.2; Isa 59.7-8 – a catena of texts following a verse (9) which offers commentators various textual and grammatical difficulties.

[9] Ps 143.2; cf. Gal 2.16.

[10] Cf. Exod 20.12-16; Deut 5.16-20. Again Theodoret is clear on the distinction between norms of the natural law, prescriptions of the Mosaic Law enshrining these, and legislation for things of symbolic but not abiding value.

[11] Again placing the argument within the wider perspective; cf. note 2 to ch 1.

[12] Theodoret sides with those moderns who see this as an objective genitive, not implying the faith *of* Jesus, though disappointing them for adopting an "inferior reading" in proceeding to include "and upon all."

[13] With Paul's own encouragement Theodoret is prepared to recognize an example of typology here – something an Antiochene would not readily do without scriptural support. His comprehensive explication of the significance of *hilasterion*, relating it also to Jesus' humanity, responds with a resounding negative to Black's tentative question, "Does 'expiation' do justice to the word here used?" It is a pity he and his tradition do not take further account of patristic commentary, which in this case offers such richness. (See note on the mention of Passover in 2 Cor 4.6-8.)

[14] Paul's word for God's treatment of sins committed in bygone times, *paresis* (occurring in the NT only here and at 2.4), for which modern commentators offer either "remission" or "passing over," Theodoret seems to take in the latter sense.

[15] His Antiochene formation again equips Theodoret for seizing upon morphological details in the text that contribute to Paul's thinking.

[16] Jer 31.31-32.

[17] Theodoret again shows his appreciation of Paul's thinking on the relation of faith and works both by avoiding the insertion of "only" after "faith" (on the part of Hilary, Ambrosiaster and later Luther) and by remarking (as James had to in NT times) that it is not works in general that are ex-

cluded from relevance to salvation but works of the Mosaic Law. Antiochene precision makes for theological exactitude.

Chapter Four

[1] Though Fitzmyer finds Theodoret's text offering a reading that is "weakly attested" and "inconsistent with Pauline teaching," the bishop finds it susceptible of an interpretation that is quite in keeping with the argument.

[2] Gen 15.6 LXX.

[3] Theodoret might have cited Jewish texts like Sir 44.50 that presented Abraham as observing the Law in advance.

[4] Pss 88.35-37; 72.11.

[5] Ps 32.1-2.

[6] Gen 12.3. Theodoret has warmed to the task of commentary, elaborating Paul's argument. He would concur with the ICC commentators, "In his rapid and vigorous reasoning St Paul contents himself with a few bold strokes, which he leaves it to the reader to fill out." The bishop cannot let the reader go unassisted.

[7] Gen 17.5. Theodoret's lack of Hebrew does not permit him – any more than Paul – to raise the quibble of modern commentators about the true significance of the name Abraham or of the nations referred to (a few specific descendants, or the Gentiles in general).

[8] Gen 15.5.

[9] Of Theodoret J. N. D. Kelly remarks, "He rejected the thoroughgoing use of the *communicatio idiomatum* advocated in the Alexandrian school; in his opinion it suggested a confusion or intermingling of the natures. But not even his worst enemies could with justice interpret his teaching as what has been traditionally designated as 'Nestorianism.'" Theodoret is uncomfortable here with the idea of God suffering, as we shall see him likewise uncomfortable with Paul's statements at 8.32, "God did not withhold his own Son, but gave him up for us all," and 1 Cor 2.8, "They crucified the Lord of glory."

[10] As often, Bishop Theodoret gives lends a sacramental dimension to the acquisition of justification. It is interesting that for Christians he always sees forgiveness of sins associated with the sacrament of baptism alone.

Chapter Five

[1] As remarked in note 17 on ch 3, Theodoret does not go the way of some few Fathers and later Reformers and insert "only" into Paul's text on the need of faith for justification; "virtue in practice" is also requisite.

[2] For the forgiving of sin, faith is associated with sacramental ritual. (No mention is made of any "original" sin.)

[3] Unlike Theodoret, modern commentators (on the basis of the next verses) prefer to take "the love of God" as a subjective genitive, God's love for us.

[4] Gal 4.4-5.

[5] Again that niggling concern of Theodoret that no one should see suffering affecting the divine nature, despite Paul's use of a term that refers more directly to divinity. Confusion of divine and human natures, as well as monophysite views, would be the object of the Council of Chalcedon a few years after this Commentary, held at the instigation of Theodoret.

[6] At this critical point in Romans, where Paul is extending his horizon to consider the situation of all people, Theodoret likewise reverts to the wider perspective, as he did at the opening of the letter; and, as there, he refers to the mystery (in the Pauline sense: see note 2 there) of the Incarnation, speaking of it both as *oikonomia* and *enanthropesis*. He closes this important chapter with a similar reference.

[7] Theodoret, like all the Greek Fathers before John Damascene, reads ἐφ᾽ ᾧ in this verse and renders it "for the reason that;" he is well aware that Paul is referring to the etiological story of the Fall in Gen 3 but does not see Adam as an antecedent to the pronoun (as likewise in commenting on Ps 51.5). Adam's sin is beyond question for him, and – without explaining how – he sees both sin and death spreading to the whole race; but he is insistent that each person's sin and not Adam's is responsible for each one's liability to death. As always, he avoids the heavy moralizing tone of preachers like Chrysostom in commenting on the Fall, as well as their tendency to transfer guilt to the woman.

[8] An interpretation at variance with that of modern commentators and, it would seem, with the following verses.

[9] Luke 16.29.

[10] 2 Cor 3.15.

[11] Matt 11.13,12. Theodoret does not explain the puzzling v.12 (except, perhaps, by inverting the order of verses), nor its relevance here.

[12] Theodoret rightly recognizes that Paul's accent falls not on the sin and death traceable to Adam but on the conquest of both by Christ.

[13] See note 6 above for the broad perspective Theodoret is maintaining in this chapter.

[14] Gen 26.4.

[15] Rom 6.7. Theodoret finds Paul's theme congenial, and readily expands on it.

CHAPTER SIX

[1] Theodoret seems to be implying that the immersion ritual of baptism reproduces Christ's death and resurrection, even if in Paul's time this ritual was not in use. His term for sacrament is *mysterion* (just as some Old Latin translators of Mark 4.11 render the word as *sacramentum*).

[2] Eph 1.17.

[3] John 2.19. Theodoret's reasoning here is involved: while as on 4.24 he attributes to the Father Jesus' raising "as man", he takes *the Father of glory* here and in Ephesians to mean the Father of the Son. Yet he also cites John's Jesus claiming resurrection for himself.

[4] Working from the model, *paradeigma*, of Christ's death and resurrection,

Theodoret warns his readers that forgiveness of sins through baptism – he envisages no other sacrament of reconciliation, clearly – is available once only. Eastern sacramental discipline (at least in Antioch) in the fifth century differs from the West, it would seem. Yet against Novatian rigorism he will uphold the possibility and need of repentance of post-baptismal sin (see comment on 2 Cor 12.21).

[5] Thus, at a convenient moment when Paul has concluded a doctrinal exposition of baptism and is about to launch into an exhortation, Theodoret closes his second *tomos*, again in the manner of a preacher.

[6] Antiochene *akribeia* allows Theodoret to develop Paul's thought by distinguishing kingship from tyranny so as to demonstrate free will's independence of the natural passions.

[7] As in commentary on the previous verse, eastern optimism about human nature and human faculties emerges, the free will, *gnome*, being the critical factor in deciding how right options will be made. There is no western dualism or sense of the impairment of human nature evident here. Theodoret no more than Paul sees it appropriate at this point to introduce the respective roles of nature and grace in these right options, though the text soon proceeds to pit grace against the Law.

[8] Again Theodoret competently develops Paul's thought, and his readers benefit from his ability to deploy telling comparisons.

[9] Matt 6.24.

[10] 1 Cor 9.7. The preface reveals that Theodoret is aware that we have two letters from Paul to the Corinthians; but with his usually casual reference to the biblical text he is not inclined to be more precise.

CHAPTER SEVEN

[1] Cf. Matt 19.9; cf. Deut 24.1-4.

[2] Bishop Theodoret is more explicit than Paul about the precise means of our dying to the Law, namely, baptism – perhaps visualizing the death-resurrection imaging that the baptismal ritual provides.

[3] Jer 31.31-32.

[4] Theodoret has shown himself unwilling to condemn the Law out of hand, or give encouragement to those who would do so, like the followers of Marcion. (Fitzmyer is clearly in error in seeing Theodoret speaking here of positive law in general.)

[5] Rom 5.20; 4.15; 3.20.

[6] For Theodoret, unlike some modern commentators, Paul is taking an example from biblical history in this use of the first person, not speaking of his own experience or Christians' generally. Also unlike Chrysostom, Theodoret allocates responsibility for the Fall equally to man and woman.

[7] Again Theodoret introduces, here and below, helpful examples to make Paul's thought clearer.

[8] An Antiochene could not pass over individual comment on each epithet. Theodoret has expanded Paul's thought, rebutting charges of an otiose or even malicious divine law, and situating the discussion within the big

picture of creation and Incarnation. (The expansiveness of the commentary contrasts with the conciseness of commentary on the Psalter, which rarely moved him.)

[9] It is at this point (only) that Theodoret sees Paul shifting the focus to the plight of human beings generally – unlike those commentators who would recognize this focus earlier in the treatment of Law, sin and grace.

[10] Whereas Paul seems simply to suggest a balance here of spiritual and carnal, Theodoret (a commentator also on the Octateuch) insists on the Spirit's role in Moses' composition of the Torah.

[11] Isa 50.1.

[12] This is becoming Theodoret's formula for commentary on Paul: the lily needs gilding. So he launches into expansive development of the apostle's thought, and (also unlike the conciseness and detachment of the Psalms commentary) applies it liberally to the lives of the reader.

[13] If Theodoret's psychology intrigues us, we have to admire again his effective example of charioteer and skittish ponies.

[14] Unlike modern commentators who prefer to take *nomos* in this verse as a principle learned from experience, Theodoret seems still to see reference to the Mosaic Law.

CHAPTER EIGHT

[1] Theodoret's reading of this verse appends a clause found also in v.4. In the next verse "you" is thought a better reading than "me;" Theodoret, perhaps aware of this, has it both ways, and Chrysostom can be quoted for both.

[2] Black also suggests Paul has baptism in mind here, not as a contrast to the Law's impotence but as implied by the earlier intriguing phrase: "'those who are in Christ Jesus' means simply 'baptized Christians.'"

[3] Again Theodoret reminds his readers that the Incarnation is the means of resolving this impasse.

[4] Gal 5.25.

[5] Cf. John 17.16. Bishop Theodoret is not for moralizing about the world's evils; as in other biblical commentaries of his, he is careful not to turn preacher.

[6] Theodoret here is reproducing a synthesis of eastern thinking on the Spirit developed particularly by Athanasius and the Cappadocians in response to the subordinationist ideas of Origen, Eusebius of Caesarea, the later Arians and Pneumatomachians. The procession of the Spirit from the Father alone, of whom the Son is Only-begotten, will later be denied by Augustine and the West (with eventual insertion of the *filioque* in the Constantinopolitan creed), though like the East (as in Theodoret's text here) acknowledging the *homoousion* of the Spirit. See also note on 1 Cor 3.16-17 below.

[7] Sharing in the optimism of the East regarding material creation (again unlike the contemporary West), Theodoret does not wish this antithesis of body and spirit to be taken in any dualistic way, as had been done in the

past. Once more he represents Paul responding to gnostic and manichean views as though posterior to them (cf. note 5 to ch 1).

[8] In almost the one breath Theodoret can remind the Jews of their deficiencies and uphold the Spirit's authorship of the Law. Unlike modern commentators, he does not develop the legal implications of adoption, *huiothesia* (a term not found in the LXX), if Paul intended them beyond simple sonship – though v.17 encourages him to distinguish inheriting from physical descent.

[9] 1 Cor 12.8-9.

[10] Matt 6.9. Theodoret, for whom Syriac (i.e., a dialect of Aramaic) is his mother tongue, speaks of children generally employing this term. He does not give color to the view (of Black, e.g.) that it survives from an Aramaic form of the Lord's Prayer; he has left us no Gospel commentary to settle the issue. The doublet occurs as a liturgical formula when the Aramaic word is taken up in Greek communities (so Fitzmyer).

[11] Ps 102.26.

[12] Cf. Zech 11.2; Pss 96.12; 114.4,6; 98.8. All the Old Testament inspired authors are *prophetai*.

[13] Cf. Luke 15.10. By including the angels in Paul's perspective and reducing his statement about material creation to personification, is Theodoret wanting to part company with commentators ancient and modern who see here affirmation of "a solidarity of the human and the subhuman world in the redemption of Christ" (Fitzmyer)? In commentary on v.20 he seemed prepared to echo the thinking of *recapitulatio* by Irenaeus and anticipate Maximus's *anakephalaiosis*.

[14] 2 Cor 12.8-9.

[15] Cf. Acts 18.9-10; 16.6-7; 22.18. Unlike modern commentators and versions like the NRSV, and in keeping with his (and Antioch's generally) concern for the human role in salvation, it is not a "divine purpose" that Theodoret sees at work here, as his comment on v.30 further reveals.

[16] In commentary on these verses, Theodoret is establishing his credentials as an exegete of Antioch by remarking on the apostle's *akribeia* and revealing his own through remark on unusual phrases.

[17] Phil 3.20-21.

[18] The term "firstborn" not unexpectedly jars somewhat with Theodoret, who has just above insisted on the term "Only-begotten" for the Son; he does not cite other biblical occurrences of the term (posterior to Romans), just the acceptance of the dogma, which he spells out for the reader.

[19] As in other places, Bishop Theodoret sees a sacramental dimension to this process of justification, baptism being for him the sacrament of reconciliation (of adults).

[20] Theodoret goes on to take issue with a viewpoint we usually regard as a later development (exemplified, for instance, in Black's remark here, "The divine 'fore-ordination' is virtually synonymous"). He maintains Antioch's accent on individualism and free will, and does not specifically consider the role of grace in the process.

[21] John 6.51 (in a reading that paraphrases the received text, found lacking in clarity also by ancient testimonies); 10.18. As we have noted, with his reluctance about the *communicatio idiomatum* Theodoret would be unhappy with the bald phrase, The Son died for us; but there is no Nestorian acceptance of two *prosopa* in Christ, and as in the *Eranistes* (against the Monophysites) he insists there is one *prosopon*, the term employed here.

[22] Are "the heretics" insisting on what we have just seen Theodoret reluctant to concede, a position he now has to admit is compatible with that "one person"?

[23] Ps 44.2. Theodoret in his Psalms Commentary (and Chrysostom in his) took this psalm to be David's work but prophetic of the Maccabees' hardships; more liberal commentators in antiquity assigned its composition to that latter period.

[24] Modern commentators tend to see these rather as astrological terms. The development that Theodoret proceeds to make on these verses arises from his taking Paul's mention of love of God as an objective genitive.

CHAPTER NINE

[1] Theodoret neatly summarizes the content of the letter's opening chapters, once more against the backdrop of the divine plan and especially the Incarnation, and touching on the themes of Law, grace and faith. He thus arrives at "the heart of Romans," as chs 9-11 have been called, stressing their relationship to the preceding part.

[2] 1 Cor 16.22.

[3] Josh 6.17.

[4] The pathos of Paul's protestation is not lost on Theodoret, who analyses it for his readers.

[5] Exod 4.22.

[5] Jer 31.31-32 loosely recalled.

[6] Gen 21.12. The argument that Paul develops and Theodoret seconds hardly endorses the latter's comment about children of God.

[7] Gen 18.10.

[8] Cf. Gen 25.1-4, the text Theodoret probably has in mind, which speaks of Keturah as Abraham's wife, whereas 1 Chr 1.32 calls her his concubine.

[9] Cf. Gen 35.22-26.

[10] Gen 25.23.

[11] Again, as in commentary on 8.30, Theodoret is so far from conceding any simple divine predestination as to uphold human influence on the divine election, despite Paul's parenthetical caveat in v.12.

[12] Mal 1.2-3.

[13] Whom does Theodoret have in mind here? Is it the Ahimelech, priest in Nob, who befriended David, and won his friendship (but still met a sticky end – and, in any case, was no slave or Ethiopian)? Other biblical Abimelechs do not qualify for godliness.

[14] Exod 33.19. Theodoret is having to make some reorientation of his argument here. After taking the biblical examples cited by Paul in vv.9-14 to

illustrate his thesis that God's favor is determined not by nature but by human freewill, *gnome*, or purpose, *prothesis*, he cannot resist Paul's continuing argument and biblical illustrations to the effect that God decides gratuitously.

[15] Exod 9.16.

[16] Is it for pastoral reasons that Bishop Theodoret is reluctant to concede the gratuity of divine election, and keeps insisting on the critical role of human free will and responsibility?

[17] 2 Tim 2.20-21.

[18] 1 Cor 3.12. Theodoret is still reluctant to labor Paul's point of gratuitous election, bringing the argument back again to human responsibility. Divine foreknowledge is as much as he is prepared to concede, and he would have no sympathy for those who later wished to use these verses to document a thesis of individual predestination.

[19] Cf. Hos 2.23; 1.10.

[20] Again Theodoret takes Paul's point of God's election (Paul, admittedly, also not fully respecting Hosea's thought) to support again the need for conversion on the part of the Jews.

[21] Cf. Isa 10.22-23. Paul's accent on the remnant does not inspire Theodoret.

[22] Isa 1.9.

[23] Cf. Isa 28.16; Rom 10.11.

Chapter Ten

[1] Perhaps one of Theodoret's less happy comparisons; the sugar-coated pill might have been more appropriate.

[2] Lev 18.5; cf. Gal 3.12.

[3] Cf. Deut 30.12-14.

[4] Theodoret does not dwell on the antique credal formula in v.9. With no particular thesis to labor in commentary on this chapter, he moves along briskly.

[5] Isa 28.16; cf. Rom 9.33.

[6] Joel 2.32.

[7] Isa 52.7.

[8] Luke 10.5.

[9] Isa 53.1.

[10] Ps 19.5.

[11] Matt 10.6.

[12] Acts 13.46.

[13] Deut 32.21.

[14] Titus 3.3.

[15] Isa 65.1.

[16] Isa 65.2. Unlike modern commentators, Paul would like to see the two verses from Isaiah referring to different peoples, Gentile and Jew respectively (with the encouragement of the Septuagint's offering *ethnos* in the former verse and *laos* in the latter, Fitzmyer notes). Theodoret does not remind him that the prophet has the one people in mind, though unac-

countably he turns to his copy of the Hexapla to note a relatively minor variant in translation of that prophetic text by those versions alternative to the LXX from earlier centuries attributed to Symmachus and Aquila. In turning to this resource (a vademecum for patristic commentators on OT texts: see my translation of his Commentary on the Psalms), did he have some concerns about Paul's use of Isaiah?

CHAPTER ELEVEN

[1] Cf. Acts 2.41.

[2] Cf. Acts 21.20, where in fact the Jerusalem community as a whole and not simply James reports to Paul on converts.

[3] Cf. 1 Kgs 19.10,14,18. What Black styles "a characteristically oriental attitude" in the mention only of males does not attract Theodoret's notice.

[4] Theodoret (with Chrysostom) preserves a longer form of v.6 than the principal manuscripts.

[5] Rom 4.4. Theodoret has no difficulty disallowing a role in salvation for works specifically of the Law; he feels no need to naunce Paul's position on that.

[6] Cf. Deut 29.4; Isa 29.10.

[7] Isa 6.10.

[8] LXX Ps 68.23-24. Fitzmyer recognizes the common element in the OT quotations as "eyes not for seeing," and adds, "One need not try to decide to what the other details refer (feasting, etc.)" – but an Antiochene like Theodoret knows that *akribeia* cannot be content with that.

[9] Matt 24.14 loosely recalled.

[10] With the mixing of the metaphors, the question arises for Paul's commentators: do first batch and root have the same reference? Origen and Theodore thought so, seeing Christ referred to; Theodoret differs in view of Paul's continuing argument.

[11] Finally Theodoret is able to make his habitual diagnosis of the problem, human free will, *proairesis*.

[12] Theodoret seems to be understanding *mysterion* in Paul's sense, not as simply a secret (like some modern commentators), but as the divine plan revealed to us – or at least to initiates, some manuscripts of the Commentary reading "to those who have insight" at this point.

[13] Matt 17.11, the reference to Elijah harking back to Paul's thought in vv.2-4.

[14] Cf. Isa 59.20-21; 27.9.

[15] Again Bishop Theodoret is ready to lend a sacramental dimension to the process of forgiveness of sin, referring specifically to baptism as the sacrament of reconciliation.

[16] With his accent on human responsibility, Theodore comes close to directly contesting Paul's position on the irrevocability of divine gifts, the instances he cites illustrating anything but. For him free will, not divine generosity, is the critical factor.

[17] Theodoret's editor Schulze gives this proviso as the conclusion of v.29

of the Pauline text; but it is more likely to be Theodoret's own paraphrase of the "threat" that follows in the next two verses. The thought is certainly in line with the commentator's thinking, not the apostle's at this point.

[18] Theodoret is in a numerous company of commentators in having difficulty with the word order and resultant sense of these verses. He has as well his continuing problem with the gratuity of divine mercy, and so can only allow any Jewish conversion on the condition of repentance of their obstinacy.

[19] Again Theodoret is being perverse here in making Paul say something he is in fact denying – namely, that God is prepared to relent only conditionally – by an argument that rests on making one key word mean something quite different, Humpty Dumpty-wise. Whatever *sunekleise* means (and commentators debate it), it is not about censure. Paul's teaching on the universality and gratuity of God's mercy leaves Theodoret dismayed.

[20] Isa 40.13. Commentators are in difficulties identifying all these quotations by Paul.

[21] Theodoret, ever the disciplined commentator, does not wax lyrical on Paul's beautiful doxology or trace its origins to stoic or hellenistic thought; in fact, he does not venture beyond paraphrase except to see its relevance to argument against the subordinationism of early and late Arianism. Likewise, against the heresiarchs he applies not polemic but simple logic.

CHAPTER TWELVE

[1] Cf. Rom 6.13.

[2] Ps 50.14,23. Just as modern commentators debate the sense of Paul's requirement that worship be *logike*, so Theodoret contrasts it with Old Testament sacrifices where irrational beasts alone were involved, a practice he says the OT constantly questioned. He would agree with Black that Paul is by no means suggesting Christian worship should be so "spiritual" as to be redundant.

[3] 1 Cor 7.31.

[4] The Antiochene coloring to his commentary appears when Theodoret can trace movements in Paul's thought based on differences in the roots of words, whether these be true indicators or false.

[5] Matt 5.3.

[6] Black remarks, "The meaning of these words has been endlessly debated, and a consensus of interpretation is no more likely nowadays than it was in patristic or Reformation exegesis, a situation which could point to a 'primitive error' in the transmitted text, although there are no significant variants." The critical issue is, does Paul speak of *fides quae* or *fides qua*? Theodoret, with his habitual accent on human responsibility, has no difficulty opting for the latter, passing on without further comment; for him, our response in faith influences God's gift of grace, and that should determine our self-esteem.

[7] Paul's celebrated teaching on love, of course, occurs at 1 Cor 13, whereas

it is in 1 Cor 12 that Paul speaks of body and members in similar terms to this passage. Is Theodoret slightly off target (again)?

[8] 2 Cor 9.7.

[9] 1 Thess 5.19.

[10] For an Antiochene like Theodoret (and Chrysostom), one makes oneself worthy or unworthy of grace and the enlightenment of the Spirit ...

[11] ... And yet, in almost the same breath, the Antiochene can admit dependence on divine grace in response to prayer.

[12] 2 Cor 8.14.

[13] Matt 5.44.

[14] 1 Cor 10.32. Apart from the occasional cross-reference to Paul's other moral dicta, Theodoret is content to move briskly through the parenesis which, as he remarked at the outset of this section of the letter beginning with this chapter, is secondary to dogmatic truth as "the summit and true foundation." He is a desk theologian, not a preacher, and is ever careful not to blur the distinction by indulging in moralizing.

[15] Cf. Deut 32.35.

[16] Cf. Prov 25.21-22.

[17] The meaning of the proverb and its import in Paul's parenesis have troubled commentators. Theodoret is interested only in discouraging any duplicitous and malicious display of liberality intended to bring the miscreant into deeper difficulties, as Origen and Chrysostom had taken Paul to mean.

CHAPTER THIRTEEN

[1] Acts 17.6.

[2] Cf. Acts 21.21. Theodoret takes the view that Paul is not simply enunciating some truisms about obedience to civil authority but is reacting to some specific abuses. "Christians may even have been refusing to pay taxes," Black surmises from the following verses.

[3] Jer 3.15.

[4] Isa 1.26; 3.4. Theodoret, writing this after decades as a bishop in a city in which he has been credited also with civic and social improvements, warms to what he takes as Paul's theme, the legitimacy and utility of secular government. He would lend no support to those, like Cullmann, who see Paul speaking of angelic or demonic powers.

[5] Cf. Deut 5.17-18.

[6] Lev 19.18.

[7] Does Theodoret presume there are no women among his readers? Not that Paul's text would correct him on this.

[8] Luke 10.27. Theodoret is right in attributing to the Lord the joining of two commands occurring separately in the Torah, though he goes on to suggest the latter is the practical implementation of the former.

[9] For Theodoret, always sacramentally alert, this verse is redolent of the baptismal liturgy and practice.

[10] Not for the first time does Theodoret hasten to take issue with dualistic heresies that impugned the value of the body.

Chapter Fourteen

[1] Theodoret cites one of the theories as to the grounds for abstinence; Cranfield lists no fewer than six such theories.

[2] Gal 1.8 loosely recalled. Bishop Theodoret is clearly not in favor of relativism in general, especially where doctrine is concerned, though he admits there is diversity in ascetical practices even in the churches of his day.

[3] Theodoret's text does not include the next clause in Paul's text.

[4] Isa 49.18; 45.23.

[5] Isa 44.6; 43.10 loosely recalled; 45.21,23. Commentators debate the reference by Paul to "the Lord" in these citations; Theodoret is in no doubt, aware perhaps that the Christological meaning emerged also from the citation of Isa 45.23 in Phil 2.10-11.

[6] Acts 10.15. The Gospel text he had in mind was probably Matt 15.11.

[7] Paul's concern is about respecting people's conscientious behavior; but Theodoret takes occasion to rule out any dishonor to Christ. What precisely prompts this observation?

[8] John 6.29.

[9] Theodoret is one of ancient witnesses to the placing of the doxology of Rom 16.25-27 in this position (only – as distinct from those who place it twice), a fact that encourages in commentators the view that the doxology was a late addition to the letter. He does not go along with Marcion and others who closed the letter at this point. Finding it in his text here, he takes the doxology as a prayer of Paul for his recipients – though dispatching it in summary fashion, perhaps aware of its controversial textual status.

[10] Theodoret here seems to resonate with the language and thinking of Eph 3 that does have similarities with the Romans doxology, confirming in some commentators its secondary character. One could, however, argue that it and Theodoret's comments are all of a piece with Pauline thought; see my "The mystery of Christ: clue to Paul's thinking on wisdom."

[11] 1 Tim 6.16.

Chapter Fifteen

[1] Ps 69.9 (a psalm given a Christological sense widely in the NT).

[2] Matt 26.39.

[3] Without elaboration Theodoret summarizes the value of Old Testament texts – inspired prediction of Christ's life, written instruction, hagiography.

[4] In defiance of the word order of the text before him, Theodoret here – and at 2 Cor 1.3 and Eph 1.3 – perversely resists Paul's thought, possibly to avoid saying the Lord Jesus has a God and Father, possibly to avoid God's fatherhood of us being spoken of as identical with God's fatherhood of Jesus. At 2 Cor 1.3 he quotes in support of his quibble Jesus praying (Luke 10.21), "I thank you, Father, Lord of heaven and earth," and comments: "He clearly teaches that, whereas he is his Father, he is maker and lord of creation" – that is, we and Jesus do not stand in the same relation

to the Father. And he has a concern with the three opening verses of Eph lest they be used by heretics to question the divinity of the Only-begotten. In short, in his view taking Paul at face value runs the risk of subordinationism, and this justifies twisting the text.

5 Ps 18.49.

6 Deut 32.43 LXX.

7 Ps 117.1.

8 Isa 11.10 LXX.

9 Rom 8.24.

10 Bishop Theodoret does not expatiate on the liturgical metaphor Paul is employing in this verse, and unlike modern commentators he sees the Gentiles as having something to offer (taking the genitive as subjective) rather than being the offering Paul makes as liturgical minister.

11 Isa 52.15 LXX.

12 Cf. Gal 2.9-10.

13 Theodoret shows no reluctance in embellishing Paul's suggestion of the riches brought by Jewish Christians from their background in Judaism.

14 Fitzmyer suggests the metaphor of the seal was to do with the grower's brand name, whereas Theodoret thinks in terms of sealing as securing.

15 Acts 20.23; 21.13.

16 While some commentators ignore the detail and others see it as a typically Jewish blessing, Theodoret properly seizes upon it to relate it to Paul's situation and the divisions in the community.

CHAPTER SIXTEEN

1 Theodoret, in simply speaking of Phoebe as a *gyne diakonos*, does not (any more than Paul) resolve the question as to whether she belonged to an order of deaconesses, or was merely one of the church assistants. He is more interested in the disparity between the degree of support she provided and the notoriety she received in return.

2 Cf. Acts 18.3. Commentators observe that the diminutive form *Priscilla* is found only in the text of Acts (18.2,26), *Prisca* in Paul here and at 1 Cor 16.19, 2 Tim 4.19. Schulze thinks Theodoret is in fact reading *Prisca* here (though the commentary suggests otherwise), admitting both forms appear in the codices. By mention of "the books" Theodoret is perhaps observing that Lucan and Pauline usage differs.

3 Acts 18.24-28.

4 As commentators observe, the accusative form *Iounian* in Paul's text could derive from a masculine name Junias (a contraction of Junianus, not otherwise attested) or feminine Junia; even Chrysostom took it as the latter, marveling that a woman could be deemed worthy of the name of apostle. Theodoret, though intent on signalling all the women who come in for commendation in these verses, clearly joins the majority of commentators who take the other option.

5 Rarely does Theodoret give "the divine apostle" his name, whereas commentary on this chapter elicits it several times, perhaps because of the personal references.

[6] Matt 22.14. Theodoret enters into no speculation as to the identity of these members of the Roman church from external evidence, developing only the hints Paul gives.

[7] Phil 3.19.

[8] Matt 10.16.

[9] Cf. Acts 16.1-3.

[10] Not all commentators agree there are grounds for presuming this Jason is the one mentioned in Acts 17.5-9 (likewise for the Lucius of 13.1 and Sosipater of Acts 20.4).

[11] Theodoret, predictably, does not enter the modern debate as to the degree of latitude accorded this scribe in the composition of this indisputably Pauline letter.

[12] 1 Cor 1.14.

[13] 2 Tim 4.20.

[14] He assembled evidence for this, including the above (even giving that tautological gloss on *xenos*, host), in the preface. It strikes the reader, after the well developed (if hackneyed) peroration, as a banal anti-climax: why insist on the fact? Editor Schulze goes out of his way to contest the authenticity of similar codicils to the Corinthian letters.

It has been a lengthy but measured commentary on this longest and most doctrinal of Paul's letters, with no sense of tedium in the commentator. Theodoret has clearly enjoyed grappling with the issues (his own as well as Paul's), admitting to a preference for dogmatic over moral topics – even if squirming at times when faced with Pauline attitudes not acceptable to an Antiochene; like a celebrated modern, he can be said to have been "wrestling with Romans."

The First Letter to the Corinthians

THEME

The divinely-inspired Paul was the first to offer the saving message to the Corinthians, and (228) he spent a considerable time among them, the Lord having given this explicit direction: "Speak and do not be silent," he said to him, remember; "there are many in this city who are my people."[1] Accordingly, a year and six months passed, and while he for his part went on his journeys to other cities for the sake of preaching, the Corinthians were caught up in argumentation and rivalry. In fact, they had split into many factions, appointing garrulous men as their teachers, and they persisted in admiration each of their own leader and in dispute among themselves over them. Now, one of those who prided themselves on their eloquence was also guilty of grave lawlessness, having intercourse with his step-mother; those of his faction, however, overlooked it, and spoke glowingly only of his eloquence.

For this very reason the divine apostle, in beginning the letter,[2] criticizes the so-called wisdom and reveals the message which, while bare of this feature, possessed great force. He also finds fault with those who wrangle over other matters amongst themselves and employ secular rulers as their judges. He also forbids them to partake of food sacrificed to idols, suggesting this also has been the practice of some. Amidst these things he also offers advice on virginity and widowhood, and of course gives lengthy treatment also to the spiritual gifts, bringing out the difference between them and urging the gift of tongues be employed not for rivalry but for benefit. He also offers them teaching about the resurrection, since some apparently tried to convince them not to accept the doctrine

158

about the resurrection of the body. And – without my speaking at length on each – some other matters he conveyed to them in writing, both of advantage to them and productive of good for all people. He did not, however, go to great length on the doctrine of the faith[3] since he had spent no little time with them and had given them precise instruction on what their position should be, and on visiting them the remarkable Apollo confirmed the apostle's teaching. Accordingly, he imitated an excellent physician, applying appropriate remedies to their ailments. Stephanas, Fortunatus and Achaicus, who were sent by the Corinthians to him, as he mentions at the end, made themselves available for the writings. In fact, he sent blessed Timothy to them, though not with a letter, and he made this clear himself, saying, "If Timothy comes, make sure he has nothing to fear among you."[4]

CHAPTER ONE

Paul, called to be an apostle of Jesus Christ (v.1). The very opening betrays the thrust of the accusation: it teaches them not to have confidence in themselves but to glory in the saving God. Hence he made mention both of apostleship and of calling, as if to say, You name yourselves after human beings, but I name myself after Jesus Christ, who calls and sends me. *By God's will.* (229) This likewise criticizes the disharmony: he gave a hint of the harmony of Father and Son. Now, at the same time he makes clear that he uses the prepositions identically: here he used of the Father the preposition *by whom*, which those adopting the position of Arius and Eunomius apply to the Son. He would not have done this, however, if he took the preposition *through whom* to suggest anything less than *from whom*.[5] *And our brother Sosthenes.* I suspect he was a Corinthian; the story of the Acts also mentions him, and blessed Luke brings out that the Greeks during Gallio's term laid hold of him and treated him very badly.[6]

To the church of God that is in Corinth, to those sanctified in Christ Jesus, called to be saints, together with all those who call on the name of our Lord Jesus Christ, in every place theirs and ours (v.2). All the things said are antidotes for the ailment; he mends the division that had unfortunately occurred. First he gives them the name *one church* and *church of God*, and adds *in Christ Jesus*, not in this person or that. He also calls them *sanctified* and *saints*, and links them with the believers throughout the world to teach them that it behooves not only them to be of one mind, but also all the believers in the saving message to have one viewpoint for the reason of belonging to Christ the Lord's one body. The phrase *theirs and ours* goes with *the Lord*, meaning, We who write and you who receive the writings have one Lord, Jesus Christ. [7]

Grace to you and peace from God our Father and the Lord Jesus Christ (v.3). It was timely for him to pray for both grace and peace for them in so far as they are divided and at odds with one another. He showed its source to be not only the Father but also the Son, bringing out also the equality of the Son. [8]

I give thanks to my God always in your regard for the grace of God given to you in Christ Jesus (v.4). Though on the point of leveling accusation, he solicits their attention in advance so that the treatment may be acceptable. The words are also free of falsity: he did thank God for the gifts given them. He also says so more clearly: *Because in every way you have been enriched in him, in all speech and knowledge, just as the testimony of Christ has been confirmed in you* (vv.5-6). These are types of gifts of the Spirit: "To one is given through the Spirit words of wisdom," he says, remember, "to another words of knowledge according to the same Spirit." [9] He constantly inserts the name of the Lord, to bring out that no one should be named by reference to anyone else than the provider of salvation. He calls preaching *testimony of Christ*: the preachers in some way give testimony. Likewise he said also in writing to Timothy, (232) "So I give testimony before God who gives life to the dead;" [10] similarly, the Lord also said in the sacred Gospels, "This good news of the kingdom will be preached to all the nations as a testimony to them." [11] He refers to the working of marvelous signs as *confirmation* of the Gospel, the truth of the message being demonstrated through them.

So that you are not lacking in any spiritual gift (v.7). In fact, they enjoyed a share of the charism of inspiration and spoke in different tongues, as he brings out more clearly in what follows, *as you await the revelation of our Lord Jesus Christ*: you enjoyed these gifts so that you might look forward to the second coming of the Savior. *He will also strengthen you to the end so that you may be blameless on the day of our Lord Jesus Christ* (v.8). He prayed for strength for them and innocence; mention of *blameless* showed they were at some stage guilty of blame. *God is faithful, and through him you were invited into the fellowship of his Son, Jesus Christ our Lord* (v.9): he who also regaled us with the gift of adoption will do this. He called adoption *fellowship of the Son*, you see; *faithful* means reliable and true. Here, of course, he used *through him* of the Father to shut the shameful mouths of the heretics and to emphasize that it is not indicative of diminution.

Having thus cajoled them with praise and commendation, he sets about the accusation, not leading into it baldly but beginning with exhortation. *So I urge you, brethren, in the name of our Lord Jesus Christ, to all say the same thing and not have divisions amongst you* (v.10). It was good for him to associate with the exhortation the name of the Lord, this being scorned by them: though they should have called themselves after it, they used the names of the leaders. *And be united in the same mind and in the same purpose.* The fault he finds with them is not difference in doctrine but quarreling and rivalry over leaders. The sense of the message is one, he says, implying this by *in the same mind*; but the disposition is not one, indicating this by *and in the same purpose*. So he urges them to think and intend the same things, not keeping their distance and idly quarreling about the leaders.

I mean, I have been informed about you, my brethren, by Chloe's people (v.11). Perhaps some household bore this name; he did not cite the informants by name lest he set them at one another's throats. *That there are quarrels among you.* He also brings out the type of rivalry. (233) *What I mean is that each of you says, I belong to Paul, I belong to Apollo, I belong to Cephas, I belong to Christ* (v.12). Whereas they named themselves after different teachers, he cited his own name and Apollo's, and also added that of the head of the apostles, to make clear that it was not right to use their names for this purpose; we shall learn this more clearly in what follows. Now, it was very clever of him to list the name of Christ with the others to show the absurdity of what was done, putting on equal ranking the master and the servants. [12]

Has Christ been divided? (v.13) Some have read this in the indicative, claiming *Christ* here stands for the Church and interpreting it this way, *You have wrongly divided the body of Christ.* I for my part, on the other hand, consider it is interrogative, the sequel bringing this out: *Surely Paul was not crucified for you? or you were baptized in the name of Paul?* What he means is something like this: Surely Christ has no sharers in his lordship and authority, and is for this reason divided, some called after him, some called after so and so? Did not he alone accept death for us all? Were you not granted the grace of baptism in his name? Surely invocations of human beings did not accord you forgiveness of sins?

I thank my God that I baptized none of you except Crispus and Gaius in case anyone claim that I baptized in my name. I did also baptize the household of Stephanas; beyond that, I am not aware if I baptized anyone else (vv.14-16). He adds to the accusation with each of his remarks, but does not strike severely those accused, substituting his own person for theirs. He is implying that some were giving themselves names not only of the teachers but also of the baptizers. He also quotes the reason why he did not baptize many. *Christ sent me, you see, not to baptize but to preach the good news* (v.17). Actually, he gave both directions: "Go, make disciples of all nations, baptizing them in the name of the Father, and of the Son, and of the Holy Spirit." [13] But preaching is more important than baptizing: baptizing is easy for those thought worthy of priesthood, whereas preaching is proper to a few, who have received this gift from a divine source. [14] At this point he then represses the sense of importance of those who pride themselves on their eloquence, saying, *not in wisdom of utterance lest the cross of Christ be rendered pointless*: if I were to have recourse to garrulity and cleverness, the power of the crucified would not be demonstrated; everyone would get the idea that the believers had been snared by rhetorical skills, whereas the preachers' lack of expertise proves superior to those taking credit for eloquence and thus clearly reveals the force of the cross. (236)

You see, the message of the cross is folly to those who are perishing, but to us who are being saved it is the power of God. It is written, remember, I shall destroy the wisdom of the wise, and the intelligence of the intelligent I shall annul [15] (vv.18-19). By *the message of the cross* he means the preaching about the cross; he refers to the unbelievers as *perishing* and the believers as *being saved*, assigning the terms on the basis of the outcome. He cited the scriptural testimony to make clear that from the beginning the God of all foretold this. Then he shows the reliability of the prophecy: *Where is a sage? where a scribe? where a debater in these days?* (v.20) The preaching of the cross conquered all these people. He gives the name *sage* to the one equipped with Greek wordiness, *scribe* the teacher of the Jews, boasting of knowledge of the Law, and *debater* the one from both groups who is proficient in skills of argumentation. Then he adds, *Has not God made foolish the wisdom of this world?* By the *wisdom of this world* he does not mean eloquence: God is the source of that, himself making distinctions in languages and assigning particular characteristics to each. So it was he who gave eminence to the Greek language; but those at least who did not use it properly made of it a deceitful bait and produced a specious fable of error. Accordingly, he accuses not eloquence but the falsity concealed in it. He says it has been refuted and shown to be folly.

You see, since in the wisdom of God the world did not know God through wisdom, God decided through the folly of the message to save the believers (v.21). He refers to two *wisdoms of God*, or rather three, showing what is considered folly to be wisdom in reality. One wisdom he refers to is that given to human beings, as a result of which we are rational, we have discernment of what is to be done, we are in possession of skills and sciences, and we are able to know God. The second is that which is involved in the contemplation of created realities: we see the magnitude of the heavens, beauty of the sun, array of the stars, expanse of earth and sea, diversity of plants and animals, and the other things, not to mention every one. The third is revealed in our Savior, which the unbelievers call folly. [16] Now, he means that human beings, having received from God knowledge of nature, ought to have been guided by creation and adored its God; but since they were unwilling to benefit from this source, the loving God achieved their salvation in a different manner, and through what is called *folly* by heedless people he freed them from error.

Since Jews require signs and Greeks look for wisdom, whereas we preach (237) *Christ crucified, a stumbling block to Jews and folly to Greeks* (vv.22-23). Jews demanded miracles from the Lord, and the evangelists make this clear to us; they probably bade the apostles as well to make a display of signs – the divine apostle says as much, in fact.

Greeks, on the other hand, mocked their lack of learning, as they said in Athens, for instance, "What does this babbler want to say?" [17] We, however, he says, scorn the stupidity of both the one group and the other, and we preach the Lord's passion, clearly aware, of course, that both the one and the other are in obvious opposition to it.

What benefit comes from the preaching? *But to those who are called, both Jews and Greeks, Christ God's power and God's wisdom* (v.24). The same thing is both wisdom and folly, both power and weakness: folly and weakness to the unbelievers, wisdom and power to the believers. The sun, after all, is light to those who see, but darkness to those who are blind; it does not itself bring darkness, of course – the disability blocks the brightness of the rays. It should be understood, however, that the divine apostle did not refer to the divinity of the Only-begotten as *wisdom and power* but to the preaching of the cross, and he utterly refutes Arius and Eunomius in their malicious attempts at this point to show the Word God given the name *wisdom* in this text; at this point, too, they are responsible for the blasphemy from the passage in Proverbs as well. [18] *Because God's foolishness is wiser than human beings, and God's weakness is stronger than human beings* (v.25). By *God's foolishness and weakness* he refers to the mystery of the cross, in the opinion of stupid people; he shows it prevailed over both the wise and the strong.

I mean, consider your calling, brethren, that not many of you were wise according to the flesh, not many powerful, not many of noble birth (v.26). He did not say, None wise, none powerful, none of noble birth: some believers did come from these, but not many, the majority happening to be from poorer classes. *But God chose the foolish things of the world to shame the wise, God chose the weak things of the world to shame the strong, and God chose the lowly and despised things of the world and what is not to abolish what is* (vv.27-28). By *foolish, weak* and *lowly* he referred to people's opinion: real folly is not lack of verbal skills but absence of faith, weakness and lowly birth are not poverty but impiety and vicious habits. The God of all, at any rate, overcame the learned through the unlearned, and the rich through the poor, and through fishermen he snared the world. (240) *So that all flesh might not boast in his presence* (v.29): if from the outset he had chosen those equipped with wealth and taking pride in rhetorical skill, and made them preachers, not only their adversaries but also the preachers themselves would have come to harm, thinking they prevailed over error through their own power.

Now, it is from him that your life is in Christ Jesus, who became for us wisdom from God, and also righteousness, holiness and redemption; as it is written, Let the one who boasts boast in the Lord [19] (vv.30-31). He used the phrase *from him* to refer not to the process of creation but to the process of salvation; Scripture says, remember, "To all who received him he gave power to become children of God for believing in his name; they were born not of blood, nor of will of the flesh, nor of will of man, but of God." [20] Since, you see, he had said that God chose the foolish things of the world and the weak and lowly, of necessity he added, *It is from him that your life is,* highlighting the nobility conferred. He also gave an inkling of the manner of the birth by saying *in Christ Jesus:* you are not named after so and so; rather, you have been thought worthy of rebirth in Christ. It is he who has given you true wisdom, [21] he who has granted you forgiveness of sins, accorded you righteousness and made you holy by ransoming you from the devil's tyranny. Accordingly, you ought glory not in human beings but in the God who saves.

CHAPTER TWO

When I came to you, brethren, I did not come not with flights of rhetoric or wisdom to proclaim to you the Gospel of God (v.1). By *rhetoric* he means eloquence, by *wisdom* skill. I used neither of these, he says, on reaching you. *In fact, I decided to show knowledge of nothing among you except Jesus Christ, and him crucified* (v.2). It was good for him to use *decided,* to make clear that he was unable even to offer them discourse about theology; instead, he delivered only instruction in the Incarnation, glorying in the Lord's passion. [1]

My presence among you was marked by weakness, by fear and trembling (v.3). I suffered excruciating torment, and I spent the time in confinement. [2] *My speech and my proclamation were not marked by persuasiveness of human wisdom but by demonstration of the Spirit and of power* (v.4): miracle working testified to the proclamation of the Spirit. But it was very appropriate for him to connect the power of the Spirit with the feelings of weakness. (241) *So that your faith might be due not to wisdom of human beings but to power of God* (v.5): this was the reason the Lord did not allow us to employ eloquence, so that your faith might be shown to be above suspicion, not falling under the power of smooth talking but guided by the power of the Spirit.

Among the mature, however, we do speak wisdom, but a wisdom not of this age nor of the rulers of this age, who are on the way to destruction (v.6). Since in what went before he called the message *foolishness*, employing the term proposed by the unbelievers, he has to show that it is *wisdom* in reality and in the usage of those who adopted a sincere and mature faith. Now, by *rulers of this age* he refers to sophists, poets, philosophers and orators as having a name for eloquence in the present life. [3] *Instead, we speak God's wisdom concealed in mystery, which God determined before the ages for our glory* (v.7). He does not mean that we speak in riddles [4] – rather, that we offer to human beings the wisdom hidden in mystery, which God did not plan now on the basis of some second thoughts, but from the very outset he determined in devising glory for us by so doing; he is the source not only of salvation but also of glory for the believers.

None of the rulers of this age realized this: if they had realized it, they would not have crucified the Lord of glory (v.8). He gave the name *rulers of this age* to Pilate, Herod, Annas, Caiaphas and the other rulers of the Jews. He says they were ignorant of the divine mystery, and hence crucified the Lord. This is surely the reason the Lord on the cross also said, "Father, forgive them: they do not know what they are doing." [5] After all, had they realized that the saving passion would, on the one hand, disperse them through the world, and on the other would give the nations a share in the salvation, they would not have been responsible for the passion. Hence the Lord judged them deserving of pardon. After the resurrection from the dead, however, the ascension, the coming of the all-holy Spirit and the various miracles of the apostles, they persisted in their infidelity and so he consigned them to the siege. [6] Now, he called the crucified one *Lord of glory*, not to associate the passion with the divinity, but to show the degree of lawlessness of the sinners. [7]

But as it is written, What eye has not seen nor ear heard nor has it entered the human heart God has prepared for those who love him (v.9). Since he had mentioned the Jews' ignorance and said the mystery

surdity of what is being done: if in my case (he is saying), thought worthy though I was of the apostolic grace and responsible for planting you, and in the case of Apollos, who provided you with water, (248) it is quite absurd for this to happen, much more is it impious and unholy for it to happen in the case of others. [1]

Who, then, is Paul, who Apollos, other than ministers to those who came to faith? [2] (v.5): not so the Lord; we are his servants, and ministers of your salvation. *As the Lord gave to each*: the difference is in us; even if we share the ministry with one another, nevertheless we are equipped with grace in a measure of some kind. *I planted* (v.6): I was the first to preach to you. *Apollos watered*: in my wake he endorsed my teaching. *But God gave the increase*: the completion came from his grace. *So neither the one who plants is anything, nor the one who waters, but God who gives the increase* (v.7): if God does not cooperate, futile is our effort.

The one who plants and the one who waters are one (v.8) as far as service is concerned: both minister to the divine will, though not in terms of the outcome nor in terms of zeal, there being a great difference among those ministering in these respects. He in fact says as much, *Each will receive wages according to each one's labor* – not simply in terms of the outcome but *according to the labor* the outcome involves: in many cases one offers two hundred to the Savior with great ease, another undergoes the utmost effort in liberating one or two from error. You can see this also with fasting and temperance: one person with the assistance of nature practices temperance without effort, another under attack from nature achieves what is desired with the greatest effort. And while the person with an ardent temperament goes fasting until evening in intense distress, another lasts two or three days without partaking of food or suffering very great hardship. Hence the just judge looks not to the outcome but to the effort. [3]

We are God's fellow workers, after all (v.9). Those holding the position of Arius and Eunomius did not assign this title to the Son, either; instead, they call him assistant. The divine apostle, on the other hand, calls even the preachers of the truth *God's fellow workers*. There is a great difference, however: whereas the Son acts as fellow worker, they carry out God's will as very well disposed servants. [4] *You are God's farm, God's building* – belonging not to this person or that, but to the God of all. *According to the grace of God given to me, like a skilled master builder I laid a foundation* (v.10). After first suggesting the divine grace, he thus called himself *a skilled master builder*. I was the first to put down the foundations of piety among you, he is saying. *But someone else is building on it. Each one must take care how to build on it: no one can lay any other foundation than the one laid, which is Jesus* (249) *Christ* (vv.10-11): one has to build on foundations, not lay them; it is impossible for anyone who wishes to build knowledgeably to lay another foundation. Blessed Peter also set this foundation in place, or rather the Lord himself: after Peter said, "You are the Christ, the Son of the living God," the Lord replied, "On this rock I shall build my Church."[5] So do not name yourselves after human beings: Christ is the foundation.

Now, if anyone builds on this foundation with gold, silver, precious stones, wood, hay, straw, each one's work will become obvious (vv.12-13). Some claim this was said by the apostle in connection with doctrines; my view, on the contrary, is that he says it about the practice of virtue and vice, and is preparing in advance the accusation against the fornicator.[6] *Gold*, of course, *silver* and *precious stones* are forms of virtue, whereas *wood, hay* and *straw* are the opposite of virtue, for which the fire of hell is prepared. Now, these depend not on the evil of the teachers but on the free will of the disciples: while the former propose the divine lessons, some of the listeners make gold of themselves, some silver, some precious stones by zealously heeding what is said. Others in turn, on the other hand, living a life of indifference, resemble the volatility of wood, hay and straw by opting for vice. It is not the present life, however, but the future that will demonstrate the difference in the materials: he said, note, *The Day will disclose it*, that is, the day of judgment.

Because it will be revealed by fire, and the fire itself will test what each person's work is like. If someone's work built on the foundation survives, they will receive pay, whereas if someone's work is burned up, they will be fined but their own person will be saved; but this will happen as through fire (vv.13-15). The teachers give lessons in the divine things, but what is to be done the listeners choose independently by their free will. On the day of the Savior's coming, however, there will be an inquiry and precise examination; some who have lived a good life, like gold and silver, the fire will make more resplendent, whereas the evildoers it will consume like wood, hay and straw. The teacher, on the other hand, who has taught what is proper, far from paying a penalty, will be accorded salvation. Paul in fact said as much, *their own person will be saved*, that is, the teacher; but *the work will be burned up*, that is, those who make an evil work of themselves.[7] Now, if we read it this way, we shall find precisely the meaning of the Scriptures: If someone's work is burned up, they will be fined; but this will happen as through fire, (252) instead of, Their work will be burned by fire, whereas they will be saved, namely, the teacher: he was not responsible for their taking a turn for the worse, having personally provided the proper teaching. If, on the contrary, someone prefers to apply *as through fire* not to the work but to the teacher, let them take it this way, He will not pay the penalty for them, and instead will be saved after being proven by fire, provided his life is in keeping with his teaching.

Now, the fact that this refers not to doctrines but to deeds the sequel also testifies: he says, *Do you not realize that you are God's temple, and the Spirit of God dwells in you? If anyone spoils God's temple, God will destroy them: God's temple is holy, and you are like that* (vv.16-17): if it is appropriate to show reverence for the temple built of wood, to a greater degree presumably is it right to consecrate the rational temples to God. Now, it ought be noted that he called *God's temples* those who have the grace of the Spirit dwelling within; in fact, the text gives witness that the all-holy Spirit is God.[8]

Let no one deceive themselves (v.18), specifically by taking pride in eloquence or in being highborn. He adds, in fact, *If any among you think they are wise in this age, let them become fools so as to become wise: the wisdom of the world is folly with God* (vv.18-19). He calls *wisdom of the world* the wisdom that is bereft of grace of the Spirit, relying on human reasoning alone. He urges them not to trust in this, but to glory in the so-called *folly* of the message. He relates scriptural testimonies to the accusation of such wisdom: *It is written, remember, Who lays hold of the wise in their roguery,*[9] and again, *The Lord knows the thoughts of the wise, that they are futile*[10] (vv.19-20).

Having thus refuted the idle boasting of the teachers, he shifts his attention to those puffed up about it. *So let no one boast in human beings: all things belong to you* (v.21). What are these things? *Whether Paul, Apollos, or Cephas, whether world, life or death, whether present or future – all belong to you, and you belong to Christ, and Christ belongs to God* (vv.22-23). He gave them a glimpse of the true wealth and (253) and the source of the wealth, and he taught them to despise things of no value. It was for your sake, in fact, he is saying, that we apostles were granted the grace of apostleship, that we might preach the word to you. To you is given the present life and the life you await. Death itself takes issue with nature for your benefit; all visible things have been created for your needs, and those awaited have been prepared for your sake. It therefore behooves us to be attached to Christ the Lord, [11] who is source of these goods, and through him to the God of all: he has been united to us in the nature he received from us, but to the Father in the divine substance. If, however, those holding the position of Arius contradict this and are unable to concede the difference in nature, let them refer to the present and the future, the apostles, life and death as of our making since the divine apostle said, *All things belong to you*. But they would not say so. Consequently, whereas these things are ours thanks to divine generosity, we belong to Christ – as man, his limbs, but as God, his creatures. Christ belongs to God, as his true Son, begotten of him according to divinity.

CHAPTER FOUR

Let a person think of us in this way, as ministers of Christ and dispensers of God's mysteries (v.1): let the one wishing to honor us honor us as ministers, respect us as dispensers, keep esteem within the bounds of nature. The divine apostle put this not only into writing but also into action: when the Lycaonians tried to offer sacrifice, he stopped them, with Barnabas he tore his clothing and shouted out, "We are mortals like you." Likewise blessed Peter said to Cornelius, "I too am a human being." [1] *Now, it is further required of dispensers that they be found trustworthy* (v.2), not depriving the master of his due but maintaining a positive attitude to the master.

To me, however, it is a very small thing to be subject to your inquiry (v.3). He makes a twofold accusation of them, not keeping honor within bounds but honoring without limits, and judging without the authority to judge, not just anyone but the teachers. You see, they would not have given preference, some to this one, others to that one, unless they had arrogated to themselves the role of judging. This is the reason he denied them the authority to judge, speaking of the lowly condition of teachers when their affairs are subject to the judgment of the disciples. Then to mollify them he generalizes: *or by a human day*, referring to the natural brevity of life as *a human day. I do not even subject myself to inquiry:* (256) *I am not aware of anything against me, but am not thereby acquitted. The Lord is my examiner* (vv.3-4). Why mention the others? he is saying. For my part, though I have a precise understanding of what concerns me and am conscious of nothing lawless on my conscience, I cannot bring myself either to judge myself or to pronounce myself guiltless; rather, I await the Lord's verdict. Now, let no one think the phrase *I am not thereby acquitted* is at variance with *I am not aware of anything against me*: it is not at variance but in keeping. I mean, it often happens that even those unaware commit sin, thinking it is right and just, but the God of all sees it differently. In fact, what follows makes this clear.

And so do not make a judgment before the right time, until the Lord comes, who will throw light on the hidden things of darkness and disclose the plans of hearts; then commendation will be given each from God (v.5). We see what is on the surface, he is saying, whereas to God even the hidden things are clear. He does not lay bare everything in this life, however, but everything will be made clear on that day. So await the righteous judgment; then you will see the righteous pronouncements. Since in what went before he put himself in focus, as well as Apollos and Cephas, to show the absurdity of what was happening with the majority, he had then to lay bare the charge. *Now, I cast myself and Apollos in this role, brethren, for your sake so that you might learn through us to adopt the attitude, Nothing beyond what is written* (v.6). If we the teachers of the teachers, we who received the message from God, did not assign titles to ourselves, and instead bade people be called after Christ, consider how extreme the impiety of this being done by them. He says as much, note, *so that you might learn through us to adopt the attitude, Nothing beyond what is written*. Now, it is written, "Let the one wishing to be first among you be last of all;" [2] and "Let each of you remain in the condition in which you were called." [3] *So that none of you will be puffed up in favor of one against another*: they had divided themselves into groups, some wanting to be called after this one, others after that, and were at odds with one another, each party striving to promote their teacher over the others.

He then addresses in turn the teachers themselves: *After all, who sees you as different?* (v.7) What party elected you? why are you not called teacher of everyone equally? *What do you have that you did not receive?* What do you have to boast of? On the contrary, it was God who made a gift of it to you. Knowledge? It, too, is a divine gift. Or wonderworking? It, too, is the work of the Spirit. *And if you received it, why boast as if you had not received it.* No one boasts of deposits made by somebody else, but watches over them so as to keep them for the giver. (257)

You have already had your fill, you are already rich (v.8): you lack nothing, you enjoyed all good things in abundance. *You became kings without us*: while we are still struggling and endure the sufferings of preaching the message, you have attained kingship. Since he expressed this ironically, he reveals the intention he has: *Would that you had become kings*: far from envying you, I even pray that you enjoy these good things. Then he calls on the depths of humility: *So that we also may be kings with you.* Actually, he generally applies this to Christ the Lord, "If we endure, we shall also reign with him,"[4] meaning that since he is truly king, his true servants will share the kingship; but here by means of his modesty he applies it to quell their conceit.

I think, in fact, that God has shown the apostles as taking last place, as though destined to death (v.9): if it is true that you lack nothing and have come into enjoyment of kingship, it would seem we have been brought into life only to be slain (the meaning of *destined to death*). *Because we have been made a spectacle to the world, to angels and to human beings*: our situation lies exposed to the scrutiny of everybody; while angels marvel at our fortitude, some people are pleased with our sufferings and others feel sympathy but are powerless to help. *We are fools for the sake of Christ*: we preach what the unbelievers have taken for folly. *But you are sensible.* And to avoid upsetting them too much, he added, *In Christ,* that is, May it be your good fortune to have true sense. *We are weak, while you are strong; you enjoy repute, while we suffer dishonor.*

He next lists his sufferings according to type: *Up to this very moment we suffer hunger, thirst and nakedness, we are beaten and go homeless, we grow weary with the work of our own hands* (vv.11-12). In all these ways he made obvious his patient endurance, and through what follows the greater maturity of his values. *When reviled we bless, when persecuted we do not resist, when slandered we speak kindly* (vv.12-13). Then he brings out the ultimate indignity: *We have become the world's garbage.* We are no different, he is saying, from what is thrown out in households as superfluous – vegetables, scraps and other things like that; [5] likewise we are reputed by most people to be worthless. *Everyone's rubbish to this very day*, as if to say, I am very grateful. [6] He said this not about the persecutors but about those who welcomed the message. Hence his proceeding, *I am not writing this to make you feel shame; rather, I admonish you as my dearly beloved children* (v.14). He also shows them as his offspring: (260) *After all, if the guardians you have are beyond counting, you still do not have many fathers: I begot you in Christ Jesus through the Gospel* (v.15). He called the other teachers *guardians* but himself *father* for being the first to offer them the evangelical teaching.

I urge you, then, brethren, be imitators of me (v.16), that is, as I am modest, be modest yourselves; what I suffer, suffer yourselves; take pride in the sufferings, not in the gifts. *For this reason I sent you Timothy, my beloved and faithful child in the Lord, who will remind you of my ways in Christ, as I teach them everywhere in every church* (v.17). He showed his affection for them by sending Timothy, and his love for Timothy by calling him *beloved child*; and he revealed the rest of his virtue by saying of him *faithful in the Lord.* He is the one, he is saying, to narrate my exploits, calling the exploits *ways.* Now, he did not say, He will teach, but He will *remind*: the term accuses them of forgetfulness; they had been witnesses of the apostolic virtue. He added that it was also his custom to offer this teaching to all the churches.

Having leveled this charge at them all in general, he then delivers his verdict on the fornicator. *Some people have become puffed up on the supposition I am not coming to you* (v.18). Knowing in advance of his repentance, the divinely-inspired apostle does not mention his name lest it become common knowledge, but speaks in general terms, *some people. But I shall come to you shortly, the Lord willing, and shall get to know not the talk of the puffed up people but their power* (v.19): I am interested not in eloquence but in performance. He goes on to confirm this: *The kingdom of God, after all, is not in talk but in power* (v.20): it is not sufficient for salvation to preach God's kingdom; one must also perform what is worthy of the kingdom. *What do you prefer – that I come to you with a rod, or with love and a spirit of gentleness?* (v.21). He gave them the choice of two, either a spiritual way or a judicial way, calling the process of correction *a rod*; with it he deprived Elymas of sight, remember. [7]

CHAPTER FIVE

There is actually a report of fornication among you (v.1). He brought out sufficiently the enormity of the impropriety; there should have been no such report, he is saying. He also shows the magnitude of the transgression: *such fornication as is not mentioned even among the Gentiles*: what (261) those versed in the teachings of the demons do not commit is committed amongst us. *For someone to take his father's wife.* Even here it is worth admiring the apostolic wisdom: he did not say stepmother, since the term arouses a kind of hostility – instead, *his father's wife*, that is, having the role of a mother, related to his father in the place of his mother, being to his father what his mother was. [1]

And you are puffed up! (v.2): you enjoy a high opinion of yourself for having a sophisticated teaching! *Did you not rather mourn to the extent of having the one guilty of this crime removed from your midst?* He does not legislate for the opposite; he did not say, Why on earth have you not expelled him? He had forbidden them above, remember, to judge the teachers. Instead, his words were, What was the reason that you did not grieve, beseeching God to be rid of this opprobrium?

For my part, though absent in body, I am present in spirit, and have made my judgment as if present (v.3): none of you wants anything else; I forthwith pass sentence *on the one guilty of this crime*. Again he brought out the enormity of the transgression. *In the name of our Lord Jesus Christ, when you are assembled and my spirit is there as well, with the power of our Lord Jesus Christ, hand over such a man to Satan for the destruction of the flesh so that his spirit may be saved on the day of our Lord Jesus Christ* (vv.4-5). He constituted a really terrifying tribunal: first he assembled everyone in the name of the Lord; then he introduced himself as well through the grace of the Spirit; and he showed the Lord seated and delivering the verdict, passing the defendant over to the bailiff and defining his limits so that he would chastise the body only, bringing to the soul a salutary remedy from the chastisement. Now, by *spirit* he refers not to the soul but to the gift of grace; I am doing all these things, he is saying, so that it may be kept safe in him until the coming of our Savior. We learn from this that on those separated from and cut off from the ecclesiastical body the devil makes an assault when finding them to be devoid of grace. [2]

Having cut him away in this fashion, he brings out the reason for so doing. *Your boasting is not commendable: are you not aware that a little yeast leavens the whole batch? So clean out the old yeast so that you may be a new batch, as you are unleavened* (vv.6-7). By *old yeast* he refers to the condition before baptism, from which he bids them be separated and be unleavened, carrying no trace of that condition. Since he had mentioned unleavened bread, and Jews were in the habit of eating unleavened bread at Passover, it was logical for him to go on, *After all, our Passover, Christ, has been sacrificed for us*: we also have a lamb, which is accepted as a sacrifice for us. [3] (264) *And so let us celebrate the festival, not with old yeast, nor with yeast of evil and wickedness, but with the unleavened bread of sincerity and truth* (v.8). He persisted with the metaphor, and showed what is called *yeast*, on the one hand, and on the other *unleavened bread*.

I wrote to you in the letter not to associate with fornicators (v.9). Not in another letter but in this one: [4] a little before he had said, *Are you not aware that a little yeast leavens the whole batch?* Then he brings out the topic on which he had written: *Not in general terms with the fornicators of this world, the avaricious, the rapacious, or idolators – otherwise you would need to take leave of this world altogether* (v.10): I impose no difficult requirement on you; I am not bidding you be completely cut off from those not of the faith, this being tantamount to dispatching you to some other world. [5] *But my written instruction now is for you not to associate* (that is, I have written to you in these terms) *with any one nominally a brother who is a fornicator, avaricious, idolator, loudmouth, drunk, or thief, and not even eat with one such* (v.11): if it is not proper to share ordinary food with such people, certainly not mystical and divine food. [6]

I mean, what business is it of mine to judge those outside as well?

(v.12): I have no authority over them. *Is it not those inside you judge? God will judge those outside* (vv.12-13). Them we leave to God's judgment; it is the others we are required to judge. *You will remove the evil from your midst.*[7] He cited a Mosaic testimony, confirming his words with divine Law.

CHAPTER SIX

Since, however, he had linked the avaricious person to the fornicators, he necessarily inserts instruction about this person as well.[1] *When any of you has a case against another, do you presume to have the case settled before the unrighteous and not before the saints?* (v.1): though you have been accorded divine wisdom, when you have a disagreement with one another you have recourse to judges beset with the handicap of impiety. *Are you not aware that the saints will judge the world?* (v.2). He used *judge* for condemn, as is clear from what follows: *If the world is judged by you, are you unworthy to sit in the lowest courts?* Thus the men of Nineveh and the queen of the south will condemn that generation; thus the twelve apostles will judge the twelve tribes of Israel[2] – that is, condemn them. But they will condemn as being of their company, believing in the Lord, having endured countless forms of death and not abjured faith in him. Likewise in turn those from the Gentiles who believe will condemn those who did not come to believe in the saving message.

Are you not aware that we are to judge angels, not to mention (265) *ordinary cases?* (v.3) Once more he used *judge* to mean *condemn.* By *angels* he means demons, for they were angels once upon a time. The saints will condemn them because, though clad in a body, they had a care for the divine liturgy, whereas those creatures, though naturally bodiless, adopted evil ways.[3] *So if you have ordinary cases, do you appoint as judges people of no account in the church?* (v.4). The person of lowest standing, he is saying, and the least in the church outranks those thought learned among them; in other words, he does not bid those of lowest standing in the church do the judging. This emerges from what follows.

I say this to your shame. There is thus not even one wise man among you capable of deciding between his brothers. Is judgment rather to be made between brother and brother, and this before unbelievers? (vv.5-

6).⁴ He brought out the many absurd features: firstly, that the one who goes to court is a believer (he calls him *brother*); then, that it is with someone of the same faith; and most grievous of all, having recourse to a judge who is actually an unbeliever. It should be understood, of course, that this is not at variance with what was written to the Romans:⁵ he is not bidding them resist the civil authorities, but obliging the wronged not to have recourse to the civil authorities; choosing to put up with the injury or to be examined by their fellow believers depended on their own free will.

Then he introduces the more advanced obligation. *It is therefore already quite a failure on your part that you bring cases against one another* (v.7): litigation in itself is regrettable. *Why not rather put up with the injury? why not rather submit to the loss?* This is a mark of perfection. He presents them, on the contrary, far from not adopting that practice, even doing the direct opposite. *You instead do wrong and inflict loss* (v.8). Then, to top it off, the worst charge: *And brothers at that*: grave as it is to wrong a stranger, much more so one's own.

Are you not aware that the unrighteous will not inherit the kingdom of God? (v.9). Then he lists the other wrongs as well, one by one. *Make no mistake.* He implies some people are saying that God in his lovingkindness does not punish; hence he adds, *Neither fornicators, nor idolators, nor adulterers, nor male prostitutes, nor sodomites, nor avaricious people, nor thieves, nor drunks, nor loudmouths, not robbers will inherit the kingdom of God* (vv.9-10). He joined less serious sins with more serious since his theme was not punishment but kingdom. Lest, however, in remembering the sins before all-holy baptism they despair of salvation, he was obliged to add, (268) *And this is what some of you used to be, but you were washed clean, you were sanctified, you were justified in the name of our Lord Jesus Christ, and in the Spirit of our God* (v.11). He clearly brought out the equality of the Son and the Spirit, and attached a reference to God and the Father: through invocation of the Holy Trinity the nature of water is sanctified and forgiveness of sins provided.⁶

He then in turn resumed attention to fornication in the words, *Are all things lawful for me?* (v.12). It must be read as a question; and then by way of response, *But not all things are beneficial.* Likewise what follows, *Are all things lawful for me? But I will not fall under the power of anything*: you say that you are not living under the Law, that you are independent and have free will; but it is not expedient for you in all circumstances to use that power. I mean, when you perform some unseemly act, you forfeit that power and become a slave to sin. *Food is for the stomach, and the stomach for food, and God will destroy the one and the other* (v.13): if you want to use your freedom in these matters, do so; food was created for the stomach. But you ought to realize that it too will come to an end: after the grave food is superfluous for human beings, and the life to come has nothing of the kind. As there will be no marrying or giving in marriage, remember, in keeping with the Lord's saying,[7] so there will be no eating or drinking. Now, he employed the word *destroy* by way of prophecy. *But the body is meant not for fornication but for the Lord, and the Lord for the body.* He often called the Lord our head; accordingly, the body is linked to him as to a head. In fact, the body was not created for fornication in the way the stomach was made a receptacle for food.

God both raised the Lord, and will raise us up through his power (v.14): do not spurn the Lord as though a corpse; he has been raised, and God who raised him will also raise us with the power of the risen one. In this way he brought out clearly that while he was raised in his humanity, as God he will raise us.

Are you not aware that your bodies are members of Christ? (v.15) Are you not joined to Christ in the manner of bride to bridegroom? *Am I, then, to take the members of Christ and make them members of a prostitute? Far be it!* He greatly heightened the lawlessness by calling our members Christ's members. They are no longer yours, he is saying, but Christ's, so how would you make them members of a prostitute? Then he brings out how this happens. *Are you not aware that the one joined to a prostitute is one body with her? The two shall be one flesh,*[8] *Scripture says, remember, whereas the one joined to the Lord is* (269) *one spirit* (vv.16-17). It was not inappropriate for him to apply what is said of the marriage union to fornication, both former and latter being the same in the kind of action involved; but he brings out the difference between the licit and the illicit. His meaning is, then, In being joined to the prostitute you make your limbs the limbs of a prostitute, whereas in being related to the Lord through the Spirit you make your limbs Christ's limbs. So if you are related to the Lord and then return to her, the injury is done to the Lord himself: you bring his limbs to the prostitute, and you make the Lord's limbs the limbs of a prostitute. [9]

Shun fornication (v.18). He did not say, Hate it and turn away, but *Shun*: knowing the ferocity of this sin he both rouses the one being pursued and urges him to flee the pursuer. He also brings out the loathsomeness of the affair: *Every sin that a person commits is outside the body, whereas the fornicator sins against the body itself*: anyone committing countless other sins – breaking oaths, defiling the tongue with blasphemy, taking what does not belong to one – is not affected by such an experience of sin; but the person who becomes a slave to licentiousness experiences the evil immediately after the sin and loathes the body itself. For this very reason they even have recourse to baths to cleanse the body from top to toe, supposing they can in this way expunge the defilement.

Are you not aware that your body is a temple of the Holy Spirit within you, which you have from God? (v.19). He said above that the body is God's temple, he said it is Christ's limbs; here in turn he calls it temple of the all-holy Spirit. Now, he calls the gift Spirit; in all of this we learn the equality of the Trinity. *And you not aware that you are not your own?* Why? *You were bought at a price* (v.20): the Lord's blood was paid for you, you belong to someone else. He said this to counter the phrase, *All things are lawful for me*, to bring out that we are in service to a master and must live according to his laws, adding in fact, *Glorify God in your body and in your spirit, these belonging to God*: God is creator of our souls and bodies; he not only made them but also freed them from the devil's lordship. It behooves us, therefore, to praise him both through the body and through the soul, doing and saying what prompts the tongues of everyone to benediction.

At this point the apostle completed the first chapter. Mindful of the exhortation, let us present our bodies as a living sacrifice, holy and pleasing to God, [9] and sanctify our soul with the remembrance of his manifold kindnesses, so that in the present life we may truly be styled temples of God and enjoy the promised (272) goods, thanks to the grace and lovingkindness of our Lord Jesus Christ, to whom with the Father and the all-holy Spirit belong glory and magnificence, now and forever, for ages of ages. Amen.

CHAPTER SEVEN

Now, concerning the matters about which you wrote me: It is good for a person not to touch a woman (v.1). He indicated clearly that he was replying to the matters on which they had raised questions. The Corinthians asked whether those who had taken wives by the marriage law and had then received saving baptism should take part in marital intercourse. Accordingly he replies, commending continence, on the one hand, and condemning fornication on the other, but allowing marital relations: after saying, *It is good for a person not to touch a woman,* he added, *On account of cases of fornication let each one have his own wife, and each woman have her own husband* (v.2). He makes the same provision for both husbands and wives, since human nature is one. Now, it was relevant for him to insert *on account of cases of fornication* since he had already leveled charges about that.

The husband is to render his wife the due regard, and likewise the wife the husband (v.3). He is making this requirement in respect of self-control, bidding both husband and wife equally to bear the yoke of marriage, not to look in other directions and destroy the bond, but to direct the due regard to each other. Now, he made this requirement of the husband first, since the husband is head of the wife.[1] Human laws, you know, tell women to be continent, and punish those breaking the law, whereas of husbands they do not require the same continence: men, being makers of the laws, were not concerned for equality, instead granting themselves license.[2]

For his part the divine apostle, by contrast, inspired by divine grace, requires continence of husbands first; but since it happens that husbands or wives in their longing for chastity withdraw from marital intercourse against the wishes of their partners, it was right for him to make a statement on this as well. *The wife does not have the say over her own body; rather, the husband does. And likewise the husband does not have the say over his own body; rather, the wife does* (v.4). Since the marriage law declared them to be one flesh,[3] it was right for him to call the wife's body the husband's, and in turn to put the husband's under the authority of the wife. Here, of course, he raised the law with the wives first, since it is particularly they who before the husbands are in the habit of embracing continence. *Do not deprive one another, except perhaps by agreement for a time so as to devote yourself to fasting and prayer, and then come together again* (v.5). People (273) have the idea they are deprived of what is given unwillingly; so it was very appropriate for him to mention the case of those choosing abstinence without mutual agreement: should the wife alone embrace it, the husband naturally gets upset, since she is abstaining against his will. The wife has the same reaction if the husband should choose the better part; so it was right of him to say, *Do not deprive one another*, and add *except by agreement*, and knowing the weakness of nature to add *for a time*. He also brought out the time in saying, *so as to devote yourself to prayer and fasting*: fasting needs dignifying with holiness. After fasting he recommends intercourse, saying, *and then come together again.* And to bring out that he suspects someone else in making this requirement, he added, *lest Satan put you to the test*; and to show that we are the ones who increase his influence against us, he went on, *owing to your incontinence*: when you are addicted to indifference and choose to be in thrall to pleasure, the devil takes the opportunity of an attack on you.

The fact, however, that he accommodated the laws to human weakness he brought out in what follows. *Now, I say this by way of concession, not command: I would like all people to be as I myself am* (vv.6-7). He both gave a glimpse of the perfection involved in abstinence, and also permitted the lesser way: while his words suggested the remedies appropriate to weakness, he proposed the example for choice of the better part; he put himself forward as an example, compelled to reveal to us the wealth of his own chastity. [4] *But each one has a particular gift from God, one of this kind, another of that.* He gave heart also to the married, calling marriage a *gift from God*: a person helped by that grace also achieves continence in marriage. Grace comes to the assistance of those who contribute the proper enthusiasm; Scripture says, remember, "Ask and it will be given to you, seek and you will find." [5]

Having replied to the Corinthians' questions and stated his requirements for what is proper for the married, he writes also for those who have not yet taken on the yoke of marriage, and for those who have taken it on but have then been parted by death and are bewailing their widowhood, as he needed to do. *Now, I say to the unmarried and to the widows: it is good for them to remain as I am* (v.8). Once again he showed himself to be in the company of the unmarried: it would not be right for anyone to place him among the widowed, since he was still young when he was given his vocation. On the other hand, let no one think that he requires celibacy of men but continence only of women after marriage: (276) he recommends both to each sex. ⁶ *But if they are not practicing continence, let them marry: it is better for them to marry than to burn* (v.9). By *burning* he refers not to the turmoil of passion but the slavery of the soul and the tendency to lower things. What he means is something like this: It is better both for you who have not yet had a taste of marital intercourse and for you who have been joined in marriage but separated by death to opt for abstinence; but if you cannot bear the onset of passion, and instead are in a weak condition of soul before this contest, lacking an ardent zeal for good, no law keeps you from marrying.

At this point he moves to a different requirement. *Now, to the married I give this direction – not I, but the Lord – for a wife not to be separated from her husband. But even if she is separated, she is to remain unmarried, or be reconciled to her husband. And a husband is not to dismiss his wife* (vv.10-11). He recalled the evangelical law; the Lord said in the sacred Gospels, remember, "Anyone who divorces his wife, except on the grounds of unchastity, causes her to commit adultery" ⁷ – hence his adding, *not I, but the Lord.* Now, the direction, *she is to remain unmarried, or be reconciled to her husband,* is not inconsistent with the direction, *do not deprive one another, except by agreement*: that was said to those separated for no other reason than abstinence alone, whereas in this case he counsels those at odds with their partner over other matters. And while he is trying to keep the marriage bond intact, he makes allowances for human weakness but recommends abstinence to the separated and thus forbids dissolution of the marriage. In fact, he opposes a union with another partner, and pressures each party to return to the former marriage.

Now, to the rest I say – I, not the Lord (v.12). The phrase *I say* means, I did not find this law written in the sacred Gospels: I am imposing it now. That the apostle's laws are laws of Christ the Lord, however, is clear to those versed in divine matters: such are his own words, "Do you require proof that Christ is speaking in me?"

and "Not I, but the grace of God in me," and "By the grace given me I say."[8] Likewise here, too, he imposes a law with the all-holy Spirit speaking through him. *If a brother has an unbelieving wife, and she is happy to live with him, he is not to dismiss her. If a woman has an unbelieving husband, and he is happy to live with her, she is not to dismiss him: the unbelieving husband has been sanctified by his wife, and* (277) *the unbelieving wife has been sanctified by her husband. Otherwise your children would be unclean, but as it is they are holy* (vv.12-14). He is not requiring anyone to take an unbeliever as a wife, nor bidding a believer be joined in marriage with an unbelieving husband: he is saying the direct opposite; shortly afterwards, note, he added the requirement of widows *only in the Lord,*[9] that is, to a believing, pious man, of modest and discreet life. Here, on the contrary, he spoke of those joined in marriage before Christian teaching. That is to say, take the case where the husband came to faith while the wife persisted in unbelief, or conversely the wife accepted the teaching while the husband was caught up in the defilement of unbelief. He recommends the healthy put up with the ailment of their partners, and be busy about saving them, saying, *The unbelieving husband has been sanctified by his wife, and the unbelieving wife has been sanctified by her husband,* that is, has a hope of being saved. If, however, he or she persists in the ailment, their offspring will have the chance of being saved. Now, he employed a degree of exaggeration in this so as to persuade them not to abandon the union.[10]

If, however, the unbeliever goes off, let them go: the brother or the sister is under no obligation in such cases (v.15). Let the believing partner, he is saying, give no occasion for the separation; but if the ailing one wants to take their leave, you are innocent and are free of blame: *God has called you to peace.* The Lord actually said, "I came to cast not peace on the earth but a sword, to divide a person from their neighbor;"[11] but the one saying is not at odds with the other. The apostle interprets the Lord's teaching: the saving message (he is saying) does not bring confusion to life; rather, it achieves true peace that is pleasing to God. First of all, however, it sunders a concord that is evil,[12] and with the discord achieves a harmony that is commendable: those who welcome the divine message are turned into teachers of the non-believers and in marvelous fashion produce the remarkable transformation, guiding households that were divided to a desirable harmony.

At this point he says as much: *After all, for all you know, wife, you may save your husband; and for all you know, husband, you may save your wife, depending on God's allotment to each* (vv.16-17). Make the effort involved, he is saying, in good spirits: you have God as an aid to your zeal. *Let each one walk in the way God has called: this is my ruling in all the churches.* Here he taught clearly that he was not recommending a union with unbelieving husbands and wives, but was determining these matters for those called in this way. He then as usual moved from the foregoing to other matters, making suitable provision for everyone. *Was anyone circumcised called? Let him not undo his circumcision. Was anyone uncircumcised called? Let him not be circumcised. Circumcision means nothing, and uncircumcision means nothing – only performance of God's commandments* (vv.18-19): let no one who is called while uncircumcised accept circumcision, nor anyone circumcised give the appearance of being uncircumcised: (280) uncircumcision is from nature, and circumcision is practiced in keeping with the Law; yet it is not the fact but the observance of the divine commandment that is commendable.[13] *Let each one remain faithful to the condition in which you were called* (v.20).

He then moved on to other matters. *Were you a slave when called? Let this not worry you. But even if you can become free, make the most of it instead* (v.21): grace recognizes no difference between slavery and lordship. So do not shun slavery as unworthy of the faith; rather, even if it is possible for you to attain your freedom, remain in service,[14] and look for reward. Now, it was not without purpose that he had recourse to this exaggeration, but in his concern lest slavery be shunned on the grounds of religion. But he also offers further encouragement. *After all, the one called in the Lord as a slave is a free person belonging to the Lord; likewise the one called as a free person is a slave of Christ* (v.22). We usually refer to someone freed from slavery as emancipated. This is the term he used of a slave granted the gift of faith; and he said the free person is *a slave of Christ*, the slave emancipated, teaching the free that they have Christ as lord, and the slaves likewise, that they enjoyed true freedom. After all, who is so free as the person rid of sin? And who suffers such harsh servitude as the one subject to the slavery of the passions?

You were bought with a price: do not become slaves of human beings (v.23). His requirement was not inconsistent with what had been said. He bade them not to have the attitude befitting a slave, neither the one called slave nor the one known as a free person. He also very clearly represented the slaves and the masters as fellow slaves, saying to the one group and the other, *you were bought with a price*: the Lord acquired us by giving his own blood. *Let each of you remain before God in the condition in which you were called* (v.24). This phrase he used as both introduction and conclusion of the exhortation. He moves on in turn to a different requirement.

Now, in regard to the virgins I have no command from the Lord (v.25). The Lord, remember, when the apostles said, "If the law about wives is like this, it is better not to marry," replied, "Not everyone will accept this teaching," and again, "Let the one accept it who can." [15] This is the very reason the divine apostle also said, *I have no command from the Lord*. So if you have no law, what is the force of your statement? *Instead, I give my opinion*: I am not laying down the law but offering advice. God, remember, after legislating for what is in keeping with nature, recommends what is over and above nature. Since, however, it was likely some people opposed the advice as a novelty, he added, *as one who by the Lord's mercy is trustworthy*. (281) He let his apostolic ranking emerge with customary modesty. I am a trustworthy adviser, he is saying, on account of the Lord's great mercy and as one entrusted with the good news. Now, what is your advice? *I consider, then, that this is good for one, in view of the present necessity, to remain as you are. Are you bound to a wife? Do not look for release. Are you free of a wife? Do not look for a wife* (vv.26-27). He used *I consider*, not out of uncertainty as to whether virginity is a good and the highest of goods. Rather, in case the exhortation should be turned into a law, he introduced a note of uncertainty; on law follows observance and transgression, after all, and punishment of the transgressors. Hence he does not make high ideals an obligation, but recommends them, and after saying *Do not look for a wife*, he went on to say, *But if you marry, you do not sin; and if a virgin marries, she does not sin* (v.28). Why on earth do you give the advice not to marry if in fact marriage is free of sin? [16] *But such people will experience tribulation in the flesh.* And why does that concern you? *I would spare you that.* He betrayed his fatherly affection, and showed the advantage of the unmarried state. Of course, we must realize that it was not in regard to those who had once and for all taken leave of this life that he said, *if you marry, you do not sin; and if a virgin marries, she does not sin;*[17] rather, it was in regard to those who had to that point not made a choice of one state or the other, but were in the middle ground between the married and the unmarried state.

He then confirms his point from another direction as well. *Now, I say this, brethren: the time left is short* (v.29): life is moving to its end; the consummation of the present age is near at hand. *So that even those with wives should be as though they had none, those who weep as though not weeping, those rejoicing as though not rejoicing, those buying as though destitute, and those dealing with the world as though having no improper dealings* (vv.30-31). Present realities are foreign to us, he is saying: we move on from here as quickly as possible;[18] accordingly, let no one lament poverty or set great store by riches, nor let those with a great number of possessions waste them on luxury and prodigality, but reap only benefit from them. This, in fact, is what he means by *and those dealing with the world as though having no improper dealings.* In Ezekiel also, God brought this charge against the rams, that they fed on the good pasture and treaded down the remainder with their feet, drank the clear water and muddied the rest with their feet;[19] the verse, *and those dealing with the world as though having no improper dealings,* is in harmony with that. Then, to show the impermanence of present realities, he went on, *After all, the form of this world is passing away*: there is no longer farming and navigation, no longer kingdoms and empires, no longer slavery and lordship, no longer crafts and disciplines, no longer poverty and riches: of these and other such the present life (284) is composed. Blessed Isaiah also said as much in prophesying future realities: "The slave will be like his master, the servant girl like her mistress, the buyer like the seller, the debtor like the one not in debt."[20]

The future life, in fact, has further differences; but the divine apostle went on, *I want you to be free of anxieties* (v.32). He showed clearly the purpose of virginity: the person practicing virginity has a soul free of idle and pointless concerns, and reproduces the future life as far as possible; he said as much in what follows. *The unmarried man is concerned with the Lord's affairs, how to please the Lord, whereas the married man is concerned with the affairs of the world, how to please his wife. The wife is also divided; the virgin in being unmarried is concerned with the Lord's affairs so as to be holy in both body and spirit, whereas the married woman is concerned with the affairs of the world, how to please her husband* (vv.32-34). [21] He briefly brought out the difference in attitude between the person choosing the yoke of marriage and the one embracing the unmarried state. It is easy to learn, if you want, the hardships and cares of those involved in this life; and we have demonstrated these at greater length in composing the treatises *On Virginity* and recommending the lovers of good to the riches involved in it.

Continuing with his advice, the divine apostle added this as well: *Now, I say this for your very own benefit, not to put a restraint upon you but to promote seemly and unhindered devotion to the Lord* (v.35). It is not under pressure, he is saying, that I lead you to these riches, as though employing a net and snaring you by force; rather, I am giving a glimpse of the benefit stemming from them. In fact, there is no other possible way for us to attend regularly to the worship of God than avoiding the shackles of this life. [22]

Now, if someone thinks he is behaving badly towards his virgin, if his passions are strong, and this is the way it must be, let him do as he wishes – he is not committing sin – let them marry (v.36): let the one who believes her celibate state to be unseemly, and for this reason wants to join his daughter in marriage with a husband, do what he decides: marriage is free of sin. Here once again his directions were in regard to those who had not yet chosen virginity. *But if someone stands firm in his resolve, is under no pressure, has control of his own desires and has decided in his heart to keep his virgin as she is, his action is reputable* (v.37). The phrase *is under no pressure* means being independent, not subject to an overlord. (285) *And so the action of the one who marries her off is reputable, and the action of the one who does not is even better* (v.38). He brought out the good in one case and the better in the other, and stopped the mouths of the heretics who malign marriage. [23]

He also thought it necessary to offer sound advice to widows. *A wife is bound by law for as long as her husband is alive; but if he is dead, she is free to marry whomever she likes, as long as it is in the Lord* (v.39)

– that is, to someone who is a fellow believer, religious, chastely, lawfully. *She is more blessed, however, if she remains as she is, in my view* (v.40). Once again, instead of citing a law, he offered advice. To make it creditable he went on, *I think I also have the Spirit of God.* The words are not mine, he is saying: they are from the grace of the all-holy Spirit; I am its instrument. It ought be noted, of course, that the woman remaining unmarried was not simply to be called blessed; instead, he called her *more blessed* to bring out that the one entering into a second marriage was not wretched but blessed in taking advantage of the apostle's law to marry: comparison made it clear she, too, was blessed. This was also adequate refutation of the followers of Novatian, who condemned a second marriage as fornication in open contradiction of the apostolic laws. [24]

CHAPTER EIGHT

After writing this in the wake of the first accusation and giving advice relevant both to marriage and celibacy and, of course, to widowhood and virginity, he goes on to deal with a second accusation, which I must preface with a summary of its argument. Some of those in Corinth who were perhaps believers and who had some acquaintances and familiars involved in error, were in the custom of having meals with them in the temples of idols, partaking of what was set before them as though it was not really sacrificed to idols, and on the basis of a conviction that it was all of God's making. To those who had not yet attained that knowledge, however, this practice on their part caused great harm: on seeing those who partook of the food sacrificed to idols doing so with no qualms, they were encouraged to do the same, and the fault became more serious. You see, the latter partook of it with a different intention from the others: they ate it as though sacrificed to idols, not enjoying the knowledge of the others. On learning this, the divine apostle condemns what was happening, and offers a range of remedies for the ailment.

Now, in connection with food sacrificed to idols, we are aware that we all have knowledge (v.1). It was with a degree of irony that he attributed knowledge to them: the fact that he did not really mean they had knowledge he brings out later, when he says, *If anyone thinks they know something, they do not yet know anything they ought to know.*

So having said, *We are aware that we all have knowledge,* he then goes on, *Knowledge puffs up, whereas love builds up*: love is more powerful than knowledge. (287) The former often makes conceited those not using it well, whereas the latter has a concern for the neighbor's benefit – hence his statement, *it builds up.* Now, his charge is directed at them for being bereft of love: if they possessed it, they would have a care for the welfare of the weaker members.

If anyone thinks they know something, they do not yet know anything they ought to know (v.2). He showed they were not only bereft of love but also deprived of the knowledge on which they prided themselves. Now, he makes the charge indiscriminately, preferring to heal rather than wound. *But if anyone loves God, they are known by him* (v.3): we need much knowledge, and it is impossible for us to attain it in its perfection in this life; let us therefore love God so as to enjoy providence on his part. He expressed this, note, with great precision: he did not say, The one who loves God knows him, but *is known by him,* that is, enjoys providence on his part. Likewise the blessed Moses also said to the God of all in person, "You told me, You found grace with me, and I know you beyond all others." [1] So the phrase *they are known by him* indicates God's greater care.

About the eating of food sacrificed to idols, then, we are aware that no idol in the world exists, and that there is no other God but one (v.4). I am aware, he is saying, what you are in the habit of saying: you learned it from me. I am aware that idols lack life and feeling, and that the one God of all is maker and Lord. *I mean, even if there are so-called gods, whether in heaven or on earth, as there are many gods and many lords* (v.5). The divine apostle intends to develop a further argument. Since he had said *there is no other God but one,* had also proclaimed Christ as God, and likewise listed the all-holy Spirit with Father and Son, there was uncertainty on the part of those who had not to that point acquired a precise understanding of the doctrine, doctrine of how God is one when the Son of God and of course the all-holy Spirit as well are listed with him. So from the adversaries' arguments he develops his own, and brings out the fact that Greeks, on the one hand, say that there are many gods, and on the other they call them also lords. These, however, have no existence of any kind, but are known by their names only: he said, note, *even if there are so-called gods, whether in heaven or on earth, as there are many gods and many lords*, being called by them both gods and lords. Now, the phrase, *whether in heaven or on earth*, he gets from Greeks' mythology: they gave the gods of heaven names, such as Zeus, Apollo, Hera and Athena, and (289) gods of earth, like springs and rivers and the so-called nymphs, and Heracles, Dionysus, Asclepius and countless others.

For us, however, there is one God the Father, from whom come all things and for whom we exist, and one Lord Jesus Christ, through whom all things come and through whom we exist (v.6). So, whereas they, beset by the gloom of ignorance, have erroneous ideas about many gods, even though they do not exist, we know one God the Father and one Jesus Christ. Now, the apostolic wisdom is worth admiring here, too: having shown in his previous remarks the title *Lord* to have the same force as the title *God*, he distinguished between them, assigning one to the Father and one to the Son, thus healing the Corinthians' failing. I mean, it is easy for any interested person to learn from his writings that he often calls the Son God: "Awaiting the coming of the glory of our great God and Savior Jesus Christ,"[2] and "From them the Christ according to the flesh, who is God over all, and in the kingdom of the God Christ,"[3] and countless other similar texts. Here, of course, he called one *God* and the other *Lord* so as not to give an occasion of reverting to the error of polytheism to those lately freed from the Greek error and learning the truth in its place.

If, however, the followers of Arius and Eunomius were to claim that the phrase *one God* excludes the Son from the Father's divinity, let them listen to what follows, *and one Lord*: if the Father alone is God, and the Son not God, neither then is the Father Lord since there is *one Lord Jesus Christ*. But let the blasphemy fall back on their own head: the divine apostle brings out the equality, applying *one* similarly to Father and to Son, and revealing the word *Lord* to have equal force with *God*. In like fashion the Old Testament also shows these titles combined: "I am the Lord your God, who brought you out of the land of Egypt," and "Listen, Israel, the Lord your God is one Lord," and "O Lord my God, you are exceedingly magnified,"[4] and countless similar texts. Therefore, the one who is God is also altogether Lord, and the one who is Lord is also altogether God. Neither is it the case that the Father is God in a different fashion: *there is one God the Father*, remember; nor is Jesus Christ Lord in a different fashion: *there is one Lord Jesus Christ*, remember. Now, the phrase *we exist for him* means, We ought be directed to him, have regard for him, constantly sing his praises; and the phrase *and through him we exist* refers not to creation but to salvation: while *all things come through him*, we who believe have attained salvation through him.[5]

The knowledge, however, is not in everyone (v.7). Not everyone knows this, he is saying. From this it is clear that what he said before, *We are aware that we all have knowledge*, was said ironically. *Some people through their awareness of the idol up to now* (292) *eat the food as sacrificed to idols, and their conscience, weak as it is, is stained* (v.7).[6] It is not the food that defiles it: the conscience is defiled through not receiving mature knowledge and being still in the grip of the idols' deception. *Food does not bring us close to God: there is no gain for us if we eat, and no loss if we do not eat* (v.8). Those priding themselves on their knowledge he warns against taking this as worship of God in treating the idols with scorn, partaking indiscriminately of food sacrificed to idols and scorning the weakness of those harmed by it.

What follows, in fact, indicates as much: *But be careful lest this freedom of spirit of yours prove a stumbling block for the weak* (v.9). He also brings out the manner of this harm: *I mean, if someone sees you with your knowledge eating in an idol's temple, is not their conscience in their weakness reinforced in eating food sacrificed to idols?* (v.10). He gave a glimpse of the enormity. *By your knowledge the brother who is weak and for whom Christ died will perish* (v.11). He exaggerated the accusation so as to bring the abuse to an end. Christ accepted death for the sake of this brother whom you scorn, he is saying, whereas you, after receiving the knowledge from Christ, use that gift to destroy the one saved by him. Once again, of course, he referred to the knowledge ironically: it is not his knowledge that he is touching on but his scorn of his brother, his gluttony and such like vices.

In sinning against your brethren in this way, and smiting their weakened conscience, you sin against Christ (v.12). It is the saying of the Lord himself, after all: "See that you scorn not one of these, the least of those who believe in me."[7] The verse touches on something else as well, that even the brother in his weakness belongs to the body of the Lord: he shares in the Lord's body, and the head makes his own the injustice done to the member. Then he proposes himself as an example of doing good, and brings out what he has refrained from doing on account of others' benefit, though capable of doing it. *Hence if eating causes the brother to stumble, I will never eat meat again lest I cause my brother to stumble* (v.13): I would choose to abstain not only from food sacrificed to idols but also all other meat, not only now but even forever, for the sake of the salvation of the brethren.

CHAPTER NINE

Am I not an apostle – that is, receiving my commission from God? *Am I not free?* (v.1), meaning, I am not exercising the authority of someone else, or discharging the role of a disciple: the world (293) has been entrusted to me. Since it was only after the Savior's assumption that he was called, and since the apostles ranked highest in the estimation of everyone for being accorded the vision of the Lord, he had to insert that as well: *Have I not seen Jesus Christ our Lord?*. Then he calls them, too, to witness: *Are you not my work in the Lord?* He says the same thing at greater length: *If I am not an apostle to others, at least I am to you* (v.2) While he put it briefly, he implied much in the one breath – the hardships involved in teaching, the struggles for its sake, the sufferings of all kinds, the miracles of grace of which the Corinthians were reliable witnesses, being observers of them. This was surely the reason he said, *If I am not an apostle to others, at least I am to you*: even if I have no one as a witness, your testimony is enough for me. *After all, you are the seal of my apostleship in the Lord*: I have your transformation as proof of my apostolic endeavors (calling the proof and the confirmation *seal*). Likewise the divinely-inspired John also said, "Whoever accepted his testimony set a seal on it – that is, confirmed it – that God is true."[1]

This is my defense to those who examine me (v.3): if anyone wants to examine my efforts, I shall call you to witness; your work suffices for testimony to my efforts. *Do we not have the right to eat and drink? do we not have the right to be accompanied by a believing wife, like the other apostles, the brethren of the Lord, and Cephas?* (v v.4-5). He means *eat and drink* from the Gospel; he wants to show that though in a position to receive his necessary upkeep from the disciples in accordance with the Lord's law, he continues working at his job and earning his necessary upkeep by his own efforts with a view to the welfare of the disciples. Now, some took the phrase *to be accompanied by a believing wife* to mean that just as women believers followed the Lord to provide necessary support to the disciples, so some accompanied some of the apostles to demonstrate a more ardent faith, hanging on their teaching and assisting the divine proclamation. [2]

Or is it only Barnabas and I who have no right not to work? (v.6). In other words, the Lord permitted those proclaiming the Gospel to live from the Gospel, and is it we alone who are deprived of the right? Then he shows this is both fair and necessary from secular practices as well. *Who at any time serves in the army at his own expense? who plants a vineyard and does not eat any of its fruit? who tends a flock and does not drink any of the flock's milk?* (v.7) Having thus shown (296) the serviceman fed from his service, the vinedresser partaking of the fruit and the shepherd earning his food from the milk of the animals, he went on: *Surely I do not say this on human authority? Does not the Law also say as much? In the Law of Moses it is written, remember* (vv.8-9). If this strikes anyone as human reasoning, let them listen to the Law declaring clearly, *You shall not muzzle the ox treading the grain.* [3] *Surely it is not for oxen God is concerned? Or does he not speak altogether for our sake? It was in fact written for our sake, because whoever plows should plows with expectations, and whoever threshes with expectations should obtain their expectations* (vv.9-10). He does not mean that God is not concerned for the oxen: he is concerned, but his concern is on our account; he also created them on our account. This is the reason blessed David also said, "He produces hay and grass on hills for the service of human beings." [4]

If we have sown spiritual things among you, is it a matter of great moment if we reap your material things? (v.11) are we in the wrong if after giving far greater things we receive far lesser things? *If others share this right with you, should not we with greater reason?* (v.12) In this he referred to those giving them poor leadership. *Instead of invoking this right, however, we put up with all hardships* – that is, we bear, endure, tolerate. Why? *So as not to put any obstacle in the way of the Gospel of Christ.* It was very appropriate for him to call the harm an *obstacle*: it does not allow the Gospel to take its course (he is saying), it impedes its progress, it hinders the salvation coming through the preaching.

Then, since he had mentioned oxen and commented on the Law, it was right for him to take issue with the charge of some people that the commentary had not been properly done. He shows more clearly the Law testifying to his thought. *Are you not aware that those who work in the temple get their food from the temple, and those who share at the altar get portions from the altar?* (v.13). Consider those serving according to the Law, offering some things at the altar and taking the benefit of other things themselves. This is what he implied, note, with *getting portions from the altar*: they placed on the altar as offerings the kidneys, the lobe of the liver and the fat in them, whereas they kept for themselves the right arm and the breast.[5] He shows the Lord had also commanded what was in keeping with the Law: *Likewise the Lord also directed those proclaiming the Gospel to live from the Gospel* (v.14). It is his own words, after all: "The laborer deserves his wages."[6] He did not say to grow rich on the Gospel but *to live*: his orders were to take only necessary sustenance. (297)

But I have invoked none of these rights (v.15), namely, by preaching among you. He says as much, remember, also in the second letter, "In what respect have you been worse off than the other churches, especially since I was no burden on you?" That is, the fact that he took from others whom he thought he was helping by accepting he teaches also in what follows: "I robbed other churches by taking a stipend with a view to serving you."[7] Likewise he also commends the Philippians frequently for attentively caring for him;[8] this is also the reason he prays for good things for Onesiphorus.[9] Understanding the Corinthians' weakness, however, he continued working, taking nothing from them; but in case any of them form the impression he had said this as though looking to receive something, he was right to add, *I did not write this so that some benefit might come to me from it: I would rather die than have anyone rob me of my boasting.* By *boasting* he means preaching gratis and surpassing the limit set.

After all, even if I preach the Gospel, that is no grounds for boasting: I am under necessity (v.16): I carry out this service as a slave to the

Lord; and no servant is conceited over discharging directions from the master. *Woe to me if I do not preach the Gospel*: to oppose the Lord is deserving of retribution. *I mean, if I do this on my own initiative, I have a reward, but if not on my own initiative, I am entrusted with a commission* (v.17). He used *on my own initiative* and *not on my own initiative* not in reference to free will but to bring out that he was fulfilling a law of the Lord. *So what is my reward? that in preaching the Gospel I bring the Gospel of Christ free of charge so as to forfeit my rights in the Gospel* (v.18). The Lord gave me the right, he is saying, to receive my necessary upkeep from the disciples, but I do not invoke this right; instead, I make a contribution of my hard work so as to reap the benefit of my effort.

He treated of all these matters [10] – those exploiting their knowledge to ill effect, heedlessly partaking of food sacrificed to idols, giving an occasion of harm to the weaker ones – in an attempt to get them to desist from their unfortunate exercise of power. This was the reason he showed that, though receiving his right from the law and from the God of all, seeing the apostles invoking it and heeding the very nature of things, he refrained from using any such rights in his concern for one thing only, the progress of the message and the benefit of the listeners. What follows is also in harmony with this. *Being under no obligation to anyone, I have put myself in the service of everyone so as to win over more of them* (v.19). He means the freedom given by grace; and he brings out more clearly what he means by *service*. *To the Jews I became like a Jew* (300) *so as to win over Jews; to those under the Law like one under the Law so as to win over those under the Law* (v.20). By *Jews*, in my opinion, he is referring to those not yet believers, and *under the Law* to those who have received the Gospel but are still bound to the observance of the Law: on account of the one group and the other, to be sure, he underwent in Jerusalem the purification prescribed by the Law, in Lycaonia he circumcised Timothy, [11] and made countless other similar arrangements. *To those without the Law I became like one without the Law (though not without God's law, being under the law of Christ) so as to win over those without the Law* (v.21). By *without the Law* he refers to those living outside the Law. Now, you can notice his varied arrangements, not only in his own writings, but also in the Acts of the Apostles: he spoke one way in the synagogues of the

Jews, and proposed his teaching in a different way in the Areopagus, offering remedies befitting each ailment. [12]

To the weak I became like a weak person so as to win over the weak (v.22). Thus in writing also to the Romans he said, "We who are strong ought put up with the failings of the weak." [13] Now, we need to grasp precisely the meaning of what is said: he was not, as some claimed in criticizing the divine apostle, changing his position to suit the occasion; rather, he made every effort for the benefit of all. He says as much, in fact, *to win over the Jews, to win over those under the Law, to win over those without the Law, to win over the weak;* and then by way of summary, *I became all things to all people so as by every means to save some,* knowing that not all would come to share in salvation, yet making every effort for the sake of a single one. *I do it all for the sake of the Gospel so that I may be a sharer in it* (v.25): the purpose of the Gospel is the salvation of human beings; this was the reason the Lord ate even with tax collectors and acceded to the sinful woman's weeping and wailing at his feet. [14]

Then he says that the effort of those preaching the Gospel is like those exercising the body, whereas the crown does not resemble that, surpassing it incomparably. *Are you not aware that in a race all run but one gets the prize? Run in such a way as to lay hold of it* (v.24): in that situation many compete, one alone is acclaimed, whereas in this case each of those competing well is rewarded with acclamation. *Now, all competitors discipline themselves in every way* (v.25), so consider the efforts of those people: instead of partaking of anything they feel like, they sample that food which the trainer provides. Having shown the effort, then, he gives evidence of the difference in crowns: *So while they do it to receive a perishable crown, we an imperishable one.* (301) And he puts himself forward as the example. *Consequently I do not run aimlessly, I am not like a boxer beating the air* (v.26): I see good things as an object of hope, my crown is not obscure nor am I shadow-boxing to no effect; instead, I land a blow on the invisible adversaries. He employed this expression by way of metaphor from the pugilists: in training they flay the air with their hands. [15] Now, what kind of blow is that? *Instead, I punish my body and keep it under in case it should happen that after preaching to others I fail to make the grade* (v.27); as diet makes the athlete energetic, so training and discipline give me strength and repel my adversary. Now, I take these means in fear and dread of completely missing the mark of the contests after teaching others their obligations.

CHAPTER TEN

Then, in his wish to make them more apprehensive, he reminds them of what happened to Israel, the extent of the good things they enjoyed and the punishments that befell them; and he referred to them as types of these things so as to emphasize that they would suffer a similar fate if guilty of a similar infidelity. *Now, I do not want you to be unaware, brethren, that our ancestors were all under the cloud, all passed through the sea, all accepted baptism into Moses in the cloud and in the sea, all ate the same spiritual food and all drank the same spiritual drink* (vv.1-4). These events, he is saying, are a type of ours: the sea resembled the font, the cloud the grace of the Spirit, Moses the priest, the rod the cross, Israel suggesting the baptized, while the Egyptians in pursuit acted as a type of the demons and Pharaoh in person was an image of the devil; after the crossing, you see, the Israelites were freed from the power of the Egyptians, as in a type they also received manna from heaven. The rock also resembled the Lord's side: streams sprang up for them unexpectedly, as he brings out more clearly, *They drank from a spiritual rock that followed them, remember; the rock was Christ.* Now, his meaning is that for them it was not the rock but divine grace which ensured that that rock unexpectedly gushed floods: if the rock followed them, or water from the rock, how did they need water ever again? [1] *With most of them, however, God was not well pleased: they were laid low in the wilderness* (v.5). Apart from Caleb and Joshua son of Nun, all those listed were consumed.

After thus showing all had enjoyed the favors, and on the other hand most had gained nothing from the divine gifts but had paid the penalty for disobedience, he went on, *Now, these things were done as types for us* (304) *lest we hanker after evil as they also did. Do not turn idolators like some of them, as it is written, The people sat down to eat and drink, and got up to play.* [2] *Let us not commit fornication as some of them committed fornication, and on one day twenty three thousand fell. Let us not try the Lord, as some of them also tried him and were destroyed by serpents. Do not murmur as some of them murmured, and were destroyed by the exterminator*[3] (vv.6-10). He cited each of the texts as bearing on the Corinthians' failings: firstly, evil desire, in which most evils find their source; then idolatry and gluttony, through which it grows: slaves to gluttony they feasted in the temples of the idols. He made mention also of fornication and mentioned the number of those destroyed on account of it,[4] instilling the dread of retribution in the mind of the fornicator. Those also were murmuring who had been granted the lesser charisms, having not been granted all of them. As well, those using the different tongues were trying, displaying these in church for notoriety rather than utility.

Now, all of these things happened to them as types (v.11), that is, as types:[5] in them our situation is recorded. *They were written down as an admonition to us, on whom the ends of the ages have come*: it was not for the sake of usefulness to them that God caused them to be put into writing; after all, what advantage could the dead derive from the written accounts? Rather, it was out of concern for the benefit deriving from them for us. Now, it was good for him to insert a mention of the end of the age, to urge and prompt them to practice of virtue. *So let the one seeming to stand firm be careful not to fall* (v.12) – that is, you who suppose you have knowledge. Since they too had suffered much abuse and contumely, and it was likely they were conceited even on that account, he went on, *No trial has overtaken you beyond what is human* (v.13), that is, insignificant: the divine apostle normally applies the term to what is insignificant, as when he says, "Owing to the weakness of your flesh I speak in human terms"[6] – that is, accommodated to your nature. *God is faithful and will not allow you to be tested beyond your power; instead, with the trial he will also provide the way out for you to succeed in enduring it*. He taught them not to trust in themselves but to ask for divine assistance.

After discoursing on all this, he returned to the previous chapter. (305) *Hence, my dearly beloved, flee from the worship of idols* (v.14). In turn he raises the level of accusation, and shows that the indiscriminate partaking of food sacrificed to idols in no way differs from the worship of idols. *I speak to you as to sensible people* (v.15). He delivers the censure along with commendation, concerned that with praise it be acceptable. *Judge for yourselves what I say*: I appeal

The First Letter to the Corinthians ❖ 201

to you as judges, aware of your good sense.

The cup of blessing which we bless – is it not a sharing in the blood of Christ? The bread we break – is it not a sharing in the body of Christ? Because there is one bread, we though many are one body: we all partake of the one loaf (vv.16-17). Enjoying the sacred sacraments, do we not have a share in the Lord himself (whose body and blood we claim they are) [7] since we all partake of the one loaf? He then reinforces the point from a different angle. *Consider Israel according to the flesh: are not those who eat the sacrifices sharers at the altar?* (v.18). Have regard also to Israel, and learn that those partaking of the victims are sharers at the altar since from the one victim they make the offering at that spot while also eating it in person. By *Israel according to the flesh* he referred to the one persisting in unbelief, the believers being styled Israel of the spirit.

So what am I claiming – that an idol is anything, or food sacrificed to idols is anything? No, I claim that what the pagans sacrifice they sacrifice to demons, not to God (vv.19-20): let no one think, however, that I am saying that food sacrificed to idols has any force and by natural power can defile the one partaking. That in fact is not what I say, but that those in thrall to superstition offer the sacrifices to the demons. *I do not want you to be sharers with the demons.* Then he instils greater dread: *You cannot drink the cup of the Lord and a cup of demons* (v.21). They were in the habit of tasting the libations, you see. *You cannot partake of the table of the Lord and a table of demons*: how can you share both in the Lord through his precious body and blood and in turn in the demons through the food sacrificed to idols? *Or are we provoking the Lord? surely we are not stronger than he?* (v.22). He used *provoking* in the sense of irritating. He reminded them also of the divine saying directed to Israel, "They provoked me with what is no god, they angered me with their idols." [8]

Are not all things lawful for me? (v.23) It should be read as a question; then in reply, *But not all things are beneficial.* (308) *Are not all things lawful for me?* And this likewise, *But not all things build up*: it is lawful for you to do everything on account of the knowledge you claim to have, but harming others is not beneficial to you nor does what is done by you build them up. You are mature, you object; but you should also have a care for the weaker ones. He added this, in fact, *Let no one seek their own advantage; instead, let each seek the advantage of the other* (v.24).

Since he had absolutely forbidden partaking of the foods sacrificed to idols, and yet at that time the cities were full of that kind of meat, it was likely that some people made an effort for the apostolic law and never bought meat, and others out of gluttony spurned the law. So he had to legislate for what was appropriate in this case, too. *Eat what is sold in the meat market without being inquisitive on the grounds of conscience: the land and its fullness belong to the Lord* [9] (vv.25-26): all are God's creatures, he it was who brought all into being; so buy without scruple, not inquiring whether it is food sacrificed to idols or not (the meaning of *being inquisitive*). *If one of the unbelievers invites you to dinner and you want to go, eat everything set before you without being inquisitive on the grounds of conscience* (v.27). He did not bid the one invited to go, nor did he forbid it: he left to the independence of those invited what should be done. It would not have been possible, either, for the unbelievers to be snared if intermingling was outlawed. [10]

But if someone says to you, This food has been sacrificed to idols, out of consideration for the one who brought it to your notice and their conscience do not eat it: the land and its fullness belong to the Lord (v.28). He cited this in connection both with eating and with not eating to bring out the fact that those who partake should be aware that all things are God's creatures, and those in turn who do not eat should also be convinced of it. [11] *By conscience I mean not your own but the other person's* (v.29): you are aware that the land and it fullness belong to the Lord, and you scorn the impotence of the idols, whereas he is in thrall to error and takes harm from it, believing you are partaking of meats sacrificed to idols. What follows, in fact, brings this out: *After all, why is my freedom subject to the judgment of someone else's conscience?* (by *freedom* referring to the grace of faith). Also in what comes after this, note, he emphasizes this: *If I partake with thankfulness, why am I misrepresented for what I give thanks for?* (v.30). It is not right, he is saying, for someone else to be corrupted through my maturity. [12]

So whether you eat or drink, or whatever you do, do all for God's glory (v.31). It was good for him to include everything – sitting, walking, (309) talking, showing mercy, teaching – so that God's glory might be thought of as the single purpose of everything. This was also the Lord's recommendation: "Let your light shine in people's presence so that they may see your good works and glorify your father in heaven." [13] He says so here, too. *Give no offense to Jews or Greeks, or to the church of God* (v.32): let no occasion of scandal come from you, neither to the unbelievers nor to those who have already come to faith. *Just as I please everyone in everything* (v.33). Admittedly, this is a mark of flatterers, but what follows is not indicative of them: *Seeking not my own advantage but that of the majority so that they may be saved.* The flatterers seek the advantage not of others but of themselves – or, rather, not themselves: they bring ruin on themselves ahead of others. The divine apostle, on the contrary, instead of looking for his own advantage, was concerned for the salvation of others, augmenting his own riches through their deliverance from disaster.

Chapter Eleven

Be imitators of me as I am of Christ (v.1): emulate the way I do things; I imitate the Lord, who dealt differently with Jews and with the apostles, and proposed different things to the mature and to the immature. [1]

Having thus concluded the criticism in regard to the foods sacrificed to idols, he corrects in turn other sins: the Corinthians' wives were in the habit of not covering their heads, even at the time of prayer; and some, taking pride in their eloquence, were even anxious to teach in church. So at this point he corrects this situation. *Now, I commend you, brethren, for all remembering me, and maintaining the traditions as I passed them on to you* (v.2). This commendation was not true, either: he rather blames them for not respecting the limits set.

But I want you to be aware that Christ is the head of every man, whereas the husband is head of his wife, and God is head of Christ (v.3). He employed these expressions in his wish to subject wives to their husbands and to emphasize that it is not appropriate for them to usurp the role of teaching which from the beginning God had bidden be exercised under the husband's authority; in other words, it was not by handing on divine doctrines or using theological arguments that he came up with this arrangement. The followers of Arius and Eunomius, on the other hand, endeavor from this passage also to demonstrate that the Son is creature and artifact: *God is head of Christ*, he says, note, so the wife, too, is the husband's artifact, insofar as the husband is head of the wife.[2] The wife, however, far from being the husband's artifact, comes from the husband's substance. Neither is the Son God's artifact, of course, but comes from God's substance. (312) Now, what the divine apostle means is that Christ is head of every man, namely, of the believers. He is our head, however, not in divinity but in humanity; we are called his body, remember. Now, the head has to be of the same stock as the body; so he is our head in humanity, and it follows God is his head in the same respect. If, however, they want it to refer also to divinity, let them realize that just as in humanity he is styled head of us who have a human nature but believe in him, being one in being with us in this respect, so the Father in being styled his head reveals the oneness in being. He is one in being with the Father in divinity, but with us in humanity. As Father and cause he is given the name head.

Every man who prays or prophesies with something hanging down from his head brings disgrace on his head (v.4). This, too, was something they were bold enough to do indiscriminately: they even wore their hair long in the Greek manner, and prayed to God with their heads covered. *Whereas any woman who prays or prophesies with uncovered head brings disgrace on her head – it is the same as being shaved. After all, if a woman does not cover her head, let her be shorn, whereas if being shorn or shaven is disgraceful for a woman, let her cover her head* (vv.5-6). He made it sufficiently clear that it is appropriate for a woman to have her head covered by hair.[3]

I mean, a man ought not have his head covered, God's image and glory as he is, whereas the woman is man's glory (v.7). The human being is *God's image*, not in body nor in soul but only in government; and so is called *God's image* in being entrusted with the government of everything on earth.[4] The woman, on the other hand, in being placed under the man's authority, is the *man's glory*, and like an image of an image: she too exercises government over the other things, but she is bidden be subject to the man. Then from another angle as well, *Man, after all, is not from woman, but woman from man* (v.8). So men have pride of place also on the basis of creation. *Man, remember, was not created for the sake of woman, but woman for man* (v.9). This also is sufficient to show the man deserving of leadership: he was not produced on account of her need, but she on account of his need.

For this reason a woman ought to have authority on her head on account of the angels (v.10). By *authority* he referred to the covering, as if to say, Let her show her subjection by covering herself, and not least for the sake of the angels, who are set over human beings and (313) entrusted with their care. Likewise also in the Acts, "It is not he, but his angel;" [5] and the Lord, "See that you do not despise one of these little ones who believe in me: Amen I say to you, their angels continually look upon the face of my Father in heaven." [6] Since, however, through what he said he had given considerable importance to men, he was obliged to go on, *Yet neither is man independent of woman nor woman of man in the world* (v.11): through intercourse and sharing the race is propagated. [7] *I mean, just as the woman comes from the man, so too the man comes through the woman* (v.12). Not content with this, he showed the one responsible for them: *But all things are from God.*

Now, once again he has recourse to judges. *Judge for yourselves: is it seemly for a woman to pray to God without covering? Does not nature itself teach that a man with long hair is a disgrace to himself, whereas a woman with long hair is a credit to herself because hair is given as a covering?* (vv.14-15): if she believes hair is an honor, and its removal dishonorable, let her think that she dishonors the one who gave the hair if she does not come with the due respect and honor. *If, however, anyone seems to be contentious, we do not have such a custom, nor do the churches of God* (v.16). This verse suffices to rebut even the very querulous: he showed these views were not those of himself alone but also of all the churches of God.

Consequently, after applying the treatment appropriate to this failing, in the manner of the finest physicians he heals a further ailment. They were in the habit in the churches, in fact, after the eucharistic ritual, of eating in common, rich and poor alike, and from this practice great consolation derived for the needy; the affluent brought provisions from home, and those in the grip of poverty shared in the good cheer on account of their participation in the faith. But with the passage of time it was not practiced as it should; instead, the better-off spurned the needy. On learning this, the divine apostle writes useful advice on this as well. *Now, in giving this instruction I do not commend you, because your coming together is not for the better but for the worse* (v.17): I am right to blame you; while you ought increase your virtue with time, you diminish it and also lessen your wealth.

Firstly, I mean, when you come together as one, I hear there exist divisions among you, and to some extent I believe it (v.18). He speaks not of doctrinal divisions, but those involving a love of power, which he criticized also at the beginning of the letter. He was very wise to moderate the severity of the accusation, saying not simply *I believe* but *to some extent I believe*. (316) *In fact, there must be factions among you so that the tried and true ones among you will become clear* (v.19). He speaks of contentious factions, not differences in doctrine. Now, the term *must* does not suggest obligation; similar is the saying of the Lord, "It is inevitable that stumbling occurs:" [8] as though foreseeing the future precisely, he foretold what he saw without himself obliging it to happen. But this will cause no harm, the divine apostle says: with the conviction of those in the grip of wickedness the caliber of the best men is demonstrated.

When you come together as one, then, it is not to eat the Lord's Supper (v.20). By *the Lord's Supper* he refers to the Lord's sacrament: [9] all partake of it equally, both those living in poverty and those boasting of riches, both servants and masters, both rulers and ruled. So the common tables should be common, then, he is saying, in fidelity to the Lord's table, which is available to all equally, but as it is you do not act this way. *I mean, in eating each one makes a start on their own supper; one goes hungry, another gets drunk* (v.21). He showed the common meals directly at odds with the Lord's meal: of the latter all partake equally, whereas in the other case *one goes hungry while another gets drunk*. He did not say "drinks" or "is satisfied" but *gets drunk*, making the double accusation, that he is alone in drinking, and that he gets drunk.

Then by way of censure, *Do you not have homes for eating and drinking? or are you showing your contempt for the church of God and humiliating those who have nothing?* (v.22): if your intention in coming is to have a good time, do it at home: in church it is insolence and blatant revelry. I mean, how could it not be inappropriate in God's temple, in the presence of the Lord, who has spread a table for us all, for you to set about having a good time, starve the needy and make them embarrassed for their poverty. *What am I to say to you? Am I to commend you for this? I do not commend you.* He employs his customary gentleness; he blames them in spiritual fashion, not in a judgmental way.

Then he reminds them more clearly of the holy eucharist.[10] *I received from the Lord, remember, as I also passed it on to you, that the Lord Jesus on the night he was betrayed, took a loaf, blessed and broke it, saying, Take, eat: this is my body broken for you; do this as my memorial. In the same way, after supping, the cup also, in the words, This cup is the new covenant in my blood; do this, as often as you drink it, as my memorial* (vv.23-25). He reminded them of that sacred and all holy night on which he brought to realization the type the Passover was, revealed the type's archetype,[11] opened the doors of the saving mystery, and shared not only with the eleven apostles but also with the betrayer both the precious (317) body and blood. He brings out that it is always possible to enjoy the good things of that night. *In fact, as often as you eat this loaf and drink this cup, you proclaim the death of the Lord until he comes* (v.26): after his coming there will no longer be need of the signs of the body,[12] his body being evident – hence his saying *until he comes.*

The divine apostle, then, cited this as an example to bring out the inappropriateness of the conduct of the Corinthians; beginning with the formula of the eucharist, he also recommends proper behavior in regard to it. *And so whoever eats the loaf or drinks the cup of the Lord unworthily shall be guilty of the body and the blood of the Lord* (v.27). Here he goads those suffering from ambition, he goads the fornicator, and with them those who had been partaking of meats sacrificed to idols without due consideration; and in addition to them ourselves also for presuming to enjoy the divine eucharist with a bad conscience.[13] The phrase *guilty of the body and the blood of the Lord* suggests that just as Judas betrayed him and Jews abused him, so do they dishonor him who receive his all-holy body with unclean hands and place it in a mouth that is accursed.

Having thus instilled fear into them, he gives them good advice. *Let people examine themselves, and thus eat of the loaf and drink of the cup* (v.28): turn judge of yourself, and as careful scrutineer of your behavior examine your conscience; only then receive the gift.

After all, those eating and drinking unworthily eat and drink judgment on themselves for not discerning the body of the Lord (v.29): not only will you not attain salvation from it if you receive the gift unlawfully, but you will also pay the penalty for drunken behavior towards it. He confirms what will happen in the future from what has already happened in the past. *This is the reason many among you are weak and feeble, and a good number are dead* (v.30). He cited this as a fact; he would not bring himself to put into writing what was not a fact, since he would know the obviousness of the lie. [14] *If we judged ourselves, you know, we should not be judged. But we are judged and corrected by the Lord so as not to be condemned along with the world* (vv.31-32): if we were prepared to do a reckoning of behavior and deliver a just verdict against ourselves, we would not receive from God a sentence. Nonetheless, the Lord corrects even those guilty of the worst offenses in measured fashion lest we be consigned to the destruction awaiting the impious.

Now, to the fact that he had given attention to the eucharist by way of example to instruct them to keep a common character to the meals in the churches with that sacred meal in mind, [15] the sequel bears witness. (320) *And so, my brethren, when you come together to eat, wait for one another. If any are hungry, let them eat at home lest you come together to your own condemnation. Other matters I shall put in order when I come* (vv.33-34). It was impossible for him, you see, to cover everything; but after writing on the most urgent things, he kept the rest for his coming. Let us also, being in receipt of benefit from this, on the one hand shun what is harmful to faith, and on the other spare a thought for attending to the needy; and cleansing our conscience in preparation let us thus participate in the divine mysteries so as to receive the good Lord to dwell within. To him with the Father and the all-holy Spirit be glory and magnificence, now and forever, for ages of ages. Amen.

CHAPTER TWELVE

Now, concerning the spiritual things, brethren, I do not want you to be ignorant (v.1). In former times those who had accepted the divine message and been vouchsafed saving baptism were in an obvious manner granted the working of the spiritual grace. Some spoke in divers tongues, which they had no natural knowledge of nor had they learned from others, some worked wonders and healed maladies, while others enjoyed the prophetic gift and foretold the future, sometimes making clear even what was hidden and thus betraying the action of the grace dwelling within. I mean, it was not possible that those who for a long time had been subject to the demons' deception and been victim to a widespread ailment would have so easily believed unlettered human beings in the grip of poverty and learned the truth had not divine grace obviously made its appearance and faith provided miracles like guarantees. The Corinthians also, along with the others who had come to faith throughout the world, enjoyed these gifts, but did not use them as they should: they gave evidence of the operation of grace for notoriety rather than for usefulness. The gift of tongues in particular gave them an exalted sense of self-importance, they spoke different tongues belonging neither to the listener nor to the interpreter, and did not do it in any order, but two or three or four at the one time. To the divine apostles, on the other hand, the grace of the Spirit had given the knowledge of tongues, since being appointed teachers of all the nations they had to know the languages of all so as to bring the evangelical message to each in their own language. [1]

About these, then, the thrice-blessed Paul wrote, teaching them the proper sense of order. *You know, when you were pagans, you were misled and went astray to idols that could not speak* (v.2). He intends also to call in question the inconsistency of Greek mythology and show as well the truth of religion; the demons appropriated the term god, assigned it to themselves and foist utter deception on human beings. The latter, in fact, left the straight and narrow, (321) abandoned the true God and offered to many the worship due to God; not convinced each was capable of everything, they supposed one was source of wisdom, another of military arts, and another of nautical skills. So the divine apostle indicated this through what he said, that before they received the light of religion and still in thrall to falsehood, they were led in this direction and that, subject to the deception of the insensate idols.

Hence I want you to know that no one speaking by God's Spirit says, Cursed be Jesus, and no one can say Lord Jesus except by the Holy Spirit (v.3). Among us harmony and consistency are of the highest value: the only-begotten Son does not teach one thing and the all-holy

Spirit another; instead, just as Christ the Lord in the divine Gospels taught the dignity of the all-holy Spirit, so the divine Spirit proclaimed his lordship. It would not be possible for the person activated by the divine Spirit to present Christ as bereft of the divine nature, nor in turn sincerely confess him to be God unless enlightened by that grace.

Now, there are differences between gifts, but the same Spirit; there are differences between ministries, but the same Lord; there are differences between activities, whereas it is the same God who activates all of them in everyone (vv.4-6). In these words he clearly revealed to us their purpose, showing the gifts given to be many and varied, but their source to be one: he said they are supplied by the all-holy Spirit, by the Lord, and by the God and Father. He named the same things *gifts* and *ministries* and *activities*, note, referring to them as *gifts* on account of their being given in divine prodigality, and as *ministries* since they were given through people assigned to this role; thus he said in the letter to the Romans as well, "Inasmuch as I am an apostle of Gentiles, I glorify my ministry," and in writing to Timothy he said in one place, "Discharge your ministry to the full," and in another, "I remind you to rekindle the gift of God."[2] He also referred to the gifts as *activities* for being activated by the divine nature: he did not claim, as some of the foolish heretics supposed, that some are activated by the Spirit, others by the God of all; rather, he showed the Holy Trinity to be supplier of the same gifts, and he teaches this more clearly in what follows. At this point, note, he says God activates them, and a little later says, *The one and the same Spirit activates all these, distributing to each one their own just as he wishes.*[3] The divine apostle made a point of this in the present case, of course, in opposition to the Greek views, on the one hand to show their inconsistency, and on the other to go further and (324) comfort those who received gifts apparently inferior, and emphasize that one group and the other are given by the same Spirit.

In fact, what follows also touches on this. *To each is given the manifestation of the Spirit for the common good* (v.7). He said, not *the grace,* but *the manifestation*: the grace even today is given to those thought worthy of all-holy baptism,[4] but not in obvious fashion, whereas in those days they immediately spoke in divers tongues and performed wonders, strengthened by them and instructed in the truth of the teaching. Now, he was obliged to say that the manifestation of the Spirit was given *for the common good*, to console those same mourners and to emphasize that the one who understands everything clearly and knows what is of benefit to each one guides everything in his wisdom.

I mean, to one is given utterance of wisdom through the Spirit, while to another utterance of knowledge in the same Spirit (v.8). By *utterance of wisdom* he refers not to eloquence but to true doctrine, the grace of which the divine apostle also received, as did the divinely-inspired John the evangelist, the most divine Peter the head of the apostles, and the first of the martyrs blessed Stephen. After all, men who were fishermen and lived by the work of their hands, who were unlettered, would not have been capable of attempting public oratory and literary composition and of making their words and writing abound in the greatest possible force if they had not received from the divine Spirit true wisdom. Others of the believers had the knowledge of the divine teachings, but were incapable of public speaking in a manner like them; it was, of course, the gift of the Spirit's grace.

To another faith by the same Spirit (v.9). By *faith* here he is not referring to the ordinary kind, but to that of which he says shortly after, *And if I have all faith so as to move mountains:* [5] on account of the unbelief prevalent then they worked many such wonders to people's astonishment, and through them led them to the truth. *To another gifts of healing by the same Spirit*. He refers to the curing of the infirm, the walking by the lame and the enjoyment of sight by those deprived of vision. These things happened at that time, and the story of the Acts testifies to it: it says of the divinely-inspired Peter that they placed many of the infirm on beds in the streets in the hope that at Peter's coming even his shadow might fall upon one of them; [6] and of the most divine Paul that the surface of his garments drove out the ailments. [7]

To another working of miracles (v.10). This gift also inflicted punishment frequently, like (325) loss of sight for Elymas and premature death for Ananias and Sapphira. [8] *To another prophecy*. Many were recipients of this gift, not only men but women as well; the story of the Acts brings this out clearly. *To another discernment of spirits*. Since, you see, there were seers at that time deceiving people, some such grace was given by the divine Spirit to some people for discerning those under the influence of the contrary spirit. *To yet another tongues of various kinds.* About this gift we have said what was needed. He put it last and the gift of teaching first, since it was with a view to the latter that this and the others were given, so that the message might be believed. *To another interpretation of tongues.* This gift, too, was spiritual: it often happened that a man who knew only the Greek language provided the listeners with a translation when someone else was speaking the language of the Scythians or Thracians. In every case, of course, he added *in keeping with the same Spirit and by the same Spirit* to bring out that though the streams were different, the source of all was one.

Instead of leaving the impression that this was sufficient, he went on: *Now, the one and the same Spirit activates all these, distributing to each person individually as he wishes* (v.11). In all this he consoles those who received the inferior gifts, teaching that these also are gifts of the divine Spirit. The divine Spirit gives *as he wishes*, and he wishes the common good; he said so in what went before, *To each is given the manifestation of the Spirit for the common good.* Hence he did not say the Spirit but *the one and the same Spirit* to emphasize that some are not from one Spirit and others from another, but both these gifts and those are from the one Spirit. Then he employs an image to make clear what is unseen from what is seen. *You see, just as the body is one and has many members, but all the members though many are one body, so too is Christ* (v.12). By *Christ* here he referred to the common body of the Church, since Christ the Lord is head of this body. So he urges us to focus on the body, and to recognize that though it is composed of different members, it is and is referred to as one body, and to learn from this that even while the Church is referred to as body of Christ the Lord, it has many different members, some greater, some lesser, some distinguished, some inferior to them, but all necessary and useful nonetheless.

He brings out also how we call all the believers one body. *In the one Spirit, remember, we were all* (328) *baptized into one body – Jews, Greeks, slaves, free – and all were given to drink of the one Spirit* (v.13): we were all renewed by one Spirit, we all enjoyed the same gift in baptism, we all alike received forgiveness of sins, we all participated similarly in the eucharist. [9] Consequently, we form one body, even if we have different limbs – he said as much, *we were baptized into one body*, that is, for the purpose of forming one body.

The body, you see, is not one limb but many (v.14): the body is not a single item, but is composed of many parts. *If the foot were to say, Because I am not a hand, I do not belong to the body, surely it would not on that account be any less part of the body? If the ear were to say, Because I am not an eye, I do not belong to the body, surely it would not on that account be any less part of the body?* (vv.16-17). Once again with these words he instructs those who had received the lesser gifts not to be troubled but to be content with what is given: if you fill the role not of a foot but of a hand, or perform the service not of an eye but of hearing, you should be aware that these also are necessary to the body. *If the whole body were an eye, where would hearing be? if the whole body were hearing, where would smell be?* (v.17): if the whole body were destined to have one member, and that the most presentable, it would be completely useless, deprived of the remaining limbs.

As it is, however, God has placed the members in the body, each one of them, as he chose (v.18). This was sufficient to convince even the resentful to be content with what was given: if God assigned activities to the body's parts, the person who does not abide by the limits set is clearly at odds with the one setting the limits. In this, of course, he showed the equal status of the Father and the Spirit: he said of the Spirit that *he activates all these as he wishes*, and of God that *he placed the parts as he chose. If all were a single member, however, where would the body be? But as it is there are many members but one body* (vv.19-20): the body would be helpless if it did not have the difference in members.

From this he proceeds to teach those receiving the greater gifts not to despise the others but honor them as necessary members. *The eye cannot say to the hand, I have no need of you, or the head in turn to the feet, I have no need of you. On the contrary, the body's members that seem to be weaker are much more necessary, and the parts of the body we think more dishonorable we clothe with greater honor* (vv.21-23). The weaker and more necessary parts are the liver and the head: their bones are more closely covered, yet they were given greater security by the creator. The feet, on the other hand, seem to be the more dishonorable of the body's parts, yet we take great care even of them, covering them with shoes. (329) *And our unseemly parts enjoy more abundant seemliness, whereas our seemly parts do not need it* (vv.23-24). While the face does not need covering, the genitalia we even cover with clothing, and nature surrounded them with hair like a kind of garment. He went on in fact to say, *But God arranged the body, giving the more abundant honor to what lacks it.* Thus he covered with the buttocks the part for defecation, whereas in common opinion it has the name of being *unseemly.*

So that there would be no division in the body, but the members would take the same care of one another: if one member suffers, all the members suffer with it; if one member is honored, all the members rejoice with it (vv.25-26). You can find this perfect sharing operative in the parts of the body: if the foot is sprained, the whole body is in pain; if a toenail is lost unnecessarily, the feeling of pain goes to all parts; if the tongue blasphemes or lies, tears flow from the eyes, and if in turn it speaks cleverly, they are wreathed in smiles, indicating appreciation.

Having brought out the image in great detail, he moves back to his former point. *Now, you are the body of Christ, and individually members* (v.27): not only you but all the believers throughout the world – hence his addition of *individually.* Then he explains the ranking in the Church. *Some God has placed first in the Church, namely, apostles* (v.28). He means not only the Twelve but also the seventy and those accorded this grace afterwards: he himself was called later and accorded this mandate, as well as blessed Barnabas and countless others in addition to them, and he calls Epaphroditus apostle of the Philippians, "Your apostle, who has met my needs."[10] *Second, prophets.* He means not those before the age of grace but those in the age of grace, among whom were Agabus, those who prophesied in Antioch,[11] and the divine apostle himself. *Third, teachers*: inspired by divine grace, these proposed the teaching about the divine doctrines and offered moral exhortation.[12] *Next, deeds of power, then gifts of healing.* He put teaching ahead of these, not idly but to bring out that they occur for its sake, not it for them: teaching procures salvation, but since they did not receive it without signs, miracles were given to those who made their approach in the manner of pledges of some sort. *Gifts of support,* (332) *gifts of leadership.* In this he indicated the organization of the churches.

Kinds of tongues. He put this gift last, not without purpose, but because they became conceited because of it and made use of it for ostentation and not out of necessity. [13] It was for this reason, in fact, that he listed the order of the gifts, saying which was first, which second, and which third, that they might give attention to the more necessary ones.

Surely not all are apostles? not all prophets? not all teachers? not all work deeds of power? not all have gifts of healing? not all speak in tongues? not all translate tongues? (vv.29-30) In these words once again he consoles those who seemed to have received the lesser gifts, and clearly explained that it was not possible for all to have the same ones and that they need one another, as the body's members need the assistance of one another. *Strive after the better gifts* (v.31). Some read this as a question, in the sense, Are you completely desirous of the greater gifts? If you really are desirous, I shall willingly guide you to them. In fact, he went on, *The way I show you is still better,* that is, I show the way of the far greater gifts; and he teaches them that love for the neighbor surpasses all these.

CHAPTER THIRTEEN

If I speak in the tongues of human beings and of angels but do not have love, I have become a sounding gong and a clanging cymbal (v.1). To make the comparison he cited first of all the gift of tongues, [1] since with them it seemed to be a greater gift than the others. They supposed it to be greater since it was given at the visit of the all-holy Spirit on the day of Pentecost to the apostles before all the others. So he means, Even if I knew all the languages of human beings, and in addition to them those of the unseen beings, but do not have love for the neighbor, I am no different from lifeless instruments. Now, by *tongues of angels* he is referring not to audible tongues but to those of the mind, with which they also sing the praise of the God of all and converse with one another; Isaiah also heard them singing praise, as did Ezekiel, and of course David heard them conversing, as also Zechariah and Micah. The divine apostle expressed this by way of hyperbole in his wish to bring out the value of love.

And if I have the gift of prophecy, and understand all the mysteries and all knowledge; and if I have all faith to move mountains but do not have love, I am nothing (v.2). Once again in comparing the truly greater gifts, prophecy and faith, to love he brought out the superiority of love. (333) Now, he cited them, not idly but in an expansive manner: whereas of prophecy he said, *If I understand all the mysteries and all knowledge,* of faith he said, *to move mountains.* But by this means he also revealed the possession of love to be preeminent. *If I give away all my belongings, and if I hand over my body to be burned but do not have love, I gain nothing* (v.3). Here by comparing love with the greatest forms of virtue – scorn for possessions, voluntary poverty, the efforts in favor of religion – he shows it surpassing even them. This, too, he likewise expressed in an expansive manner: he said of his belongings, *If I give away all my belongings,* that is, if in my own person I distribute what is mine and care for the needy; and in the case of martyrdom he did not simply mention death but the burning of his body, this seeming to be worse than the suffering of the other punishments. Perhaps someone inquired how the person doing these things could lack love. So it is necessary to realize that the righteous judge looks not to the righteous deed alone but also to the intention of the deed; but there are many people who are mostly concerned about human opinion, and it is likely that persons dispossessing themselves do so to win people's opinion, or likewise on account of the divine law or desire for the kingdom of heaven, and not out of care and attention to the needy. It should be realized, of course, that the divine apostle expressed many things in hyperbolic fashion to strengthen the point in hand; for example, in writing also to the Galatians he said, "Even if I or an angel from heaven should write to you what is at variance with what you received, let them be anathema:" [2] he knew that it is impossible that some angel would teach the opposite to the divine message, but he put that to teach them not to believe anybody proposing any different teaching, even if completely worthy of trust.

Love is longsuffering (v.4): it bears nobly the neighbor's deficiencies. *It is kind*: it employs gentleness and courtesy. *Love is not jealous*: it does not experience the passion of envy. *Love does not pry*:[3] it does not concern itself with what is not its business, which is what *prying* is; it does not meddle with measuring the divine being, nor call in question its arrangements, as some are inclined to do. The one who loves refrains from doing anything unseemly (*love* meaning the person who has love). *It is not puffed up*: it is not overbearing towards its brethren. *It feels no shame* (v.5): it declines to do nothing lowly or humiliating for the benefit of the brethren (336) in the belief that such an action is unseemly. [4]

It does not look for its own advantage. The divine apostle frequently said as much: "Looking not for your own advantage but for that of many so as to save them." [5] *It is not provoked*: even if something offensive is done by someone, it bears it with longsuffering on account of the affection it feels. *It gives no thought to evil*: it pardons the fallen, supposing this happened with no evil intent. *It does not rejoice in iniquity, but joins in rejoicing in the truth* (v.6): it hates lawlessness, it finds happiness in the good. *It endures everything* (v.7): it puts up with offenses out of love. *It believes everything*: it regards the beloved as guileless. *It hopes everything*: even if it sees someone taking a turn for the worse, it awaits their change for the better. *It bears everything*: nothing that happens to this person can deter them from love.

Having described these individually, and perceiving his tongue did not measure up to the task of praising love, the divine apostle went on briefly: *Love never fails* (v.8), that is, is not disappointed, but always remains firm, stable and immovable, abiding forever. *Even if prophecies are done away with, if tongues come to an end, if knowledge is done away with.* The life to come has no need of these: prophecy of present affairs is unnecessary. Tongues, too, will be useless, with the removal of differences between them; and the lesser knowledge comes to an end with the provision of the greater. He went on to say as much, in fact: *You see, partly we know, and partly we prophesy; but when what is complete comes, then what is partial is done away with* (vv.9-10): knowledge of youngsters is superfluous for mature people. The divine apostle also employs this image, note: *When I was a baby, I spoke like a baby, I thought like a baby, I reasoned like a baby. But when I became a man, I did away with the things of the baby* (v.11): those equipped with ready wit and understanding on attaining mature age have no need of youthful knowledge. So he compared the knowledge given us in this life to the knowledge of babies, and the knowledge to which we look forward to that of mature men, once again in these words teaching those sundering the body of the Church not to feel a sense of importance in the knowledge. [6]

I mean, for the time being we look through a mirror, dimly, whereas then face to face (v.12). The present is a shadow of the future, he is saying: in (337) all-holy baptism we see the type of resurrection, whereas then we shall see resurrection itself; here we perceive the symbols of the Lord's body, there we shall see the Lord himself – the meaning of *face to face.* [7] We see, however, not his invisible nature, which cannot be seen by anyone, but the nature received from us. *For the time being I know partly, whereas then I shall know fully, even as I am known fully.* He does not mean, As I am known, I shall know him, but I shall see him more precisely in being related to him; he put *I am fully known* to mean I am related. He said in similar fashion also to Moses, "I know you more than all the others;" [8] and the apostle, "The Lord knows those who are his," [9] that is, he accords them greater providence.

But as it is there remain faith, hope, love – these three; and love is greater than the others (v.13). He showed the gifts coming to an end, and love alone abiding. He also showed it surpassing the achievements of knowledge: faith is superfluous in the future life, when realities are utterly clarified. After all, if "faith is the substance of things hoped for," [10] there is no use for faith when realities are clarified. Likewise hope too is superfluous there: "Hope that is seen is not hope: what is left to hope for in the case of someone who sees?" [11] Love, on the other hand, has greater power there, in any case, with the passions gone, bodies made incorruptible and souls no longer choosing this at one time and that at another.

CHAPTER FOURTEEN

Pursue love, and strive for the spiritual things, and especially that you may prophesy (v.1): since love, then, is thus the most important thing we need, set great store on possessing it without neglecting the spiritual gifts; in any case, make prophecy your own before the others. Once again, note, he represses the sense of importance given to the gift of tongues. *You see, the person speaking in a tongue is speaking not to human beings but to God: no one hears it – they are speaking mysteries through the Spirit* (v.2). He does two things at once, criticizing their self-importance and bringing out the need of the gift. You see, this gift was made to the preachers on account of people's different languages so that on reaching the Indians they would use their language in offering the divine message; and likewise in speaking with the Persians, Scythians, Romans and Egyptians they might use languages of each in preaching the evangelical teaching. So for those speaking in Corinth it was unnecessary to use the language of Scythians, Persians or Egyptians, because they were unable to understand. [1] This was surely the reason the divine apostle also (340) said the one speaking in tongues was speaking not to human beings but to God; in fact, he went on, *no one hears it*, and in case the gift be thought useless, *they are speaking mysteries through the Spirit.*

The one who prophesies, on the other hand, speaks to human beings, giving upbuilding, exhortation and comfort (v.3): all hear what they say. *Those who speak in a tongue build themselves up* (v.4): those present did not understand what was said. *Whereas the one prophesying builds up the Church*: on seeing the revelation of thoughts and the manifestation of things done secretly they received the highest benefit. And lest anyone suspect he was driven by envy to say this, he felt obliged to proceed, *Now, I wish you all spoke in tongues, but more so that you would prophesy: the one prophesying is greater than the one speaking in a tongue, unless someone translates for the Church to receive upbuilding* (v.5). He clearly explained why he used *more*: I am not denigrating the gift (he is saying), but looking to its usefulness; with no translation available, prophecy is better, offering greater value.

In the present case, however, brethren, if I come to you speaking in tongues, what benefit shall I be to you unless I speak to you by way of revelation or knowledge or prophecy or teaching? (v.6). Once again he submerged his own personal position to encourage those accused of this. What advantage would I bring to you, he is saying, if I came to you and used different forms of language unless at some time I gave attention to teaching, revealing to you the hidden mysteries, guiding you to divine things and advising you on your duties? He also adopts an image suited to the topic in hand. *Lifeless instruments that emit sound, such as the flute or the harp – how will what is played on flute or harp be recognized if they do not produce different notes? If the trumpet produces an uncertain sound, who will get ready for battle?* (vv.7-8): you yourselves know that flute and harp need someone's rhythm and artistry; receiving this, lifeless though they be, they emit a harmonious sound, whereas if someone plays them in defiance of this, what is produced is meaningless. Likewise with the trumpet: unless it gives the battle call, it does not ready the soldiers for fighting.

Likewise in your own case, if you do not produce intelligible speech, how will what is said be understood? You will be speaking into the air, in other words. There are I don't know how many kinds of language in the world, and no race is without its own language (vv.9-10). What a harmonious rhythm is to a harp, and a call to battle to a trumpet, translation is to languages: when those present do not understand them, the words melt into the air to no purpose. (341) *So if I do not know the force of the word, to the speaker I shall be a foreigner, and the speaker a foreigner to me* (v.11). He made the same point in different ways. *Likewise in your case, since you are eager for spiritual things, seek to excel in them with a view to the upbuilding of the Church* (v.12). It was ironically he referred to them as *eager for spiritual things*. He bids them do everything for the Church's benefit.

Hence let the one speaking in a tongue pray to be able to translate it (v.13). Beseech the one who has given you the gift of tongues, he is saying, to supply as well that of translation so that you may offer benefit to the Church. *I mean, if I pray in a tongue, my spirit prays but my mind bears no fruit* (v.14). The speaker's *fruit* is the benefit to the listeners; he said as much also in the letter to the Romans, "So that I may have some fruit among you also as I did among the other Gentiles as well." [2] In other words, if I speak in a different tongue and do not provide the translation to those present, I have no fruit since they gain no advantage.

So what to do? I shall pray in the spirit, and I shall pray in the mind as well; I shall sing in the spirit, and I shall sing in the mind as well (v.15). By *spirit* he refers to the gift, and by *mind* to the clarity of what is said. He means that the one speaking in a different tongue, either in hymnsinging or prayer or teaching, ought translate for the benefit of the listeners or use an assistant in teaching capable of doing it. *The reason is that if you give a blessing in the spirit, how will the one occupying the place of an outsider say Amen to your thanksgiving? He does not understand what you are saying* (v.16). By *outsider* he refers to the person among the ranks of the laity, since even those who are out of the front line are normally called *outsiders.* [3] *After all, you give thanks alright, but the other person is not built up* (v.17). I am aware, he is saying, that under the action of divine grace you sing God's praises; but the person who does not understand the language does not grasp the meaning.

Then by way of exhortation, *I thank my God that I do not speak in tongues more than all of you. Instead, in church I prefer to speak five words in my mind for your instruction than a myriad words in a tongue* (vv.18-19): I was thought worthy of this grace prior to you; through me you also received the grace. Still, in my concern for the benefit of the majority I prefer clear teaching to profane. [4]

Then by way of censure. *Brethren, do not turn into children in your thinking; rather, be infants where evil is concerned, but be grownup in your thinking* (v.20): do not (344) emulate children's ignorance but their innocence; do not possess grownups' wickedness but their shrewdness. *In the Law it is written, In foreign tongues and on alien lips I shall speak to this people, and yet they will not hearken to me in this way, says the Lord* [5] (v.21). It is an inspired text from the Old Testament; he gave the name *Law* to the Old Testament. After quoting the testimony, he proceeds to the commentary: *And so the tongues act as a sign not for believers but for unbelievers* (v.22): the difference in the tongues alarms the unbeliever. Those assembled in Jerusalem on the day of Pentecost also experienced it; so they immediately said, "Are not all those speaking Galileans? How do we hear them, each in our native language, Parthians and Medes" and the rest? [6] *Prophecy, on the other hand, is not for unbelievers but for believers.* The apostle had one purpose, the welfare of the majority; this was surely the reason why he also bade the Corinthians choose prophecy, contributing as it did to the common good.

If, then, the whole church were to assemble together and all speak in tongues, and outsiders or unbelievers were to enter, would they not say that you are in a frenzy? (v.23). Here he gave the name *outsiders* to the uninitiated, and explains that, not understanding what is said, they will gain the impression of them that they are out of their mind. *Whereas if all were to prophesy, and some unbeliever or outsider were to enter, he would be reproved by all and examined by all; and thus the hidden things of his heart would become manifest, and thus he would fall down and adore God, proclaiming that God is really among you* (vv.24-

25). This was the way fear fell upon all when Ananias and Sapphira were the object of accusation. It should be remarked, of course, that here he clearly called the all-holy Spirit God: the working of prophecy was from the divine Spirit; *the one and the same Spirit activates all of these, distributing to each person individually as he wishes,*[7] remember. Yet here he used the expression, *he would fall down and adore God, proclaiming that God is really among you,* calling the all-holy Spirit God. Likewise blessed Peter also said, "Why did Satan deceive your heart to lie to the Holy Spirit? You did not lie to human beings but to God."[8]

After thus bringing out the difference in the gifts, he explains also the good order appropriate to them. *So what is to be done, brethren? When you come together, each of you has a psalm, a teaching, a tongue, a revelation, an interpretation: let it all happen for upbuilding* (v.26). Once again he brought out the body and (345) the body's limbs: through the term *come together* he emphasized the one body, through the term *each of you has* this and this the difference in the limbs; then in turn the contribution of each to the common good, *let it all happen for the common good. If anyone speaks in a tongue, let there be two or at the most three, and taken individually* (v.27): do not speak all together: this is a mark of disorder and confusion; nor in great numbers: two are sufficient, but draw the line at three speakers. *And let one translate*: those present need to understand what is said. *But if there is no translator, let them be silent in church, and speak to themselves and to God* (v.28): it is most inappropriate to employ the divine gift for publicity and not for usefulness.

Let two or three prophets speak, and let the others make a judgment (v.29). The divine apostle had already catalogued the distinction of some spiritual gifts from other spiritual gifts. So he makes the statement here as well for those accorded this gift to make a judgment of what is said as to whether it is said by the working of the divine Spirit: as the devil ranged the false prophets against the prophets, so the false apostles against the apostles. He brings this out also in the second letter to the Corinthians, "The false apostles are like this, deceitful workers."[9] *If a revelation is made to someone else seated there, let the first keep silent* (v.30). If the grace of the Spirit moves another person, he is saying, let the one who has begun to speak give way.

After all, you can all prophesy one by one so that all may learn and all be exhorted (v.31): let nothing happen in disorderly fashion, nothing in a confused fashion; it is possible for you all to offer the prophecy to those assembled and be the cause of gain for them from it. This orderliness has continued in the churches up to the present time, some of the teachers speaking to the people on this festival, others on another.[10] *Spirit of prophets is subject to prophets* (v.32). By *spirit* he refers to the gifts. Joshua was likewise subject to Moses, Elisha likewise to Elijah, the band of the prophets likewise to Elisha himself, Timothy and Titus and the rest likewise to the apostle himself. *You see, God is not a God of disorder but of peace, as in all the churches of the saints* (v.33): we prescribe nothing new: we teach you the laws of the churches, which the prince of peace himself imposed.

Since, however, not only men but also women enjoyed (348) grace – God himself foretelling it also through the prophet Joel, "I shall pour out my spirit on all flesh, and your sons and your daughters will prophesy"[11] – he had to legislate for the latter as well. *Let your women stay silent in the churches: their role is not to speak but to be subject, as the Law also says* (v.34): God said to Eve, "Your yearning is for your husband, and in turn he will have dominion over you."[12] *But if they want to learn something, let them ask their own husbands at home: it is disgraceful for women to speak in churches* (v.35). Then again by way of censure, *Or did the word of God proceed from you, or find its way to you alone?* (v.36): you were not the first nor indeed the only ones to receive the evangelical message; so do not be content with your own ideas but follow the prescriptions of the churches.

If anyone claims to be a prophet or spirit-filled, let him acknowledge what I write to you as the Lord's commandments (v.37). Those with the divine Spirit dwelling within he called *spirit-filled*, whereas the person lacking this grace cannot understand. Hence he proceeded, *But if anyone does not recognize it, let them not be recognized* (v.38). Then by way of exhortation, *And so, my brethren, be zealous for prophesying, and do not forbid speaking in tongues* (v.39). Once again he showed one gift to be of higher status, and the other also to have some usefulness in it, suggesting this by *do not forbid. But let everything be done in seemly fashion and according to order* (v.40). He emphasized order in what preceded. Let us also maintain this good order and follow the apostolic requirements[13] so as to share fellowship with the lawgiver, thanks to the grace and lovingkindness of our Lord Jesus Christ, to whom with the Father and the all-holy Spirit belong glory and magnificence, now and forever, for ages of ages. Amen.

CHAPTER FIFTEEN

After concluding the instruction on the spiritual gifts, the divine apostle thought it useful also to give a treatment of the resurrection; some deceivers were misleading them with the claim there would be no resurrection of bodies. Being replete with spiritual wisdom, he brings out not by chance but in first place the purpose of the Lord's incarnation, and shows the Savior's cross, passion and resurrection happening with a view to the resurrection of all in common. [1] This we shall learn from the text itself.

Now, I draw to your attention, brethren, the Gospel I preached to you, which you also received, in which you also stand firm, by which you are also saved, and the language I used in preaching to you (vv.1-2). Again he combined commendation with instruction to win their attention – hence his saying *in which you stand firm* and adding to strengthen their standing *by which you are also saved*. He means this: I want you to remember the Gospel preached by me among you, which you received enthusiastically, and you look forward to the salvation stemming from it. Now, I call it to your mind in my wish to bring out its scope (this being the meaning of *the language I used in preaching to you*). Then he goes on, *If you hold it fast, unless you believed in vain*: if the resurrection of bodies is beyond belief, the preaching of the Gospel is pointless.

I passed on to you, remember, first of all what I received (v.3): I did not devise the message, nor did I follow human reasoning; instead, I received from the Lord instruction in this. Now, what did you receive? *That Christ died for our sins, in keeping with the Scriptures*: the prophets also foretold this, Isaiah crying aloud, "He was wounded for our iniquities, and crushed for our sins, the chastisement of our peace upon him." *That he was buried*: the prophets foretold this, too, "His tomb will be in peace." [2] *That he was raised on the third day, in keeping with the Scriptures*: the divine David also says, "You will not abandon my soul in Hades, nor let your holy one see destruction." [3] The Lord brings Jonah to the fore: [4] the type contains a number of the three days.

That he appeared to Cephas (v.5). The personage is worthy of giving testimony, but he is solitary – hence his proceeding, *Then to the Twelve*. And in case anyone suspect that out of love for their teacher these men preached the resurrection that had not happened,[5] he felt obliged to add, *Then he appeared to more than five hundred brethren at once* (v.6) – not one by one but to all at the same time: the testimony of so many is beyond suspicion. And lest anyone suspect he was not telling what really happened he added, *Most of whom are alive to this day, though some have died*. Anyone interested, he is saying, can learn this from those same people. *Then he appeared to James* (v.7). This personage was significant, not from his kinship alone, being styled "brother of the Lord,"[6] but also from his own virtue, being known as "righteous." *Then to all the apostles.* Once again he gave the name *apostles* not only to the Twelve, having already mentioned them, but to all those who had received such a commission.

Lest he seem to mention this as hearsay, however, he also lists himself among the witnesses, adopting his customary modesty of attitude in the words, (352) *Last of all, as to one untimely born, he appeared also to me* (v.8). Choosing to present himself as inferior to other people, leaving aside all those who had come to full term in the womb and then been born according to the law of nature, he compared himself to a miscarried embryo, which is not included in the list of human beings.[7] Then he explains the reasons for this: *After all, I am the least of the apostles, unfit to be called an apostle because I persecuted the church of God* (v.9). In case he should by this account render his own testimony unreliable, he went on, *But by the grace of God I am what I am* (v.10). He tries to conceal the riches, and is obliged to lay them bare, though he still did not state clearly their nature – only, *I am what I am. His grace in my regard has not proved to be empty*: it was not in vain that he had mercy on me; he knew what he was doing. *On the contrary, my labors were more abundant than all of theirs*. Under no obligation to make a clean breast of his own history, he had a sense of complete self-satisfaction: he conceals the marvels and reveals only the labor, saying this was an effect of divine grace. In fact, he added as much: *It was not I, however, but the grace of God that is with me*.

Then he shifts his focus to what preceded. *So whether it was I or they, this is what we preach and this what you came to believe* (v.11): if the resurrection of our God and Savior is the gospel preached both by me and by the other apostles, you also received it enthusiastically. Having laid this down like a foundation, he builds his discourse regarding the shared resurrection, employing very compelling arguments. *Now, if Christ is preached as raised from the dead, how is it that some among you claim that there is no resurrection of the dead?* (v.12). We preach Christ, he is saying, not only as God but also as man: "Though he was in the form of God," remember, "he took the form of a slave." [8] We have said both that he died and that he was raised. But it is clear that while the divinity is immune from suffering, the body is subject to suffering: he both handed it over to the cross and raised it from the dead. So how is it, he is saying, that the resurrection of the body is under question with some people whereas the resurrection of Christ the Lord is believed? *If, however, there is no resurrection of the dead, then Christ has not been raised* (v.13): if the former is impossible, the latter has not happened, Christ the Lord having a body. *But if Christ has not been raised, surely our preaching is pointless, and your faith is also pointless* (v.14): if Christ did not really rise, it is futile for us to preach at great risk, and futile for you to believe what is preached.

We are found to be giving false witness to God as well, because we testified of God that he raised (353) *Christ, whereas he did not raise him* [9] (v.15): we are liable on the score of calumny for presuming to claim God raised Christ, whereas he did not raise him. Then in turn he reverses the same ideas, intent on strengthening faith in the resurrection with further arguments, saying, *After all, if the dead are not raised, neither has Christ been raised. But if Christ has not been raised, your faith is futile: you are still in your sins* (vv.16-17): baptism is a type of the Lord's death, but the type has no force if it does not involve the forgiveness of sins; so the burden of sins is still to be carried. He included this in view of the statement, *Christ died for our sins, in keeping with the Scriptures.*

Surely also those who have fallen asleep in Christ have perished (v.18): it was to no purpose, apparently, for the triumphant martyrs to lose their life for confessing Christ; while they eagerly accepted the contest, they lost the crown. If resurrection goes, after all, victory celebration goes with it. *But if our hope in Christ affects this life only, we are the most pitiable people of all* (v.19): we pass through this life exposed to dangers of all kinds, pinched by hunger, constantly abused, moving from one of the world's prisons to another, homeless, refugees, coping with unceasing tempests.

But it is not like this: we are buoyed up with sound hopes, and have the Savior's resurrection as pledge of our own resurrection. He said as much in proceeding, *As it is, however, Christ has been raised from the dead, he became first fruits of those fallen asleep* (v.20): he was the first to destroy the power of death; the whole mass follows without exception the first fruits. He confirms the point with an example from former times. *You see, since death came through a human being, resurrection of the dead also came through a human being* (v.21). Then he moves from the nature to the persons to make his point clearer in this way. *That is to say, as in Adam all die, so too in Christ all will be made alive* (v.22): look at the foundation of the race and see the progeny following the progenitor, and all made mortal since he took on mortality. Likewise the whole human race will follow Christ the Lord and share resurrection: he is also firstborn of the dead, as the other was firstformed human being. Now, it was right for him to call him a human being, though knowing him to be God as well, so that by bringing out the commonality of nature he might strengthen the point about resurrection. [10]

Since, however, he said all will be made alive, but after the resurrection there will be a separation between those who have lived a temperate life and those who have passed their life in licentiousness, between those who have been a victim of unbelief (356) and those distinguished for their faith, and between those who have devoted themselves (to put it in a nutshell) to what deserves praise and to what deserves accusation, he felt obliged to proceed: *But each in proper order* (v.23). Likewise the Lord also teaches in the sacred Gospels that he will make the lambs take their place at his right hand and the goats at his left. [11] *Christ the firstfruits* – that is, he rose first – *then, at his coming, those who are Christ's*, at the time of the consummation. Now, he calls *Christ's* not only those who have come to faith in him after the Incarnation but also those conspicuous for piety and virtue under the Law and before the Law.

Then the end (v.24), that is, the resurrection shared by all: when it happens, everything will find its end, both present realities and the prophecies of the prophets. *When he hands the kingdom over to the God and Father, when he will do away with every ruler and every authority and power.* In handing over the kingdom to the God and Father he is not himself stripped of the kingdom; rather, he brings into subjection the tyrannical devil and his assistants, and forces all to do obeisance and acknowledge the God of all. *He must reign, you see, until he has put all the enemies under his feet* (v.25). The phrase *until* here does not suggest time, but brings out that he will subject absolutely everyone. This reminds us of what was said by David, "The Lord said to my lord, Sit at my right hand until I make your enemies a footstool for your feet." [12] If, however, those who adopt the position of Arius and Eunomius claim this expression applies only to the Son, let them listen also to God himself saying, "I am, I am, and until you grow old I am:" [13] if it is taken in that sense, the God of all will be found to have his existence commensurate with the old age of human beings – which is the raving of maniacs. After all, the God of all is eternal, and co-eternal with him is his only-begotten Son. He also has an eternal kingdom; the most divine Daniel also taught us this, "His kingdom is an everlasting kingdom, which for all time will not be destroyed." [14]

The last enemy that will be done away with is death (v.26): after dispatching the devil and his assistants to exterior darkness, he will bring death to an end, and will raise up all the dead: *He has put all things under his feet,* [15] *remember* (v.27). Here he said the Father put all things under him, and in the letter to the Philippians he says he has done it: after saying, "He will transform the body of our lowliness so that it be conformed to the body of his glory," he went on, "by (357) the power that enables him also to put everything under him." [16] In other words, the one able to put everything under himself, he is saying, will also bedeck our perishable bodies with imperishability.

Now, when he said, All things are subjected, it is clear this excludes the one subjecting everything to him. When all things are subjected to him, then also the Son himself will also be subjected to the one subjecting everything to him (vv.27-28). This text those adopting the position of Arius and Eunomius are accustomed to bandy about unceasingly, supposing the status of the Only-begotten is diminished by it. [17] They ought realize, however, that the divine apostle in this text has written nothing about the divinity of the Only-begotten: in an exhortation to belief in the resurrection of the flesh, he endeavored to demonstrate its resurrection from the Lord's resurrection. It is clear that his confirmation arises from like applied to like: that was his reason for referring to him as *firstfruits of those fallen asleep*, calling him *a human being* and by the comparison with Adam bringing out the common resurrection happening through him, so that after showing the resurrection of the one of the same nature he might convince the opponents to believe that all human beings will share in the same resurrection. Accordingly, it should be understood that the natures of Christ the Lord are two, and that the divine Scripture speaks of him sometimes from the viewpoint of humanity, and sometimes of divinity: even if it speaks of him as God, it does not deny the humanity; even if it calls him man, it confesses at the same time the divinity. Now, it is impossible to say everything in elevated terms about him on account of the nature he has assumed from us. I mean, no matter how lowly the expressions, some people deny the assumption of the flesh; clearly more would suffer from that ailment were nothing lowly said. What on earth is the meaning of *and then he will be subjected*? It resembles, in fact, the situation of those who rule as despots at the present time: if he will then be subjected, he has not yet been subjected. Consequently, the blasphemers make the sinful mistake of trying to subject the one who has not yet accepted the limits of subjection; there is need to wait and learn the manner of the subjection.

We have spoken at great length about them, however, in our efforts against them; so we should be brief in commenting on the apostle's purpose. He was writing to the Corinthians, who had just recently been liberated from Greek mythology; their mythology is replete with utter intemperance and iniquity. Not to mention other aspects and defile my tongue, they worship gods that murder parents, and they say the children revolted against the parents, drove them out of their kingdom and snatched power for themselves. Since, then, he made great claims about Christ the Lord, that *he would do away with every ruler, every authority and power, would bring death to an end* and *put all things under his feet*, (360) he was obliged, lest they be spurred on by that dreadful mythology and suspect he does to the Father that begot him those things that the demons they worship were responsible for, to go further after saying, *It is clear this excludes the one subjecting everything to him*, and add, *the Son himself will also be subjected to the one subjecting everything to him*. That is to say, not only will he not subject the Father to himself, but he will personally even undergo the subjection proper to the Son. Consequently, the divine apostle in his suspicion of the harm stemming from Greek mythology added those words, employing rather lowly expressions for their benefit. For their part let the opponents explain the kind of subjection involved in that. Actually, if they are prepared to acknowledge the truth, here and now he gave evidence of subjection in becoming incarnate and procuring our salvation; so how will he then be subjected? how will he then also hand over the kingdom to the God and Father? In fact, if this is the position adopted, the God and Father will now be found not to possess the kingdom. The claims made by them are shot through with such absurdity.

You see, he also made his own our condition in that we are styled his body and he is called our head. "He has taken on our sins, and borne our ailments." [18] Likewise, too, he says in words of the psalm, "O God my God, hearken to me, why have you abandoned me? The words of my failings are far from saving me." [19] Admittedly, he did not commit sin, nor was guile found in his mouth; but he becomes the mouthpiece of our nature in becoming firstfruits of our nature. Likewise he makes his own both our disobedience here and now and our subjection in the future, and once we are subjected after the freedom from corruption he himself will be said to be subjected.

What follows, in fact, leads us to this understanding: after the divine apostle said, *Then the Son himself will be subjected to the one subjecting everything to him*, he went on, *so that God may be all in all*. That is to say, now he is everywhere in his substance: he has a nature uncircumscribed, and "in him we live and move and have our being," [20] according to the divine apostle. As far as his good pleasure is concerned, on the other hand, he is not in everything: "He takes pleasure in those who fear him, and in those who hope for his mercy." [21] Yet in them he is not all: "No one is rid of uncleanness," [22] remember, and "No one living will be justified in his sight," [23] and "If you take note of sins, Lord, Lord, who would hold their ground?" [24] So he takes pleasure in those who do good, but does not take pleasure in those who fall. In the future life, when corruption comes to an end and immortality is conferred, there will be no place for the passions: with them completely eliminated, no form of sin will any more be at work. In this way God then *will be all in all*, all people freed from falling, converted to him and under no inclination to the worst. (361) Now, what the divine apostle said here of God elsewhere he referred to Christ; he speaks this way, "Where there is no longer Jew or Greek, circumcision or uncircumcision, barbarian, Scythian, but Christ is all in all." [25] He would not have applied to the Son what belongs to the Father if their equality had not been taught to him by divine grace.

Let us, however, proceed with the remainder of the commentary. *Otherwise, what will they do who are baptized for the dead if the dead do not actually rise? why are they baptized for the dead?* (v.29). The baptized person, he is saying, is buried with the Lord so that, having shared death, they may also become sharers in the resurrection. [26] But if the body is dead and does not rise, why on earth are they baptized? *Why are we also hourly at risk?* (v.30). After making this general remark, he speaks of his own situation: *By my boasting of you in Christ Jesus our Lord, I die daily!* (v.30). He both indicated the extraordinary degree of risk and also revealed his own care. Constantly, he is saying, I consigned myself to deaths foreseen. By his *boasting* he referred to their faith, thus urging them to have faith.

If in human terms I fought wild beasts in Ephesus, what good was it to me if the dead do not rise? (v.32). In human terms, he is saying, I became the prey of wild beasts, but against hope I was saved. So what fruit did I reap from this danger if there is no resurrection of the dead? *Let us eat and drink: tomorrow we die.* [27] While the words are inspired, he cited them appropriately, meaning more or less this: fasting is pointless, temperance is pointless; let us enjoy the things of the present life, there being no reward laid up for the lovers of virtue. Then by way of exhortation, *Do not be deceived. Evil company corrupts good behavior* (v.33). By *good* here he means easy-going, what is easily led astray. [28] *Come to your right senses and do not sin: some people are ignorant of God. I say this to your shame* (v.34). As though to people who have lost their way and are besotted with unbelief he used the phrase *Come to your right senses.* Very sagely he referred to lack of belief in the resurrection as *ignorance of God*: the one who confesses to knowing God believes he is righteous, and reward is due to the righteous one; but we do not see the right reward in the present life. So the one confessing faith in God must await the resurrection.

Then he cites a question proposed by the unbelievers. *But someone will ask, How are the dead raised?* (364) *with what kind of body do they come?* (v.35). The question is twofold, about the manner of the resurrection and about the future quality of the body. He then explains both from human experience, and calls stupid the person incapable of understanding it. *Fool? What you sow does not come to life unless it dies. And what you sow is not the body that will come to be but a bare seed, perhaps of wheat or one of the others* (vv.36-37): consider the seeds, and have regard for the furrows resembling graves, and the seeds being buried like graves, then sprouting and growing. In other words, you are not sowing the body that is to be – that is, the ear of wheat – but the bare seed, whether of corn or one of the others. Now, it was very appropriate for him to use different terms: he did not say, It does not sprout unless it dies; instead, he used our terms of the seeds to bring out from them our resurrection. The Lord likewise also said, "Unless the grain of wheat falls into the ground and dies, it remains alone, whereas if it dies, it bears much fruit." [29]

Having thus brought out the manner of the resurrection, he shows also the quality of the bodies. *But God gives it a body as he chooses, and to each of the seeds its own body* (v.38): as wheat grows from wheat, lentils from lentils, and each type from its own seed, likewise also our bodies rise as they were, though with greater glory, and with incorruptibility and immortality. This can also be seen happening with the seeds: what is sown as bare seed grows up with splendid vesture. So he explains both things, the manner of resurrection and the quality of the bodies.

Then he mentions also the difference in those who rise. *Not all flesh is alike: flesh of beasts is one kind, of fish another, and of birds another* (v.39). The nature of flesh is one, he is saying, being composed of the four elements; but there is a difference in appearance. Likewise, therefore, resurrection of all is one, as also the change of bodies into incorruptibility; but the difference in manner causes also the difference in reward. *There are both heavenly bodies and earthly bodies, but the glory of the heavenly is one thing and the earthly another* (v.40): those worthy of heaven are clad in a glory befitting heaven, whereas those with an earthly attitude will take on the clothing suited to their choice. Having thus made the distinction, he brings out also the difference in the heavenly bodies: not all the righteous will share the same lot, but will receive the reward commensurate with their good deeds. The Lord also forecast this in (365) the sacred Gospels: "There are many mansions in my Father's place."[30] Here, too, in similar terms: *The glory of the sun is one thing, of the moon another, and of the stars another: star differs from star in glory* (v.41). Likewise, too, some of the righteous will shine like the sun, some like the moon, while some will resemble the splendor of the brightest stars, and others will be like the more obscure.

Having thus brought out also this distinction, he shifts his attention to the topic of the common resurrection. *This is the way, too, with the resurrection of the dead* (v.42) – that is, like the comparison of the seeds. *It is sown in corruption, it is raised in incorruptibility*: in two or three days it undergoes a noisome decay, but it is freed from decay and rises incorrupt. *It is sown in dishonor, it is raised in glory* (v.43): what is so dishonorable as a corpse? *It is sown in weakness, it is raised in power*: what is weaker than that awful gore and dust? Yet it will have an indestructible power. *It is sown a physical body, it will be raised a spiritual body. There is a physical body, and there is a spiritual body* (v.44). In each case he used *is sown* to encourage them to be confident that what is sown sprouts. Now, by *physical*[31] he refers to what is governed by the soul, and by *spiritual* what is managed by the Spirit. Those worthy will receive this manifold grace – hence the reason that what is here and now given is called a pledge, since the grace given there is manifold.

Scripture also speaks in these terms, Adam the first human being became a living soul,[32] *the last Adam a life-giving spirit* (v.45). The first truth we read in the Scriptures, the second we came to know through experience. Now, he did not call the second Adam a living spirit but *life-giving*: he is the source of eternal life for all. *It is not the spiritual that is first, however, but the physical and then the spiritual* (v.46): on account of the weakness of the physical the spiritual remedy was brought into play. *The first human being was of the earth, earthy; the second human being the Lord from heaven* (v.47). He indicated his second coming: it is from there he will come to us. *As the earthy one is, so too are the earthy ones; and as the heavenly one is, so too are the heavenly ones. And as they bore the likeness of the earthy one, we too shall bear the likeness of the heavenly one* (48-49): just as we shared the curse of the earthy first parent and participated in death, so we shall share the glory of the heavenly Lord. (368)

This is what I am saying, brethren, that flesh and blood are powerless to inherit the kingdom of God (v.50). By *flesh and blood* he refers to mortal nature; it is impossible for it, mortal as it is, to attain the heavenly kingdom. In fact, he went on to say, *nor does decay inherit incorruptibility.* It is clear, however, that once made incorruptible it will enjoy the promised good things. *Lo, I am telling you a mystery* (v.51). What is not made clear to everyone but confided to friends alone is called a mystery. So he consoles them by revealing hidden things. *While we shall not all die, we shall all be changed*: Not only will the dead rise incorrupt, but as well those still alive will be clothed in incorruptibility.

In an instant, in the twinkling of an eye (v.52). He brought out the suddenness of the resurrection, referring by *instant* to the tiniest body visible in daylight, which owing to its extreme smallness is indivisible,[33] and by *twinking of an eye* to the movement of the eyelid. By these terms he brought out God's power: not even a brief time will pass between God's command and the resurrection of the dead. *At the last trumpet.* This will be, he is saying, when the final trumpet will sound: *It will sound, and the dead will be raised incorrupt, and we shall be changed.* We referred not to himself but to the people still alive at that time.

You see, this corruptible body must put on incorruptibility, and this mortal body immortality (v.53). He explained clearly that what rises is nothing other than the decaying thing itself; he gave us a glimpse of this in his use of this expression like some finger, saying *this corruptible body* and *this mortal body. When this corruptible body puts on incorruptibility and this mortal body puts on immortality, then the scriptural saying will be fulfilled, Death has been swallowed up in vic-*

tory. [34] *Death, where is your goad? Hades, where is your victory?* [35] (vv.54-55). As though perceiving reality itself and seeing the Lord's victory and the resurrection of the dead, the divine apostle sings the inspired song like someone chanting a victory song over the enemy. *Now, death's goad is sin* (v.56): this it was that handed nature over to death. *And the power of sin is the Law*: sin is not reckoned when there is no Law.

But thank God for giving us the victory through our Lord Jesus Christ (v.57). He was obliged to close the treatment of resurrection with a hymn. (369) *And so, my dear brethren, be firm, immovable* (v.58). He makes this recommendation to them as though they were unsteady. *Always excelling in the work of the Lord*: gather the riches of piety diligently. *Aware that your labor is not in vain in the Lord*: the judge is righteous, and he weaves crowns for the athletes and bestows rewards on the laborers.

CHAPTER SIXTEEN

After making the recommendation in this way, he urges them to have a thought for the care of the saints. *Now, concerning the collection for the saints: as I instructed the churches of Galatia, do likewise in your own case as well* (v.1). By *collection* he refers to the sum of money. It was not without purpose that he made mention of the Galatians, but to indicate that he had also urged them to do this. *On the first day of the week let each of you put something aside, saving whatever you can spare* (v.2). He leaves the amount to good will, teaching that God cooperates with souls choosing the highest things, implying as much by *whatever you can spare*. The Lord's day, observed on account of the resurrection, was also suitable for the work.

So that when I come, collections will not then take place. Instead, when I arrive, I shall send those you approve with letters to take your gift to Jerusalem. If it seems worthwhile my also traveling, they will accompany me (vv.3-4): it would not be seemly for a collection to be made in my presence;[1] my task is to send it to the saints with those you choose. If, however, I see the contributions to be generous, I too shall take part in the ministry. He did not say, note, I shall take the money, but *they will accompany me*: he is the first to do what he recommends to the others, and gives no offense to Jews or Greeks, or to the Church of God. He indicates to them also the time of arrival: *I shall come to you when I pass through Macedonia* (v.5); and in case they should be irked by the preference given the Macedonians, he went on, *I am in fact passing through Macedonia. Perhaps I shall stay with you, or even spend the winter, so that you may send me on my way wherever I am going. In other words, I prefer not to see you only in passing; rather, I hope to spend some time with you if the Lord allows* (vv.5-7). He does not want to do anything without the Lord's approval; instead, he prefers to be led by that right hand. Of course, he consoled them a good deal by these words, promising to stay with them for a while. [2]

He also explains why he does not arrive immediately. *But I shall stay in Ephesus till Pentecost: a wide door for effective work has opened for me, and adversaries are numerous* (vv.8-9). There were many making an approach to the message, and also many opponents, (372) trying to prove a hindrance to their salvation. *If Timothy comes, see that he has nothing to fear from you* (v.10), that is, welcome him, look after him, let him meet with no trouble. *After all, he is doing the Lord's work like me.* The testimony suffices for moving even the indifferent to look after the disciple. *So let no one despise him* (v.11): instead of looking down on his green years, recognize in him the apostolic labors. *Send him on his way in peace so that he may come to me: I am expecting him with the brethren.* He included this as well to move them to look after the disciple, meaning, He will come to me, and will report on your general situation.

Concerning brother Apollos, I strongly urged him to come to you with the brethren. He was not altogether keen on coming to you at this point (v.12). Apollos was famous, and acquainted with them; so he adopts a conciliatory tone towards them, explaining that he had exhorted him to come. He did not go so far, however, as to say he refused; instead, he left it all to God's providence. *He will come when he has the opportunity.* He consoled them with hope.

Be vigilant, stand firm in the faith, have courage and strength. Let all you do be done in love (vv.13-14). He said *Be vigilant* on account of the impostors, and *stand firm, have courage and strength* on account of the obvious conflicts: the religious people were being persecuted by the ungodly. He said *Let all you do be done in love* with a view to those dividing the body of the Church, those in the grip of the passion of ambition, those partaking of food sacrificed to idols and scorning the people taking offense at it.

Brethren, you know the household of Stephanas and Fortunatus, that they are the first fruits of Achaia for Christ and made themselves available for ministry to the saints. I urge you to put yourselves at the service of such people and of everyone working and laboring with them (vv.15-16). He gave double commendation, their being the first to accept the saving message, and their throwing open their home to the saints and providing them with every attention. This is the reason his instructions are that they and like-minded people be accorded great respect. *I rejoice at the coming of Stephanas and Fortunatus and Achaicus because they made up for your absence, refreshing my spirit and yours. So give recognition to people such as them* (vv.17-18). The Corinthians sent letters with them and asked the apostle about married people; and he in turn dispatched his letter with them. That is to say, blessed Timothy did not, as some presumed, carry the letters; rather, though he was sent to (373) them, it is likely that after fulfilling a different function in another city he then reached them. In fact, what the letter says about him suggests as much, *If Timothy comes, see that he has nothing to fear from you.* [3] He commended them all the more keenly lest the Corinthians presume they had turned their accusers and do them harm.

The churches of Asia greet you (v.19). He included this for their benefit to show the progress of the preaching. *Aquila and Priscilla greet you warmly in the Lord along with the church that is in their house.* The divine apostle stayed with them; they also were tentmakers by trade. Out of their great virtue they made their house available as a church, giving preference in their actions to what the Church required. *All the brethren send greetings with a holy kiss* (v.20). He had expelled their hostility, and he bound them together with the holy kiss.

The greeting is in my own hand, Paul's (v.21). I dictated the letter, he is saying, and added the greeting by hand to indicate by the script that the whole contents are mine. [4] *If anyone does not love the Lord Jesus, let them be accursed* (v.22): let the person with no ardent affection for Christ the Lord be alienated from the common body of the Church. By this remark he instilled fear in those already under accusation. There are some persons who have love but are not prepared to have anyone share the love, whereas the divine apostle is anxious to have all people as fellow lovers, and he excises from the Church those who are not like this. *Maran atha*. This is not from Hebrew, as some supposed, but from Aramaic; in translation it reads "The Lord has come." [5] He included it to depress the conceitedness of the Corinthians with a name for eloquence, and to highlight the fact that their need was not for learning but for faith.

The grace of our Lord Jesus Christ be with you. My love to you all in Christ Jesus. Amen (v.23-24). While it was habitual with him to beseech the grace of the Lord Jesus Christ for them, it was not idly that he included his own love, but to emphasize that he had employed harsher language than usual under the impulse of love for them, in the manner of a father's affection and in his longing for their salvation. For our part let us draw benefit from this, and love the loving Lord so as to have no share in the apostolic curse but rather be thought worthy of the apostolic tabernacles, [6] in Christ Jesus our Lord, to whom with the Father and the all-holy Spirit be honor and (376) magnificence, now and forever, for ages of ages. Amen. [7]

Notes to the *First Letter to the Corinthians*

CHAPTER ONE

[1] Acts 18.9-10. Theodoret is following indiscriminately the evidence of Acts (for details like this vision and Paul's length of time in Corinth) and of the contents of the letter (for the nature and concerns of the Corinthian community). He cannot allow himself to adopt the attitude of caution of modern commentators to the degree of correspondence between these Lucan and Pauline sources, nor their view that Paul wrote other letters to the Corinthian community no longer extant (cf. his comment on 5.9).

[2] Theodoret touches on some of the issues and topics covered in the letter, roughly in the order of their appearance.

[3] This is a comparative remark in the wake of the more formally doctrinal Romans, made in the light of the particular pastoral concerns Paul here addresses, though the apostle in at least one celebrated pericope summarizes "what is of first importance" for all believers.

[4] 1 Cor 16.10. Theodoret here implies that Stephanas and friends took Paul's letter back to Corinth (the verb is *diakonein*; cf. 2 Cor 3.3), and not Timothy (a contrary view held by some commentators known to him), as he insists again in commenting on 16.17-18. Modern commentators see these men as rather bringing a letter of concern (cf. 7.1) to Paul that prompts this response, whose bearers are not specified (though Kümmel allows the possibility they were the same men).

[5] Theodoret is always on the alert to prevent the reader taking Pauline expressions in a way supportive of the subordinationism of early or later Arians, making here precisely the same point he made on Rom 11.36 – though without similar grounds, surely.

[6] Cf. Acts 18.12-17, some mss including mention of Greeks in v.17. Modern commentators would agree Theodoret is right to be tentative about identifying the two men.

[7] Theodoret conveniently omits reference here to the phrase "in every place" that is located close to "theirs and ours" in the text but is hardly its antecedent (despite Schulze's punctuation).

[8] Again (as also on v.8) Theodoret shows that he is both looking in the text for Pauline reference to the situation of the Corinthians and reading into it guidance on his own current theological concerns – exegesis and eisegesis together.

[9] 1 Cor 12.8.

[10] Cf. 1 Tim 6.13, where, however, at least in the received text, a different verb, "charge," occurs.

[11] Matt 24.14 loosely recalled – a habit of Theodoret's.

[12] Kümmel traces the history of modern attempts to identify the "parties" listed by Paul, concluding, "Nothing suggests that Paul has himself formulated the slogans in 1.12" – yet this is just what Theodoret not unconvincingly puts forward: to bring out the impropriety of calling cliques after their teachers, Paul cites a few others of true eminence (including his own), and as a *coup de grace* adds Christ.

[13] Matt 28.19.

[14] A significant recognition by a bishop of the pride of place to be accorded the ministry of the Word over liturgical ministries, one being of divine origin, the others an accidental adjunct arising from human appointment. Chrysostom the preacher could understandably make such a ranking (and he does so dignify that ministry); it is less predictable in Theodoret the desk theologian.

[15] Cf. Isa 29.14 LXX.

[16] Theodoret appropriately distinguishes the various meanings of wisdom that apply in Paul's treatment of Jews' and Greeks' response to the divine plan: human sagacity, cosmic design, the incarnation and death of Jesus. He might have gone further and recalled the rabbinic attribution of wisdom *par excellence* to the Law, which Paul is also classing as folly here.

[17] Acts 17.18.

[18] Theodoret probably has in mind the celebrated personification of wisdom at Prov 8.22-31, a favorite text of the Arians for proving the Word's creatureliness, and one he (unlike many commentators) also finds irrelevant in commenting on the Christological hymn at Col 1.15-20. Is his resistance to any application of *sophia* to the divinity due also to this term's occurrence in gnostic cosmology, which he thinks Paul may have found current with some Corinthians (especially with that use of *aion* in v.20 and 2.6)? Considering Paul's plain statement that Christ is God's wisdom, his denial is perverse, as is his ignoring Paul's repetition of it in v.30.

[19] Cf. Jer 9.24; 2 Cor 10.17.

[20] John 1.12-13.

[21] Theodoret, with his mind on Arian abuse of Old Testament Wisdom texts, is not prepared to go along here with modern commentators like Barrett, who claims, "Thus Christ crucified himself becomes the personal figure of Wisdom, God's agent in creation, but especially (as far as the present passage is concerned) God's means of restoring men to himself."

CHAPTER TWO

[1] Does Theodoret see Paul as a model here in choosing biblical narrative over speculative reasoning (hardly his own choice)? *Oikonomia* here, as often, means not simply the divine plan but its highpoint, the Incarnation, the life of Jesus.

[2] Theodoret seems to be taking Paul's terms in the sense of physical suffering, not simply emotional turmoil.

[3] Paul's mention again of this age, *aion*, and the mature, part of gnostic terminology, does not this time strike a chord with Theodoret. See note 18 on ch 1.

[4] As we should do in our time, Theodoret does with his readers – dismiss any simplistic notion both of mystery and of wisdom to imply mere secrets, *pace* NRSV and other versions that should know better. For Paul, as Theodoret recognizes, the mystery (of Christ) is that eternal design of God of which the culmination is the Incarnation and Paschal *Mystery* of Jesus, which bring us salvation and glory. See my "The mystery of Christ: clue to Paul's thinking on wisdom."

[5] Luke 23.34.

[6] Again Theodoret, perhaps seeing here an invitation to lay the blame for Jewish misfortunes on the crucifixion (as he and Chrysostom frequently do), passes up the option taken by some commentators of regarding the rulers of this age to be supernatural beings in gnostic cosmology.

[7] A further instance of Theodoret's perversity in resisting Paul's plain statement out of his unhappiness with the *communicatio idiomatum*: he cannot bring himself – or allow his readers – to say God suffered, God was crucified.

[8] Since Paul is not quoting precisely any biblical text (cf. Isa 64.3 LXX), commentators busy themselves with locating the source of this citation. Theodoret is impatient with such efforts: *akribeia* does not reach to impugning the apostle's veracity – and in any case, he adds, we do not have access to all inspired works, *propheteiai*, citing Chronicles in support (perhaps some such statements as 2 Chr 18.9; 24.19).

[9] 1 Cor 4.5. Commentators have trouble following Paul's thought here and identifying its background. Theodoret's principal concern is to avoid any suggestion of ignorance on God's part or of inequality in talk about God and the Spirit, and this rather than Paul's statement gets his attention.

[10] Not from Father and Son, be it noted.

[11] This phrase of Paul also has the commentators suggesting a variety of interpretations. Bishop Theodoret takes it to refer to the Scriptures and the sacraments (*mysteria*), nicely linking Old and New Testaments as spiritual realities, and in particular finding OT types for NT sacraments.

[12] Cf. Isa 40.13; Rom 11.34.

[13] Theodoret has little difficulty seeing the relevance and value of these verses, which puzzle and even dismay modern commentators (Barrett despairing of a rendering of *psychikos* that is adequate, opting for "natural" only because of "the difficulty of finding an alternative," Murphy-O'Connor suggesting darkly that Paul's principle "has had a most pernicious influence in church history"). Theodoret, on the contrary, whose text of v.15 reads "everyone" (not "everything") as the object of the spiritual person's discernment, sees Paul's confidence well-grounded and consistent with the theme of the chapter.

CHAPTER THREE

[1] Theodoret adheres to his simple and plausible understanding of the parties in Corinth, not having (like Barrett) to explain why the names Cephas and Christ do not occur again or how many the parties were.

[2] Modern commentators make much of the neuter pronoun opening the verse ("to underline the instrumental character of ministry," in the view of Murphy-O'Connor), but Theodoret's distinctive text reads differently, without losing the nuance Murphy-O'Connor discerns.

[3] Perhaps from his own experience in the apostolate, Theodoret passes quickly over Paul's accent on unity in the first part of the verse – the drift of the chapter so far, after all – to weigh into the second part on individual differences between effort and outcome in apostolate and the practice of virtue. It is a rare excursus on the part of this desk theologian scrupulous about the limits to his role.

[4] While modern commentators debate whether Paul is accentuating here divine-human cooperation or the need for harmony among the evangelists in Corinth, Theodoret seizes upon the denial of the term to the Son by Arian subordinationists. He would have preferred Paul not to employ it here.

[5] Matt 16.16,18. Without relating Paul's warning on foundations to any Cephas party at Corinth, as do some modern commentators like Barrett, Theodoret sees the connection with the pericope of the Petrine confession, interpreting it more benignly.

[6] After just above deserting Paul's thought to joust with heretics, Theodoret surprises us by showing more interest in a moral than a dogmatic interpretation of these verses. Guinot, however, reminds us that Chrysostom likewise declines to follow those preferring the latter, and may be responsible for the change.

[7] The apocalyptic character of these verses has commentators struggling to find a clear reference, so Theodoret is not on his own in this. His editor Schulze is at pains to show that the (true) text does not show him taking Paul's mention of fire as a reference to purgatory, unlike Latins ancient and medieval. His concern, rather, is that no one should present teachers in a poor light: he clearly has an esteem for the role, just as above he promoted the ministry of the Word over (mere) baptizing.

[8] We have seen Theodoret before, as on Rom 8.11, anxious to uphold the *homoousion* of the Spirit.

[9] Job 5.13.

[10] Cf. Ps 94.11.

[11] Theodoret discerns the connection of these concluding verses of the chapter to its opening about divisions in the Corinthian community, but cannot resist leaving Paul's thought for a further tilt at Arian positions with the mention of the interrelation of Christians, Christ and God. Modern commentators like Lightfoot and Barrett join him in this.

CHAPTER FOUR

[1] Acts 14.14-15; 10.26.

[2] A conflation of Mark 9.35; 10.44.

[3] 1 Cor 7.24. Taking his text at face value, Theodoret makes as good a fist of the puzzling phrase as did modern commentators until J. Strugnell in 1974 demonstrated that it is merely a marginal comment of a copyist whose copy lacked the negative, prompting him to insert it and remark, "the *not* is above what is written."

[4] 2 Tim 2.12. Like modern commentators, Theodoret recognizes Paul's use of irony here; but unlike Murphy-O'Connor he does not see this extending as far as v.13.

[5] Barrett, whose otherwise thorough commentary could be improved by some reference to patristic insights, would have benefited in this case from Theodoret's understanding of this unusual word before coming up with a version "scapegoats."

[6] How Theodoret discerns gratitude on Paul's part in this context is not easy to see.

[7] Cf. Acts 13.6-11.

CHAPTER FIVE

[1] In telling fashion Theodoret teases out the implications of Paul's less explicit statement of the irregularity (cf. his comment on 2 Cor 7.12). Modern commentators, by contrast, devote their attention to determining whether to translate *porneia* in this case as incest, adultery or fornication.

[2] For a pastor, of course, schism from the community was the way to perdition, membership of the community being the means to grace (at least in Antioch's incarnational thinking).

[3] Theodoret resonates with Paul's Passover analogy, detailing references to unleavened bread and sacrificial lamb; but he speaks of the Passover as an observance, not of the Jews of his time, but of the Old Testament, mentioning also its Christian counterpart. Likewise on Romans 3.25 he could speak at length on the mercy seat of OT times and suggest its NT realization, but not pick up Paul's reference to a current Jewish observance of the Day of Atonement. Was he not in touch with the Judaism of his day, or did he prefer not to acknowledge it?

[4] We have seen Theodoret before (as a matter of principle?) declining to entertain the possibility (recognized by modern commentators) of other letters now lost having been written to the Corinthian community.

[5] We have also seen Theodoret elsewhere adopting this Pauline principle in opposition to dualists like Marcion and the manichees who represented the world as evil.

[6] A gloss of Theodoret's own, though not without support from Paul's thinking at 10.16-21, e.g. Barrett concurs: "This prohibition will evidently include (though it will not be confined to) his exclusion from the church's common meal" – a phrase more in keeping with Barrett's "low" sacramental theology than Theodoret's.

[7] Deut 17.7.

CHAPTER SIX

[1] Theodoret seems to be taking Paul's *pleonektes* of 6.11 in the sense of litigious and not simply grasping.

[2] Matt 12.41-42; 19.28.

[3] Cf. 2 Pet 2.4; Jude 6.

[4] Editors and commentators differ on the punctuation of the verses, but with Theodoret agree on Paul's drift.

[5] Cf. Rom 13.1-7.

[6] Barrett speaks of the "unconscious Trinitarianism" of the phrasing, Murphy-O'Connor maintains "the thought is not yet trinitarian," but for Theodoret with the baptismal formula in mind Paul could not be more explicit.

[7] Matt 22.30.

[8] Gen 2.24.

[9] Theodoret has no false prudery in spelling out the full significance of the immorality the Corinthians felt free to engage in; never wordy for words' sake, he explicates Paul's thought with telling starkness.

[9] Rom 12.1.

CHAPTER SEVEN

[1] Cf. 1 Cor 11.3. Theodoret is reading a text of 7.3 that includes *eunoia* as what is due to each partner.

[2] In commentary on vv.2 and 3 Theodoret insists on sexual equality based on nature, at least as far as marriage rights are concerned, lightly chiding society for its inconsistency in this regard despite the evidence of nature. He does not proceed to chide Paul for some encouragement of discrimination in exclusivist word usage in v.1, *anthropos* being used where *aner* would be appropriate (though admittedly in the slogan being quoted). Likewise in his Commentary on the Psalms, Theodoret takes the psalmist to task in the opening of Ps 1, "Blessed is the man," insisting both men and women are in focus – though his own word usage is not always precise in what follows.

[3] Cf. Gen 2.24. Theodoret continues in his sage recognition of the more or less lax attitudes to marital fidelity of husbands and wives, respectively. He impresses as a shrewd observer of contemporary mores.

[4] At this point (but cf. his comment on v.8) Theodoret does not quite resolve the debate as to whether Paul, in putting himself forward as an *archetypos*, is suggesting he is single (Murphy-O'Connor), celibate, widower (J. Jeremias), or "possessing the capacity for resistance to sensual allurements" (P. Bachmann). He says only that Paul is betraying his own *hagneia*; and he reveals his own pastoral breadth by admitting the married have their own charism. Except for the phrases "the lesser way ... the better part," we find the bishop's thinking on marriage and celibacy quite contemporary.

[5] Matt 7.7, preceded by a typically Antiochene statement of the need for

human cooperation with – even preparation for – grace.

[6] Another manuscript adds, "both celibacy and the abstinence of widow-hood after marriage." Commentators like Fitzmyer warn against the harmonizing of data from this letter and from Acts (as Theodoret is doing here in referring to Luke's phrase "a young man named Saul" in Acts 7.58 – that is, someone under 40) in determining Paul's age and marital status.

[7] Matt 5.32. The bishop clearly does not envisage divorce or annulment, only temporary separation – at least in Paul's thinking grounded on a dominical law, if not in the church of Cyrus. (It is interesting that Theodoret has imperceptibly shifted the onus from Paul's separated wife to a sepa-rated husband.)

[8] 2 Cor 13.3; 1 Cor 15.10; Rom 12.3.

[9] V.39, though modern commentators like Lightfoot apply the phrase to the widow, not the intended husband.

[10] Bishop Theodoret, who in this discussion of ticklish marital situations has shown the signs of an experienced and sage approach, is perhaps sug-gesting Paul is overly optimistic in his expectations of such mixed marriages.

[11] Matt 10.34.

[12] The Migne text here, mistakenly, prints *kalen* for *kaken*, whereas Theodoret – himself overly sanguine, perhaps – is expanding on the division that acceptance of the faith can bring to households before harmony eventu-ally prevails.

[13] Theodoret does not take advantage of Paul's evenhandedness to launch into a disquisition on the valueless character of circumcision; while insist-ing with Paul on the true basis of its value, he concedes it real merit as response to divine law.

[14] Theodoret sides with modern commentators like Conzelmann and Barrett in taking Paul's vague phrase as a recommendation to slaves to decline an offer of freedom (if an "exaggeration"), unlike Moule and Murphy-O'Connor. His decision is supported by rationalizing, not by tex-tual evidence: would the mores of the time be responsible for his option and argument? The bishop finds no conflict between religion and slavery, and further develops his moralizing justification of slavery.

[15] Matt 19.10-12 loosely recalled.

[16] The question is relevant, and Theodoret might also have delved into the sense of the phrase in the previous verse, "in view of the present neces-sity," with its implications for Pauline eschatology. But, willy-nilly, it has escaped him.

[17] With his experience of monastic living at Apamea, he would be aware that this chapter is a *locus classicus* for the spirituality of consecrated life; and he wants to make it clear that Paul in this verse is not dealing with people in that situation.

[18] Where we might have preferred Theodoret to discuss Paul's eschatology as revealed in these verses, he takes them instead as encouragement of detachment from this-worldly realities in the manner of Heb 13.14 and

The Epistle to Diognetus that could smack of dualism – something not typical of him, nor does he expand on the theme.

[19] Ezek 34.18.

[20] Isa 24.2.

[21] The text of v.34 is represented in a great range of forms. Theodoret's is divided in a way that allows him to discern Paul's general theme of the detachment possible for virgins who make a profession of virginity, such as religious women (and men); consecrated virginity, he says, has both a pragmatic and an eschatological value. His work on virginity that he proceeds to cite is no longer extant, unfortunately (he speaks of it as *logoi* – homilies? – though not delivered but composed, *suggraphein*).

[22] We should like to read Theodoret's work on virginity to see how he develops those pragmatic and eschatological aspects, and whether he avoids an impractical dualism if speaking, as here, to people living in the world.

[23] Theodoret feels none of the uncertainty that dogs modern commentators about the case proposed by the Corinthians for Paul to deal with. Assisted by a reading of v.38 in his text, *eyyamizein*, marry off (where later commentators read *gamizein* to mean take in marriage), he understands Paul to be referring to a man and his daughter, and to be regarding marriage as a reputable state (unlike the heretics, whether at Corinth or of Theodoret's time), if less reputable than virginity. No comment, predictably, on the daughter's rights in the situation.

[24] Theodoret is scrupulously faithful to Paul's thought in distinguishing the relative status of widows, giving no encouragement to rigorists like Novatian's followers. (Chrysostom had written a short work against remarriage by widows.)

CHAPTER EIGHT

[1] Exod 33.12. Theodoret does not generally see it his task to document Paul's thought from other biblical statement – simply to explicate (and sometimes merely paraphrase) it, occasionally showing its bearing on current theological issues. But in these verses he is about to joust with a key Arian heresy, and looks to Scripture for ammunition.

[2] Titus 2.13. The Corinthians' misunderstanding of idols and their claim to divinity has no malice in it, Theodoret says; it simply arises from imperfect *theologia*, an "imprecise understanding of the doctrine" of the Trinity taught them by Paul himself. So he rehearses some simple teaching based on other Pauline statements and comparisons with Greek mythology. When he comes to the error of heresiarchs, however, he finds no saving feature, classing it simply as blasphemy.

[3] Rom 9.5 in a reading different from that on which he commented at its place in the letter.

[4] Exod 20.2; Deut 6.4; Ps 104.1.

[5] While we may not be happy with the distinction Theodoret makes, a version such as the following leaves also a modern commentator like

Barrett dissatisfied, "through whom all things, including ourselves, come into being." Barrett observes, "This rendering, in bringing out the relation, tends to obscure the distinction between *all things* and *ourselves* – Christ is the agent of creation, and also the agent of redemption, and it is as the product of redemption that we come into being."

[6] Theodoret's text reads *syneidesei*, awareness (and later in the verse in the sense of conscience), for *synetheia*, association; but he sees no significance for Paul's thought in the difference.

[7] Cf. Matt 18.10.

CHAPTER NINE

[1] John 3.33.

[2] According to Guinot, this interpretation is that of Severian, fellow Antiochene of Theodoret, who however does not pursue it, having already taken a position on Paul's marital status.

[3] Deut 25.4.

[4] Ps 147.8 LXX. Like other commentators, Theodoret is unwilling to leave Paul giving the impression that animals do not fall within God's care.

[5] As a priest Theodoret is naturally interested in the provisions for Old Testament priests as listed in Lev 7 and Num 18.

[6] Luke 10.7.

[7] 2 Cor 12.13; 11.8 – not quite in sequence, as Theodoret thinks.

[8] Cf. Phil 4.10,15-16.

[9] Cf. 2 Tim 1.16.

[10] Though his text is divided into chapters like ours (cf. his comment on 10.14), Theodoret has been seen to divide Paul's material into larger sections. Within these he can pause at times to review the progress of thought and look ahead – a helpful exercise for his readers.

[11] Cf. Acts 21.26; 16.3. Theodoret (whose text of v.20 omits the phrase "though not myself under the Law") notes what should strike a commentator as a difficulty, but is in fact passed over without remark by moderns like Barrett and Murphy-O'Connor – namely, how does the second category in the series of three differ from the first. Unlike them, he does not presume the first and the second are identical; he admits the difficulty implicitly by offering his personal solution, and makes a good fist of it, if not wholly convincing, by distinguishing two responses by Jews to the Gospel, rejection and incomplete acceptance.

[12] Theodoret would have in mind the different approaches adopted by Paul to a Jewish congregation in Pisidian Antioch in Acts 13, for instance, and to the Areopagus in Athens in Acts 17.

[13] Rom 15.1.

[14] Cf. Matt 9.11; Luke 7.37, the incident of the sinful woman at Jesus' feet, whom Theodoret – unlike Chrysostom – does not go on to present as a prostitute, as often portrayed in later Christian tradition.

[15] A good metaphor is not lost on Theodoret, whom we have seen employing his own to good effect.

CHAPTER TEN

[1] For one already disposed to appreciate biblical imagery, Theodoret relishes the encouragement of Paul to recognize in all these Old Testament realities types of New Testament – and specifically sacramental – persons, events and rituals (though it is interesting that he does not develop the eucharistic associations).

[2] Exod 32.6.

[3] Cf. Num 25.1,9; 21.4-6; 17.10.

[4] Theodoret does not pick Paul up on the number wrongly cited from Num 25.9 (24,000 in fact).

[5] Schulze admits the verse is quoted differently by Theodoret elsewhere, which perhaps accounts for this repetition.

[6] Rom 6.19, a text not quite supporting his reduction of "human" to "insignificant" – a demeaning comment.

[7] The Greek could be read to mean, "whose body and blood we claim to be," but the argument depends on the meaning given above – as does good theology. His argument goes thus: as the Jews (and the pagans) offered and also consumed the one victim, so by celebrating the eucharist Christians offer and consume the body and blood of the Lord. Paul's argument goes one step further, that it is impossible for Christians to claim that though consuming the pagans' victim, they are not linked with them in offering the victim.

[8] Deut 32.21.

[9] Ps 24.1.

[10] A disarming admission by the bishop of his agenda in mixed social intercourse.

[11] The psalm verse recurs here in Theodoret's Koine text in use in Antioch, and he rationalizes its double occurrence without in either place noting (or being aware of?) its use by Jews to recommend the recital of grace at meals, something that Paul (who would have known of the practice) touches on again in v.30.

[12] Not quite Paul's thought, who has moved to a defense of the strong – the mature, in terminology Paul also uses.

[13] Matt 5.16.

CHAPTER ELEVEN

[1] Theodoret implicitly takes the position of many commentators that this verse is retrospective, not belonging to the material that follows. So he moves quickly to Paul's new focus of attention.

[2] Theodoret lets himself be drawn away from Paul's general drift here into Christological debate in which the verse was caught up (the term *homoousios* figuring prominently). The result is that the issues that interest modern commentators – whether *kephale* has the meaning of head or simply source, and whether the verse bears on marital relations or on equality of the sexes generally – receive little attention.

³ *Pace* Barrett, and in line with the interpretation of the NRSV and other commentators, Theodoret presumes Paul is referring to a current fad (not necessarily associated with homosexuality, in his view, *pace* Murphy-O'Connor and Byrne) of men adopting the practice customary with women of letting their hair grow long. Not inclined to gild Paul's lily, he curtly disallows it, at least in church.

⁴ Taking his cue from Paul, Theodoret looks to Gen 1 and 2 for a biblical basis for the relation of the sexes in connection with hair styles. He takes the traditional interpretation of the human being's creation in God's image to mean succession to a governmental role, as 1.26 suggests (and our fuller knowledge of the background of the Hebrew terms in it confirms), but then shows that he – like Paul – is taking the *anthropos* of that verse to mean the male only, a careless reading that encourages his understanding of woman's role as subordinate. His reading of Gen 2 confirms this understanding.

⁵ Acts 12.15.

⁶ Matt 18.10. Does the scriptural documentation really explain the mention of angels (which has modern commentators guessing as well)?

⁷ Theodoret, no more than Paul, has shown how a topknot – long hair or veil – is a symbol of acceptance of authority. His comment on Paul's subsequent insistence on the interdependence of man and woman is affected by his reading "in the world" (*kosmo*; "in appearance"?) in his text in place of "in the Lord," encouraging a simply biological view of the relationship.

⁸ Matt 18.7.

⁹ Literally, "By the *kyriakon deipnon* he refers to the *Despotikon mysterion*" – Paul's term for the eucharist not identical with that in use in Theodoret's time.

¹⁰ Literally, "the sacred mysteries."

¹¹ The bishop sees the eucharist primarily in paschal terms (perhaps even quoting from the Easter liturgy), at least in this context where the community's behavior at the supper is the issue.

¹² Sacraments, as signs rather than mysteries, will be otiose when the body signified re-appears.

¹³ Is the bishop respecting Paul's intention in this, in the light of the chapter's drift (to do with "lack of loving concern," in Barrett's words), or rehearsing his own usual pastoral directives about readiness for reception of the eucharist?

¹⁴ As we do, Theodoret finds this fatalistic comment of Paul somewhat out of character; unlike some preachers, he does not exploit it for moralistic purposes, feeling only the need to justify it.

¹⁵ Theodoret would thus not be happy with the subheading for vv.17-24, The Eucharist, listed by Murphy-O'Connor.

CHAPTER TWELVE

¹ While Paul does not concentrate on the gift of tongues among the charismata enjoyed by the Corinthians, its abuse is clearly in Theodoret's sights

– a reflection of his own experience, despite his reference to "former times"? He returns to the charge in commentary on vv. 10,31.

[2] Rom 11.13; 2 Tim 4.5; 1.6. An Antiochene like Theodoret, never prepared to admit that lexical distinctions are otiose, could not agree with Barrett that in the use of these terms Paul is merely "varying his speech" and that *diakonia* "has nothing to do with 'ministry' in the technical sense."

[3] V.11. Again Theodoret moves from Paul's precise point to his own theological agenda in the wake of trinitarian debates since the apostle's time.

[4] Western Christians would note that Theodoret does not speak of a sacrament of confirmation as a moment of conferring of the Spirit independent of baptism.

[5] 13.2.

[6] Acts 5.15.

[7] Cf. Acts 19.12, though Theodoret could have made a stronger point if he had read the verse more precisely, the healing agent being Paul's skin rather than the garments brought into contact with it.

[8] Acts 13.11; 5.5-10.

[9] Again we are reminded that for Theodoret and his church initiation into the Church at baptism (as adults?) meant all this – reception of the Spirit, forgiveness of sins, reception of the eucharist (literally, "the divine mysteries"). Unlike the West he does not articulate stages of initiation as baptism-confirmation-eucharist, nor does he labor deletion of the stain of an original sin as distinct from personal sins.

[10] Phil 2.25.

[11] Cf. Acts 11.27-28.

[12] Theodoret customarily makes this distinction between dogmatic and moral teaching.

[13] Cf. note 1.

CHAPTER THIRTEEN

[1] Theodoret would not concur with the view of commentators like Conzelmann and Barrett that ch 13 is an insert from elsewhere in Paul's writing and placed here to make a comparison of love with the charismata as a way of testing them. With his readiness to see the gift of tongues already under question, he finds the comparison completely sequential, involving none of the "awkwardness" Barrett detects.

[2] A conflation of Gal 1.8-9.

[3] The text reads (and the context would suggest a term like) "boasts," *perpereuetai*; and though Theodoret insists he has the right word, the meaning he gives to it is in quite another direction.

[4] Again Theodoret seems to be taking a verb, *aschemonein*, "to be rude," in a sense other than intended (and different also from the way he understood it at 7.36).

[5] 1 Cor 10.33.

[6] Theodoret wants his readers to see a connection between this chapter on love and earlier chapters on divisions in the community.

[7] The bishop, if not Paul, finds the graduation to perfect knowledge in heaven exemplified in the cessation of need for sacramental signs. While not responding to Murphy-O'Connor's *monitum*, "There is no reference to the beatific vision," he does warn against expecting vision of God's invisible nature, ever respectful of divine transcendence as he is.

[8] Exod 33.17 LXX.

[9] 2 Tim 2.19, citing Num 16.5.

[10] Heb 11.1.

[11] Rom 8.24.

CHAPTER FOURTEEN

[1] Again Theodoret warms to the theme of the relative unimportance of the gift of tongues. He appears to understand the glossolalia as a functional thing, and therefore wasted on Corinthians residing in Corinth, and does not comment on the mysteries spoken through the Spirit.

[2] Rom 1.13.

[3] The term *idiotes* calls for explanation from commentators, Barrett finding its original meaning to be "one who stands outside a particular activity or office," a meaning which Theodoret would find acceptable. He applies it here to the laity, an understandable – though surely anachronistic – application in a member of the hierarchy (if not in keeping with our contemporary models of Church), with an equally understandable parallel with military service. In v.23 the outsider is the one not initiated into the Church's rites.

[4] Theodoret (unlike modern educators) finds no particular significance in Paul's use of *katechein* for instructing; it is his teaching with comprehension that is important. It is also important that Paul not be thought lacking the glossolalia, though the text does not go so far.

[5] Cf. Isa 28.11-12.

[6] Acts 2.7-9.

[7] 1 Cor 12.11.

[8] A precise of Acts 5.3-4. The sequence is a little confused here owing to Theodoret's theological agenda never far from his commentary on the text. The mention of falling down in Paul's text reminds him of the fate of Ananias and Sapphira; but consulting the text of that ch 5 in Acts reminds him that it is the Spirit they are accused of deceiving. This takes him back to an earlier chapter in Paul's letter where the Spirit's role in the gifts is acknowledged, which enables Theodoret to use Spirit and God interchangeably, confirming the probity of the interchange from the text of Acts again. Status of both Son and Spirit is never far from his mind, if not to the forefront of Paul's.

[9] 2 Cor 11.13 – though Paul is not speaking for the moment of true and false apostles.

[10] As suggested in note 3, Bishop Theodoret is inclined to see Paul instructing the Corinthians to have the kind of structured and orderly church he is acquainted with "at the present time," whereas we associate their

church with a less structured but bubbling vitality which normally succumbs to later and inevitable institutionalization. Pastors naturally find this vitality "confusing."

[11] Joel 2.28 Grk (3.1 Heb). Theodoret does not agree with those editions, versions and commentators who would like to see v. 33b referring ahead to vv. 34ff.

[12] Gen 3.16. Theodoret does not expand on these stern words. Having first found his own biblical justification for women's share in the Spirit's gifts, he dutifully locates the text from the Torah Paul probably has in mind as his, but offers no comment – perhaps (as modern commentators are) aware of the acknowledgment of women's role of public praying and prophesying in 11.6. He would be unlikely to discuss the possibility of a deutero-Pauline character to vv.34-35. It should be noted that his text of v.34 includes "your," which could encourage a translation "wives" instead of women in general – a palliative of his?

[13] In the concluding part of commentary on this chapter, Bishop Theodoret concurs with some Pauline accents in particular – the need to follow church practice, to adhere to good order in church, and to downplay the gift of tongues. Commentators, including pastors, are not above holding preferences.

CHAPTER FIFTEEN

[1] A typically helpful overview of the chapter by the commentator, identifying the aberration that elicited Paul's treatment of the topic.

[2] Isa 53.5; 57.2 LXX.

[3] Ps 16.10.

[4] Cf. Matt 12.40.

[5] Theodoret acknowledges and rejects an interpretation of the resurrection as merely subjective. Murphy-O'Connor remarks of this verse: "The emphasis is on the initiative of Jesus, not on the subjective experience of the beneficiaries."

[6] Gal 1.19, if Paul is in fact referring to this James. As to the bearer of the name *dikaios*, does Theodoret have in mind the Joseph of Acts 1.23 who bore the name *Ioustos*?

[7] Again Theodoret is at pains to ensure the image is not lost on his readers.

[8] Cf. Phil 2.6-7, "the form of a slave" being a favorite term for Jesus elsewhere in Theodoret's writings with his Antiochene accent on the humanity.

[9] Theodoret does not comment on the following phrase, "if in fact the dead are not raised," found in our text.

[10] Theodoret, unlike some other commentators ancient and modern, is right to see Paul's accent as Christological in these verses 21-22 rather than highlighting the Fall.

[11] Cf. Matt 25.33, which in fact speaks of sheep rather than lambs.

[12] Ps 110.1.

[13] Isa 46.4. Theodoret, of course, has already detected in v.25 what a modern like Barrett perceives: "There is a strong vein of subordinationism in

this passage." And, with his theological agenda, he is girding himself for worse to come.

[14] Dan 7.14.

[15] Ps 8.6.

[16] Phil 3.21.

[17] The passage is clearly one that subordinationists would make play of (though Kelly does not list it among the Arians' armory of texts). Theodoret goes to unusual lengths to establish their misuse of it, though claiming his comment on Paul's handling of a difficulty of the Corinthians pales beside his engagement in the whole subordinationist controversy elsewhere.

[18] Isa 53.4; cf. Matt 8.7.

[19] Ps 22.1; cf. Matt 27.46.

[20] Acts 17.28, though "the divine apostle" is in fact quoting Epimenides (did Theodoret realize?).

[21] Ps 147.11.

[22] Job 14.4.

[23] Ps 143.2.

[24] Ps 130.3.

[25] Col 3.11, Theodoret omitting – conveniently in his situation? – "slave and free."

[26] Theodoret knows nothing of what is called "some kind of vicarious baptism" by Barrett, who cites Chrysostom as witness to a practice of baptizing deceased catechumens. Theodoret seems simply to be saying that if resurrection does not occur, the symbolism of death, burial and rising in the ritual of baptism is flawed and the rite futile.

[27] Isa 22.13, though the prophet is not citing the epicurean sentiment with approval (Theodoret might have noted).

[28] Likewise here there is no suggestion that Theodoret has recognized the source of the sentiment, a play by Menander; instead, he feels obliged to give an unlikely gloss on *chrestos*.

[29] John 12.24.

[30] John 14.2.

[31] Literally, "ensouled," *psychikon*.

[32] Gen 2.7.

[33] Theodoret's point is clearer in the Greek term, *atomon*.

[34] Cf. Isa 25.8.

[35] Cf. Hos 13.14.

CHAPTER SIXTEEN

[1] The bishop is sensitive to Paul's situation when asking for financial assistance.

[2] It has been a long letter, and Theodoret – who sets a high store by conciseness – is not about commenting at length on a mere postscript devoid of doctrinal considerations unrelated to his own theological agenda.

[3] V.10, the critical locus for Theodoret in discussing the question of the letter's transmission also in his introduction to commentary on it.

[4] Theodoret is unlikely to open up the possibilities of ghost writing in

connection with Paul's letters; strict dictation would be as much as he would be likely to concede, constricting though this method was found to be.

⁵ Guinot sees here a reference to Chrysostom. Theodoret, Syriac (i.e., a dialect of Aramaic) speaker by birth (Canivet tells us), knows better, and would presumably also know if his text read rather *Marana tha*, "Our Lord, come," as do modern texts and versions. Need we agree with Theodoret that Paul includes it as a linguistic flourish?

⁶ An odd phrase, *skenoi apostolikoi*, considering that Theodoret has just reminded us that Aquila and Prisc(ill)a were tentmakers, *skenopoioi*, like Paul, and that the only other use of *skenos* by Paul is of the (earthly) body at 2 Cor 5.1,4. The bishop is not much for puns, we have found.

⁷ Editor Schulze includes in his text of the Commentary the following codicil, "The first letter to the Corinthians was dispatched from Philppi with Stephanas, Fortunatus and Achaicus," but notes as well: "That this codicil is Theodoret's is not established even by the statement that at this point the letter is said to have been written at Philippi, when Theodoret unambiguously states it was written at Ephesus in the course of the latter part of the letter to the Corinthians and in the preface to Paul's letters."

The Second Letter to the Corinthians

While the Corinthians drew great advantage from the first letter, those men, excellent and admirable in every way, added to their benefit – Timothy in first place, and after him Titus, both men having been sent to them. But in due course some of those who had come to faith from Jews, clinging to the ways of the Law, went about in all directions misrepresenting the apostolic teaching, labeling the divinely-inspired Paul apostate and lawbreaker, and urging everyone to observe the Law. They did the same in Corinth, too.

Consequently, the divine apostle, who had by then got as far as Macedonia, writes a letter, and firstly develops a defense for not yet arriving there. Not because he had broken his promise: he had promised to see Macedonia first and after that come to them. He said so in the first letter: "I shall come to you when I pass through Macedonia; in fact, I am passing through Macedonia, whereas I shall perhaps stay with you or even spend the winter so that you may send me on wherever I am heading." [1] So he had done nothing contrary to his promises.

But having been delayed in Ephesus he explains the reason for the delay. He grants pardon even to the one responsible for that awful transgression. Then he compares the Old covenant with the New, not to disparage the former, but to show the latter to be superior. After that he lists his own hardships, not as a victim of the passion of self-importance but for the sake of disproving the lies of the deceivers. He also recommends them to be sensitive to the needs of the saints, prompting them to a generous provision by mention of the Macedonians. He also includes the list of his own sufferings, (377) to bring out that this is a mark of the preachers of the truth.

While this, then, is the theme of the letter, verse-by-verse commentary will bring out more precisely the sense of the text.

CHAPTER ONE

Paul, apostle of Christ Jesus by God's will, and brother Timothy, to the church of God that is in Corinth, together with all the saints that are in the whole of Achaia. Grace and peace to you from God our Father and the Lord Jesus Christ (vv.1-2). Both men had been sent to them, Timothy and Titus, but he did not include blessed Titus in these pages since he had deputed him to be their bearer, dispatching this letter with him. He calls them *the church of God*, once more binding them together in harmony and presenting him as Lord and benefactor. With them he associated as well all the believers in that race, making one body of all those thought worthy of salvation.

Blessed be the God (a break must be observed here) *and Father of our Lord Jesus Christ* (v.3): our God but Father of our Lord Jesus Christ. The Lord also taught us this distinction, and said in the sacred Gospels, "I confess to you, Father, Lord of heaven and earth," [2] bringing out clearly that while he is his Father, he is maker of creation and Lord. *The Father of mercies and God of all consolation,* that is, source of mercies, fount of compassion and agent of fatherly mercies in our regard.

Who consoles us in all our tribulations so that we may be able to console those in any tribulation with the consolation with which we ourselves are consoled by God (v.4). Narrating the trials that happened to him, he cited first the remedies for the trials; he shows the God of all offering comfort commensurate with the trials. Likewise blessed David also said, "To the number of the pangs in my heart your consolation gave joy to my soul." [3] Adopting in his usual fashion a modest attitude, he spoke of the comfort being attained not for his sake but for the sake of the peoples. *Because just as the sufferings of Christ are abundant for us, so through Christ our consolation is also abundant* (v.5). He used *abundance* both of the sufferings and of the consolation to bring out the magnitude both of them and of it. [4]

If we are suffering tribulation, it is for your consolation and salvation, which is active in endurance (380) *of the same sufferings as we also suffer. Our hope for you is firm: if we are consoled, it is for your consolation and salvation, for we know that as you are sharers in our sufferings, so too in our consolation* (vv.6-7): [5] for your sake we encounter the manifold trials: if we had not wanted to offer you the saving message, no one would have inflicted the same sufferings on us; but since we are concerned for your salvation, we are the butt of dire consequences at the hands of the adversaries, though earning comfort from the Lord God. And so we are the recipient of both the one and the other for your sake. You share both with us in so far as you make your own our situation.

You see, we do not want you to be unaware, brethren, of our tribulation that beset us in Asia, our being extremely weighed down beyond endurance so as to despair even of living (v.8). In many cases he brought to light the magnitude of the perils, the terms *weighed down, beyond endurance* and *extremely* suggesting it, and in addition to them *despair even of living*. He means, The peril was so great that we were at a loss and gave up even on life. Now, I am inclined to think he is referring to the riot over Demetrius the silversmith. [6] *But we ourselves had already uttered our death sentence so as not to rely on ourselves but on the God who raised the dead* (v.9): but the Lord did not allow us to experience the sentence of despair; rather, he made the threat of death impinge on our thinking lest we trust in our own resources instead of looking for his assistance. By *death sentence* he refers to the verdict of capital punishment. It was very appropriate for him to mention the resurrection of the dead so as to bring out that liberation from those extreme perils was equivalent to raising the dead.

He rescued us from those deaths, and he will rescue us (v.10). Then, as though taking the past events as a pledge of the future, he went on, *In him we have set our hope that he will still rescue us.* And in customary manner he gives a lesson in modesty by proceeding, *You cooperate by praying for us so that on the part of many people thanks will be given on our behalf for the gift given to us through the prayers of many* (v.11): once this happens, many will sing God's praises in our regard on seeing us travel through dangers and escape them, thanks to divine assistance. [7]

This, in fact, is our boast, the testimony of our conscience (v.12): the witness of conscience provides us with confidence. Now, what does conscience tell him? *That we have conducted ourselves in the world – and the more so towards you – with guilelessness and sincerity, not from wisdom of the flesh but by God's grace.* What we learned from divine grace, he is saying, (381) we offer openly to everyone, not adding anything of our own to it. By *wisdom of the flesh* here he is implying not eloquence but villainy; he is referring to those awful rogues on the grounds of their corrupting the message and preaching their own views.

I mean, we write to you nothing other than what you read and under-stand. I hope that you will understand it to the very end, as you have partly understood us, too (vv.13-14): we do not think one thing and preach another, as some people endeavor to misrepresent us. The facts bear this out: what I taught you when present is what I also write now absent, and what I hope to preach all the time from now on. Now, it was not without purpose that he added *you have partly understood us,* but to goad them for not completely rejecting the calumnies directed at him. *That we are your boast as you also are ours on the day of our Lord Jesus.* He consistently observes the rule of his own modest attitude, and at this point puts himself and the disciples on the same level: he said they take credit in him and likewise he in them on the day of the Lord's coming.

With this assurance I wanted to come to you first so that you might enjoy a double favor, both to come to Macedonia via you, and in turn come to you on the way back from Macedonia and be sent on my way to Judea by you (vv.15-16). Some thought the apostle contradicted him-self, since in the first statement he promised to see the Macedonians first, then to visit the Corinthians;[8] but they did not take note that in one case he made those promises, whereas here he revealed his own preference, saying, *I wanted to come to you first, then to come to Macedonia via you and in turn come to you from there so that you might enjoy a double favor,* that is, a twofold joy in welcoming me twice. But while I wanted this, certain factors prevented me. These he brings out a little later, offering his defense in several ways.

So, in making these plans, surely I wasn't giving in to levity? surely my plans are not made according to the flesh so that with me it is Yes, yes and No, no at the same time? (v.17). He posed two contrary attitudes, the first being, I am not frivolous nor do I have sudden changes of mind so as to choose now one course of action, now another. The second is, I am not a victim of passion, either, so as to satisfy my longings in every way, the meaning of *surely my plans are not made according to the flesh so that with me it is Yes, yes and No, no at the same time?* Whoever follow the longings of the flesh, after all, are at the mercy of their own ideas, even if these are quite out of place, whereas those making sober plans do not put the plans into effect if they sense that the plans, good though they may be, (384) are not likely to benefit others. On the other hand, to the fact that we eagerly and without scruple propose what we perceive to be of benefit to you the message gives testimony: in proposing it to you on many occasions we made no change in what we had to say.

This, in fact, is what he proceeded to say: *God is my witness that our words to you were not Yes and No* (v.18). He spoke this way to support the statement *surely I wasn't giving into levity?* by calling them to witness that he consistently proposed the message to them in unambiguous fashion, consistently taught the same thing, and refrained from changing anything. *I mean, the Son of God, Jesus Christ, who was preached among you by us – by me, Silvanus and Timothy – was not Yes and No: in him it is always Yes* (v.19). He cited him as the message, meaning, The word about the Son of God that we preached – I, Silvanus and Timothy – contained no inconsistency, nor did we preach one thing at one time and another at another time; instead, we constantly proposed the same teaching to you. Now, in my view *Silvanus* refers to Silas; he also shared his prison term in Philippi, Paul left him behind in Beroea in Macedonia and got to Athens, Silas reaching him in Corinth in the company of Timothy and proving a fellow worker in preaching.[9] We also find changes in other names; for example, he called Priscilla Prisca in the letter to the Romans.[10]

All God's promises, in fact, are a Yes in him, and in him is the Amen to God for his glory through us (v.20):[11] God's promises are many – resurrection of the dead, incorruptibility of the body, unending life, kingdom of heaven – but these the God of all has supplied through the only-begotten Son. Hence also through him we offer the hymn of thanksgiving to him as well. Now, it was not without purpose that he included *Amen* here:[12] it was to emphasize that not only does the priest in saying the prayer offer the hymn, but also the person adding the Amen shares in the offering of praise.[13] *But it is God who establishes us with you in Christ and anointed us, both sealing us and giving the pledge of the Spirit in our hearts* (vv.21-22): God is the cause of these good things; he also granted us a steadfast faith in Christ, he anointed us, and accorded us the seal of the all-holy Spirit, granting us this grace like a kind of pledge of the good things to come. (385) Through the word *pledge*, of course, he hinted at the magnitude of what would be given: a pledge is a small part of the whole.

Then he brings out more clearly why it was that while he wanted to see them first, he promised to come to them after the Macedonians. *But I call God to witness against my spirit that it was to spare you that I still did not come to Corinth* (v.23). In his wish to persuade them that his words were true, the divine apostle called the overseer of thoughts to witness. Then he checks the asperity of his expression: it was a harsh and quite threatening remark to say that it was by way of sparing them he postponed his journey to them, and he says, *It is not that we are domineering where your faith is concerned; we work together with you for your joy* (v.24). He included this by way of surmise: some were probably saying, Why, then? what reason was there for us to come to believe, only to accept domineering behavior and be subject to your dictatorial correction? So he was obliged to add, I said this not as a tyrant over you but as a fellow worker for your spiritual happiness. *You stand firm in the faith, to be sure.*

Chapter Two

But I reached this decision, not to come to you once more in grief (v.1). He omits the term *though* from the construction, *Though you stand firm in the faith, to be sure*, but his meaning is, Though I have no fault to find with your faith, invested with its soundness as you are, yet there are other failings on your part which require some correction;[1] but I did not decide to come to you to give grief to the sinners. Now, *once more* goes with *my coming*, not *in grief*. *After all, if I grieve you, who is there to cheer me up but the one grieved by me?* (v.2): what so cheers me up as acquaintance with those under accusation? It is in fact proof positive of the benefit coming from accusations.

But I wrote this very letter so that on coming I should not have grief from those who should be my source of joy, believing as I do of all of you that my joy is the joy of you all (v.3): this is the reason the letter preceded my arrival, that healing should come of it and thus procure happiness for me. You too share in it, judging our fortunes to be your own. *I mean, in great distress and anguish of heart I wrote to you with many tears, not to grieve you but for you to know the love I have in great measure for you* (v.4). In the former letter he upbraided them very severely. So he emphasizes that his wish in writing was not simply to grieve them but to bring about the cure of the miscreants on whose account he had also suffered greatest pain; and he wrote with confidence, mentioning the affection he has for them.

Then he lays bare also the reason for the grief. (388) *If, however, anyone has caused grief, it is not me they have grieved but to some extent (not to exaggerate) all of you* (v.5). He wanted to say rather more and show the whole body of the Church sharing the grief; but leaving aside the others he mentioned them alone, as is clear from the phrases *to some extent* and *not to exaggerate*. Then he lays bare his fatherly feeling: *This punishment by the majority suffices for such a person. So by contrast you should rather forgive and encourage lest such a person be somehow overwhelmed by excessive grief* (vv.6-7). On the one hand, he brought out the extent of the repentance by mentioning the excessive grief; on the other hand, he mentions the forgiveness so as to show the sin to be worse than the repentance: all shunned the person as he ordered. Tentmaker though the writer was, he was capable of such an effect owing to the power within him.[2] By *overwhelmed* he referred to despair and utter loss of faith. *So I urge you to give clear evidence of your love for him* (v.8): unite the member to the body, attach the sheep to the flock, demonstrate ardent affection for him.

It was for this I wrote to you, after all, to put you to the test and know whether you are obedient in everything (v.9): you should cooperate with me not only in cutting off but also in attaching. *If you are in any way forgiving, so am I* (v.10). When he passed the sentence of punishment against him, he gave them no authority for any pardoning, seeing as he did that they would perhaps not maintain the balance of justice. But on learning that they had benefited from his letter, he gives them latitude for generosity in the words, *If you are in any way forgiving, so am I: for my part, if I have in any way forgiven, I have done so for your sake.* The remark implies they had presented a request on behalf of the sinner through the blessed men Timothy and Titus. And in case anyone suppose that he had neglected justice as a favor to human beings, he added *in the presence of Christ*: I am doing this as though Christ were watching and were satisfied with what has been done. He tells the reason, *lest we be circumvented by Satan: we are not unaware of his schemes* (v.11). The scheming enemy knows how to concoct desperate plans on many occasions, and by such means devise their utter ruin.

After this digression he returns to the thread of the previous narrative: having outlined what happened to him in Asia, (389) he felt obliged to mention how sincerely he preached to them the divine Gospel. From that point he laid bare his love for them, having said that he wishes to see them before the Macedonians. Then after bringing out the reasons for the delay, mentioning the grief and reinserting into their ranks the one separated from the Church, he went back to the thread of the narrative.[3]

When I arrived at Troas for the Gospel of Christ, a door opened for me in the Lord. But I had no ease in my spirit, not finding my brother Titus; instead, I took my leave of them and left for Macedonia (vv.12-13). Having reached Troas for no other purpose than simply preaching the message, he is saying, I was very distraught, on the hand seeing many people making their approach to the message, but on the other having no assistant in the work of looking after them. In other words, Tituts had not yet reached us, though I had sent him to you to have an eye to your welfare. This was the reason, having no one to share the work, that I left them and made off. It was not without point that he mentioned the thrice-blessed Titus at that time; rather, since he was due to bear this letter, he wanted to bring out the man's virtue. This he did adequately, explaining that in his absence, despite many people making their approach to the message, he was incapable of doing what was required. Hence his calling him *brother* as well, giving him the title to bring out the close relationship.[4]

But thanks be to God, who always leads us in triumphal procession in Christ, and through us in every place makes evident the fragrance of knowing him (v.14). In every way, nonetheless, we sing the praises of God, who in his wise conduct of our affairs leads us hither and yon, making us obvious to everyone, and through us offering the knowledge of godliness. By *fragrance of knowing* he referred to the knowledge in this life, teaching two things at the same time, that this is an insignificant part of perfect knowledge, and that while the latter now eludes us it will at the appropriate time be made manifest, after the manner of incense, which in many cases when mixed with fire in a bedroom spreads its fragrance even outside; those who catch it, while not seeing it, enjoy its sweet smell. [5]

Because we are the fragrance of Christ to God in the case of those being saved and those perishing: to the one group a stench of death to death, to the others a fragrance of life to life (vv.15-16): we offer everyone the sweet fragrance of Christ, but not all given a share in it enjoy salvation. To those with bad eyes the light is treacherous and unkind, but it is not the sun that causes the harm. It is also said that vultures shun the fragrance of perfume, yet perfume is still sweet-smelling, even if the vultures give it a wide berth. Likewise, too, the saving message brings about salvation for those who believe, but inflicts ruin on the unbelieving. *Who is up to this?* (392) It is not ourselves, however, who are responsible for this achievement, but the grace of the Spirit through us; we do not even consider ourselves worthy of this ministry.

We are not, after all, like the others, peddling the word of God; rather, in Christ we speak in a sincere manner, as sent by God and in the presence of God (v.17). At this point he proceeds to take issue with the adversaries, and brings out that whereas he proposes teachings coming from the operation of divine grace, they peddle the divine word, turning it into a fanciful story and contaminating the grace with their own ideas, like those who mix water with pure wine, according to the inspired verse, "Your peddlers mix water with the wine." [6]

CHAPTER THREE

Then, since he had on the one hand dealt them a blow, and on the other given true testimony of himself, he felt obliged to proceed, *Are we beginning to commend ourselves again?* (v.1): it was not for us to say this; rather, it was for you, who know precisely our performance and theirs. He continues goading them in word: *Surely we do not need, as some do, letters of recommendation to you or from you?* In this he suggests that some of those impostors had been recommended by others to them, and by them had been introduced to others by letters of recommendation. And since his words were sufficient to stun them, in what follows he offers a balm in the words, *You are our letter, written on our hearts, known and read by all people* (v.2): we have need of nothing in writing; the facts themselves bear witness to us. As a living letter commending our behavior to you we have your faith, celebrated everywhere on land and sea; we it was who freed you from error and brought you to the light of the knowledge of God.

What follows makes this clear, in fact. *You show that you are a letter from Christ, delivered by us* (v.3): why do I say *us*? You are in fact a letter from our Savior in person: the words of the message are his, we are simply deliverers of the text, *written not in ink but with the Spirit of the living God, not on tablets of stone but on tablets of hearts of flesh.* Leaving aside those teaching the opposite, he shifts his attention to facts and shows the difference in the two covenants: one was carved on tablets of stone, the other was inscribed on rational hearts.

Now, we have such faith through Christ in reference to God. Not that we are sufficient of ourselves to claim anything as coming from us (vv.4-5). It was timely of him to make mention of the God of all, since those preaching contrary doctrines claimed God was interested in the observance of the Law. So he says, We have confidence in the God of all, Christ having given us this confidence. We place no store in ourselves, nor do we offer the message by making it up from our own ideas. *Rather, our sufficiency is from God, who also made us sufficient ministers of the New covenant, not of letter but of spirit* (vv.5-6): the God of all personally supplied us with power enough to serve the grace of the Spirit; it is not the ancient letter of the Law we offer but the new gift of the Spirit. *The letter kills, after all, whereas the spirit gives life.* He presented both from the viewpoint of their end: the Law punished the transgressors, whereas grace gives life to believers at least.

Then he brings out the contrast more clearly. *Now, if the ministry of death in writing, chiseled on stone, came in glory such that the children of Israel could not look at the face of Moses on account of the glory of his face, a glory now faded, how will the ministry of the Spirit not surpass it in glory?* (vv.7-8). He called the ministry of the Law a *ministry of death* since the Law punished the transgressors. So if from a source of punishment, death and letters carved on stone, he is saying, the person mediating them was invested with glory of countenance such that it was impossible for the viewers to bear the brightness coming from it, how much more those ministering to the divine Spirit will enjoy greater glory. By *ministry of the Spirit*, note, he referred to those ministering to the Spirit, as likewise by *ministry of death* those ministering to the Law, namely, Moses: he makes a comparison between Moses and the heralds of grace, and shows him bringing inscribed tablets and them supplying the grace of the all-holy Spirit, the Law punishing and grace giving life, the glory coming to him lasting for a short time and theirs continuing forever, in one case Moses alone sharing in the glory and in this case not the apostles alone but also all those who have come to faith through them. [1]

He then develops the comparison at greater length to bring out the superiority of grace. *After all, if the ministry of condemnation was a source of glory, much more does the ministry of justification abound in glory* (v.9). The Law condemned the sinners, whereas grace accepts them and justifies them through faith: it leads them to divine baptism and grants them forgiveness. [2] So if the one ministering to the former shared in glory, much more those serving the latter will enjoy it to a greater extent. *You see, what once had glory has no glory* (398) *in this respect, on account of the superior glory* (v.10): such is the glory reserved for them that you could rightly say no glory accrued to Moses when you consider them. I mean, at night the lamp seems the brightest of lights, but in full daylight it is invisible and is not thought to be a light at all. *After all, if what has faded came in glory, much more will the permanent come in glory* (v.11). By *what has faded* he referred to the Law as having no force with the coming of Christ the Lord, and by *the permanent* the gift of grace as not coming to an end. So if the former was granted glory, he is saying, clearly also the latter will attain it many times over.

Having such hope, therefore, we bring to bear great confidence (v.12): we know the greatness of the glory, and are in no uncertainty; rather, with confidence we demonstrate the extraordinary degree of grace. *Not as Moses covered his face with a veil lest the children of Israel should look at the end of what was fading* (v.13): we do not need the veil as they did; we are speaking to believers, and all the believers enjoy the brightness of the intellectual light. Now, the verse makes clear that the divinely-inspired Moses prefigures the Jews' infidelity in covering his face with a veil, bringing out that they will be unable to see the end of the Law; "Christ is the end of the Law," remember, "for justification for every believer." [3] This, in fact, is what is implied by *lest the children of Israel should look at the end of what was fading*. He said, in fact, the Law was fading, that is, ceasing to have force, but the end of the Law is Christ, concealed under the Law.

But their minds were hardened (v.14): no one else was responsible for the hardening; they themselves gave evidence of the passion of their own free will. *To this very day, in fact, at the reading of the Old Testament the same veil remains unlifted, being set aside in Christ* (v.14): the Law bears the semblance of Moses to this day, and the veil lies over those trying to read it without faith. *But to this day when they read Moses, a veil lies over their heart* (v.15). By *Moses* he referred to the Law, and by *a veil* to unbelief; he also explains how it is impossible for the veil to be removed. *But when there is a turning to the Lord,* (397) *the veil is removed* (v.16): in speaking to the people Moses had the veil in place, but in approaching God the veil was removed. Likewise, then, if you wish to gaze upon the Lord, you will be freed from the veil of infidelity.

But who is it on whom one must cast one's gaze? *Now, the Lord is the Spirit* (v.17). He brought out the equal status of God and the Spirit. Now, in his wish to show new realities superior to old, he would not have made mention of the Spirit if he actually knew the Holy Spirit to be a creature: if he were a creature, as the followers of Arius and Eunomius hold, and we subscribe to him but Moses to God the Father, our way is surely far inferior to theirs. If, on the contrary, it is not inferior but greater, and far greater, then the Holy Spirit is not a creature but equal in power and status. But in their effrontery they claim that the Lord is called Spirit here, not the Spirit in person Lord. This, however, betrays folly and effrontery: the divine apostle made a complete comparison of the letter and the Spirit, saying, *written not in ink but with Spirit of the living God*, and again, *not of letter but of Spirit*, and further, *the letter kills but the Spirit gives life*, and again, *how will the ministry of the Spirit not be in glory?* Consequently, it is clear that the divine apostle called the all-holy Spirit Lord. [4]

What follows also gives testimony: *Where the Spirit of the Lord is, there is freedom*. Now, if he had called the Lord Spirit, he would have said, Where the Lord is. But this is not the expression: he spoke of the Spirit as Spirit of the Lord since through him the Lord's grace is provided. And in case anyone should suspect the Spirit is a servant, he was obliged to add that the Spirit is Lord. *All of us, with face unveiled, beholding the glory of the Lord, are being transformed into the same likeness, from one glory to another, as from the Lord the Spirit* (v.18): Moses alone enjoyed glory, whereas in this case all the believers; he had a veil because of the Jews' weakness, whereas in offering instruction to the faithful we do not need a veil, but behold the Lord's glory with bared face, not being affected by the eyesore of unbelief.[5] From this we derive no little beam of glory, which is peculiar to those of a pure heart: as clear water cleanses the face of the onlookers, the orb of the sun and the vault of heaven, so the pure heart is like an impression or mirror of divine glory. The Lord also spoke in these terms: "Blessed the pure (400) in heart because they shall see God."[6] Now, by *from one glory* he means the divine Spirit's, by *to another* ours, meaning the source from which we receive – hence the addition of *as from the Lord the Spirit*. From this it is clear that he called the Spirit Lord also in the preceding verses.

Chapter Four

Hence, having this ministry as a result of God's mercy, we are not giving up (v.1). He made no secret of the fact that to the preachers he gave the name ministry of the Spirit, and said he attained to it through lovingkindness alone. This is the reason, he is saying, that we nobly bear the troubles that befall. *We renounce what shame keeps hidden* (v.2). He means circumcision, which the believers from Gentiles publicized. He says so elsewhere as well: "But whatever profit I had I consider as loss for Christ's sake," and again, "So I even regard everything as rubbish so as to gain Christ."[1] *Not conducting ourselves with cunning nor falsifying God's word, but with the openness of truth commending ourselves to the conscience of everyone before God* (v.2). Again he accuses those people who were corrupting the divine message with contamination from the Law, practicing guile and not presenting instruction pure and simple. We on the contrary, he is saying, have as our witnesses both those people who are of right mind and also the inspector of conscience himself.

Then, since he had said, "All of us with face unveiled behold the glory of the Lord,"[2] and yet there were many affected by the eyesore of unbelief and incapable of perceiving the things of God, he was obliged to go on, *Even if our Gospel is veiled, it is veiled to those who are perishing* (v.3). He said as much above as well: "To the one group a stench of death to death, to the others a fragrance of life to life."[3] *To them God* (a break must be observed here)[4] *blinded the minds of the unbelievers of this world lest they be enlightened by the illumination of the Gospel of the glory of Christ, who is God's image* (v.4). He brought out that unbelief is confined to this world; in the next life truth is clearly revealed to everyone. God blinded them, not imparting unbelief to them, but perceiving their unbelief and not allowing them to see the hidden mysteries. "Do not give holy things to dogs," he says, "nor cast your pearls before swine," and again, "The reason I speak to them in parables is this, that looking they do not see, and listening they do not understand."[5] Knowledge and belief are necessary, after all, for sharing in the light; the sun, remember, is inimical to weak eyes. Now, he called Christ *God's image* as he is God from God: (401) in himself he reveals the Father – hence his saying, "The one who has seen me has seen the Father."[6]

I mean, it is not ourselves we preach but Christ Jesus as Lord and ourselves as your slaves for Jesus' sake (v.5). He had said this also in the first letter, "Let a person think of us this way, as Christ's assistants and dispensers of God's mysteries."[7] Here, too, he said rather humble things about himself: he called himself the slave not only of Christ but also of the faithful out of love for them, saying as much, *for Jesus' sake. Because the God who said the light shone out of darkness*[8] *is the one who shone in our hearts as a light of the knowledge of the glory of God in the face of Jesus Christ* (v.6). The one who of old brought light into being by a word, he is saying, and said, "Let there be light," illumined our minds now not with that light but with his own so that we might perceive his glory through Christ himself – the meaning of *in the face of Jesus Christ*. Since the divine nature is invisible, it is perceived (to the extent possible) through the humanity that was assumed, resplendent with the divine light and sending out lightning flashes.[9] It is also clear from this that God did not instil unbelief in the unbelievers, having abundantly regaled everyone with the brightness of intellectual light as he has;

instead, they were the ones who were enamored of unbelief, whereas he did not send his rays to them in their refusal to see them.

We have this treasure in clay vessels, however, so that the extraordinary degree of power may come from God and not from us (v.7). Since great things had been said about the preachers of the New covenant whereas they were seen to be suffering a very harsh lot, he felt obliged to emphasize that this also proclaimed God's power. He likens the grace given by the Spirit to a treasure and the nature of the body to clay; it is a wonderful sign of God's power that it does not lose the treasure despite sustaining countless blows.

Then he goes through the list of trials, and shows God's assistance commensurate with them. *Afflicted in every way but not depressed, at a loss but not desperate, persecuted but not abandoned, struck down but not perishing* (vv.8-9): if none of these assaults had come our way, the greatness of the divine power would not have been demonstrated. But like plants that are germinated by fire we preach the power of God's protection through what we suffer while being kept unharmed. Now, *at a loss but not despairing* means, We find ways to salvation in situations where there are none. (404) *Always carrying about in the body the dying of the Lord Jesus so that the life of Jesus may also be manifested in our body* (v.10). He speaks in similar terms elsewhere as well: "If we suffer with him so that we may also be glorified with him." [10]

Constantly, you see, we the living are being given up to death for Jesus' sake so that the life of Jesus may also be manifested in our mortal body (v.11): this is the reason we willingly undergo risks involving death for the Lord, that we may also share his life, and by giving up the temporary life we may receive in its place the incorruptibility of the flesh. Now, the term *constantly* has to do with precision in composition; *we the living* is his main thrust. *And so death is at work in us, but life in you* (v.12): we undergo the risks for the sake of your salvation; we are at risk in offering you instruction, and through our being at risk you enjoy life.

Now, since he mentioned immortal life, which is a matter of hope, and since what is hoped for is not visible, [11] he recalls an inspired Old Testament statement to bring out the fact that the saints of old were also distinguished for their faith. *Since, however, we have the same spirit of faith, according to the text, I believed, therefore I spoke,* [12] *and since we believe, therefore we also speak* (v.13). It was very relevant for him to cite this testimony: blessed David in the previous psalm had said, "He rescued my soul from death, my eyes from tears and my feet from stumbling for me to be pleasing in the sight of the Lord in the land of the living" [13] (though this land was not seen), he began the next psalm with the words, "I believed, therefore I spoke." The same Spirit, he is saying, spoke also through them, and speaks through us.

Aware that the one who raised the Lord Jesus will also raise us through Jesus, and will present us in company with you (v.14): the Lord accepted death for the sake of all so that we might all share resurrection with him. Consequently, we believe that he will also through him render us superior to death, and present both you and us together before the fearsome tribunal. *Everything is for your sake, after all* (v.15) – that is, the believers: he refers not only to the Corinthians but to all who have accepted the message. *So that grace may increase on account of thanksgiving by the greater number and abound to God's glory*: concerned for the salvation of all in common, he arranged things in keeping with Christ the Lord; so he was obliged to repay him unceasingly in thanksgiving hymns.

Hence we are not giving up (v.16): far from being distraught or depressed, we bear everything nobly. *Rather, our outer self is decaying, our inner self is being renewed day by day*: the soul gains greatest advantage from recourse to courage. [14] He then compares the troubles of the present life to the good things awaited in the future: *The slight momentary tribulation is preparing an everlasting weight of glory for us beyond all measure* (v.17). On the one hand he brings out through *momentary* the brevity and temporary character, while on the other he contrasts *everlasting* with *momentary*, and *weighty* – that is, valuable – and *beyond all measure* with *slight* and *light*, and not repose but *glory*, which is far greater, with *tribulation*.

Since the latter are visible but the former not apparent, he was right to proceed, *We consider not what is seen but what is not seen: what is seen is temporary, what is not seen is eternal* (v.18): it is not only the tribulations that are temporary but also the repose of the present life; so we should not be attached to the passing things, but look forward to the enjoyment of the eternal goods. [15]

CHAPTER FIVE

You see, we are aware that if the earthly tent that is our dwelling is destroyed, we have a building from God, a dwelling not made by hand, eternal in the heavens (v.1). By *earthly dwelling* he refers to existence in the present life, and by *tent* to the body. So if the present realities come to an end, he is saying, we have as a dwelling the one not made by hand, the eternal, the heavenly; he contrasted the heavenly with the earthly, the eternal with the destroyed, the one not made by hand with the one formed by human beings. *In this tent, after all, we groan, longing to be clothed with our habitation from heaven* (v.2). Here by *habitation* he referred to incorruptibility, speaking of it as *from heaven* since the gift is dispatched to us from there. Now, he did not say *put on* but *be clothed*, since instead of putting on another body, this corruptible one is clothed with incorruptibility. [1]

If, that is, even when we put it on, we will not be found naked (v.3): while all people will wear the garment of incorruptibility, not all will share the divine glory; so he calls those divested of the glory *naked*, amongst whom the apostle ranked himself, teaching both the Corinthians and all people to be humble. *I mean, we groan under the weight of it because we want not to be unclothed but to be clothed* (v.4): we groan, not out of a longing to be rid (408) of the body, but desiring to be free from its passions; we aspire not to strip off the body but to be clothed with incorruptibility. [2] We shall know what this will be like: *so that what is mortal may be swallowed up by life*: as dawning day puts darkness to flight, so indestructible life spells the end of corruption. *The one who has prepared us for this very thing is God, who also gives us the pledge of the Spirit* (v.5): from the beginning the creator arranged our condition this way, and foreseeing Adam's transgression he prepared in advance a remedy suited to the wound. [3] Now, he mentioned this to show the truth of the promises about the future from the marvels worked through the Spirit.

Always confident, then, and aware that while at home in the body we are away from the Lord, walking as we do by faith, not by sight. We are confident, and we prefer to be away from the body and at home with the Lord (vv.6-8). He does not say, We are at a distance from the Lord in still being joined to the mortal body; [4] rather, We do not see him here and now with the eyes of the body, whereas then we shall see and be in his company. In other words, here and now, he is saying, we do not see the things we look forward to as they are; this is surely the reason we long to be away from the body and at home with the Lord. Now, in this his teaching is not to fear death but to desire freedom from this life.

Hence we are also anxious, whether at home or away, to be pleasing to him (v.9): faith is not sufficient for salvation; rather, it is necessary to serve the benefactor in everything. [5] He used *We are anxious* with the meaning, We make it our concern. He shows the possession of virtue to be necessary on other scores as well. *We must all, remember, appear before Christ's tribunal* (v.10). He did not say, take our place, but *appear*. This is sufficient to make those suffering from insensitivity feel dread and attend to the wounds of sin, the thought that these would be made obvious to everyone. And he goes on to increase the dread on another score: *so that each may receive recompense for what was done in the body, whether good or evil*: the judge, righteous as he is, will award to each one due recompense for the actions of their life. He brought out at the same time the receipt of recompense by souls, both those honored and those punished, along with their bodies.

Knowing the fear of the Lord, then, we persuade people but lie open before God (v.11): having this (409) dread hanging over us, we try to correct those with false opinions of us and explain our true situation, knowing clearly as we do that the God of all is overseer of all things. *I hope we also lie open before your consciences*: I think you do not need our explanation to realize precisely our purpose. *We are not commending ourselves further to you, but providing you with a basis for boasting of us so that you may be able to deal with those who boast in outward appearance but not in heart* (v.12). Once more he mollified them, testifying to their affection for him. It is not for your sake that I am saying this, he means, but for you to learn how you should plead the cause of your teacher and refute the falsehood of the adversaries, who think one thing and say another.

I mean, if we are deranged, it is for God; if we are of sound mind, it is for you (v.13). By *sound mind* here he referred to humility, by *derangement* the account of virtuous deeds; in doing both my intention is correct, he is saying. *The love of Christ urges us on, you see, deciding as we have that one died for all, so all died. He died for all so that the living might live no longer for themselves but for the one who for them died and was raised* (vv.14-15). He linked this with the preceding theme: after saying, *Hence we are also anxious, whether at home or away, to be pleasing to him,* he was obliged to give an insight into the reason. We are on fire with the love for Christ, [6] he is in fact saying, considering that while all of us are subject to death, he alone accepted death for us so that the Spirit might secure life for us. This is the reason we judged it right to live for him and conduct our lives in accordance with his laws; it is a debt we owe him.

And so from now on we take no one from a human point of view: even if we did take Christ from a human point of view, we do not take him that way now (v.16): having learned that death was destroyed by the Lord's death, we now realize no human being is mortal. I mean, even if Christ had a body that was subject to suffering, yet after the passion he made it incorruptible and immortal. *And so if there is any new creation in Christ, the old things have passed away, lo, all has become new* (v.17): it therefore becomes the believers in Christ to live their lives, as it were, in a new creation; renewed (412) by all-holy baptism, we have put off the senility of sin. [7]

Now, all this is from God, who reconciled us to himself through Jesus Christ and gave us the ministry of reconciliation (v.18). He indicated God's ineffable lovingkindness: he was not reconciled to us (he is saying), although he it was who was insulted by the Fall; rather, he reconciled us to himself, not employing a human being as mediator, but making the only-begotten Son a mediator of peace. To us he also entrusted the good news of reconciliation. *Namely, God it was.* A break must be observed here. [8] *In Christ reconciling the world to himself* (v.19): the God of all it was who by means of Christ achieved reconciliation with human beings. Now, what is the manner of this reconciliation? *Not reckoning their falls against them, and assigning to us the preaching of reconciliation*: he granted the forgiveness of sins, and commissioned us as ministers of peace.

We act, therefore, as ambassadors of Christ (v.20). Since he claimed to have been appointed minister of reconciliation, he was obliged to set out the ambassadorship; and to show its trustworthiness he went on, *since God's exhortation comes through us.* Now, what is the message he brings as ambassador? *We beg you in Christ's name, be reconciled to God.* The words are sufficient to make even the most unfeeling be ashamed: he said first that with the execution of Christ he not only did not bear resentment but sent us as ambassadors to win all people over, respect his longsuffering, be ashamed at the murder of Christ, and be reconciled to the Creator, God and Lord. He goes on to add to the aforesaid the dishonor of the passion. *After all, the one who did not know sin he made sin for our sake so that in him we might become the righteousness of God* (v.21): though free of sin he underwent the death of sinners in order to undo people's sin, and bearing the name that we have he gave us the name of what he himself is – that is, he regaled us with the riches of righteousness.

CHAPTER SIX

In cooperation we urge you not to receive the grace of God in vain (v.1). Since he had said, *We act as ambassadors of Christ*, he is obliged to stress that the ambassadors combine to assist the very ones who are exhorted so that they may reap the benefit of divine grace and not give the impression that the plan is without point or purpose by giving evidence in their life to the contrary. *He says, remember, At an acceptable time I hearkened to you, and on a day of salvation I helped you* [1] (v.2). By thus invoking the inspired testimony he confirms the exhortation. *Lo, now is an acceptable time; lo, now is a day* (413) *of salvation*: life draws to an end; even if here and now we are not sharing in salvation, we shall not be deprived of it after departure from here.

Then he describes his own hardships for their benefit: *Providing no obstacle to anyone lest our ministry be faulted; instead, commending ourselves in every way as God's ministers* (vv.3-4): our concern is not to be a source of the slightest scandal to anyone, but rather in every way to show ourselves worthy of God's ministry. Now, what are the forms of this ministry? *In great endurance, in tribulations, in hardships, in difficulties, in beatings, in imprisonments, in riots* (vv.4-5). He spoke variously of the troubles befalling him from outside, and to the involuntary ones he adds also the hardships willingly undertaken. [2] *In hard work, in watching, in fasting, in integrity, in knowledge, in longsuffering, in kindness, in Holy Spirit, in unalloyed love, in truthful speech, in the power of God* (vv.5-7). In other words, far from being content with the troubles befalling him from outside, he also devises discipline for the body, not only fasting and watching but also work with his hands, implied by *in hard work*. By *integrity* he refers to scorn for possessions: from the Corinthians he had not accepted even basic necessities. By *knowledge*, in my view, he refers to teaching: it, too, was a labor. Then *longsuffering* in regard to outsiders, *kindness* to his own, the worship of the all-holy Spirit: he followed its bidding. By *unalloyed love* he refers to the sincere and genuine kind, not what appears on the outside but what is confirmed in action; by *truthful speech* to the preaching of godliness. He attributed them all to God's power: with his help he achieved what he mentioned.

Through the weapons of righteousness in right hand and left, in honor and disrepute, in blame and praise, as impostors and yet true, as unknown and yet well known, as dying and, behold, we live, as chastised and yet not at death's door, as grieving but always rejoicing, as poor and yet enriching many, as having nothing and yet possessing everything (vv.7-10). All are the direct opposite of one another – honor and disrepute, blame and praise, life and death, happiness and grief – yet he presented the one and the other as *weapons of righteousness*, and blended the one virtue from opposites. Honor did not puff him up, note, nor disrepute deject him; praise did not go to his head nor blame upset him; instead, moving from one opposite to another he remained unchanged. By *right hand* he refers to what seems pleasing, by *left* the opposite, giving the names from common opinion. Now, his final remarks are also worthy of note: after saying *as poor* he did not go on to say Well off for necessities, but *enriching many*; (416) he collected money from everybody, remember, and dispatched it to the needy, and though having nothing he was in charge of every religious household.

Our mouth was open to you, O Corinthians, and our heart expanded (v.11): I am forced to say this by my affection for you; I carry you all in my thoughts. Such, you see, is the nature of love: it makes the hearts of those possessing it open wide. What follows indicates as much: *You are no lower in our esteem*: the person ill-disposed to someone drives out from the mind the very thought of them. *The loss of esteem is on your side, deep within you.* He brought the severest charge against them, showing he received them all in his heart magnanimously, and on the other hand faulting them for not being prepared to respond in like manner but reducing their esteem for him. Hence his further remark: *Respond as you receive – I speak to you as though to children*. Since he had affected them by his accusation, he mollifies them with the term *children. Be expansive on your part also.*

Do not enter a false association with unbelievers (v.14): repay me with equal love. Do not resemble oxen that go in a different direction and twist the yoke by preferring the error of the unbelievers to our teaching. *After all, what is there in common between righteousness and lawlessness? what fellowship is there between light and darkness? what concord between Christ and Beliar? what part does the believer have with the unbeliever? what agreement does the temple of God have with idols?* (v.14-16). In all these ways he brought out the contrary position of the teachers of lawlessness, sources of darkness and ministers of the devil, calling the devil *Beliar. You are the temple of the living God, remember.* He then demonstrated the truth of his thesis with an inspired testimony: *As God said, I shall dwell in them and walk among them, and I shall be their God and they will be my people .*[3] *Therefore leave their midst, cut yourself off, says the Lord, and touch nothing unclean;*[4] *I shall welcome you and be a father to you, and you will be sons and daughters to me, says the Lord almighty*[5] (vv.16-18).

CHAPTER SEVEN

Having thus taught them through the inspired teaching to avoid association with the adversaries and consoled them with the divine promises, he also on his own account offers his encouragement. *Having these promises, then, beloved, let us cleanse ourselves from every defilement of flesh and spirit, bringing holiness to perfection in fear of God* (v.1). By *spirit* here he refers to the soul, (417) by *defilement of spirit* to association with idols, and by *defilement of flesh* to lawlessness in behavior.

Let us in: we have wronged no one, we have ruined no one, we have defrauded no one (v.2). He is not at variance with his own words, praising them at one time and accusing them at another:[1] they did good and committed faults like all human beings, and he praises the former and charges them with the latter. His purpose in both the praise and the blame is to train them in values of the highest kind. At this point he implies some were led astray by those impostors and accepted the calumnies against him – hence his reply in defense, *we have ruined no one, we have defrauded no one*, that is, we neither used deceitful words, clothing malice in false colors, nor preached for profit. By *let us in* he refers to their loss of esteem and lack of love; he had said above as well, *Be expansive on your part, too.*

Since he said, *We have defrauded no one*, he was obliged to proceed, *I say this not by way of condemnation* (v.3), that is, I did not say this to reproach you for pettiness. *I said before, remember, that you are in our hearts to die together and live together.* He continues mollifying them: *I have great confidence in you* (v.4), as a father in his children, as a teacher in his students. *I have great pride in you*: I boast of you and everywhere proclaim your faith. *I am filled with consolation, I overflow with joy in all our tribulations*: memory of you proves an occasion of complete consolation for me.

Then he outlines once more the trials. *When we reached Macedonia, remember, our flesh had no rest; instead, we were distressed in every way, contests without, fears within* (v.5): not only did the struggle with the adversaries give us trouble, but also concern for those of weaker disposition took its toll. He was afraid, you see, of a turn for the worse on their part. *But God, who consoles the lowly, consoled us with the arrival of Titus* (v.6). Here his purpose is to show the virtue of blessed Titus and to enkindle in them love for him, Titus being the one who delivered this letter. This was the reason he said that his appearance was sufficient to dispel the effect of the troubles. *Not only by his arrival, however, but also by the consolation by which he was consoled in your regard, reporting to us your longing, your lamentation, your zeal for me* (v.7): he increased my satisfaction also by the accounts of you, telling me how you long to see us, how you lament the faults committed, (420) and the degree of zeal you have shown against the adversaries on my behalf.

So that I rejoiced further. Because even if I grieved you with the letter, I am not sorry, even if I was sorry (vv.7-8): on learning this I experienced great happiness, even if quite distressed that I was forced to cause you grief through the letter. [2] *For I see that that letter, if only for a time, grieved you. Now I rejoice, not because you were grieved, but because you were grieved to the point of repentance: you were grieved with a godly grief so that you lost nothing on our account* (vv.8-9): even if that letter annoyed you for a while, still it was the cause of great benefit. I am now glad to see not mere grief but the fruit of grief:

that grief gave rise to praiseworthy repentance. *Godly grief, after all, produces repentance unto salvation, whereas the world's grief produces death* (v.10): lamenting one's falls brings about true salvation. By *the world's grief* he refers to grief at the loss of money, on the death of children or wives; its excess can bring on death.[3] This is the reason that even those who mourn beyond measure often repent, whereas those who bewail sin, even if mourning excessively, reap happiness while not undergoing repentance.

I mean, take note of this, what enthusiasm has been produced in you by godly grief, what self-justification, what indignation, what fear, what longing, what zeal, what vindication! (v.11): accepting the letter's censure, you brought total enthusiasm to the task of self-justification, you summoned anger to fight against the sinners, you brought godly fear to bear, you even longed for us more ardently than of old, and adopting a righteous zeal you deplored the transgression of laws. *In every respect you have shown yourself upright in every matter:* you have demonstrated clearly that you are not satisfied with their evil exploits (the meaning of *upright*). *So even if I wrote to you, it was not on account of the wrongdoer or on account of the wronged but for the sake of having our zeal for you made known to you in God's sight*[4] (v.12): as the outcome demonstrated, we wrote that letter for your sake so as to reveal our feeling for you. By *the wrongdoer* he means the fornicator, and by *the wronged* the man's father: though dead he was wronged by the violation of the marriage bed.[5]

Hence we are consoled by your consolation. We have more abundant joy still at the joy of Titus, because his spirit was refreshed by all of you. Because if I boasted somewhat about you to him, I was not let down (vv.13-14): I am especially glad that (421) he carries about with him memory of you, bruiting abroad the love of all of you; he learned from experience that the words often spoken by me about you are true. *But as everything we said to you was true, so too our boasting to Titus proved true:* we could never bring ourselves to say anything untrue; rather, we also proposed to you true doctrine and embellished your praises with truth. *His feelings are all the stronger for you as he recalls the obedience of you all in accepting him with fear and trembling* (v.15): he is very well disposed to you, and bears a lasting remembrance of you, describing how you yielded to his exhortation and how much honor you showed him, reverencing him as a father and respecting him as a spiritual ruler. *So I rejoice because I have every confidence in you* (v.16): I am filled with satisfaction because I am confident in reproving and censuring you. Likewise I am not wide of the mark in commending you.

We too, therefore, both in learning and in teaching, should take a salutary lesson from this. The teachers should imitate the world's teacher, giving timely censure, rebuking as appropriate, encouraging, exhorting and prompting with praise. Those in receipt of the teaching should obey the teachers, accept the teaching with longing and fear, and through such watering bear fruit to Christ the Savior, to whom with the Father and the all-holy Spirit be glory, honor and might, now and forever, for ages of ages. Amen. [6]

Chapter Eight

Now, I bring to your attention the grace of God given to the churches of Macedonia (v.1). Having discoursed on the situation of Titus, and sufficiently mollified them in advance with words of commendation, he went on, *I rejoice because I have complete confidence in you.* He brings out his confidence in detail, and offers exhortation about the care of the saints. Firstly, he describes the sincere faith of the Macedonians, their efforts in its regard and their magnanimity in need. He called possession of good things *grace of God*, not to exclude the independence of their free will but to bring out that with divine assistance it was possible to assemble the riches of virtue. [1] *Because in a severe testing by tribulation the abundance of their joy and their extreme poverty have overflowed in the riches of their generosity* (v.2). He came up with the highest commendation for them, presenting them as satisfied with their dissatisfaction, and in their extreme need rich in generosity; beset with billows (424) from all directions, they rejoice as though borne up on fair winds, and though lacking bare necessities they give evidence of magnanimity as though wealthy and affluent.

Because according to their means, I testify, and beyond their means they responded, with great earnestness begging us for the grace of sharing the ministry to the saints (vv.3-4): I testify of them that in their enthusiasm they exceeded their needs and anticipated our exhortation, begging us to be mindful of the care of the saints. By *grace of sharing* he referred to such care, bringing out through both words that it is profit for the giver, the carers sharing with those being cared for. *It was not what we expected: they gave themselves first to the Lord, and by the will of God to us, so that we might urge Titus to bring to perfection among you as well this grace as he had begun it* (vv.5-6). The phrase *not what we expected* refers not to their good will but to the amount of money: from a distance we expected some trifling amount to be collected, but magnanimity exceeded need. Now, the cause of this was love of God: they dedicated themselves to God, and likewise to us as God's ministers. On perceiving this enthusiasm of theirs, therefore, we urged Titus to make haste to you in turn and bring to realization the teaching that had preceded him.

Having thus stirred them up with compliments to the Macedonians, he then begins his proposal. [2] *But as you abound in everything, in faith, in word, in knowledge, in complete enthusiasm, and in your love for us, may you also excel in this grace* (v.7). He reminded them of the spiritual gifts: "I mean, to one is given utterance of wisdom though the Spirit, to another utterance of knowledge in the same Spirit, to yet another faith by the same Spirit." [3] He testified to them also about love for one another, securing magnanimity with compliments. *I speak not by way of command, but also testing the genuineness of your love by others' enthusiasm* (v.8): I say this not as a command but by way of advice and out of a wish to have you seem reputable: this is the reason I adduced the eagerness of the Macedonians. He then introduces his strongest example: *You know, of course, the grace of our Lord Jesus Christ, who though rich became poor for your sake so that you might be rich by his poverty* (v.9): have an eye to the maker and Lord of all, (425) the only-begotten Son of God, who experienced extreme need for the sake of our salvation, securing for us the riches that stem from penury.

I am giving my view in this: it is appropriate for you, who began last year not only to take action but also to wish to take action, to complete that action now so that just as you have the eagerness to wish it, so you may bring it to completion from what you have (vv.10-11): I say this in my concern for what is advantageous to you, and aware of your eagerness; in the past you made it clear to me. So there is need to add the witness of action to the eagerness (indicating eagerness by the word *wish*). His commentary is to this effect in what follows, note. *If the eagerness is forthcoming, you see, the gift of what you have is acceptable, not of what you do not have* (v.12): eagerness must come to fruition, though the God of all is accustomed to measure the offering by the capacity; it is not quantity but the quality of free will that he is interested in.

That is to say, it is not meant to bring relief to others and tribulation to you: it is a matter of balancing your abundance with their need at this present time so that their abundance may also assist your need to achieve a balance, as it is written, The one with much did not have too much, and the one with little did not have too little [4] (vv.13-15). The Lord defines perfection as utter contempt for possessions and voluntary penury; and yet he taught also that without perfection it is impossible to attain eternal life. When asked by the young man, "What do I do to inherit eternal life?" [5] he did not immediately propose to him the teaching about perfection, but reminded him of the other commandments; when he replied that he had observed them all, however, it was then he urged him to choose a life free from cares and possessions. Having learned this lesson, the divine apostle does not make demanding requirements; rather, he accommodates the laws to the limitations of their good will. Hence he said, *it is not meant to being relief to others and tribulation to you,* he bade them share what is over, and gave a glimpse of the advantage stemming from it, *so that their abundance may also assist your need.* The best reward will follow, he is saying: giving least you will receive most; you will join them in sharing commendable endurance. Now, it was very timely for him also to cite the testimony; the Lord suggested this balance also at the gathering of the manna: the one who gathered more gained no advantage, the generous giver linking moderation to the gift.

Thanks be to God, who gives the same (428) *zeal for you in the heart of Titus, because he accepted the recommendation, and being more zealous he went off to you of his own accord* (vv.16-17). Once again he made clear Titus's love for them, thus making them more amenable to the man's appeals. *We sent in his company the brother who is famous for preaching through all the churches, and not only that: he has been appointed by the churches as our fellow traveler with this gift, which is administered by us for the Lord's own glory and a sign of our good will* (vv.18-19). The words apply to the thrice-blessed Barnabas: he it was who was also granted the mandate in Antioch with blessed Paul by the words of the divine Spirit, "Set apart for me Barnabas and Saul for the work I have assigned them." [6] And later in Jerusalem along with him he made an agreement with the divine apostles: "Peter, James and John, who were regarded as pillars, extended the right hand of fellowship both to me and to Barnabas so that we should go to the Gentiles and they to the circumcised, on the sole condition that we remember the poor." [7] He did make mention of them in this case, saying, *he has been appointed our fellow traveler with this gift, which is being administered by us* – that is, for the care of the saints – and then adding, *for the Lord's own glory and a sign of our good will*.

He also explains the reason why he dispatched such a man. *Taking pains lest anyone find fault with us in this abundance being administered by us* (v.20): we are afraid someone on seeing the amount of money collected may come to some other conclusion – hence my taking more than one man, and above suspicion at that, to share in this ministry. *Making the proper arrangements not only in the sight of God but also in the sight of people* (v.21): not content with the testimony of the Lord alone, we also want people both to acknowledge what is good in us and also to draw benefit from it. *We sent along with them our brother, whom we have often tested and found zealous in many matters, and who is now far more zealous because of great confidence in you* (v.22). Though he praised him, he did not say who he was; some claim he was Apollos, since in the first letter he also promised to send him.

As for Titus, he is my partner and (429) *fellow worker for you; as for our brothers, they are apostles of churches, the glory of Christ* (v.23): I say this, then, about Titus, he became my partner in preaching and is a fellow worker for your benefit; and about the others, they are my brothers, apostles of churches, and glory of Christ the Lord: those who see the splendor of their virtue sing the praises of the God proclaimed by them. *Therefore, show them in the sight of the churches the proof of your love and of our boasting of you* (v.24): lay bare all the riches of your love, then, and confirm my commendation of you; in this way you will bring honor on all the churches.

CHAPTER NINE

It is superfluous for me to write to you concerning the ministry to the saints, knowing as I do your eagerness of which I boast to the Macedonians, saying that Achaia has been ready since last year (vv.1-2). Having discoursed of the matters to do with those ministering to the need, he spoke of the exhortation about generosity as *superfluous*, not supposing it to be really superfluous but by such a style of speech prompting their generosity further. Hence he had testified also to their eagerness, and claimed to have told the Macedonians of it in the past so that the Corinthians might also become thereby more eager on that account. He goes on in that vein, in fact, *Your zeal stirred up most of them*. Now, the divine apostle deserves our admiration when we perceive his spiritual wisdom: he encouraged to the practice of good the Macedonians through the Corinthians, and the Corinthians through the Macedonians. [1]

I sent the brothers lest our boasting of you be to some extent thought hollow and, as I said before, for you to be ready. Otherwise, if some Macedonians come with me and find you not ready, we would be ashamed, not to mention you, as to the grounds of our boasting (vv.3-4). He showed himself to be exercised and afraid there be grounds for the compliments proving false, anxious that they have an eye to their own reputation and that of their teacher and be generous in their share of the money. *So I thought it necessary to recommend the brothers go on ahead to you and make sure your promised alms is ready as an alms and not as an extortion* (v.5). At no place did he call the sharing lovingkindness – only gift, fellowship, alms. He directs it be done with joy, saying as much, *as an alms and not as an extortion*: the extortioner is peeved, the generous giver is pleased.

Since, however, he had left the measure of giving to the exercise of free will, he necessarily makes recommendations as to suitability in this connection as well. (432) *Consider this: the one sowing sparingly will also reap sparingly, and the one sowing bountifully with also reap bountifully* (v.6). It was very appropriate for him to apply this metaphor, calling such generosity sowing, and referring to the manifold fruit of beneficence. He also pointed a finger at those having recourse to stinginess in saying the harvest corresponds to the amount of sowing. Then he once more concedes the role of free will: *Let each one give as they choose in the heart, not with reluctance or under compulsion: God loves a cheerful giver* [2] (v.7). He said as much also in writing to the Romans, "The merciful in cheerfulness:" [3] satisfaction of soul ought lead the way to the offering of funds.

Then he prays for them, betraying fatherly affection. *God can ensure every grace comes to you in abundance so that by always having enough of everything you may excel at every good work, as it is written, He scattered abroad, he gave to the needy, his justice abides for ever* [4] (vv.8-9). He begged for the riches of the divine gifts for them, and abundance of the works of virtue, calling the gifts *every grace* and the forms of virtue *good work*. It was timely for him also to cite the inspired testimony to bring out clearly that contempt for money gives rise to everlasting righteousness.

May the one who provides seed for the sower supply bread for eating, multiply your seed and increase the produce of your righteousness. May you be enriched in every respect with a view to complete simplicity, which is responsible through us for thanksgiving to God (vv.10-11). It was not without purpose that he associated the prayer with the exhortation; rather, he meant to bring out the riches of divine power and the fact that he it is who can supply good things in abundance to everyone. He it is, in fact, who also gave human beings the seed from the beginning, he it is who also nourishes it once sown in the soil and from it furnishes people with nourishment. Yet in his concern for our welfare he wants the needy to enjoy necessities by means of us. By *seed* he once again referred to beneficence, by *produce of righteousness* the benefit springing from it, and by *simplicity* generosity: the person who employs words in superfluity invites the passion of niggardliness. [5]

Because the service of this ministry not only meets the needs of the saints but also abounds in many thanksgivings to God; through the testing of this service you glorify God (vv.12-13). Do not think, he is saying, one good result issues from this work, attention solely to the neediness of the saints: it gives rise to many other benefits, being responsible (433) for the praises of the God of all being sung by everyone. He mentions also what is the basis of this song of praise: *By the obedience of your confession to the Gospel of Christ, by the simplicity of the sharing with them and with everyone, and by their prayer for you in their longing for you on account of the surpassing grace of God in you* (vv.13-14): seeing how you accepted the divine message and how you submitted to the Lord, and perceiving as well the generosity to the saints, not only those living in Jerusalem but also those everywhere, they offer the hymn of praise to the God responsible for these things. Reap the benefit yourselves as well of the prayers offered by them for you; they love you dearly, learning of God's generosity in your regard.

Thanks be to God for his indescribable gift (v.15). It is customary for the apostle to sing God's praises whenever he discourses on any of the divine arrangements. How could you comprehend the being of the one whose gift is indescribable?

CHAPTER TEN

After this treatment of the care of the saints, he then begins to develop the criticism of those impostors; and he touches also on Corinthians themselves, suggesting that some of them had been caught up in their falsehoods. *I, Paul exhort you in my own person through the gentleness and kindness of Christ – humble as I am with you face to face, but bold when at a distance. I ask that when present I will not have to show the boldness of thinking it necessary to stand up to some of those who think we are conducting ourselves according to the flesh* (vv.1-2). Those who had come to faith from Jews, urging adherence to the way of life of the Law, denigrated the divine apostle, calling him a vile and ignorant fellow, and saying he kept the Law in secret but in public did not do so on account of the weakness of those who had come to faith from Gentiles. [1] He used *conducting ourselves according to the flesh* to mean living in accordance with the Law. The phrase *I, Paul, in my own person* carries the weight of the apostolic status: he reminds them of the wonders worked among them and of the gifts brought to them through him. He called to mind *the gentleness and kindness of Christ* to bring out that in imitation of him he has adopted an attitude of restraint, and does not bring to the fore his apostolic authority.

In fact, we conduct ourselves in the flesh, but do not wage war according to the flesh (v.3): though clad in the flesh, we are not victims of the passions of the flesh. *That is to say, the weapons of our warfare are not of the flesh; rather, they have the power of God for destroying* (436) *fortresses* (v.4): as weapons we have the gifts of the Spirit, by which we prove victorious and subject the adversaries to the Lord. Then he explains more clearly the fortresses: *Destroying arguments and every eminence lifted up against the knowledge of God, and capturing every notion for the obedience of Christ* (v.5). Just as he called the saints temples of God, so those in thrall to impiety *fortresses* of the devil. Leading them away from the battle line like some kind of captives, he is saying, we present them to the king of all and make them follow his laws. *Holding all disobedience in readiness to be avenged whenever your obedience is complete* (v.6). He indicated the cause of longsuffering: we expect to convince the majority by word and exhortation, then to punish in this fashion those endeavoring to hold out longer.

Are your eyes on what confronts you? (v.7). It should be read as a question. [2] Do you wish, he asks, to put every detail about us to the test and examine our affairs? Do it with precision, then. *If you are confident you belong to Christ, take further stock of this, that as you belong to Christ, so too do we.* As things stand, he is saying, we do not fall short of what that claim implies: we too are distinguished by the name of Christ. Now, it was very wise of him to leave till last the comparison of performance and raise in first place equality on the basis of names. He then proceeds: *I mean, even if I boast a little too much of the authority the Lord gave me for your upbuilding and not destroying, I am not ashamed* (v.8). He showed that he is willing to leave aside the riches of the gifts, but he claimed to have received the authority for upbuilding and not for destroying, bringing out they were doing the opposite and were unwilling to build up yet endeavoring to destroy the work of others.

Lest I give the impression of frightening you with the letters, some saying the letters are forthright and strong whereas his bodily presence is weak and his speech beyond contempt (vv.9-10). Those employing calumnies against him were in the habit of saying this of him, When absent he is full of words whereas when present he is insignificant and quite unlearned. *Let such people consider this, that the kind of people we are with words in our letters, so we are too in action* (v.11): we can make clear the grandeur of the apostolic rank and give evidence of deeds in keeping with the written words.

You see, we are not rash enough to promote or compare ourselves with some of those who commend themselves. But when they measure themselves by one another, and compare (437) *themselves with one another, they are not showing sense* (v.12). He wrote this whole section vaguely, being unwilling to censure those responsible by name. His meaning is this: With eyes only for themselves, they formed the impression they alone were of great importance; far be it from us to make a judgment of ourselves as they do. He brings this out more clearly in what follows. *We shall not boast immoderately but according to the measure of the norm God has set us so as to reach as far even as you* (v.13). By *measure of the norm* he referred to the grace given by God: the munificent giver distributed it to the believers; he said as much also in writing to the Romans, "To each according to the measure of faith God has assigned." [3] He means, We lay low any immoderate way of thinking and have regard only to the grace given, and we know that our course has stretched as far as you.

What follows also brings this out. *I mean, in reaching you it is not as if we were overstepping our limits: we were the first to reach as far as you in the Gospel of Christ, not boasting beyond measure in others' labors but having hope as your faith grows of going from strength to strength among you within our limits so as to preach the good news in lands beyond you without boasting of what has already been done in someone else's area* (vv.14-16): we apply the set limit, and measure our situation against it. [4] We know that we even got as far as you, and proposed to you the divine Gospel. We also hope to advance further – that is, when you are confirmed in the faith and provide testimony to our efforts; far be it from us to take credit for others' sweat (the meaning of *without boasting of what has already been done in someone's else's area*). Now, he is referring to those who while not choosing to preach to those not yet believers, tried to corrupt those who had accepted the message.

Since he had often said, *We boast*, he was obliged, lest anyone believe he was really getting carried away, to add, *Let the one who boasts boast in the Lord* [5] (v.17): far from feeling self-important, we rejoice in the divine gifts. *After all, it is not those who commend themselves who are approved, but the ones the Lord commends* (v.18): we should not testify in advance to our own virtue, but await the divine verdict.

CHAPTER ELEVEN

Then, since he was on the point of recounting plaudits of himself, he ensured proper reception in advance by calling his action *foolishness. I wish you would bear a little with my foolishness* (v.1). I am aware, he is saying, that those gifted with sagacity should not recount plaudits of themselves; but I have no choice. So put up with a little foolishness. (440) Then with a little more urging, *But do bear with me*. He reveals also the point of the words: *I am jealous for you with the jealousy of God: I betrothed you to one husband to present you as a chaste virgin to Christ. But I am afraid that as the serpent deceived Eve with his cunning, so in place of simple devotion to Christ your thoughts will be corrupted* (vv.2-3): I am your matchmaker, and arranger of the wedding; through me you received the bridegroom's presents. That is the reason I am showing jealousy, in fear and trembling lest your simple devotion be overcome by their villainy. He called the whole Church *virgin*, of course, referring in this way to the integrity of faith: not all the believers profess virginity, but all must be adorned with the sincerity of faith. Now, it was very appropriate for him to mention not the devil but the *serpent*, bringing out that these people also had become instruments of the devil in similar manner to the serpent. The damage itself he called *corruption* since he gave them the name *virgin*.

I mean, if someone comes and preaches a different Jesus from the one we preached, or you receive a different Spirit from the one you received, or a different Gospel from the one you accepted, you have no trouble in putting up with it (v.4). He shifted the accusation to those deceived, and brought out clearly the absurdity of the deception. Why on earth were you led astray? he is saying. They preached to you a different Jesus; they provided you with different gifts of the Spirit; they proposed a different Gospel. *After all, I think I am in no way inferior to those super-apostles* (v.5). But it is unnecessary to compare our situation to theirs: I believe we do not fall short of the great preachers of the truth. [1] He tempered this with modesty: he did not say, I am equal to the super-apostles, but *I think*, that is, I consider I am not inferior to them. *Even if I am a simpleton in speech, not so in knowledge* (v.6). He was not in a position to call the leaders of the apostles simpletons; rather, while saying nothing of them, of himself he makes the claim, I may have an unskilled tongue but a mind equipped with knowledge of God. *Instead making it clear to you in every way and in all things*: you too are witnesses of this, our strengths being well known to you.

Did I commit a sin, humbling myself that you might be exalted? because I preached to you God's Gospel free of charge? (v.7): apparently I bear this accusation because I exercised great humility in your presence, and in preaching the Gospel to you I did not accept from you even necessary upkeep. *I plundered other churches to get pay for the ministry to you* (v.8): to offer the Gospel to you, (441) I availed myself of necessary upkeep from others. *Pay* was well put since he had spoken of *military service* previously. He claimed to have *plundered other churches* since he was kept by them in preaching among the Corinthians.

When I was with you and in need, I was a burden to no one: my needs were met by the brothers coming from Macedonia (v.9). In every way he brought out both their niggardliness and his generosity. I was among you, he is saying, offering the divine message, and I was in need but could not bring myself to burden you; Macedonians met my needs. This is the most serious charge against the Corinthians: the apostle, though living among them, was kept by others. But lest they think he was saying this so as to get something, he was obliged to go on, *I kept myself from being a burden to you in any way, and shall continue to do so.* And in case anyone should suspect he was only playing with words, he added an oath: *As the truth of Christ is in me, this boast will not be silenced in the regions of Achaia* (v.10). No one will stop my mouth, he is saying, or prevent my boasting of this generosity. Then, in the knowledge of the gravity of his words, he offers a palliative: *Why? Is it that I do not love you? God knows I do* (v.11). With this testimony he drove out all suspicion.

So why do you take nothing? *What I am doing I shall continue to do in order to remove the claim from those wanting to claim to be recognized as our equals in what they boast of* (v.12): I do this with the adversaries in mind to undermine their excuses for maligning us. He showed them to be bragging, but stealthily lining their pockets, saying as much shortly after: *I mean, you put up with it if anyone makes slaves of you, preys upon you, rips you off.* [2] *Such people are false apostles, workers of deceit, disguising themselves as apostles of Christ. No wonder: even Satan disguises himself as an angel of light. So it is not remarkable if his ministers also disguise themselves as ministers of righteousness, whose end will be in keeping with their actions* (vv.13-15). It is the devil's practice to imitate divine characteristics, and for false prophets to come out in opposition to the prophets, to take on the guise of angels and deceive human beings. So it is not remarkable if these people also adopt for themselves the facade of the title of apostle, and employ trickery as an aid in deceiving people. But they will before long reap the fruit of their schemes. (444)

I repeat, let no one think me a fool; otherwise, if you do take me for a fool, concede that I too may boast a little (v.16). Often when bent on describing his own efforts for the benefit of the disciples, he was then restrained by his own good sense. So here too he urges them not to form the impression he is acting like a fool. But if you do not believe it, he is saying, at least put up with me as a fool. *In maintaining this boast, what I am saying is not in the Lord's style but spoken like a fool* (v.17). There is a law of the Lord which teaches, "When you do all this, say, We are useless servants because we have done what we are obliged to do."[3] This is the reason the divinely-inspired Paul said, *What I am saying is not after the Lord's manner*, that is, I say this at variance with his law. Lest, however, anyone suspect all his teaching was called foolishness, he was obliged to add *in maintaining this boast*: I class myself as a fool (he is saying) with respect to these words. *Since many boast according to the flesh, I too shall boast* (v.18). By *according to the flesh* here he referred to external things – wealth, noble birth, eloquence: the adversaries, being of Hebrew descent, had a sense of importance and gave prominence to the patriarch Abraham.

After all, you gladly put up with fools, wise as you are: you put up with it if anyone makes slaves of you, preys upon you, rips you off, puts on airs, slaps you in the face. I speak in terms of insults (vv.19-21). He showed that it was idle for them take pride in scorn for money – hence his adding *if anyone preys upon you* and *if anyone rips you off*; the phrase *if anyone slaps you in the face* means, If anyone spits on you, abuses you. He added as much, remember, *I speak in terms of insults*, that is to say, I said this on account of the insults inflicted on you by them.

As though we did not have what it takes: you presume it was because of weakness that we did nothing of the kind. *Whatever anyone dares to boast of – I am speaking foolishly – I too boast of*. He mitigated his statement, calling it *foolishness*; but he explains that he did not reach to insulting them or preying upon them or ripping them off – only to letting them see his own efforts. At the head of the list, of course, he puts what they had proposed as important, to bring out that not even in these matters do they have anything more than he. *They are Hebrews; so am I. They are Israelites; so am I. They are Abraham's offspring; so am I* (v.22). He cited what been said by them about themselves; and while bringing out his equality with them, he shows his superiority in acts of free will. *They are ministers of Christ – I speak as a madman – I am more so* (v.23). Again he said *madman* to bring out that he was forced to say so against his better judgment. (445)

He mentions also the basis of the superiority, not adducing wonderworking, the dead come to life, the lame walking, exorcism, salvation of the world, but the sufferings for the sake of the Gospel. *In hardships more frequently, in scourging to a greater degree, in prison more often, near death frequently. Five times I received from Jews forty lashes less one, thrice beaten with rods, once stoned, thrice shipwrecked, day and night I was adrift at sea* (vv.23-25) – in other words, I spent all night and day with the ship adrift, being tossed hither and yon by the waves. Jews usually inflict forty lashes less one. *Frequently on journeys* (v.26): I undertook the labors of travel for the sake of preaching. *At risk from rivers*: in my journeys I was forced to cross them. *At risk from bandits*, who attack along the way. *At risk from my people*. He had the Jews in mind. *At risk from Gentiles*. The statement is obvious. *At risk in the city*. He referred to the riots stirred up against him. *At risk in the wilderness*. He was often forced to pass through deserted places. *At risk at sea*. He used sea travel in his anxiety to fill both islands and mainlands with godliness. *At risk from false brethren*: from the outset the devil sowed the weeds.

In hardship and trouble (v.27) of teaching, of working. *In many a sleepless night*. Not even in prison did he get any sleep, as the events in Philippi confirm. [4] *In hunger and thirst*, an example of involuntary hardship; *in frequent fasting*, an example of voluntary hardship; *in cold and nakedness*, an example of need and utter penury. *Apart from all the rest* (v.28): I am forced to list a few of many. *My daily pressure*: my daily round includes meetings, prisons, courts. *The care of all the churches*: should my pursuers ever take a rest, the very care of the churches would use up all my energies, carrying about with me as I do the care of the whole world. *Who is weak, and I am not weak?* (v.29). He did not say, I am weak with them, but *I am weak*: as I am beset with the weakness itself, so I suffer pain and anguish. *Who is made to stumble, and I am not inflamed?* When others are made to stumble, I catch fire and burn.

If I must boast, I shall boast of what my weakness involves (v.30). Though he explained he was in a position to let people see the effects of grace, (448) he judged that examples of patient endurance were more appropriate for him. *The God and Father of our Lord Jesus Christ , who is blessed forever, knows that I do not lie* (v.31). Once again he distinguishes *God* from *Father*: he is our God, but Father of the Lord. [5] *In Damascus the governor under King Aretas guarded the city of Damascus with the intention of arresting me, and I was let down in a basket through a window in the wall, and so escaped his hands* (vv.32-33). He indicated the severity of the danger by the manner of the flight.

CHAPTER TWELVE

Boasting really does not become me; I shall move on to visions and revelations of the Lord (v.1): while to me treatment of these matters is of no value, it is helpful for you; so out of a concern for your welfare I am obliged to say what I regard as unbecoming to me. [1] *I know a person in Christ who fourteen years ago – whether in the body I do not know, or out of the body I do not know: God knows – such a person was caught up to the third heaven. I know such a person – whether in the body I do not know, or out of the body I do not know: God knows – that he was caught up to paradise and heard ineffable words, which a human being may not utter. I shall boast of this person, but of myself I shall not boast – only of my weaknesses* (vv.2-5). Though he had had many revelations, as he even admitted himself, *I shall move on to visions and revelations,* yet it was under pressure that he spoke of one, and that one he attributed to someone else, saying, *I know a person,* not myself. He also mentions the time so as to bring out that it was for their sake he was forced to talk of these things: fourteen years had elapsed without his divulging what it had been vouchsafed him to see. By the phrase *to the third heaven* some claim he meant the third part of the distance from earth to heaven, such a person being caught up and hearing the ineffable words, which he did not say a human being may not hear but may not utter; after all, if a human being may not hear them, how was it he heard them? He did hear them, but dared not divulge them. Some claim the *words* are things: he saw the beauty of paradise, the choirs of the saints in it, and the utterly harmonious sound of the hymnsinging. But as to precisely what they were the one who beheld them alone knows; as for us, we should proceed with the remainder of the commentary.[2]

I mean, if I were prepared to boast, I would not be a fool, speaking the truth as I would (v.6). Since he often called himself a fool, he was obliged to bring out the truth of these matters in case anyone should on that account suspect his words to be false. *But I refrain lest anyone think of me beyond what they see of me or hear of me*: (449) this is the reason I am afraid of telling it all, lest anyone form an opinion of me beyond what is appropriate to a human being (as happened also in Lycaonia:[3] thinking him to be a god, they were for sacrificing bulls, but he tore his garments and made plain the nature he had). *To prevent my being carried away by the extraordinary nature of the revelations, a thorn in the flesh was given me, a messenger of Satan to buffet me lest I be carried away* (v.7). He admitted once more in this that he had been accorded great revelations. For this reason, he is saying, the Lord in his care for my welfare apportioned me manifold trials, restraining my pride in this way and not allowing me to form notions of grandeur. By *a messenger of Satan*, in fact, he referred to the abuse, violence and rioting of the mobs.

His commentary is clearer on this in what follows. *Three times I appealed to the Lord about this for him to remove it from me, and he said to me, My grace is sufficient for you: my power is made perfect in weakness* (vv.8-9). He showed the weakness of nature, saying, I begged to be freed from the trials. He showed also the Lord's comforting: he said the abundance of grace was sufficient for consolation, while the weakness and patient endurance of the preachers brings out also the power of what is preached. *I shall therefore boast more gladly of my weaknesses so that the power of Christ may come to dwell in me.* He had explained what it was he called *a messenger of Satan*; but in case anyone should get the idea the weakness was a bodily passion, he brings out its features more clearly.[4] *Hence I take satisfaction in weaknesses, in insults, in times of need, in persecutions, in hardships for Christ's sake: when I am weak, then I am powerful* (v.10). He did not say, I endure, but *I take satisfaction*, that is, I rejoice, I am happy, I accept with pleasure what befalls: the apparent weakness is the source of real power in me.

Having given this explanation, he went on, *I was a fool to boast* (v.11); and he explains the reason for it, *You forced me*, that is, by believing the calumnies against me (as the sequel makes clear). *I ought to have been commended by you*: I should have had you as advocates and witnesses to my lifestyle. *After all, I am not inferior to the super-apostles*. Once again he kept praise to a minimum; having undergone greater labors than all the others, he was not prepared simply to put himself on a level with the apostles but claimed to be in no way inferior to them. Once again he returns to his characteristic modesty: (452) *Even if I am nothing, yet the signs of the apostle were worked among you in great endurance, in signs and wonders and miracles* (vv.11-12): have no regard for me, but weigh up the effects of grace; you were witnesses of the apostolic dignity and are observers of the spiritual testimony. Now, he was right to put *endurance* ahead of *signs*, since proof of good intentions carries much more weight.

I ask you, in what way are you worse off than the other churches except for my not being a burden to you? (v.13) What kind of spiritual gift did you not receive from us except for not finding fault with us for our not being in receipt of bodily ministrations from you? Then by way of irony, *Forgive me this fault*: I confess, I was in the wrong, and I ask pardon. But in case anyone should form the impression that he was putting this forward by way of blame and was interested in gain, he promises to adhere to his resolve in the future. *See, I am ready to come to you a third time, and I shall not be burden to you* (v.14).[5] Then he mitigates the harshness of his expression. *I am looking not for what is yours but for you*. He employs also a proverb from nature: *Children are not bound to save up for their parents, remember, but parents for their children*: my longing is not for money; I am after your souls, knowing that fathers always store up riches for their children, but promising to do something even greater than natural fathers. *I shall in fact most willingly spend and be spent for your souls* (v.15) – that is, I give even myself for you – *even if in loving you more fully I am loved less*. An accusation joined with solicitude: he annoyed them by charging them with stinginess in love, whereas he gladdened them by showing his intense interest in them.

Be that as it may, I was no burden to you; being devious I took you in by deceit. Surely I did not defraud you by any of those I sent to you? I urged Titus to go, and sent the brother with him: surely Titus did not defraud you in any way? Did we not behave in the same spirit? did we not follow in the same footsteps? (vv.16-18): but perhaps someone might say that I employed devious behavior, taking nothing from you when present but accepting something from you through those I sent to you. So tell me in very truth if Titus or anybody else exploited the authority given to the preachers. By *fraud* he referred to the offering, since it is natural for the person giving against their will to speak of being defrauded even if discharging a debt.

Having thus treated of these matters by way of refuting the false apostles, he brings out for their benefit the dignity of teaching. *Do you again get the impression that we are mounting a defense for you?* (v.19) Perhaps, he is saying, (453) you consider the defense also to be a sign of baseness. *We are speaking before God in Christ*: we, on the contrary, are saying it with God as witness, illumined by the commandments of Christ the Lord (*in Christ* meaning according to the laws of Christ). His law, remember, is, "If you are offering your gift at the altar, and there you remember that your brother has something against you, leave your gift before the altar, and go off and first be reconciled to your brother, and then come and offer your gift;" and again, "Let your light shine in people's sight so that they may see your good works and glorify your father, who is in heaven." [6] He says this here in his own right as well, *Everything, beloved, is for the sake of your upbuilding*: if we lower ourselves or say sublime things, if we deliver accusations or commendations, our concern in everything is for your welfare.

You see, I am afraid that when I come I may not find you as I wish, and that I may not be found by you as you wish (v.20). He mentions the possibilities and deplores them with them: *quarreling, rivalry, anger, fights, calumny, gossip, conceit, disorder*. He had accused them of this in the first letter as well. *I am afraid that when I come again my God may humble me before you, and I may grieve over many who sinned previously and have not repented of the impurity, fornication and licentiousness they committed* (v.21). By his *humbling* he referred to their lawlessness, confirming what he had said previously: *Who is weak and I am not weak? who is made to stumble and I am not inflamed?* [7] He claimed to be grieving, not simply over sinners but over those who after the sin had not applied the remedies of repentance. Now, the apostolic teaching clearly levels an accusation at the imposture of Novatus. [8]

CHAPTER THIRTEEN

This is the third time I am coming to you. Every charge will be established on the testimony of two or three witnesses [1] (v.1). He put facts before reputations, protesting against those who made little of repentance and putting fear into them. *To those who had sinned before and to all the rest I made it clear previously and I make it clear, during my second visit and now in writing, that if I come again I shall not be lenient* (v.2). He brought to the fore the apostolic authority in an attempt to stem the vehemence of sin by fear: it was easier for them to correct their own and punish outsiders. The most divine Peter, remember, had dispatched to death Ananias and his partner, (456) who were of the number of the disciples, while Elymas, an infidel and adversary, the blessed Paul consigned to darkness by extinguishing the sense of sight. [2]

Are you are looking for proof that in me it is Christ who is speaking, who is not weak in your regard but powerful in you? (v.3): evidently you want to test whether Christ is making pronouncements in me, clear though your knowledge of his power is. *That is to say, if he was crucified in weakness, yet he is alive by God's power* (v.4): even if he underwent the suffering of the cross owing to the natural mortality of the body, yet he is alive, and his life is that of God and Son of God. Resembling this is the statement, "Destroy this temple, and in three days I shall raise it up." [3] Now, if in one case the divinity of the Only-begotten is said to have raised the body, and in another case the Father himself, it makes no difference: the divine Scripture often applies to the Father what is done by the Son. Thus the Only-begotten is called creator of everything, while his Father is likewise also called creator. Let us, however, proceed with the rest of the commentary. *After all, we are weak in him, but we shall live with him in your regard by God's power*: we shall likewise share with him the sufferings as well, having endured them on his account, and we shall participate in life with him. God's power is a pledge of resurrection, you see.

Examine yourselves to see if you are standing firm in the faith, test yourselves (v.5): examine not our situation but your own, and see if you are really established in the faith. *Do you not realize that Jesus Christ is in you, unless you have failed the test?* You ought to know that you have Christ the Lord himself dwelling within you: the one without this knowledge is devoid of faith (the meaning of *failed the test*). Since he had said shortly before, remember, that Christ was making utterances in him, he explained to them that he dwells and moves about in them, according to the inspired oracle. [4] *I hope that you will come to know that we have not failed the test* (v.6). He expressed this in threatening fashion as though about to provide them with a demonstration of spiritual power; but it is a further revelation of particular affection.

We pray to God, however, that you may do nothing wrong – not that we may appear to have passed the test but that you may do the right thing, failure though we may be (v.7). My prayer, he is saying, is that you take no occasion from us for a demonstration of the apostolic grace. Rather, I pray that you be distinguished for all good deeds, and we keep authority out of sight. (457) *We are not capable, after all, of anything against the truth – only in favor of the truth* (v.8): how could we take punitive measures against you when you are involved in seemly behavior? *We in fact rejoice when we are weak but you are strong. This we also pray for, your betterment* (v.9). He said the same thing in different ways to bring out the love he had for them. *Hence I am writing this while away from you so that when present I may not be severe in using the authority which the Lord gave me for upbuilding and not for destroying* (v.10). He made clear that punishment is also upbuilding: from the chastisement of one or two the assembly reaps benefit. Thus, when Ananias and Sapphira received punishment, fear fell on all those who heard of it, Scripture says.

At this point he brought the harsh words to a close and offered them beneficial exhortation. *Now, brethren, rejoice* (v.11): joy belongs to those who practice virtue. [5] *Better yourselves*, that is, complete what is lacking. *Encourage one another*: enjoy consolation from one another in times of trial. *Be of one mind*: join together in harmony, let there be one mind among you. *Be peaceable* – to us, to one another, and before all to the saving God. *And the God of peace and love will be with you*: seeing these good deeds he will accord you complete providence, since it is he who requires them. *Greet one another with a holy kiss* (v.12), that is, guilelessly, chastely, as members of one another and body of Christ. *All the saints greet you.* He joined to them also the believers throughout the world.

The grace of our Lord Jesus Christ, the love of God and the fellowship of the Holy Spirit be with you all. Amen (v.13). It was not by way of division that he expressed it this way, nor did he apportion some things to Christ, some to the Father and some to the Holy Spirit. Frequently, in fact, he spoke of love in connection with the Spirit, fellowship with the Son and grace with the God and Father. Thus also in the first letter he spoke of operation in connection with the Father, and shortly after spoke of it in connection with the Son.[6] Now, he also cited the order of the persons in a different fashion, not to overturn the order cited by the Lord[7] but to bring out that the order of the names does not indicate diversity of nature or power or difference in status. Let us also pray to be accorded the apostolic blessing and attain the promised goods, thanks to the grace and lovingkindness of our God and Savior (460) Jesus Christ, to whom with the Father and the all-holy Spirit be glory and magnificence, now and forever, for ages of ages. Amen.[8]

Notes to the
Second Letter to the Corinthians

CHAPTER ONE

[1] 1 Cor 16.5-6.

[2] Luke 10.21. With his ever present theological concerns, Theodoret insists (as he does at the letter's close) on the distinction being observed in understanding the Father's relationship to us and to Jesus (he would not be rash enough to raise the question of a modern commentator like Bultmann as to the legitimacy of reading "God of our Lord Jesus Christ," as the Greek would allow). He is not equally interested in the Old Testament background to the phrases "grace and peace," "Father of mercy, " "God of consolation."

[3] Ps 94.19.

[4] Theodoret is not disposed to explicate this fully packed and tightly balanced thought, nor to comment on the repetition of key terms that so obviously marks these verses.

[5] The text of these verses has undergone drastic variations, so that Theodoret is not commenting on the form found in modern versions but on a form thought to be original.

[6] Cf. Acts 19.23-40, the perilous incident that suggests itself to modern commentators as well.

[7] Theodoret expresses Paul's thought more clearly than the apostle in a verse of which Murphy-O'Connor remarks, "As yet no one has succeeded in unraveling the syntax."

[8] Theodoret (like Chrysostom) is not ready to admit Paul could change his mind, as the Corinthians in fact accused him of doing. Nor could he allow for the possibility that a missing letter had informed the Corinthians of a change of plan. (Are the "some" here later commentators, as Guinot presumes, or members of the Corinthian community?)

[9] Acts 15-18.

[10] Rom 16.3.

[11] A different reading from the majority.

[12] Repeatedly Theodoret's Antiochene style of commentary is marked by *akribeia* in noting diverse forms of names, finding inclusion of details to be deliberate on the author's part, etc.

[13] Bultmann remarks: "The liturgical custom of speaking the Amen in

worship is assumed;" cf. 1 Cor 14.16. In this Commentary and others we have noted Bishop Theodoret prepared to acknowledge that clerics do not have a monopoly on worship.

CHAPTER TWO

[1] As a good Antiochene, Theodoret knows that every *de* should have its *men*.

[2] A perceptive (and rare sociological) comment that would help the readers appreciate the impact of Paul's correspondence on the Corinthian community.

[3] Another helpful synopsis by the commentator of the letter's structure for his readers.

[4] Does this lengthy and rather repetitive justification of Paul's unintended departure from Corinth in the absence of Titus reflect some sense of unease on Theodoret's part about the turn the letter is about to take, such as convinces moderns like Bornkamm and Bultmann to divide 2 Cor into several letters and at this point move directly to 7.5-16? Or is it simply that Paul's behavior is felt to need some explaining, and repetition helps?

[5] Again Theodoret shows his readiness and ability to explicate the full force of an image in the biblical text. And not above gilding the lily, he proceeds to add figures of his own in support.

[6] Isa 1.22.

CHAPTER THREE

[1] Theodoret does not take occasion from Paul's remarkable reference to the Old covenant as a ministry of death and condemnation to gild the lily and embark on an anti-Jewish diatribe. Nor, on the other hand, is he concerned to depth his readers' understanding of "glory" by explication of its Old Testament and Hellenistic background.

[2] The bishop supplies a sacramental dimension to justification that Paul chooses not to.

[3] Rom 10.4.

[4] Theodoret is more concerned to establish the status of the Spirit than to present Paul distinguishing Lord and Spirit, a concern of other exegetes.

[5] Throughout commentary on this chapter Theodoret – predictably – has not drawn attention to Paul's inconsistency about the placement of the veil, whether over Moses' face or the people's.

[6] Matt 5.8. Theodoret resists any temptation to become moral at this point; his concerns are more dogmatic.

CHAPTER FOUR

[1] Phil 3.7,8.

[2] 3.18.

[3] 2.16.

[4] The interjection was made also at 1.3; 5.19 when the commentator wanted the text divided properly. Here, almost as though aware that modern commentators like Bultmann would highlight the gnostic concept of "the god of this world," Theodoret insists Paul is not speaking in these terms.

[5] Matt 7.6; 13.13.

[6] John 14.9. Again Theodoret invokes the credal terminology of Constantinople.

[7] 1 Cor 4.1.

[8] Cf. Gen 1.3.

[9] Paul is contrasting the face of Christ with that of Moses as a development of his comparison of the two dispensations, whereas Theodoret takes the opportunity for further Christological reflection.

[10] Rom 8.17.

[11] Cf. Rom 8.24.

[12] Ps 116.10 in the reading of the LXX, where it is numbered 115.1.

[13] Ps 116.8-9 (LXX 114.8-9). In his commentary on this psalm, Theodoret does not refer to Paul's citation of it, a fact that perhaps strengthens the generally held view that (*pace* Parvis and Viciano) his Psalms Commentary precedes this one.

[14] Theodoret is not inclined to recognize and expatiate on the gnostic background to Paul's distinction in terms in the manner of a modern commentator like Bultmann.

[15] For all his unwillingness to find a gnostic element to Paul's thinking that attracts some moderns, Theodoret would be dismayed to find a similarity to his comment here in Saying 42 of The Gospel of Thomas, "Be passersby."

CHAPTER FIVE

[1] Whereas a commentator like Murphy-O'Connor debates whether these images should be taken anthropologically and individualistically, or instead existentially, an Antiochene like Theodoret looks for (unfounded?) clues in morphology (playing, for instance, on the difference between *endusasthai* and *ependusasthai*). *Akribeia* has its shortcomings.

[2] Theodoret is keener than Paul to preserve a positive value for the body.

[3] The Fall (which Paul hardly refers to here) is presented by Theodoret, if not as a *felix culpa*, at least as no longterm obstacle. For an eastern theologian the accent falls more on healing than on the wound.

[4] Again Theodoret is reluctant to regard bodily existence as an obstacle to union with the Lord, not treating this view (as do some commentators) as one proposed by the Corinthians.

[5] If it was for statements like this from Chrysostom that Luther dismissed him as "only a foolish babbler," Theodoret would not appeal to him, either, for this Antiochene insistence on the (delicate) balance between grace and human effort in the process of salvation.

[6] Theodoret, perhaps predictably in the light of the previous note, is taking the genitive in Paul's text as objective. Modern commentators are

inclined to see Paul speaking of Christ's love for us, in line with other statements such as Rom 8.35-39, Gal 2.20, 2 Cor 13.13.

[7] Schulze's text omits the comma in the opening clause of the verse usually included in modern NT editions, leading to versions such as "If anyone is in Christ," and prompting commentators to speak of a mystical sense of "in Christ." Bishop Theodoret, on the other hand, again gives Paul's thought a sacramental dimension, and Bultmann agrees with him: "That person is 'in Christ' who was received by baptism into the community as the 'body of Christ'... The 'in Christ' is thus not a formula of mysticism, but rather of eschatology, or it has an eschatological-ecclesiological sense." Theodoret's punctuation, not to mention his pedestrian spirituality, discourages his debating the mystical dimension of the phrase.

[8] As we have seen before (cf. 1.3; 4.4), this rubric is an index of theological caution on Theodoret's part regarding proper division of a verse. Bultmann is equally categorical: "The connection can scarcely be 'God was in Christ,' so that 'reconciling' would be attributive or in apposition, since for Paul, after all, the 'being' of God 'in Christ' is an inconceivable idea" – not quite the way Theodoret would have put it. Scholastic theologians would speak rather of different forms of causality, formal and efficient, and this is more in keeping with the bishop's thought, if not his terminology.

Chapter Six

[1] Isa 49.8.

[2] For the guidance of his readers, Theodoret comes up with a division of Paul's hardships as helpful as other commentators', and makes as good a fist as they of explaining some puzzling items in the list.

[3] Cf. Lev 26.12; Ez 37.27.

[4] Cf. Isa 52.11.

[5] Cf. 2 Sam 7.14. The final verses of a short chapter with their challenging antitheses and lengthy OT documentation Theodoret passes over with little comment, though there is nothing to suggest he would agree with a modern commentator like Bultmann in seeing them as an insert, perhaps from a lost letter.

Chapter Seven

[1] Theodoret, too, like some modern commentators, is feeling a lack of sequence here.

[2] Whereas modern commentators are inclined to take this letter, mentioned also at 2.4, to be a lost letter, Theodoret at its earlier mention identified it with 1 Cor. His position on (NT) Scriptures does not include speculation on lost letters (or Gospels, doubtless).

[3] The relationship between grief and death has puzzled commentators, and Theodoret does not shirk the challenge, even if we find his own comments themselves somewhat puzzling.

[4] Most texts and versions, on the contrary, speak of "your zeal for us."

[5] Cf. note on 1 Cor 5.1.

[6] Theodoret, not inclined like modern commentators to divide 2 Cor into two letters, finds an appropriate break at this point. Speaking as a pastor, he finds in Paul, "the world's teacher" (a phrase found also in Chrysostom), a model for his teaching ministry, and in the Corinthians exemplary recipients. Today's educators would look in vain for a hint at the possibility of teachers learning from those they teach. It is a brief moral peroration; he knows the limits to a desk commentator's role.

CHAPTER EIGHT

[1] Theodoret characteristically would not want his readers to think the Macedonians were prompted to generosity only by divine grace: their own free will, *gnome*, had a role as well.

[2] Theodoret does not agree with those commentators who see v.7 closing the opening section rather than beginning a new movement of thought.

[3] 1 Cor 12.8-9.

[4] Exod 16.18, the context being the giving of the manna, on which Theodoret will proceed to comment.

[5] Matt 19.16-22. The interpretation Theodoret gives to Jesus' reply to the (rich) young man smacks of cenobitic spirituality, which Theodoret had earlier sampled. Fitzmyer remarks that Jesus' reference to perfection (in Matt, not Mark or Luke) "became the springboard for a certain interpretation in the Christian tradition that distinguished precepts and counsels and which found support in it for the monastic/religious vow of poverty" – though Theodoret sees that life characterized rather by freedom from cares and possessions.

[6] Acts 13.2. While Paul's text is not specific, and modern commentators are content to leave the question open, Theodoret makes a plausible case from scriptural data for this man's being Barnabas, whereas below he is content merely to cite earlier commentators' claims for the second fellow traveler's being Apollos, citing some inconclusive scriptural support.

[7] Gal 2.9-10.

CHAPTER NINE

[1] A datum of the letter strikes Theodoret as it does modern commentators, leading to quite different conclusions. For Bultmann it is clear proof of structural confusion: "In Chapter 8 the Macedonians were the model for Achaia, and now Achaia is the model for the Macedonians. This makes sense only if Chapter 9 was written earlier than Chapter 8." For Theodoret, who of course does not entertain such a possibility, it is grounds for admiring the apostolic letter writer. Did the former ever read the latter?

[2] Prv 22.8 LXX.

[3] Rom 12.8.

[4] Cf. Ps 112.9.

[5] Theodoret is trying to trace the semantic development of *haplotes* occur-

ring here in Paul's text from simplicity to liberality (though he had accepted that development without comment in Rom 12.8).

CHAPTER TEN

[1] Predictably, Theodoret has no difficulty with the letter's sequence at this point such that leads even those unconvinced of the efforts of commentators like Bornkamm to divide the letter into five to concede, like Murphy-O'Connor, "Chapters 10-13 cannot be the continuation of chaps 1-9; it is psychologically impossible that Paul should suddenly switch from the celebration of reconciliation (1-9) to a savage reproach and sarcastic self-vindication (10-13)." Theodoret's opening survey of the letter likewise did not take account of psychological problems, needless to say.
[2] Modern editors and commentators on Paul's text likewise have to decide how to take the verse, Bultmann agreeing with Theodoret.
[3] Rom 12.3.
[4] Theodoret takes this vague, rambling period of Paul's and breaks it down into intelligible sections for easier assimilation by his readers, making it also more concrete.
[5] Cf. Jer 9.24, a text cited already in 1 Cor 1.31.

CHAPTER ELEVEN

[1] Does Theodoret think Paul is ironical in his seemingly complimentary references to the rogue evangelists? Perhaps (as his further comment suggests) he sees Paul respectful of their minders in Jerusalem, an alternative Murphy-O'Connor also proposes.
[2] V.20.
[3] Cf. Luke 17.10. The rarity of this item of scriptural documentation, cited only because Paul's text implies it, shows that the commentator on Paul feels it inappropriate and unnecessary to gild the lily, his task being simply to explicate the plain statement of the text. His procedure here thus differs from that employed on a (figurative) Old Testament text like the Psalms, where meaning had to be established with support from other biblical loci.
[4] Cf. Acts 16.24-34.
[5] Once again, as at the letter's opening, Theodoret insists we make the proper theological distinction here, whether Paul intends it or not. He will have to make the same insistence at the opening to the hymn in Eph.

CHAPTER TWELVE

[1] The Koine, or Byzantine, text of this verse found in Chrysostom and Theodoret differs from that occurring in modern editions and versions, rendered "Boasting is necessary; while it does not become me, I shall move on..." – a sense Theodoret seems to give to his text.
[2] Guinot assiduously traces the opinion about the third heaven to Severian,

but is unable to trace that to do with the words the visionary heard; he adds, "Jean Chrysostome un peu curieusement néglige de préciser ces deux points." Perhaps Chrysostom's lack of interest is not so "curieuse;" Theodoret himself is less interested in arriving at "précision" on these details than in the fact of a mere human being's access to these ineffable realities, and with some impatience he presses on, leaving such matters better undecided. Divine transcendence is in question.

[3] Cf. Acts 14.8-18.

[4] Commentators have differed as to the nature of this thorn, Satan's messenger, varying from a physical ailment (so Bultmann) to persecution (so Murphy-O'Connor). Theodoret, who does not in this case canvass the opinions of his predecessors, opts for the latter, being quite insistent no sense of physical *pathos* should be entertained – lest the divine apostle be thought any the less of?

[5] Theodoret is not going to get caught up in discussions of the number of Paul's visits to Corinth and the relation of the letters to them, in the manner of modern commentators; or it may be he sees no problem.

[6] Matt 5.23-24,16.

[7] 11.29.

[8] The *Nouatus* here is probably the same rigorist as the *Nouuatus* Theodoret mentions at the close of 1 Cor 7 as prohibiting second marriages, namely, the Roman presbyter Novatian in the third century, who also denied the possibility of post-baptismal pardon. Theodoret, we have often noted, does not speak of a sacrament of reconciliation beyond baptism, and it is rather the Christology of Novatian against which Antioch, including Nestorius, inveighs.

CHAPTER THIRTEEN

[1] Deut 19.15; cf. 1 Tim 5.19.

[2] Acts 5.1-11; 13.8-11. Sapphira's name is not thought worth a mention at this point.

[3] John 2.19. The *testimonium* is really a digression, as Theodoret sheepishly admits shortly after in resuming the commentary; but with his ever-present theological concerns he has strayed again into Christological debate.

[4] Namely, the conflation of Lev 26.12 and Ezek 37.27 already cited at 6.16.

[5] Theodoret (with Bultmann and others who debate the number and structure of the letters sent to Corinth) does not support the NRSV in taking *chairete* in the sense of farewell here – though on semantic, not structural, grounds.

[6] Cf. 1 Cor 12.6,11, though in commentary there Theodoret was concerned to show the text referring both to (not the Son but) the Spirit and to the Father.

[7] Theodoret probably has in mind an evangelical locus like Matt 28.19. We note there is nothing Nestorian in Theodoret's use of *prosopa* for the persons of the Trinity here.

With that double trinitarian caveat thus raised in relation to Paul's greeting, about appropriation and about the order of the persons, Theodoret can now close his commentary.

[8] As at the close of 1 Cor, editor Schulze includes in his text a codicil whose authenticity he nevertheless questions: "The second letter to the Corinthians was sent from Philippi with Titus and Luke." He comments: "I have little doubt this codicil is not to be attributed to Theodoret. Above in the preface to Paul's letters he says nothing of the place where this letter to the Corinthians was written except that Paul while writing it was living in Macedonia. But nothing there of envoys; and indeed on 8.18 of this letter he says clearly that Barnabas was sent with Titus, perhaps even Apollos (on v.22), not Luke."

General Index

Index of Biblical Citations

Index of Modern Authors

Made in the USA
Middletown, DE
22 October 2023

41237788R00196